Rabindranath Tagore

Selected Writings on Literature and Language

THE OXFORD TAGORE TRANSLATIONS

Rabindranath Tagore

Selected Writings on Literature and Language

General Editor

SUKANTA CHAUDHURI

Advisory Editor

SANKHA GHOSH

Introduction by

SISIR KUMAR DAS

Notes by

SISIR KUMAR DAS AND
SUKANTA CHAUDHURI

OXFORD
UNIVERSITY PRESS

OXFORD
UNIVERSITY PRESS

Oxford University Press is a department of the University of Oxford. It furthers the University's objective of excellence in research, scholarship, and education by publishing worldwide. Oxford is a registered trademark of Oxford University Press in the UK and in certain other countries

Published in India by
Oxford University Press
YMCA Library Building, 1 Jai Singh Road, New Delhi 110001, India

First Edition published by Oxford University Press in 2001
jointly with Visva-Bharati
Oxford India Paperbacks 2010
Eighth impression 2015

ISBN-13: 978-0-19-806968-3
ISBN-10: 0-19-806968-5

Typeset in Adobe Garamond
by Guru Typograph Technology, New Delhi 110045

General Editor's Preface

This preface must begin with a general point relevant to every volume in the series. It is an obvious point, yet worth stating: that these volumes are part of a series; each one, a combined effort by several translators and scholars. They have had to follow a common programme and adopt certain uniform strategies. I am grateful to all the translators in this volume for their generous cooperation in this regard.

The most basic principle, however, is that there can be no uniform strategy. Literary translation proceeds by a series of particular, contingent judgments, virtually a species of inspired adhocism. For a start, it soon becomes imperative to break the translator's shibboleth that the same word in the original must always be rendered by the same word in translation. The need for variation and adaptation takes on special urgency in these essays on literature and language, as in all critical and discursive writing. The factors governing the translator's choice are unusually complex here.

The reason is not hard to seek. Conceptual terms, even more than other words, are unique in coverage from language to language. No abstract noun in one language has a true equivalent in another. The correspondences that we assume are no better than conventions or compromises, often creating serious distortions of perspective. It is almost a blessing when even such suspect equivalence proves impossible. Here the translator must employ a combination of words where the original had one; or confine himself to the most salient implications in that particular context, relinquishing many secondary nuances.

Yet such loss is clearly serious. Conceptual words, if used to any purpose, must carry a more or less precise meaning: they are all, in an extended sense, technical terms. Even a partial loss of meaning subverts their function. One can try to minimise the loss through supportive words or explanations, at some risk to the feel and impact of the original. The translators in this volume have had to chart their course through such challenging terrain.

Although Rabindranath's critical writings are radiantly non-technical in idiom, they draw heavily on certain crucial concepts of Indian aesthetics, which have virtually passed into common parlance: *rasa, bhava*, or *rupa*, for instance. One might argue for retaining these terms in translation, as the only way to preserve their full implications. But that would be an exercise in tautology. It would obscure the dominant significance in a given context and disfigure the lucid grace of Rabindranath's writing with the scars of a hybrid register. We have therefore rendered these terms by various words and phrases according to context. A note on pages xi–xiii explains the general import of the terms and the means used to render them.

The other challenge for the translator of these essays is posed by Rabindranath's packed and intricate sentences, their branching veins laden with rich ore of concept and image. It is difficult to match such constructions in English; doubly so where the pivotal elements have no English equivalent, so that whole phrases and clauses are needed to render a single word. In these cases, it has sometimes been necessary to favour meaning over syntactic nuance: sentences have been split up or reorganised while making every effort to preserve not only the overall sense but something of the formal impact.

We have adopted another practice that calls for explanation. In some basic respects (such as the forms of pronouns), Bengali is less gender-specific and gender-biased than English. In particular, Rabindranath often uses the common Bengali words for a human, *manab* and *manush*, in contexts that are clearly gender-neutral. While a certain masculinist nuance cannot be ruled out, to translate as 'man' would imbue the text for today's reader with an unwarranted gender bias. We have therefore used a variety of renderings: 'human being', 'humanity' or 'humankind' where feasible, but also constructions in 'we' and 'one'. The latter strategy might involve restructuring the original sentence—the better, we hope, to preserve its basic intent. Masculine pronouns have been used where the context implies male identity or attributes. The rendering of *balak* (commonly 'boy', but basically 'child') has been explained in the headnote to 'Children's Rhymes'.

Throughout this series, place names and mythological names have as a rule been standardised, even where the original text uses a variant. Of course, the exact term has been preserved where its significance affects the surrounding text—for example, through a quibble or metaphoric use. English words embedded in the original Bengali text have been put in italics, except where used so naturally or unobtrusively as not to warrant such signposting.

Explanations and annotations have, as a rule, been placed in notes. But to reduce distracting references on minor matters, small explanations have sometimes been worked into the translation. Words or passages carrying a note have been indicated by an obelisk (†) in the text.

A new question facing today's translator is how to render the name of the source language. We have preferred 'Bengali' to 'Bangla': it is still the commoner form by far, and accords better with Rabindranath's formal register.

The transliteration of Bengali and other Indian words is a major challenge. Where familiar English spellings exist, they are inconsistent. Attempts at standardisation run into many problems. Standard Bengali pronunciation seldom agrees with the original Sanskrit or its closer approximation in Hindi; none of these can be conveyed by the English (Roman) alphabet; efforts at logical equivalence offend against familiar practice and, hence, acceptability.

Diacritical marks solve most technical problems but create others of access and reception. A working compromise seems the only feasible solution. We have rendered Bengali names and terms according to current standard Bengali pronunciation rather than the original Sanskrit one. Given the paucity of vowels in the Roman alphabet, this (or indeed any) practice harbours ambiguities, especially as the single vowel *a* must perforce render both অ and আ. (The alternative would be to use *o* for both অ and ও, which is equally misleading and less familiar.) The combination *ey* has sometimes been used instead of simply *e* to render the এ at the end of a word, where the influence of the silent final *e* in English might otherwise have proved overriding.

Following common practice, শ and ষ have both been rendered by *sh* and স by *s*, though the difference has virtually ceased to matter in Bengali; and the *k+sh* ক্ষ compound been spelt as *ksh* though invariably pronounced as *kh* in Bengali. Following general practice again, the *j+n* compound জ্ঞ has been rendered as *gn*. In transliterating Sanskrit, the nasal *anusvar* has been uniformly rendered by *m*.

Yet classical Sanskritic names and terms must be retained in familiar spellings based on the Sanskrit pronunciation. *Rasa* has been so spelt as an accepted term in English aesthetic terminology. Certain proper names in other languages have also been rendered in traditional Sanskritic spellings. To depart from these would confuse readers; at the same time, the Sanskritic forms clash with those of their Bengali versions or derivatives. We thus have *Vidyapati* but *Arabinda* (Ghosh) or indeed *Rabindranath; Rama* but *Ram Babu.* This is clearly unsatisfactory, but a perfect solution seems impossible.

By the same rationale, Sanskrit works have been cited by their original titles rather than the Bengali forms used by Rabindranath. The sole exception is *Shakuntala* for *Abhijnanashakuntalam* in the essays on that play, in aid of brevity as upheld by common practice.

Where Rabindranath cites Sanskrit quotations with Bengali translation, we have included the Sanskrit text (in approximate Roman transliteration without diacritical marks), followed by an English version adhering to Rabindranath's Bengali. Where he offers only a Bengali translation, we have rendered it by an English version, again following his Bengali. Where he cites the Sanskrit alone, this has been included in the text, followed by an English rendering in square brackets. Special practices demanded by particular essays have been explained in the headnotes to those essays.

* * *

As with the other volumes of the series, the selection of pieces was made by Shri Sankha Ghosh with suggestions from the translators. I am grateful for his perceptive yet discreet advice regarding every aspect of this volume. I am also grateful to Dr Tapobrata Ghosh for his detailed review of the translations, and to Professor Pabitra Sarkar, Shrimati Abhaya and Ajaya Dasgupta, Dr Nrisingha Prasad Bhaduri, Professor Supriya Chaudhuri, Dr Bijoya Goswami, Dr Sarbani Ganguly, Dr Pradyot Datta, Shri Sarvananda Chaudhuri, Dr Amlan Das Gupta, and Shrimati Tasneem Suhrawardy for help with queries and references. The members of Rabindra Bhavan, Shantiniketan, have been uniformly helpful; I must specially thank Dr Prashanta Kumar Pal, Shri Anathnath Das and Shrimati Supriya Roy for their informed advice. Thanks also to Rabindra Bhavan and Kala Bhavan for providing illustrations.

Professor Swapan Chakravorty and Dr Tista Bagchi have rendered considerable assistance with the notes. We hope these extensive notes will be of use even to those who do not need to read Rabindranath in translation.

A Note on the Contributors

TISTA BAGCHI is Reader in Linguistics at Delhi University.

BHAWANI-PRASAD CHATTOPADHYAY retired as Senior Lecturer in English, Itachuna College, West Bengal.

SWAPAN CHAKRAVORTY is Professor of English at Jadavpur University.

SUKANTA CHAUDHURI is Professor of English at Jadavpur University.

SISIR KUMAR DAS is Professor of Modern Indian Languages at Delhi University.

SANKHA GHOSH is a noted Bengali poet and critic. He retired as Professor of Bengali, Jadavpur University.

A Note on the Style of Dates

Many dates cited in this book, beginning 12 . . ., 13 . . . or 14 . . ., are based on the Bengali era (*Bangabda*). The international equivalents according to the Christian era are always given alongside, but the Bengali dates can be important as establishing chronology or helping to pinpoint a reference. A general rule for converting Bengali years to international ones is to add 593 (i.e. add 600 and subtract 7). But because the Bengali year begins in mid-April, one should add 594 for dates after the middle of Poush, the ninth month of the Bengali calendar.

The Text

The Bengali text followed is that in the original Visva-Bharati edition of Rabindranath's Collected Works (*Rabindra-Rachanabali*), Calcutta, Ashwin 1346– (September 1939–). Departures, if any, and a few important variant readings have been indicated in the notes.

Some Basic Terms and Concepts, and Their Renderings

The following terms often occur in the original Bengali text of these essays: they indicate the governing concepts of one or more pieces, or of Rabindranath's thought generally.

RAS (Sanskrit *rasa*): Like the archaic English term *humour, ras*(*a*) literally means a fluid or juice. In classical Indian poetics, it signifies the mood, vein or spirit that a work of art is intended to arouse. Usually, nine rasas are postulated:

1. *shringar* or *adi rasa*: the erotic
2. *vira rasa*: the 'heroic'—not only martial, but active or enthusiastic in matters of piety, generosity, good works, etc.
3. *karuna rasa*: the sad or sorrowful
4. *raudra rasa*: the wrathful or violent
5. *adbhuta rasa*: the marvellous or wonder-arousing
6. *bhayanaka rasa*: the fearsome or horrific
7. *vibhatsa rasa*: the rasa of revulsion or detestation, felt towards the ugly, repellent, or perverse
8. *hasya rasa*: the comic or humorous
9. *shanta rasa*: the serene or renunciatory

The *shanta rasa* is sometimes merged with the *karuna*. On the other hand, *vatsalya*, the rasa of filial affection, is sometimes proposed as an additional rasa.

As a concept in aesthetics, *rasa* is a recognised term in English, and has been commonly used in this volume. Simpler or less intensive uses of the word have sometimes been rendered as 'emotion', '(aesthetic) pleasure' or even 'joy'.

RUP (Sanskrit *rupa*): Combines the ideas of 'form' and 'beauty'—sometimes roughly on a par, sometimes foregrounding one or the other. In this volume, it has sometimes been rendered compositely as 'form and beauty'; more often by one of these words according to context, but even here the other association might be present in some measure.

Rup(*a*) can also signify 'image', or even 'kind' or 'manner'. These words, or suitable equivalents, have been used in appropriate cases.

BHAB (Sanskrit *bhava*): Combines the sense of idea, concept, or theme—i.e. something intellectually perceived—with that of mood, feeling or sentiment. The two implications are often present in equal measure, requiring a composite rendering such as 'feeling and idea'. Elsewhere, one or the other sense dominates, allowing an appropriate single-word rendering.

DHARMA: Though commonly used as an equivalent for *religion*, *dharma* has much wider implications. In its most basic sense, it means the distinctive nature, property, or propensity of a creature or object: it is the dharma of fire to burn, of water to flow, and of the tiger to hunt. Hence the word can mean a total ethos or way of life, especially as governed by virtuous law or values. A good man follows dharma not only as formally enjoined by religion, but as his own innate or ingrained imperative of virtue. Ultimately, the word can signify the deified principle of righteousness, the god Dharma.

In this volume, 'virtue' or 'righteousness' has often been adjudged the best rendering of *dharma* in a particular context. Sometimes, of course, the word refers simply to institutional religion and can be rendered accordingly. In a few cases, the original term *dharma* had to be retained in the absence of a viable English equivalent.

LILA: Literally 'play', but seldom used for actual play or sports. Sometimes refers to playful or sportive behaviour in humans; but classically to the 'sport' of providence, some deity or the world-order, in a free, often irrational and inscrutable exercise of its forces. Strictly, the term refers to activity undertaken in pure pleasure and out of no need or want—which can be postulated only of the divine. However, not all uses of the word, in Rabindranath or elsewhere, are quite so serious or precise.

Usually rendered here as 'play' or 'sport'.

SADHANA: Rigorous endeavour impelled by the contemplation or cultivation of a desired end, often with a specific sense of spiritual discipline or self-fashioning. Here rendered variously by words like 'effort', 'endeavour', or 'striving'.

DHYAN (Sanskrit *dhyana*): Meditation and, by extension, the intense contemplation or cultivation of some object, principle, or pursuit. Can imply ascetic rigour, but less markedly than *tapasya* (see below).

TAPASYA: Ascetic meditation. The implications of meditation or contemplation (at its highest point, a trance-like state), and of ascesis or severe self-discipline, are equally important. Such a demanding exercise usually has a specific spiritual end; hence the word can carry the extended meaning of rigorous endeavour (see *sadhana* and *dhyana* above).

TAPOBAN (Sanskrit *tapovana*): A hermitage or spiritual retreat in the forest. The sense of spiritual withdrawal and contemplation is combined, especially in Rabindranath, with that of a peaceful retreat in nature exerting its own spiritual influence.

The first element in the word is akin to *tapasya*, but the tapoban is not necessarily a place of severe ascesis. Life there is simple and spiritually ordered, but devoid neither of pleasure nor of human relationships including marriage and family life.

MANGAL (Sanskrit *mangala*): the power of good, especially good or beneficence as befalling a person or community. Usually translated here as '(the) good' or 'beneficence'; occasionally as 'benign(ity)' or 'the benign'.

KALYAN (Sanskrit *kalyana*): Combines the sense of happy circumstance and beneficence with a stronger association of prosperity and well-being than in *mangal* (see above). Usually translated here as 'beneficence', sometimes as 'prosperity' or '(the) good'.

Contents

List of Illustrations

Introduction

Rabindranath Thakur or Tagore's place as a critic has been partially eclipsed by his fame as a creative writer. Yet he is undoubtedly one of the makers of modern Bengali criticism and among the most perceptive critics in the language, if not the best. His corpus of critical writings is considerable, comprising more than one hundred essays of varying length. If his various other observations on art and literature, distributed in different works including his English writings, are taken into account, the corpus would be substantially larger. His engagement with the central issues of criticism, as well as with literary theory and aesthetics, spans almost his entire literary career.

Between 1888, when he was 26, and 1941, the year of his death, Rabindranath published at least eight books of different length devoted to literary criticism and theory. His early essays—that is those written and published during the last two decades of the nineteenth century—were originally written as book reviews. Some of them did, of course, take up certain theoretical issues that dominated literary debate at the time in India as well as in Europe. Two strands—not always easily separable—can be traced in these early writings. One concerns the assessment of contemporary Bengali literature; the other problematises more general issues. Literary criticism and literary theory both held attraction for Rabin-dranath, though he was not particularly anxious to construct a theory of his own, nor perhaps temperamentally equipped to do so.

It must clearly be understood that Rabindranath did not have any rigorous formal training in either philosophy or the history of the arts. On the other hand, not only was he a voracious reader in these subjects, but he was deeply involved in them, both as a creative writer and as a leading intellectual of his time. He had a natural impatience towards all formalism: he did not formulate his methods of literary analysis in precise terms, nor did he identify his critical tools with any objectivity. His approach to art was intimately linked to his philosophy of life; and like his philosophy, his view of art was free from rigidity, never aspiring to the condition of a system.

Rabindranath's first book of criticism, entitled *Samalochana* (Criticism), was published in 1888—about seven years after the successful production of his musical drama *Valmiki Pratibha*, which had established him as a poet and playwright of merit. Two popular works of his verse had also appeared by that time. Recognised though he was as a poet, Rabindranath did not consider his activities as critic detrimental to the creative spirit. In this he differed from the popular Bengali opinion of his day.

Sixteen of the essays included in *Samalochana* were written between 1880 and 1884. Most of them (except 'De Profundis') relate to Bengali texts. Rabindranath's critical evaluations of these texts, whatever be their value today, were not regulated by any parochial standard. His reading was wide and diverse, not confined to Bengali literature (which, although in ferment at the time, could still be considered a minor literature). His love for Sanskrit literature and his extensive reading in English ensured an enlargement of taste that was reflected in these early writings in ample measure.

Most of these essays went beyond their immediate contexts and addressed problems and concepts of general interest, such as 'silent' and 'natural' poets, historical and psychological changes in the evolution of poetry, the internal constituents of the epic, and issues of genre. But what appears most interesting is Rabindranath's privileging of one kind of poetry: his criticism had a specific function in respect of his own creative activities. Perhaps that was not unexpected in the case of a critic who was also a poet. His criticism was at the same time an apologia for his own poetry.

II

When Rabindranath began his career as critic, Bengali criticism was only a few decades old. Critical writings were still very few, and the reading public was hardly interested in criticism as a serious intellectual enterprise. On the one hand, there had been a complete break with the indigenous critical tradition; on the other, the Indian exposure to Western critical literature was still too limited and feeble to fill the vacuum. There was a long and rich tradition of Indian poetics, known as *alamkara shastra*, which goes back to Bharata's *Natyashastra*, a seminal work on dramaturgy dating from very early in the Christian era. This work, comparable to Aristotle's *Poetics* in its critical insight, intellectual rigour, and theoretical formulations (as well as its impact on later generations), was followed by a long series of texts and commentaries through many centuries. Like the ancient Indian grammarians, the exponents of poetics displayed acute powers of analysis and ability for system-building. Several schools of literary thought flourished in ancient India: animated debates on critical issues concerning language and meaning continued vigorously till the tenth century, when early Indian poetics reached its point of consummation.

Among the various schools of *alamkara* pursuing such concepts as *rasa*, *dhvani*, and *vakrokti*, the most renowned and arguably most singular was the school of *dhvani*, propounded by the ninth-century Kashmiri scholar Anandavardhana in his celebrated treatise *Dhvanyaloka*. The *dhvani* school was certainly the most influential, but other schools were no less important. After the tenth or eleventh century, the intellectual vigour of the discipline began to decline: it was slowly reduced to barren exercises in ingenuity.

From this time, the failure of the scholarly tradition of Indian poetics lay in its inability to go beyond Sanskrit to the literatures produced in the living languages of the country. If one ignores a few sporadic instances of critical analysis, mostly of a rudimentary nature, known as *dosha-guna-vichara* (examination of faults and virtues), there was no criticism at all in most Indian languages till the mid-nineteenth century. In Bengal, there was never a dearth of scholars specialising in poetics, but none included Bengali literature within his purview. Rupa Goswami's *Ujjvala Nilamani*, a sixteenth-century work on Vaishnava poetics, was undoubtedly a fine piece of scholarship. It became a model for the classification of Vaishnava lyrics in Bengali and other Indian languages, but did not reflect any interest in the emerging Vaishnava literatures in these languages at that time. In Bengali literary activity, criticism was a nineteenth-century innovation, mainly if not entirely an enterprise of the English-educated Bengali.

The Sanskrit scholars, of course, maintained the continuity of *alamkara* studies in Bengal. Some of their basic terms and concepts naturally permeated the literary vocabulary of other educated Bengalis. In the preface to his poem *Padmini Upakhyan* (The Tale of Padmini, 1858), Rangalal Bandyopadhyay (1827–87), an English-educated poet, quotes the famous aphorism *Vakyam rasatmakam kavyam* (Poetry is speech imbued with rasa) from *Sahitya Darpana* (The Mirror of Literature), the well-known fifteenth-century work by Vishvanatha. Rangalal's preface was a defence of a new poetry inspired by the English poets; yet he refers to the theory of rasa, which is peculiarly Indian. His friend Michael Madhusudan Datta (or Dutt, 1824–73), on the other hand, found the sanctions of Vishvanatha generally unacceptable, and did not show any interest in Indian literary theory. In 1873 Bankimchandra Chattopadhyay (or Chatterjee, 1838–94), almost universally held to be a champion of Hindu nationalism, dismissed Sanskrit poetics in general and the theory of rasa in particular with unconcealed contempt. He charged it with being too mechanical and narrow to deal with the infinite shades of emotion that constitute literature.

Whether Bankimchandra, with a critical vision newly acquired from European scholars, was right in this pronouncement need not concern us now. What is important is that despite the continued presence of certain concepts of Sanskrit poetics in the literary traditions of Bengal, it was European critical thought that became most influential in Bengali literary circles. It was possible for Michael to assert the superiority of the *Iliad* over the *Ramayana* and the *Mahabharata* without any qualms. His terms of reference for judging epics derived not from Vishvanatha but from Aristotle, whom he eulogised as the master of *alamkara* (*alamkara-shastra-guru*) of the Western world.

In fact, by the end of the 1870s, when criticism had taken roots in Bengali mostly in the form of book reviews and popular articles, it was totally under the sway of European criticism. Traces of Sanskrit poetics, mostly in terminology rather than in concepts, lingered on for some time, but no one talked about literary texts within the defined framework of any *prasthana* or critical school. What resulted from the encounter between Sanskrit and English was not, however, the establishment of an eclectic school of criticism, but a general widening of the area of literary enquiry.

The critics, like the creative writers themselves, felt that Bengali criticism could gain vitality and substance only through constant contact with European literature. It began with Rangalal: his preface to *Padmini Upakhyan* is an eloquent example. Michael Madhusudan advanced the trend by his occasional and at times flippant comments comparing the Indian epics with the Greek and Indian drama with Shakespearean. The process culminated in Bankimchandra. His essays *Shakuntala, Miranda o Desdemona* (Shakuntala, Miranda and Desdemona), and *Atiprakrita* (The Supernatural) are fine instances of an emerging interest in the comparative criticism of three literatures—Sanskrit, English, and Bengali, forming a single literary universe for the Bengali reader. The hierarchy of these literatures was naturally governed by the existing power-relationship among them. Sanskrit literary theory had to be content with a humble position.

By the time Rabindranath started writing criticism, Bankimchandra had already presented what we may call a sociological theory of literature. A keen student of Auguste Comte (1798–1857), Bankimchandra was familiar with the positivists' idea of literature. The positivist influence on him is clearly discernible in his analysis of Bengali poetry: particularly in his comments on the erotic Sanskrit poem *Gitagovinda*, relating it to the indolence of his contemporary society, which suffered from a strong sense of defeatism. He talks of the highly deterministic methodology of Henry Buckle (1821–62), who demonstrated the direct relationship between literature and external conditions such as physical features and climate, political and religious movements. John Stuart Mill (1806–73), whom Bankim revered, was another major influence. Bankim worked certain utilitarian tenets into his view of literature, without however compromising his belief in beauty as a basic factor of literary creation.

Despite his strongly sociological approach to literature—something new in India and never addressed in Sanskrit poetics—Bankim's was not a mechanical and reductive approach. Not only did he introduce biographical criticism in Bengali, but he also hinted at the possibility of exploring the creative process by privileging the author's mind and personality. His statement that the 'understanding of the poet is no less important than that of the poetry' opened up a new horizon in Bengali critical thought.

Bankim's literary career was not very long. His interest in criticism, though serious, was subservient to his creative faculty. Yet he almost singlehandedly laid the foundations of Bengali criticism. When Rabindranath emerged as a critic, he found Bankim had made criticism a respectable area of intellectual enquiry. Rabindranath acknowledged the historical role played by Bankimchandra. Like his predecessor, he probably thought it was the responsibility of the writers themselves to contribute to the growth of a healthy critical tradition.

III

The extent of Rabindranath's familiarity with Sanskrit poetics is not very clearly known. Except for *rasa*, he rarely used any technical term from Sanskrit poetics. Even his use of the term *rasa* is very general. His knowledge of European aesthetics and criticism was certainly wider, but he refused to follow any particular school too closely. As has already been observed, he abhorred any academic approach to art, and was temperamentally opposed to theorising. Like Oscar Wilde, he could have said, 'I am tired of my expedition into the dim dull abyss of facts.'

In a poem written in 1895, Rabindranath describes his conscientious exercises to master the theories of art and his disillusionment with them all; and how, finally, joy came to him through a direct contact with art that defied all formulation and analysis. On a lonely evening, the poet sat reading criticial theories about the nature of beauty and the poetic art, categories to which Shelley and Goethe and Coleridge might subscribe. All these exercises ended in fatigue and weariness. The poet felt they were devised by pedants, and were all false and baseless. As he closed the book and extinguished the lamp, the room was flooded with moonlight, and all his problems about the nature of beauty were resolved. He could now speak with a new realisation:

> O universal goddess of bounty, how could you hide yourself behind a tiny lamp? How could a few futile sentences out of a book rise to my charmed ear and obscure your wordless utterance extending across the worlds?[1]

Despite such dismissal of scholarly works on art and aesthetics, Rabindranath maintained a steady relationship with them. His impatience with methodological rigour and the demands of theory surfaced from time to time, asserting the supremacy of artistic enjoyment and experience over analysis and categorisation. This was a predicament of his creative life that remained more or less unresolved to the end. That partly explains the weakness as well as the strength of his critical writings: they lack in rigour of analysis, but are full of the joy of creativity.

In the mid-1930s, when Rabindranath was a target of attack for the modernists in Bengal, he wrote in an essay: 'The criticism of literature consists in its interpretation, not its analysis.'[2] For him, analysis only separated the components of a text but failed miserably to convey the delight it produced. It also failed to explain how the disparate elements came together to produce that delight. His criticism was not intended for the academic world. His target reader was the intelligent layman, the reader of literature, and the creative writer himself. Criticism was yet to attain sovereignty, claiming a metalanguage and a readership of initiates: Rabindranath shunned the specialised language of criticism.

[1] *Purnima* (The Full Moon), in the collection *Chitra* (1896).

[2] From *Sahitye Bichar* (Judgment in Literature), in *Sahityer Pathe* (On the Road to Literature), 1936.

His critical writings fall into two broad and slightly overlapping phases, the first concerned with interpretation and assessment and the second with theory. The first phase begins in 1880 and extends up to the first decade of the next century. It is an extremely interesting phase, in which he first emerges as an apprentice displaying skill and talent, and then slowly establishes himself as the foremost critic in the language.

Nothing is known about the reception of the first collection of this phase, *Samalochana* (1888), whose essays had been written in the early 1880s. Rabindranath himself was not very kind to this youthful work: he did not allow it to be reprinted. It had the marks of mere precocity, but also flashes of original thought and the courage to express it clearly. His critical insight and innovation became fully manifest in *Adhunik Sahitya*, *Prachin Sahitya*, and *Loksahitya*, three slender volumes all published in 1907. The thirty-five essays collected in these three books had been written over nearly two decades.

Adhunik Sahitya (Modern Literature) contains sixteen articles. Three of them review books which are not strictly literary: one on the history of Muslim rule in India, another a polemical work on modes of worship, and a third written by Bankimchandra, on Krishna. In this self-proclaimed collection of essays on contemporary writings, the only incongruous piece is on Radha as represented by Vidyapati, the great Maithili poet of the fifteenth century. The article—almost certainly the first by an Indian—on the French writer Joseph Joubert (1754–1824) is also rather out of place, though interesting and informative. There is also an essay on 'De Profundis', a perceptive interpretation of Tennyson's poem celebrating the birth of his son, reprinted from the 1888 volume *Samalochana*.

The rest of the book comprises three fine tributes to senior contemporaries—Bankimchandra, his elder brother Sanjibchandra (1834–89), and the poet Biharilal Chakrabarti (1835–94); reviews of two novels; and reviews of three books of verse written by Dwijendralal Ray (1863–1913), a dear friend later turned strident foe. Among these essays, the one on Biharilal is the most significant. In Biharilal, Rabindranath discovered a new voice, differing radically from that of poets engaged with the epic, Michael Madhusudan in particular.

Rabindranath's critical power and insight are at their best in the essays in *Prachin Sahitya* (Ancient Literature), dealing with some major texts of Sanskrit literature: the *Ramayana*; Kalidasa's *Kumarasambhavam*, *Abhijnanashakuntalam* and *Meghadutam*; and Banabhatta's *Kadambari*. There is also a highly appreciative review of a Bengali translation of the

Dhammapada from the Pali. It is an instance of Rabindranath's profound interest in and veneration for the Budha and his thought. No other Indian writer of the modern period has written so extensively on the Budha and Buddhism, or responded to them so creatively. Among the six essays devoted to Sanskrit literature, three are on Kalidasa, the poet Rabindranath most admired.

The collection is remarkable for the way it rescues the great Sanskrit texts from the morass of philological and rhetorical commentary to present them as living works. For the first time in many centuries, Kalidasa appears before the modern reader as a poet of great imagination and power, his voice still fresh and vibrant. For Rabindranath, Sanskrit literature is not a venerable mummy to be preserved in a mausoleum, but a presence still alive and beautiful, capable of speaking to the modern reader. He does for Sanskrit literature what European classicists had done for Greek and Latin, renewing them for the modern sensibility through critical analysis in modern European languages. However, he has not historicised the texts at all; nor does he concern himself with the ontological status of the work of art. His responses to Sanskrit literature emerge from an ambience created partly by European Romantic theories of poetry and partly by the Arnoldian view of poetry as a criticism of life.

The essay on *Meghadutam* is a perfect example of the creative response of a modern poet to an ancient poem. It also offers a fine example of 'the critic as artist' as conceived by Oscar Wilde. Written in prose of haunting beauty, it may not be accepted as criticism proper, being too subjective and too 'poetic'. But it undoubtedly captures the beauty and magic of Kalidasa's poem in a way no 'criticism' could have done. Another remarkable work of innovative and creative criticism is *Kabyer Upekshita* (Neglected Characters in Poetry), foregrounding certain characters in Sanskrit literature to whom, feels Rabindranath, their creators have not done justice.

As a critic in the more usual sense of the term, Rabindranath is at his best in the essays on *Abhijnanashakuntalam* and *Kumarasambhavam.* His readings of both works are free of all traces of the ancient traditions of textual scholarship as well as the paradigms of Indian poetics. But he contextualises the works in the Indian ideals of love and duty, pleasure and sacrifice. This was the time when he had started his school at Shantiniketan, which enshrined a strong revivalist fervour at the start. His reading of Kalidasa was influenced by his deep involvement with ancient Indian ideals as interpreted by the nineteenth-century Brahmo Samaj, to which he belonged. From the mid-nineteenth century, Bengali critics had undertaken the comparative study of texts from different cultures and linguistic traditions. The comparison of *Abhijnanashakuntalam* with *The Tempest* marks the culmination of this practice. Rabindranath does not employ any linguistic analysis, nor the customary analysis of plot and character. His parameters are defined by cultural values. His understanding of the texts is guided not solely by literary merit nor by aesthetic criteria, but by the value systems implicit in the texts.

Rabindranath is not as euphoric over Shakespeare as are many of his compatriots, including Bankimchandra and Shri Arabinda (Aurobindo), who found Sanskrit drama wanting in power to represent the complex problems of life in comparison to the Shakespearean or the Greek. Rabindranath's differing view is not owing to parochialism of taste and certainly not to any cultural chauvinism. It is chiefly because of his understanding of the relation between humankind and nature and the place of violence and peace, power and contentment in human society and the cosmic order. Like most of his contemporaries, Rabindranath had great admiration for the abundance and variety of the Shakespearean world, and he accepted it as a model for his dramatic writings. The change in his response to Shakespeare is neither abrupt nor coloured by revivalist prejudice; it is gradual, concurrent with his evolving views on the role and function of art. The change appears as much in his critical writings as in his conception of drama, which in his young days was formed by models from English literature. There too, Rabindranath gradually abandoned the Shakespearean model.

Equally significant, and perhaps more unorthodox, are the essays on Bengali nursery rhymes and rural literature, collected in *Loksahitya* (Folk Literature). The nineteenth-century Bengali literary canon, elitist and Westernised as it was, was strongly prejudiced against folk literature. The occasional interest shown by individuals was largely of an anthropological nature. When in 1883, Lal Behari De compiled a collection of Bengali fairy tales translated into English, he thought that, like the *Märchen* of the Grimm Brothers, the *Icelandic Legends* of Jon Árnason, or the *Highland Stories* of Campbell, his work would be a contribution to folklore and comparative mythology, 'proving that the swarthy and half-naked peasant on the banks of the Ganges is a cousin . . . to the fair-skinned and well-dressed Englishman on the banks of the Thames'.[3] Rabindranath was more eager to present this non-canonical and marginal literature, in

[3] Lal Behari De, Preface to *Folk Tales of Bengal* (1883), as in *Bengal Peasant Life, Folk Tales of Bengal, Recollections of My School Days*, ed. M.P. Saha (Calcutta, 1969), p. 265.

which he discovered great beauty and depth, to his countrymen indifferent and ignorant of their literary heritage, than to prove any relationship between the peasants of Bengal and their white masters. For the first time in our literature, the subaltern was valorised.

These three books, then, present three worlds of literary creation: ancient, contemporary, and folk. None of them employs analytical methods involving philology or social anthropology; nor was Rabindranath much interested in the philosophical dimension of literature. He relied almost exclusively on a strongly subjective intuition and taste.

Rabindranath's approach to literature and art was holistic, his emphasis being on the ultimate impact or rasa. He saw criticism as interpretation: at times a mediation between the reader and the text and at times a tribute, an acknowledgement of the delight that the reader draws from the text. In his essay on the *Ramayana*, he writes, 'True criticism is an act of worship. The true critic is a worshipping priest, who merely gives expression to his own mingled wonder and adoration or that of the public at large.' This metaphor of worship (*puja*) must be understood in its context. It is applied to a classic of the stature of the *Ramayana*, a text that has survived the ups and downs of literary taste through centuries, inspiring a thousand poems and plays and moulding the social and domestic ideals of millions of men and women. Is not the Greek criticism of Homer or the Roman criticism of Virgil a *puja*? T.S. Eliot declared that the greatness of literature cannot be determined solely by literary standards. The concept of *puja* is not an extraneous issue in criticism, but very much a part of its history.

Closely linked with *puja* is interpretation, which can be both an empathic understanding of the text or the author and a mediation between the text and the reader. In his essay on Biharilal, Rabindranath celebrates a little-known poet; in 'De Profundis' he explains the significance of a poem, the sublimity of its theme in particular, to a rather dismissive audience. In the whole corpus of his critical writings, perhaps the only instance of an aggressive attack is his assessment of Michael Madhusudan Datta's *Meghnadbadh Kabya*, a non-conformist epic in both spirit and structure. For Rabindranath, epic is not a mere narrative of exciting events but an exposition of the greatest ideals of a given time. He does not allow Michael's poem to determine its own genre, but judges it in terms of a framework imposed upon it. He condemns the poem for failing to conform to his prescriptions of the epic. But fortunately, he soon realised that if criticism was to be distinguished from rhapsodic expressions of the self, it should also eschew verbal attack. It must be a dignified exercise.

IV

The second phase of Rabindranath's critical writings can be identified with the essays collected in the book *Sahitya* (Literature), also published in 1907. None of the eleven essays relates to any specific literary text. One can say with some justification that with these essays, Rabindranath entered a different area of intellectual discourse, that of literary theory. After a long gap, he produced another such book, *Sahityer Pathe* (On the Road to Literature) in 1937, while a further collection appeared posthumously in 1943 under the title *Sahityer Swarup* (The True Nature of Literature); but he hardly produced any more readings of specific texts. The year 1907 therefore marks a watershed in his career as critic.

But before we talk about his literary theory, we must mention another important publication, *Panchabhut* (The Five Elements, 1897): a delightful work, containing dialogues and debates on various issues of life and literature between five characters representing the five elements.[4] The elements are characterised by touches of impish humour. Fire and water are feminine: lively, gleeful, and restless. The others are masculine: earth solid and pedantic, air a die-hard idealist, and space a votary of spirituality. The narrator is also a participant in the exercises, at times initiating, at other times provoking a discussion.

What is important for us, however, is not the brilliance and wit of *Panchabhut* but the substance of the essays where Rabindranath addresses certain issues of literary theory. His interest in theory is clearly reflected in three essays: two on comic laughter or mirth, and one on the significance of poetry. Written in a light vein, this last piece touches on several issues of interpretation and problematises them without pedantry. It obliquely raises such questions as the stability of the text, the relationship of text and meaning, and the validity of the readers' construction of the text. The significant part of the debate is the defence of hermeneutics and the acceptance of a plurality of interpretations. This was remarkable for its time, when texts were supposed to have only one meaning and the role of the reader in creating different meanings was hardly recognised. The importance of the reader may not be anything new; it is recognised

[4] For an explanation, see notes to 'A First Acquaintance'.

in both the Aristotelian concept of katharsis and the Indian concept of *rasasvada* (the savouring or experiencing of rasa). But to concede, as Rabindranath did, the right of the reader to construct his text and the validity of each possible interpretation, was not easy. Removed as he was from the indeterminacy of our time, he could not readily talk about the intentional fallacy or the death of the author.

One thing, however, is clear. Rabindranath wanted to liberate criticism from the restrictions of all structured approaches to literature and art. His concept of literature, its nature and function, and consequently his literary theory, is deeply rooted in the etymology of the word *sahitya*, the Sanskrit term for literature. It is derived from *sahita*, which carries the sense of togetherness. Some ancient scholars explained the term *sahitya* as the togetherness of *shabda* (sound, word) and *artha* (meaning).[5] Rabindranath extends that interpretation beyond the relation of sound and sense to a larger human relationship. According to him, not only literature but all the arts seek to ensure the relationship between human beings. Literature brings them closer to one another: the reader to the writer, one country to another, the ancient times to modern times. This concept of togetherness being central to Rabindranath's literary theory, he rejects the doctrine of art for art's sake, as well as the idea of absolute artistic freedom, untempered by any concomitant ideal of *mangal* (the good or beneficent). It is this 'togetherness' that draws him to the idea of literature as communication as well as expression. Literature becomes an institution like language itself, created and sustained by a community.

Like the European expressionists, Rabindranath can advocate the free and unbridled expression of states of mind; but he cannot accept the view that self-expression is the final goal of literature. 'The writer's main target is his audience,' he writes.[6] When a person is alone, there is no need of literature; literature becomes inevitable and imperative when one is part of a larger community. *Sahitya*, then, is an instrument to achieve togetherness. Of course, it is created by individuals out of their urge for self-expression, which Rabindranath accepts as innate in humankind; but it is created not for the self alone but for all humanity. In his own words:

> For man, as well as for animals, it is necessary to give expression to feelings of pleasure and displeasure, fear, anger and love. In animals, these emotional expressions have gone little beyond their bounds of usefulness. But in man, though

[5] *Shabdarthau sahitau kavyam* (Sound and word together make up poetry): Bhamaha, *Kavyalamkar*, 1.16.

[6] Translated from *Sahityer Samagri* (The Materials of Literature), 1903.

they still have roots in their original purposes, they have spread their branches far and wide in the infinite sky high above their soil. Man has a fund of emotional energy which is not all occupied with his self-preservation. This surplus seeks its outlet in the creation of Art, for man's civilisation is built upon his surplus.[7]

It is the surplus in the human condition that finds expression in art and literature. It is not an expression of egotism but of personality. Man 'feels his personality more intensely than other creatures, because his power of feeling is more than can be exhausted by his objects. This efflux of the consciousness of his personality requires an outlet of expression. Therefore, in Art, man reveals himself and not his objects.'[8]

Such a view of art is naturally critical of all mimetic theories, since it holds art to reveal the personality rather than the phenomenal world. But Rabindranath reconciles the phenomenal world and the human personality by making the former a part of the latter. He writes: 'This world, which takes its form in the mould of man's perception, still remains only as the partial world of his senses and mind. It is like a guest and not like a kinsman. It becomes completely our own when it comes within the range of our emotions. With our love and hatred, pleasure and pain, fear and wonder, continually working upon it, this world becomes a part of our personality.'[9]

But it needs reiterating that what we express is not only personal emotion limited to one's own self. It belongs to all humanity: that is what makes communication possible. Humankind becomes free only when we go beyond our biological existence and respond to the world of perceptions and emotions. Like the creator himself, humankind too is *lilamay*, a participant in a joyful sport. The history of art is the history of this *lila* or play.[10]

Rabindranath does not accept literature as imitation of the external world. But he does not deny that the world is the cause of literature. In *The Religion of Man*, he writes that art is the response of the creative human soul to the call of the real. It is not an imitation of external reality but a response to that reality. He refers to a verse in the *Atharva Veda* where the world has been described as the poem of God, *devasya kavyam*. The ancients used to call the poet *prajapati*, creator, and his creation

[7] From *Personality* (1917), as in *The English Writings of Rabindranath Tagore*, ed. Sisir Kumar Das (Sahitya Akademi, New Delhi, 1994–96), vol. 2, pp. 351–2.

[8] Ibid., p. 352.

[9] Ibid., p. 353.

[10] See note on p. xii.

another world, fictional but based on the fundamental rules of nature. The difference between the two worlds is that in the world where we live, we are regulated by biological necessity and all our activities are utilitarian; in the world created by poets, we are free: we see ourselves there in various configurations. The first world is the poem of God; the other the poem of humanity. It may be pointed out that according to Rabindranath, reality is not something transcendental and impersonal. It is a creation of our personality: in other words, its existence is valid only in relation to the existence of humankind.

The basic urgency of expression—and hence the creation of literature—comes from the surplus in the human state. The whole purpose of human creation, like God's, is *ananda* (joy). The Upanishads, says Rabindranath, never tire of talking of *anandarupamamritam yadvibhati* [the being that shines forth in joyous and immortal form].[11] From a speck of dust to the stars in the heavens, everything is the manifestation of truth and beauty, joy and immortality. Both beauty and joy are guiding concepts in Rabindranath's idea of art; but beauty, as he sees it, does not depend on just external form or symmetry, structure or design, which can give only visual pleasure. Beauty is founded on more profound principles. Like joy, it is not a matter of sensory pleasure, since beauty in art includes the unpleasant, the ugly, the painful, and the distorted as well as what is conventionally considered lovely. Here Rabindranath is clearly in agreement with the theory of rasa which stipulates the transformation of the *bhavas*, the mundane emotions (which are universal), into rasa or aesthetic joy, the ultimate delight produced by literature.

The ancient theorists argued that what shocks, pains or terrifies in life can turn into objects of beauty and joy in art. When represented in art, death and separation, the two most painful things in life, pass from *bhava* to *rasa*, from the *laukika* (mundane) to the *alaukika* (supra-mundane, i.e. aesthetic) plane. The saddest thoughts of real life thus become the sweetest songs in literature. Rabindranath would argue that beauty and delight are identical; and he also identifies beauty with the good or beneficent. Beauty cannot be the aim of art and literature unless it is good, he declares—much to the discomfort of scholars who see in this a confounding of ethics and aesthetics. He writes:

> . . . whatever is beneficent is in deepest unison with the whole world, in secret harmony with the mind of all humanity. When we see this absolute accord of the true and the beneficent, the beauty of truth no longer eludes our perception.

[11] See 'The Sense of Beauty'.

Compassion is beautiful; so are forgiveness and love. . . . In our puranas, Lakshmi is the goddess of not only beauty and riches, but also beneficence. The image of beauty is the fullest manifestation of the good, and the image of the good the consummate self of beauty. ('The Sense of Beauty')

Along with beauty, which he equates with the good or beneficent, Rabindranath also considers the age-old question of the truth value of poetry. Not only does he reject Plato's objections against poetry, that it does not have any truth-value and that it feeds the lower passions; he goes one step beyond Aristotle, who countered his preceptor by claiming poetry to be more philosophical than history and to manifest universal truth. Rabindranath argues that the truth of literature does not depend upon its power to reflect reality but its power to distinguish truth from facts. Facts can be proved and verified, measured and catalogued; truth is the principle that upholds the facts and links them. Facts are fragmentary and isolated; their greater unity is revealed in truth.

When within the fact of the individual 'I', I express the truth 'I am human', I am lit by the radiance of eternity emanating from the light of the great One. Expression, properly speaking, is the expression of the truth within the fact. As expression is the basic function of literature and the arts, their chief task is to afford our minds the savour of truth in the vessel of fact. This savour is the savour of the One, of the unbounded.[12]

What is here referred to as 'the savour of truth' is identical with the 'savour' of the One and of the *asim* or unbounded—a poetic way of describing Brahma, the supreme consciousness. Scholars have written at length on the nature of rasa as conceived by the Indian *alamkarikas*, to explain how the experience of beauty in art makes one progressively conscious of the illusoriness of the empirical world and how aesthetic experience leads to the attainment of a higher form of experience. Art is an instrument to attain *ananda*, joy, which is identical with *brahmasvada*, the 'savour' or perception of the supreme reality. Rabindranath uses the same terms to express his ideal of the ultimate 'savour' of art; but he does not accept the Vedantic position on the theory of rasa, nor does he negate the empirical world as illusion. As in philosophy so in art, he uses the metaphor of *sima* (boundary) and *asim* (the boundless) to indicate how the two complement each other. The joy of attaining the infinite within the finite is one of the recurring themes of Rabindranath's creative writings and philosophical thought. The central theme of his philosophy, as Abu Sayeed

[12] Translated from *Tathya o Satya* (Fact and Truth), *Sahityer Pathe.*

Ayyub puts it, 'emerges as the notion that art is a bridge across the chasm which normally separates the individual from the world around'.[13]

VI

Towards the end of his life, Rabindranath was attacked by the modernists in Bengal for his idealistic interpretation of art, and particularly his view of good and evil as making up the 'symphony of the universe'. This smacked strongly of the Upanishadic doctrines which the moderns regarded as obsolescent. They criticised his philosophy of art as too mystical and inadequate to account for the modern disillusionment that would deny the ultimate goodness of the universe. With their emphasis on the forbidding presence of evil in life, they found Rabindranath's equation of beauty and truth an empty platitude and his theory of art all too obfuscating.

Unshaken in his faith, Rabindranath deplored the modernists' valorisation of the ugly and the repulsive as the only reality. He saw in such a stand 'a subjective reaction and a passive perversion of the spirit'. He writes: '. . . if there is a theory of modernity, and if we describe it as a theory of the impersonal, it must be said that this arrogant mistrust and vilification of the world is also a perversion of personal feelings caused by a sudden upheaval.' ('Modern Poetry').

The emphasis in modern literature on suffering and evil, and its challenge to theories privileging beauty and the good as both substance and end of literature, result for Rabindranath from a biased understanding of the nature of reality. He feels that the modernists have not acquired the detachment to separate the aesthetic from the biological plane of existence.

It is not difficult to find contradictions in Rabindranath, whose ideas on art and literature had evolved slowly and gradually through five decades, concurrently with his primary development as a creative writer. At times he would emphasise the role of a given culture in the representation of reality: for example the Buddha in Gandhara art or the sculpture of Rodin as reflecting the European temper, while in the Indian mind 'the real appears in its ideal form of fulfilment' without care for anatomical accuracy.[14] If this binary division of East and West appears too reductionist, there is another voice in Rabindranath which declares, 'There is no

[13] Abu Sayeed Ayyub, 'The Aesthetic Philosophy of Tagore', *Rabindranath Tagore Centenary Volume* (Sahitya Akademi, New Delhi, 1961), p. 81.

[14] 'The Meaning of Art': *English Writings*, vol. 3, p. 585.

such thing as absolute caste restriction in human cultures.'[15] If his ideals of art and literature have a strong Upanishadic foundation, it is also important to realise that he rejected all blind adherence to the past. He writes:

When in the name of Indian art we cultivate with deliberate aggressiveness a certain bigotry born of the habit of a past generation, we smother our soul under idiosyncrasies unearthed from buried centuries. These are like masks with exaggerated grimaces, that fail to respond to the ever-changing play of life.[16]

It is difficult to consider Rabindranath's thoughts on literature and art without reference to his other writings; but such an exercise serves to indicate a certain hiatus between Rabindranath as critic and as artist. It makes his critical writings doubly interesting: they celebrate the intimate relation between creativity and critical power, while also pointing towards the area where the twain shall never meet.

VII

A few words must be added about Rabindranath's writings on language. These are partly the outcome of his concern with style, diction and standardisation, and the role of language in society. But a substantial part also grows out of his abiding interest in linguistics proper and its pedagogy. This may seem contrary to the traditional image of the poet deriding the grammarian. But when one thinks of Rabindranath's involvement with so many 'unpoetical' activities rural reconstruction, agriculture, and the management of a school—and the wide range of subjects he studied and wrote about, his interest in grammatical studies appears natural.

It is not widely known that Rabindranath wrote primers of English and Sanskrit. His Bengali primer *Sahaj Path* (Easy Reading) is, however, a classic. None of these primers is the amateurish work of a poet; they are products of careful planning and graded arrangement of linguistic material, imbued with a strong urgency to introduce an alternative method of language teaching. *Sahaj Path* has not even today lost its utility: quite recently, it was the subject of a heated controversy over its alleged ideological moorings.

These works reflect a lifelong engagement with the study of language. It began as early as 1885, when Rabindranath was deeply involved with experiments towards a new poetic idiom, as well as with establishing a

[15] Ibid.

[16] Ibid., p. 587.

new line of Bengali criticism. Around that time, he wrote an essay on the erratic features of Bengali pronunciation—or, more accurately, the imperfect correspondence between the phonic structure of the language and its alphabet and orthography. That essay ended with the observation that though several Bengali grammars had been composed, they were all mere modifications of Sanskrit grammar: 'Of real Bengali grammar, there is nothing.'[17] This was the beginning of Rabindranath's investigations into the nature of the Bengali language, based on observed practice and free from any preconceived notions. Over the next twenty-five years, he frequently wrote on various aspects of the language, chiefly its sound system and morphology and sometimes also etymology. These pieces were collected in the book *Shabdatattwa* (Linguistics) in 1909. By that time, he had already won distinction as a literary critic.

Again in 1938 at the age of 77, he produced a monograph, *Banglabhasha-Parichay* (Introduction to the Bengali Language), now regarded as a classic both for its insight and originality of thought, and for its attractive prose. These two books, different in origin, structure, and design but unified by their acumen and originality of thought, substantially present Rabindranath's writings on language and linguistic issues.

Like most intellectuals of his time, Rabindranath was aware of the great achievement of nineteenth-century European scholars in historical and comparative linguistics: in particular, the impact on linguistic studies of the idea of evolution. Like poetics, linguistics too had a glorious tradition in India; but again like poetics, this had been reduced to sterile academic exercises. The Sanskrit pandits, despite their familiarity with Panini's *Ashtadhyayi,* remained engrossed with the subtleties of Sanskrit, without any interest or concern for the living languages of the country. Except for the ancient Tamil grammar *Tolkappiyam,* no formal grammar had been composed for any modern Indian language before the nineteenth century. A Bengali grammar had indeed been produced in the mid-eighteenth century by a Portuguese padre for the use of Christian missionaries; but it was published in Lisbon and remained quite unknown in Bengal.

The first recognised grammarian of Bengali was the Englishman Nathaniel Brassey Halhed, a friend of the playwright Sheridan. Halhed, who came to India as an officer of the East India Company, produced his work for the benefit of the British in Bengal. He modelled it on the English

[17] 'Bangla Uchcharan' in *Shabdatattwa* (*Rabindra-Rachanabali,* Visva-Bharati, vol. 12, p. 342).

grammars of the time, which were prescriptive in nature and governed by Latin rules. When Bengali scholars felt the need to prepare grammars of their language for use by native speakers, they squarely based themselves—with a few noted exceptions—on Sanskrit grammar, overlooking the features which distinguished the two languages. With exemplary boldness, Rabindranath rejected this Procrustean resort to Sanskrit. All his essays on Bengali morphology are strong pleas for recognising Bengali as an independent language-system with its own rules of operation.

It is also significant that Rabindranath had only a marginal interest in historical linguistics, although he grew up in a milieu where it was a dominant force. Bishop Robert Caldwell's *A Comparative Grammar of the Dravidian or South Indian Families of Languages* (1856) and John Beam's *A Comparative Grammar of the Modern Aryan Languages of India* (3 volumes, 1872–79) had opened up new horizons in Indian linguistics. Rabindranath admired these works, but his own field of inquiry fell almost entirely within synchronic linguistics. He was interested in the living language, its structures and functions, and not in historical change.

Rabindranath's essays on Bengali enclitics, the plural number, the case system, inflexions, and suffixes are products of this interest. His finest achievements as a linguist are surely the comprehensive lists he prepared of Bengali verb roots and of onomatopoeic words in Bengali. No one before him had so meticulously collected the onomatopoeic words abounding in Bengali, or written so illuminatingly on their functions, indicating their wide semantic range and expressiveness. The essay remains unsurpassed even today: unfortunately, its close references to Bengali vocabulary and usage make it unsuitable for translation. It forms a corollary to the essay on 'Children's Rhymes' included here. Both pieces indicate his attachment to the language of the people, as opposed to the formal, ornate, recondite Sanskritic mode.

This strong advocacy of a new approach to Bengali grammar, free from the hegemony of Sanskrit, generated a healthy debate in contemporary Bengal. The only other scholar who took up the cause of Bengali as a living language in its own right was the renowned Sanskritist Haraprasad Shastri. A contemporary hailed them both as the true heirs of Panini. This may be an exaggerated eulogy, but it testifies to the impact of Rabindranath's thought on the scholarly world.

Banglabhasha-Parichay treats of technical matters with rare clarity and ease. It is remarkably free of technical terms, and follows no specific model of linguistic analysis. The book is divided into twenty-three short sections and, after some general introductory comments, devotes itself to various issues: the expressive and 'counter-factual' aspects of the language, the arbitrary relation between sound and meaning, the symbolic nature of words, the relation between language and reality, and the role of language in the creative and social activities of humankind. These matters have been addressed by philosophers of language over the centuries, but only very recently have they been integrated with formal linguistics. Properly speaking, Rabindranath is the only Indian author of our times to foreground these issues and create a new space within the field of linguistic study.

What is most striking in this work is Rabindranath's distinction between his own approach and that of professional linguists. The latter group is represented by Sunitikumar Chatterji, the most eminent scholar of the day in this field. Rabindranath dedicates the book to him, describing him as a 'geographer' who inquires in detail into the different 'regions' of language and presents his data and speculations according to an organised methodology. Rabindranath himself, on the contrary, is a 'traveller', walking along the paths of language; his writings narrate his experience of such travel. What attracts him most is the *adbhuta rasa*, the wonder and mystery of the language.

The book is not, however, an exercise in the philosophy of language. It deals with specific problems of Bengali grammar: its sound system, its gender, number and case systems, its suffixes and inflexions among other matters. Being free from the demands of a precise methodology, Rabindranath moves freely from one linguistic 'region' to another: issues of style, metre, spelling, etc. all find their place within a comprehensive treatment of the language. *Banglabhasha-Parichay* exemplifies an approach to language that may fitly be called holistic. It aims to present the Bengali language in its totality.

It is possible to reconstruct Rabindranath's entire concept of language on the basis of these two books, along with other observations scattered through his works, including some of his poems. His thinking about language has been described as both 'counter-factual' and 'expressive'. It has been linked with the idea of 'surplus', an essential element in his critical and philosophical thought, as well as with the Vedic view of *vak* [word or speech].[18] It is also possible to discover similarities, sometimes

[18] See Pabitra Kumar Roy, 'Tagore's Concept of Language', in Bhudeb Chaudhuri and K.G. Subramanyam (eds), *Rabindranath Tagore* (Indian Institute of Advanced Studies, Shimla, 1988).

quite striking ones, between his observations and certain premises of modern linguists. It has recently been shown how his idea of a comprehensive Bengali grammar, taking account of its various dialects, has remarkable resemblances to the 'panlectal' or 'polylectal' grammar proposed by a modern language planner.[19]

Scholars may debate these issues. What is beyond dispute is that both these works, *Shabdatattwa* and *Banglabhasha-Parichay,* remain to this day a source of thought for professional linguists, and of joy and illumination for the common reader.

SISIR KUMAR DAS

[19] See Mrinal Nath, 'Language Treatment by Tagore', *West Bengal* 32.9 (Calcutta, 16 May 1990).

Silent Poet, Untaught Poet

Rabindranath includes a Bengali rendering of Marlowe's poem 'The Passionate Shepherd to His Love' in this essay. In the present translation, the original English has been quoted, in the version followed by Rabindranath. While reworking or reordering a few details, he preserves the material of Marlowe's poem in largely intact form.

The word is going round that everyone is a poet. Anyone who has feelings, who cries for sorrow, and laughs for happiness, is a poet. The idea is novel. It is not the general idea of a poet. When we hear something contrary to the general idea, we are sometimes delighted. Young people these days are often heard to say that any person of sensibility is a poet. It is not too much to say that this extended meaning of the word 'poet' has become fashionable these days. Even such an expression as 'a silent poet' has entered into circulation and come to gain currency day by day: so much so that if I make the point, which is not novel at all, that there is no such thing as a silent poet, it will strike people as a new idea.

What I wish to say is that one who is silent is not a poet at all. Unfortunately, my opinion is shared by most people in their heart of hearts. So they protest, 'That's what everybody says. How nice it would be if you could prove the contrary.' They would no doubt like it, but this question is such as to admit of no second opinion. The word 'poet' is not so problematic as to invite intellectual contortions; it is not a dialectician's toy, like the puzzle of which came first, the tree or the seed. People have given a particular object a particular name for convenience of expression. That is the name by which everybody calls it and has done for a long time. What room can there be for argument? Whom do people call a poet? One who expresses, through language, ideas and feelings of a particular kind (which we call poetry).[1] 'Silent' and 'a poet' are contradictory terms. If you marry the adjective 'silent' with the noun 'poet', you bring together such a

[1] It would n ot be appropriate for this essay to set about giving an abstruse definition of poetry, with a great show of elaboration. Hence we desist from doing so.

mutually destructive couple that no sooner do their eyes meet during the wedding rites† than they both give up the ghost. Each reduces the other to ashes by its sight. Such sighting can only be termed inauspicious. Must we bring about such a union?

It is, of course, quite possible that you think of somebody as a poet while I do not. On those grounds, you could certainly argue that, different persons being regarded as poets by different people, we cannot say that they all mean the same thing by the word 'poet'. My point is that they do all mean the same thing. When you call Ram Babu, author of *The White Lotus of Poetry*, a poet and I do not, while I call Shyam Babu,† author of *The Moonbeams of Poetry*, a poet and you do not, the real argument between us is this: what is so poetic about Ram, or conversely about Shyam, that one can call him a poet? Both Ram and Shyam go to the same school, the only question being who is in the senior class and who in the junior. Now, what is the school to which they both belong? The school of expression. What do they have in common? The act of expression. In what do they differ? In their manner of expression.

However, it is only a good poem that we call a poem *per se*. If it is bad, we call it a bad poem. If it diverges still further from good poetry, we can call it verse, or doggerel, or whatever we wish. We call the highest creature on earth a human; the ape, that comes close to it, we call a forest-human. The monkey, which deviates further still, we call merely a humanoid.† Have you ever heard anybody argue whether Wordsworth is a better poet than Bhajahari,† who does not know what a pen looks like? Thus, you see, nobody can be called a poet without publishing poetry. Going by your view, all human beings can be called artists. There is no one whose mind is not full of innumerable pictures. Why then do we not use 'artist' as another name for a human?

My point is very simple. Feelings and emotions not expressed in language are not poetry, and one who has not so expressed them is not a poet. Those who have invented the phrase 'a silent poet' regard the whole universe as poetry. Ideas of that kind look well in poetry; they are out of place in unadorned prose or in a debate. If we use a word in various senses in this way, the unwelcome consequence is that it sprouts a pair of wings: it cannot be held down to one spot, but gets out of hand. It is then of no use; it turns feral and will not return to its cage when called.

I am trying to say that I am not a painter just because I have a picture of my lady-love in my mind, any more than the lady is a painting because, if one had the talent, one could paint her.

There are many who hold that the entire human race consists of poets, children† and the uneducated especially so. This idea has not gained such wide currency as the last, but it often crops up in argument. That children are not poets has already been demonstrated. They do not express their feelings in the language of poetry. Many men have poetic feelings and enjoy poetry. You could perhaps stretch a point and call them poets, but you cannot call children poets by any means. Children do not have poetic feelings; they do not enjoy poetry, at least not as grown-ups do. Everyone has feelings; even animals feel pleasure and pain. But how many people feel poetically? How many can tell what is truly beautiful and truly ugly, and distinguish between them? Most men are incapable of discerning and appreciating beauty. To know what makes a beautiful thing beautiful, to compare it with all other beautiful things and give it its due place, to see one beautiful object and recall ten others, to imagine how the beauty of a beautiful thing can vary according to circumstance—do all these lie within everybody's power? Can all eyes see the incorporeal in the corporeal?

Everyone has the faculty of imagination, some more and some less; and who more than the lunatic? A powerful imagination does not by itself make a poet. It must be a trained and refined imagination of a high order. There should be the intellect and the taste to employ the imagination to good purpose. How many children are there in whose imagination the full moon can smile and the moonbeams sleep? If a child is extraordinarily imaginative, he might think of the full moon as a pancake and the half-moon as some sweet of that shape. Their imagination lacks coherence. It takes a great deal of training to see what goes with what, which objects when juxtaposed illuminate each other, how an object must be viewed to yield up its essence and its beauty.

There are many ways of looking at an object. Scientists look at the world in one way, philosophers in another, and poets in yet another. The same object can be viewed in three different ways by these three persons. Do you think that to master two of the three ways requires training but not the third—not only does not require it, but is positively destroyed by it? The philosopher, the scientist, and the poet—it is the task of all three to determine, with the utmost accuracy, the category to which every object belongs and the affinities and oppositions between them. An object has three aspects to it, and these three persons each has charge of one of them. That is the only difference between them; is there any other?

Many good poets have, in places, betrayed their lack of training by failing to judge which feelings and emotions belong together. This can be seen in Marlowe's well-known poem,[†] 'Come live with me and be my love'.

Come live with me and be my love,
And we will all the pleasures prove
That valleys, groves, hills and fields,
Woods, or steepy mountain yields.

And we will sit upon the rocks
Seeing the shepherds feed their flocks
By shallow rivers, to whose falls
Melodious birds sing madrigals.

And I will make thee beds of roses,
And a thousand fragrant posies,
A cap of flowers, and a kirtle
Embroidered all with leaves of myrtle.

A gown made of the finest wool
Which from our pretty lambs we pull;
Fair lined slippers for the cold,
With buckles of a purest gold.

A belt of straw, and ivy buds,
With coral clasps and amber studs:
And if these pleasures may thee move,
Come live with me and be my love.

Thy silver dishes for thy meat,
As precious as the gods do eat,
Shall on an ivory table be
Prepared each day for thee and me.

The shepherds' swains shall dance and sing
For thy delight each May morning.
If these delights thy mind may move,
Come love with me and be my love.

This poem does not express a single integrated idea or emotion. It breaks down in the middle. The comprehensive imagination that reflects an emotion in its wholeness, that has no seams or patches, is not in evidence here. The shepherd who has access to all the pleasures offered by the woods, mountains, and fields, who holds out the allurements of a bed of roses, a cap of flowers, and a kirtle of leaves—where would he lay his hands on 'fair lin'd slippers' with buckles of the purest gold', 'silver dishes', and 'ivory tables'? Does coral suit a belt of straw? In the Kabikankan's† 'Kamaley Kamini',† a beautiful woman of sixteen is shown as alternately swallowing and disgorging an elephant. This is so incongruous as to offend our sense of beauty.[2] To an imagination that is trained, sober, and refined, a beautiful young woman can never be associated with the swallowing and disgorging of an elephant.

The imagination too, like everything else, requires training. An imagination without proper training revels in the extravagant, the impossible, the preternatural. A mirror with a curved surface shows a disproportionately large nose with a forehead and a chin that are much too small. In the ill-formed mirror of an untrained imagination, natural objects lose their proportions: the nose becomes too large and the forehead too small. People of such imagination cobble together ill-sorted objects and produce a monster. They are incapable of seeing incorporeal dimensions in a corporeal object. If you still maintain that children are poets, you are talking like a child.

Much good poetry was composed in ancient times. That may be what has led to the idea that uneducated people are particularly poetical. Will you tell me how many readable poems there are in the Tahitian or Eskimo language? Can you name any nation not civilised that has good poetry? The age when the *Ramayana* and the *Mahabharata* were composed was no doubt ancient, but was it uneducated? Can anyone who has read the

[2] There are many who suggest that what Dhanapati the merchant saw was Durga kissing Ganesh† again and again: from a distance, it appeared to him like the swallowing and disgorging of an elephant. But this cannot be the true explanation, since in Kabikankan's *Chandimangal* itself it is said that of the sixty-four yoginis,† each becomes a petal of a lotus flower and Jaya† assumes the form of an elephant. Thus it has nothing to do with Ganesh. Others argue that, it being the poet's purpose to create a sense of wonder, he aims at the fantastic. But this is nonsense. The rasa of wonder† is not inimical to a pleasing fancy.

When the poet places a beautiful sixteen-year-old in a bed of lotus flowers, adorned with swans, amidst a vast ocean, everything in such a place is beautiful—the blue waters, the lovely lotus flowers, the sweet smell, the hum of bees. With all this around, why bring in the gulping down of an elephant to deal such a fearsome blow to our imagination? Can anything produce such a sense of poetic wonder as a beautiful object can do? A woman of sixteen seated in a lotus bed on the boundless ocean—would that not be sufficient cause of wonder?

two epics ever think so? And the great poets born in England in the nineteenth century—do we not notice an influence of the nineteenth century on them? Copleston[†] says, 'Never has there been a city of which its people might be more justly proud, whether they looked to its past or its future, than Athens in the days of Aeschylus.'

Many think that poetry flourishes especially in an untaught state: one reason being, in their opinion, that when you do not know the true nature of something, your imagination can play around it in a thousand ways. Truth is one, falsehoods innumerable. Hence falsehoods can feed the imagination much more plentifully than truth. The number of inedible things on earth is vast, compared to things that are edible. For each substance that we can eat, there are a thousand that we cannot. But have you heard any scholar suggest that the human race will die out if it does not eat the inedible?

The fact is, there is much more poetry in truth than in falsehood. The imagination can knock on the doors of a thousand falsehoods, but in all likelihood will not extract even a small handful of poetry by way of alms. On the other hand, you have only to go to one truth, and see if you do not get ten times as much in the form of poetry. And why should it be otherwise? It is nature that has taught us poetry, and nature never lies. Can we ever imagine that the grass that soothes our eyes is flaming red? Is there more poetry in the notion of a stationary earth and a heaven studded with immobile stars, or in the motion of all the stars, travelling each with its own family? So measured are their steps that an astronomer can tell where a planet will be today if it was in a particular place yesterday. Firstly, one cannot create anything more poetic than nature can. Secondly, we cannot apprehend a beauty lying outside the existence into which we are born.

There are many lies that we find sweet in poetry. That is because when they were first written, they were thought to be true, and have passed for truth ever since. Now I have found them out to be false, which means I have banished them from the realm of knowledge. But they have sent their roots so deep into my heart that there is no way I can uproot them. What is signified by the fact that a poet who does not believe in ghosts still describes them? It signifies that a ghost, even though not a material truth, is a truth in our hearts. When we imagine ghosts, it strikes somewhere deep in our hearts. What ideas does it bring in its train: darkness, loneliness, cremation grounds, a supernatural thing silently dogging our steps—all such fancies from our childhood days. Who but a poet can perceive such truths?

Even though the truth is one, it is not as if ten poets might not see ten different kinds of poems in it. See what a variety of colours the earth can assume in the light of a single sun. Poetry does not lie in the mere fact of a river's flow. What is indeed poetic is the truth of the particular feeling aroused in our hearts at the sight of the flowing river. Think, then, how many different kinds of feelings the same river can inspire at different times. Sometimes we hear it singing a melancholy song; sometimes it warbles merrily, filling us with joy as it dances along. The moonlight never actually sleeps: that is to say it does not lie down with its eyes shut, nor has anyone ever heard it snore. But it is nonetheless true that on a quiet night, the moonlight does seem to be asleep. Let them discover every minute scientific fact about the moonlight, let them even demonstrate that it is not a substance at all; people will still say that the moonlight sleeps. Which master scientist will dare call that a lie?

TRANSLATED BY BHAWANI-PRASAD CHATTOPADHYAY

'De Profundis'

This essay provides Bengali paraphrases of many portions of Tennyson's poems, as well as quoting them in the original English. The latter (in the readings used by Rabindranath) have been printed in italics; the paraphrases are rendered in English following the precise phrasing of Rabindranath's Bengali, which might differ (substantively, at one or two points) from Tennyson's original.

The above poem by Tennyson has not met with the appreciation it deserves. Some English critics think it is unworthy of the poet, and many Bengali readers go one better. The English humorous weekly 'Punch' published a parody of the poem and titled it 'De Rotundis'. We by no means approve of such scoffing. It is the English way. They find it amusing to satirise a well-known poem of noble theme. Some of them think it is a matter of pride for the poet if we mutilate a well-known and estimable poem, paint its face like a clown's, and stand it by the roadside for a clutch of idle frivolous passers-by to grin at. This shows up the sadly mutilated state of an aspect of the English psyche. This is not the way we, as a nation, conduct ourselves. If someone stands up in a gathering and, with contorted voice and gestures, mimics the heartfelt utterances of an elderly, respected man in order to humiliate him, those who are amused by this supposed wit ought, we think, to be ostracised.

One reason why Tennyson's 'De Profundis' has not found favour is that its subject is grave and serious. Another reason is that it contains ideas and feelings which the English do not ordinarily understand; we are the right people to understand them properly. Many educated Bengalis, learned in English, are afraid to criticise English poetry in the Indian way, for fear that their criticism should be at odds with what English critics say. Suppose that is so. If what the English critic says is valid in the English way, what the critic of our country says will be valid in ours. The two may be different, yet both may be correct. If a rose, because its neighbouring leaves turn green in the sunlight, thinks it too should be green, that to turn green is the ultimate aim of its life, the society of flowers will surely question its sanity.

'De Profundis' was written on the birth of the poet's son. One's expectations about a piece written on such an occasion are belied by this poem. Its subject is not a tender face, or sweet smiles, or baby talk. A tiny newborn baby has another quality besides sweetness and freshness, which many fail to observe but the thinking poet does not. There is, in a child just born, an illimitable sublime idea, an unfathomable mystery. This is what Tennyson expresses. The ordinary reader cannot comprehend it, or grasp the unfamiliar idea with his heart.

Tennyson has called this poem 'The Two Greetings'. That is, in it he has addressed his son in two ways: first as a father, then distancing himself; first with reference to the child's earthly life, then to his very being; first partially, then as a whole. He views his child in two aspects: he has affection for one and veneration for the other. The first greeting is one of affection, the second of adoration. In both parts of the poem, the poet's vision extends far, from horizon to horizon.

In the first part, the child is born. From where does it come? the poet at once begins to wonder. Just as the Vedic poet-sages, on seeing the youthful sun rise from the great world of darkness, from the ocean's womb, asked reverently, 'Whence does it come?', the poet too asks with the same reverence, 'Whence does it come?' He crosses the bounds of present time and place. What distances does he cover, what heights does he ascend as he speeds to that great peak of the past, as towards the source of the Ganga! What place more suitable for the poet to roam in? He sees that the child born on this earth is the sibling of the earth itself. It is twin brother to the sun and the planets. Addressing the child, he says, 'O my son, from the great ocean where all-that-will-be, contained in all-that-was (that is to say the future contained in the past, the fully formed in the unformed) whirled for a million aeons through the vast desert of countless eddying masses of light—from there have you come. It is from there that the sun has come, and the earth, and the moon, and its siblings the other planets.' The poet has entered the womb of that ancient dawn and found there, whirling, the amassed causes of the unmanifested earth and the amassed causes of today's newborn child. The two are of the same age; it is just that one was quicker to manifest itself to our eyes, while the other took longer.

Out of the deep, my child, out of the deep,
Where all that was to be, in all that was,
Whirl'd for a million aeons thro' the vast
Waste dawn of multitudinous eddying light—
Out of the deep, my child, out of the deep,
Thro' all this changing world of changeless law,
And every phase of ever-heightening life,
And nine long months of antenatal gloom,
With this last moon, this crescent—her dark orb
Touch'd with earth's light—thou comest, darling boy.

Having talked about the past, the poet comes to the present. He looks at the child. He discovers who it is that the past has nurtured with such care: it is none other than his son, dearer to him than his own life. It is his son that the past, his mother, had held in her womb along with the sun, the moon, the stars, and the planets, rocked in the same luminous cradle, nursed at the same breast, and today handed over to him. He who is today the poet's son, so dear to his heart, had so long been Nature's treasured darling. To him the poet says, 'You are our very own treasure. Your limbs and shape, perfect in every detail, foretell the perfectly formed adult man you will one day be. My face and form, and those of my wife, have been wedded in you with an indissoluble tie.' The poet sees that this child is their very own: his frame, his limbs are made out of the two of them. Then the poet looks towards the boy's future and continues:

Live, and be happy in thyself, and serve
This mortal race thy kin so well, that men
May bless thee as we bless thee, O young life
Breaking with laughter from the dark; and may
The fated channel where thy motion lives
Be prosperously shaped, and sway thy course
Along the years of haste and random youth
Unshatter'd; then full-current thro' full man;
And last in kindly curves, with gentlest fall,
By quiet fields, a slowly-dying power,
To that last deep where we and thou are still.

Now the child is no longer theirs at all. Now he has developed his own identity and has his own work to do. The poet reviews three stages of the newborn's earthly life. First he considers the original cause of his mortal existence; then he talks about his birth, or his assuming the human body;

and finally he examines his earthly life. This is where it all ends. The first greeting is over. In this the poet hails the mortal being. As long as he is a human being, he is the poet's own; the past has formed him in order to present him to the poet. When he has taken shape, the poet sees that the child is like him. This part talks only of the body, of mortal life. 'Live, do your work, let your life attain fulfilment, and finally let it end very gently and gradually.' That is the substance of the poet's greeting. The poet addresses the mortal part of his son, hence the above benediction can be implicitly applied to his earthly life.

Well, this is the end of it all. Life has begun, life has ended. Then, mounted upon life's memorial column, the poet gazes across vast distances. He sees that while life ends, and his son no longer is, the course whose flow had brought him his son does not end. Now he can see that a traveller on the path of eternity has lodged on the way as a guest in the poet's house, here upon this earth. While he is a guest on this earth he is called a son, a human being. The sojourn ends, the son is no more, the human being is no more, but the traveller endures. The poet had first greeted the guest; now he addresses the great wayfarer—no longer the guest of the earth but the guest of all time. Now he discovers that the traveller is elder brother even to the sun and the planets. In the first greeting he had talked of millions of aeons and the manufactory of eddying light, of ever-surging life in this unchangeable world of change, and said:

With this last moon, this crescent—her dark orb
Touch'd with earth's light—thou comest.

That is, when a human being is born, he is like the crescent moon: one part of his existence is gradually lit up by earthly life, earthly intelligence. In the second part the poet addresses one whose origin he does not explore by measuring time or enumerating the materials of which he is made. Now he says:

Out of the deep, my child, out of the deep,
From that great deep, before our world begins,
Whereon the Spirit of God moves as he will—
Out of the deep, my child, out of the deep,
From that true world within the world we see,
Whereof our world is but the bounding shore—
Out of the deep, Spirit, out of the deep,
With this ninth moon, that sends the hidden sun
Down yon dark sea, thou comest, darling boy.

The ocean the poet talks of here is not an ocean of light; it has no shores in the past or the future; it subsumes past, present, and future. He refers to the soul of the world, the true world within the world. The exterior world only sets a bound to the world within.

Out of the deep, Spirit, out of the deep,
With this ninth moon, that sends the hidden sun
Down yon dark sea, thou comest, darling boy.

You have emerged from this sea. Letting the radiant sun sink in the ocean, the moon rises with its pale light. You have risen with it, leaving behind the great effulgence. The man the poet addressed earlier had passed from incompleteness to completeness; the soul he now hails has passed out of its fullness into a state of incompleteness.

For in the world, which is not ours, They said
'Let us make man' and that which should be man,
From that one light no man can look upon,
Drew to this shore lit by the suns and moons
And all the shadows.

What a profoundly mysterious utterance! There is nothing we can fix upon, nothing whose limits we can discern clearly. That world 'is not ours': what world is that? Who knows? Is it the mental world of the great First Poet? '*They said*': who are 'they'? Who knows? The denizens of that Poet's mental world? His ideas? His imaginings? It is all a mystery. In a world of light, the poet has been blinded and has lost his way. He cannot see anything clearly. Hence his words are obscure but pregnant with high meaning. We have a vision of a child of the earth, cast into a world without bounds, radiant, ineffable. He is bewildered, bedazzled, rapt, speechless. The poet says: 'In a world which is not ours, They said, "Come, let us be men."'[†] 'Out of that single radiance that no human eye can endure, the human-to-be has arrived on this shore of light and shadow.' They have come from that *one light*, one supreme luminescence. They are a part of that light. What can Christian critics make of all this?

O dear Spirit half-lost
In thine own shadow and this fleshly sign
That thou art thou—who wailest being born
And banish'd into mystery, and the pain
Of this divisible-indivisible world
Among the numerable-innumerable
Sun, sun, and sun, thro' finite-infinite space

In finite-infinite Time—our mortal veil
And shatter'd phantom of that infinite One,
Who made thee unconceivably Thyself
Out of His whole World-self and all in all—
Live thou!

Where have you come from, O soul? What were you, and what are you now? The world where you now are can be divided up till nothing remains. The integrated world where you were earlier was a world beyond numbers. In the world where you now are, you can count the number of suns and stars, even if you cannot finish counting them. Earlier, you were in infinite space and infinite time; in the space and time to which you have now been banished, there are limits though we cannot find them. It is infinity divided into finite parts.

Think what you were before and what you now are! Earlier, you were part of a single infinity; now you are merely its spectral shadow, a shattered fragment. But that is not your final end. You have come an infinite distance away from infinity; over an infinity of time, you will again draw nearer and nearer to it. What more can I say to you?

Live thou! and of the grain and husk, the grape
And ivyberry, choose; and still depart
From death to death thro' life and life, and find
Nearer and ever nearer Him, who wrought
Not Matter, nor the finite-infinite,
But this main-miracle, that thou art thou,
With power on thine own act and on the world.

In my first greeting, addressing you as man, I said,

Live, and be happy in thyself, and serve
This mortal race thy kin . . .

Live, be happy, make your fellow creatures happy, and in the end die gently without pain. What greater blessing can one wish upon a man? But in the second greeting, I say to you, 'Live.' Here to live does not mean to live on earth; it means consciousness without end. In every incarnation, take what is good and reject what is evil; and at every step, cross the portals of death one after another on your way to deathlessness. Why did I bless you in two different ways in the two greetings? Because in the first instance I was addressing *matter* and the finite-infinite. In the second, I address you '*Who art not Matter,*† *nor the finite-infinite, but this main-miracle, that thou art thou, with power on thine own act and on the world.*'

What realm of infinity has the poet entered by casting his eyes on his own son! In this temple of infinity, whom does he see? What song does he burst into? It is the song the Vedic sages used to chant:

Hallowed be Thy name—Halleluiah!
Infinite Ideality!
Immeasurable Reality!
Infinite Personality!
Hallowed be Thy name—Halleluiah!

We feel we are nothing—for all is thou and in Thee;
We feel we are something—that also has come from Thee;
We know we are nothing—but Thou wilt help us to be.
Hallowed be Thy name—Halleluiah!

Infinite conception, immeasurable truth, illimitable divine being. We are at a vast distance from the infinite idea. Try as we may, we can never approach it. When at last we know as truth what was merely an idea, a sense, He comes closer to us. But we are not satisfied by merely knowing Him as truth. To know of Him only as a blind cause, a blind force, a blind truth is not complete knowledge. When we realise that He is a being without limits, that He has an identity—then He comes close to us, then we can love Him. Then can we hail Him, saying 'Praise be to you!'

'*We feel we are nothing—for all is Thou and in Thee.*' But that concerns the past. When we were within You, we did not feel that we were anything: You were everything. This was merely our idea. We were merely ideas within You. Then, when at last we emerged from You, we began to feel that we too were entities. '*We feel we are something*—that *also has come from Thee.*' This concerns the present: this is the truth for us. Now we have become something, we have become true. '*We know we are nothing—but Thou wilt help us to be.*' That concerns the future. We know we are nothing—You are gradually forming us, making us manifest! Through death, You teach us new truths and new wisdom, and build us up towards fully formed beings. We can never be that: always, '*Thou wilt help us to be.*' We shall ever have the joy of advancing from incompleteness towards completeness. Praise be to you! Even on earth we have instances of this kind of progress. Humanity was once a part of a great mass of vapours, immanent in the first material cause of the whole universe. Slowly, gradually, it separated itself and was born as human. Then, the more it grew and gained in experience, the more it began to acquire an identity. In the same order, the poet first sees God as infinite idea, then as immeasurable truth, and finally as illimitable Being.

This is where the poem ends. Where could it go from here? This is the ultimate limit. It is strange that those who gape in admiration when a giant is called a mountain and a giant's staff a tall tree, cannot appreciate the sublime idea of such a great poem. Perhaps their imagination can only cope with material greatness: they cannot grasp a sublimity that is beyond matter. If they would, they would have adjudged this short poem to be greater than *Paradise Lost.*

TRANSLATED BY BHAWANI-PRASAD CHATTOPADHYAY

On Changes in the State of Poetry

In European literature, the days of the epic are past. No poet writes an epic; many readers do not read one; many do so only because it is on their school course, and many because they think it their duty. Many critics mourn the fact that nobody writes an epic any more, that the age of true poetic qualities is gone. Many scholars think that the more civilisation throws up sandbanks, the more the shores of poetry will erode. As proof, they cite the fact that epics were composed in the infancy of civilisation, and they no longer are. Perhaps they think that a time will come when no poetry will be written at all.

It seems probable that poetry will change as every aspect of civilisation is changing. Poetry is not something removed from civilisation, a pie in the sky. It is not utterly ethereal. Its estates are not all in the sky; it has plenty of landed property on earth.

One feature that marks civilisation is that in a civilised state, no one person can become all-in-all. A country does not mean one or two persons; nor does a system of government. The individual is scaled down, while the community expands. One man is no longer a legion in himself. Now, when talking about the government, it is not enough to talk of the whims, the training, and the mentality of a single king: we have to take a larger view, look at a great many people. If you look at one part of a machine and say it does very little work, you are mistaken. You must observe the whole machine.

In a civilised society today, you have to add many quantities and make a single aggregate. Poetry is no exception to this rule. Nowadays if you wish to talk about the poetry of a civilised country, do not look at just one poem or one poet. If you do, you will only say to yourself, 'What is this? This is not much. Is this all the poetry they have in this country?' Dissatisfied, you might turn to ancient literature. If you happen to come across the *Mahabharata*, the *Ramayana*, or some Greek epic, you would say, 'This is enough. This is plenty.' A *Mahabharata* or a *Ramayana* will by itself give you a total idea of ancient literature. But those days are no more. Today a single book of poetry read on its own leaves your reading incomplete. Think of England, for example. You must take all the poets of England together and consider them as one. Those in England who read poetry have each compiled an epic in one's heart. They have taken poems by different poets and mentally bound them together in a single volume. A vast epic poem called 'The Human Heart' is being composed in English; many poets over many years have been writing it a little at a time. It is the readers who are the Vedavyasa of this epic.† They have collected the elements and compiled them in their own minds to turn them into one. Whoever looks at only one part of it, or at the different parts separately, falls into a grave error. He says that poetry is not advancing in step with civilisation. What he does is to look separately at the various functionaries constituting the machinery of a republic. He finds no one with the ample powers of a king, no one who has a king's total authority, and jumps to the conclusion that the governance of the country is on the decline. 'It is true', he thinks, 'that civilisation is advancing; but I see no improvement in the way the country is being governed, rather the contrary.' But to say that civilisation is advancing is to say that knowledge is advancing and poetry too is advancing.

When the polity becomes too complicated and far-flung, the need for a republican system is particularly felt. So long as it is small in size and direct in its methods, there is little need for something as elaborate as a republican system of government. But when rule by one monarch no longer serves, the days of the monarch are numbered. This is what has been happening in Europe. The realm of poetry has spread far and wide. From the broadest to the most minute, from the most complex to the most explicit, all apprehensions are finding their way into poetry. Today's poetry is touched by the play of shadowy, insubstantial imaginings such as men of old could not conceive of, or common men reach out to. It contains recondite ideas commonly supposed to lie outside the province of poetry. In the poetry of old, only a few garden flowers such as the rose and jasmine, malati and mallika used to bloom; no other flower was considered worthy of a place in poetry. In today's poetry, the tiniest wild flower hidden in the grass, unnoticed by the common eye, finds a place. In a word, today's poetry unfolds, broadly and deeply, the secret depth of objects that are usually belittled or totally ignored because of familiarity or some defect of vision. On the other hand, things that men were afraid to touch as being too awesome or too remote are brought within reach by today's poetry. Hence no single person can or does write an epic suitable for modern times.

This is the age of division of labour. That is the foundation on which civilisation rests. The division of labour has started in poetry as well. Poetry has come to require it.

Formerly, there was nothing a man of learning did not know. He was expected to answer any question that was put to him; else how could he be called learned? The same Aristotle wrote of philosophy, politics, and also medicine. In those days, all branches of knowledge jostled with each other, helter-skelter. They lived, as it were, in a joint family with a savant as the paterfamilias. For all their different natures, they were nourished by the same food. Now they have separated, and each has a separate household. There is not room enough for them to live together, nor is it convenient. If people of different natures are housed together, they harm each other. We should not look at one of the households and conclude that the progeny of knowledge have decreased. They have so multiplied that one head cannot accommodate them all. Those who were once young have grown up, those who were single now have children.

With the progress of civilisation, multiplicity of events, and growing complexity of circumstance, varied and dynamic traits begin to develop in the heart. The epic can no longer cope with them, nor can a single person possibly write an epic commensurate with the times. Thus the need arises for shorter poems and lyrics. Whether the lyric was already there before the epic is a question we shall later take up. There are many lyrics and shorter poems latent in brief undefined form within an epic. Many poets have brought them out and given shape to them. *Abhijnanashakuntalam*† and *Uttararamacharitam*† are cases in point. When shorter poems and lyrics grow to the stage where they cannot have full play within the confines of an epic, they detach themselves from it. There is nothing in this to cause concern about the future of poetry.

The solar system was first only a ring of gases. Then parts of it tore away and became planets and satellites. There was not such great variety then as there now is. That solar epic only contained the seeds of the various types of shorter poems and lyrics that we find today. But that does not mean there was spring and rain, woods and mountains and oceans, beasts and birds and insects. There were only the primordial causes of all these. Now the solar system has split up and achieved fullness. Nobody should think that the universe is dwindling because no part of it is equal to that first immense solar disc. If we now wish to have an idea of the immensity of the solar system, we must regard as one this vast kingdom, torn asunder but still held together by the force of gravitation. We shall then be in no doubt that the solar system today is more developed and advanced. There is division of labour in the progress of the universe too. The solar system today has so much more work to do that it could not do without such division. If we went back some distance farther, beyond even the reach of modern science, to imagine a state where the gases had not yet combined together, it would be a state in which the disparate primordial substances moved confusedly and clashed with one another—what in English is called *chaos*. First disparate non-coherence, then combination, and finally a harmonised separation of parts: the same law applies in the world of intellect. First we have isolated truths in a state of disorder; they are then ordered in a disciplined rank, and lastly they flower as separate entities. This law is true of society as well: first disorganised individuals, then their union under a single firm rule, and finally controlled autonomy for each person in appropriate measure. In poetry too, the law holds good: first disparate effusions without any order, then their conglomeration in epics, and finally distinct, full-blown lyrics. The poetry of an advanced literature must be looked at as we look at the poetry of the solar system, or else we fall into error.

Swept onward by the tide of civilisation, our whole society is shooting forward like an arrow; no one should suppose that poetry is going against the current. Because the individual is losing importance, one must not imagine that the world is shrinking. As Tennyson said,† 'The individual withers and the world is more and more.'

There is a school of thought which holds that poetry flourishes so long as ignorance prevails; hence it will disappear in the daylight of civilisation. Very well. Let us agree. Let us suppose for argument's sake that poetry is a night bird. The truth, however, is that the more we pursue knowledge, the more there prevails the darkness of ignorance. Can anyone deny it? What does the light of science do? It only 'makes the darkness visible'. Science discovers new areas of darkness every day. The atlas of darkness expands by the day; the great Columbuses of science keep discovering new continents of darkness. What could be a happier time for that nocturnal bird, poetry? It loves mystery; was there ever so much mystery? No sooner have you uncovered one than ten others take its place. God has enfolded mystery within mystery. As we slay one demon of mystery,† each drop we shed of its blood gives birth to a hundred thousand demons. That is the boon Lord Shiva† has given the demon Mystery. It is deathless.

Just as there are some so ignorant that they do not even know their own ignorance, so also in the old benighted times, we did not know mysteries as mysteries. It is a special characteristic of ignorance that it ascribes to a mystery imaginary shape and dimensions, a life-story and a horoscope, and takes them to be real. That is to say, ancient poets used to make idols of mysteries and worship them; today's poets break those idols with the instruments of knowledge and make the mystery more mysterious still. Hence the earlier state of ignorance was not so conducive to poetry. We can easily see this if we look at the creations of the Puranas.† They have been with us for a long time and thus struck root in our hearts. They have thereby taken on the character of poetry, because they arouse many feelings in our heart. But let the reader only consider how a poet of today might give concrete form to dawn or dusk, making it a truth by so conceiving of it. If everybody were to accept this projection worshipfully as the literal truth, how narrow the kingdom of poetry would become! So many people, in their imaginations, see the dawn and the dusk in so many forms and shapes, now one and now another. If they all proceeded as above, their imaginations would all form identical worlds. When the dawn and the dusk were placed in these moulds, they would emerge with a single fixed shape.

The more knowledge expands, the more the realm of poetry expands. The more it expands, the more necessary it is to have division of labour, and the more lyrics and shorter poems come to be written.

TRANSLATED BY BHAWANI-PRASAD CHATTOPADHYAY

Baul Songs

A review of the book *Sangit Sangraha: Bauler Gatha*†

We have heard of poets who begin by imitating others. Such a poet may write many poems, indeed many good poems, but they seem to be set to an unvarying raga. They sound sweet, but do not strike us as original. He writes on like this, groping his way, till he suddenly hits upon the centre of his being. Henceforth he cannot perish. Now, when he sings, we say amazedly, 'What is this we hear? Who is singing? What raga is this?'

Hitherto he had been playing on pipes borrowed from others; they could not express all the tunes his heart wished to play. He could not imagine why he was unable to play what he wished. It was the fault of the pipe! Desperately searching hither and thither, he suddenly discovered that he has a musical instrument within his soul. He touched its chords and at once his heart leapt up in joy. 'What is this?' he asked himself in wonder. 'Why do my songs not sound as if they were somebody else's? How is it that at last, after all these years, I can hear all the music of my heart, that my tongue can utter the very words I wish to say?'

The joy of the man who has found his own words, and has learnt to express himself in his own words, knows no bounds. How delighted is he just to speak! Each word that he utters is a living child to him. We have an example near at hand. When Bankimchandra was writing *Durgeshnandini*† he had not yet truly found himself. He did not write badly, but he was not able to play his own tune throughout the book. We would not be greatly surprised if someone proved *Durgeshnandini* to be a translation or an adaptation by a powerful writer, of some other novel. But if anybody was to tell us that *Bishabriksha*,† *Chandrashekhar*,† or the writings of Bankim Babu's last years were imitations, we would not listen to him.

What is true of individuals is also true of nations. If we look around us, it will seem that we have failed to determine the true language of the Bengali race; we have no adequate notion of the shape that ideas and feelings take in the Bengali heart. Hence we seldom find anything really distinctive in what is being written in Bengali these days. When we read it, we do not get the feeling that it was written by a Bengali, or that, if translated into the language of some other nation, they would find in it something new born of a Bengali heart. What is being written nowadays, whether good or bad, gives the impression that such things are written, or might have been written, in English or some other language.

The main reason for this is that we have not been able to hit upon the true ideas and feelings or the true language of a Bengali. The Sanskrit scholars will cry, 'How true! In what is being written today we find no Sanskrit compounds, no cherishing of pure Sanskritic words. You call this Bengali?' We say to them, 'Your language is not Bengali, nor is that of the English-wallahs. Bengali is not to be found either in the Sanskrit or in the English grammar: it is there in the Bengali heart. You are acting like somebody searching the town for his son while holding the child in his arms. You are moving heaven and earth in your search for Bengali, turning Sanskrit and English upside down, but you have never looked into your own hearts. The book under review has a song:

> I have yet to know who I am.
> 'Myself, myself,' I say, and yet my self remains unknown.
> I count my coins and check the score,
> Counting them over, four by four,
> But never calculate from where I came.

If it is our wish to learn our language, our ideas, and sentiments, we must look for it where the Bengali speaks out of his own heart.

Those who have become foreigners at heart are often heard to say that feelings and emotions are the same everywhere. There is nothing over which a race can claim proprietory rights. This sounds very liberal, very broad-minded; but we confess to a doubt. We suspect that only those who have nothing of their own are eager to abolish the property rights of others. The idea mentioned above sounds like a plausible pretext for felony. Only they who rapaciously plunder the English language with both hands and make Bengali a stranger in its own home, can maintain that an individual language has nothing to distinguish it. It is they who strut about in borrowed jewels. I may have no jewels, but I do not therefore, on some plea or the other, display other people's property as my own. I am a beggar, which is demeaning enough; but the other course would be barefaced theft.

Commonalities and differences must both be taken into account. Without differences, the world could not go on. It is true that all men are equal, but they are nevertheless different from each other. It is impossible to find two men cast in the same mould, with the same feelings and ideas. Nobody can deny this. Similarly, two nations might share a common humanity, but at the same time they are different. And that is all to the good: that is what allows literary exchange, traffic, and commerce. If the temperature were to be the same everywhere, winds would not blow, rivers would stop flowing, and life would cease. For everything to merge in one would mean total extinction. If our literature wishes to remain alive, let it learn how to be Bengali.

The language of feelings and ideas cannot be translated. You can make replicas of the language of dry knowledge by casting it in a mould; but it is the heart's milk that nourishes the language of feeling. It is rocked in the cradle of the heart's joys and sorrows, and so grows to manhood. Hence it is a living thing. You can cast a lifeless image of it in a mould; but such an image cannot move, it weighs on the heart like a dead stone. *The force of gravitation* might be rendered without detriment as *bharakarshanshakti*, but the English words *liberty* and *freedom* evoke feelings and ideas that cannot be exactly conveyed by the Bengali *swadhinata* and *swatantra:* there is a slight gap that separates them. In English they say, *free as the mountain air.* If we translate it literally into Bengali, does it touch a chord in our hearts? Nowadays we translate English expressions for feelings and ideas into Bengali, and imagine we are preserving the English sense; where is the proof of that? In our literature these days, English-wallahs read what English-wallahs write; they mentally translate what they read into English. Whatever they like, they like because it accords with the English. But ask somebody who does not know English to read it. If the words enter his heart, then alone can we say, 'Yes, what was English has truly become Bengali.' Otherwise, what is English does not necessarily become Bengali by mere translation.

Therefore, the more we collect Bengali feelings and ideas, and Bengali expressions for them, the better for our literature. That is why all lovers of Bengali literature owe a special debt of gratitude to the publishers of *Sangit Sangraha* [A Collection of Songs].

Such lofty notions as *universal love* sound very pleasing when foreigners talk about them; but when a mendicant sings about them from door to door among our own homes, why does it fail to reach our ears?

Jagai and Madhai,† come, O come,
Join our dance as we sing Hari's† name.
Come!
You have hurt me once, and may again;
But I shall sing you Hari's name.
They've hit me with a broken pot,
But shall I not give them of love?
Come, O come!

The Baul sings:

To love like this, you have to die.
The self-absorbed seek such love fruitlessly.

First of all, you must die. There is no love without destruction of the self. (Already, in another song, we have heard:

He whose self has died, has found his goal,
Won reward for the good deeds of ten million births.)

The Baul now goes on to say:

One who stakes his life to wear
The jewel of love, does not fear
Yama, god of death.

He who has died is no more afraid of death. He loves the world, therefore becomes the world. He is no longer the petty 'I' that needs to fear death; he is the whole universe.

One who does not love would ask, 'What does one gain from such love?' If you ask a flower, 'What do you gain by giving off scent?', it will answer, 'I cannot but scatter scent. It is my nature to do so. My life seems to lose all purpose if I cannot give off scent.' Likewise the lover will say, 'It is my nature to die. I know no happiness except in dying.'

The covetous, full of desires, will say 'What's this?
By dying for another, here's one seeking bliss!'

The Baul sings in reply:

Each man will do what in his nature lies.
Can one who is not a lover, know what love is?

Says the Baul, there is an instrument on which we can hear the music of the whole world:

There is a strange instrument in Gour's† house:
An instrument of feeling
Along whose single string,
Its single string of love, it brings
The news of all the endless universe.

Along this string of love there flow the electric currents of the infinite universe, carrying news of the universe straight to the heart in an instant. When you are sitting close to someone you love, electric currents flow between you along the invisible string of love, signals from her soul reach yours every instant. So also, if your soul is wired by love to the soul of the universe, nothing that goes on in its private chambers escapes you. Who has ever sung like this of the glory of love?

Why do we not steep ourselves in love for the world? It is because we are anxious to hold on to our egos; we wish to protect the separate identity of a person called 'I', never to let it go. The net of love enmeshes the world. Day and night, the world is striving to make you one with itself. It does not want that any part of it, any wave, should independently run against the current. It wishes that all its waves should move as one current, sing in unison. Then alone can there be harmony throughout the universe, no discord in its grand music.

That is why he who stands up and asserts his ego in opposition to the universe cannot last long. One's needs cannot be fulfilled within the narrow limits of one's puny self. Buffeted by grief and loss, the self finds shelter in the bosom of the earth and can then, at last, breathe with ease. How long can a fish live in a fistful of water? Its food is soon exhausted, the water fouled; it pines for the ocean. Unless it can get to the ocean, if it is a big fish, it soon dies; if small, it can survive for some time. So also, those with large souls cannot long live confined within their own selves; they want to extend their beings across the world. Chaitanyadeva† affords proof of this. Those with smaller souls can live with their own selves for a long time, but not for ever. The 'I' does not have within it food enough to last through eternity. Starved at last, such souls leave their homes and start to wander. All that I have said is to be found in the following song:

Bird of the mind, what more tricks will you play?
Won't you be caught in the net of God's love one day?
You stay far off, and warily move,
You break the net, and fool us and fly away.

Some day you'll be caught, and your wiles come to nought:
Without water and food, you'll wail in your dismay.[†]

The book has so many songs of such love, and each song puts one in mind of so many things, that if one were to quote all the songs and say all there is to say about them, it would make this screed too long.

We have only one quarrel with the publisher. Why did he allow Brahmo songs[†] and songs of modern English-wallahs into the book? We did not buy this book in order to read good songs. What we wanted was simple songs of genuine untutored hearts. The publisher has, in places, greatly impeded our quest.

And there was very good reason why we particularly wanted songs composed by men of old, and men without English education. Today's educated men are all much of a kind. We go to the same school, our hearts are nearly all cast in the same mould; so we are not astonished to find echoes of our own feelings in the hearts of modern men. But what joy, what surprise if we find in old literature something in tune with our own hearts! Why the joy? Because we discover in a flash of lightning the vast and enduring foundations of our heart. We see that this heart of ours is not drifting like a shipwrecked wretch, clutching the flotsam of the habits and education of a transient age; it has its home in the infinite human heart. This perception restores our faith in our own hearts. We are then able to see the bonds that unite one age with another. Does the water with which I quench my thirst come from the narrow muddy well of my own heart, or from the river source that rises like the Ganga among the lofty peaks of the human heart and has flowed so long through the green fields of the past—the water that all humanity imbibes? Once we learn the latter to be the case, how glad it makes our hearts!

That is the gladness we experience when we discover in the old poetry a kinship with our hearts. The heart in which that ancient current has dried up is a desert indeed.

Have I now come to Vrindavan?[†]
Nitai,[†] my treasure, tell me where I am.
Why do I not hear Vrindavan's birds and beasts?
Where are the sacred banyans, grove of tamal trees?
O what has withered the plants of Vrindavan?
Where are the springs of Radha and Shyam,[†] the hill of Govardhan?[†]

Why this lament? Because the Vrindavan of old is not be found in the

Vrindavan of today; because the present is totally divorced from the past. O that it were not so, that we could catch a glimpse of a creeper from that ancient arbour! How many of the charms of ancient Vrindavan might that slender creeper have captured for us! How it would have recalled to us the charms of the Vrindavan of those days!

TRANSLATED BY BHAWANI-PRASAD CHATTOPADHYAY

Literature (1889)

The essence of literature does not allow itself to be trapped within a definition. It is like the essence of life: we know what it cannot exist without, but what it is we do not know. Life is generated by life, fire must be lit from fire—so too living literature is born when vitality flows out of a pen from the poet's inmost soul. Words like 'life' and 'vitality' may appear *mystic* when applied to literature, but one cannot put the matter more clearly. Literature incorporates a certain life: that life seeps out from the hidden centre of the writer's human existence, achieves perpetuity in language, and endows language itself with perpetuity. All this must be grasped more or less conjecturally on the basis of one's own intimate experience.

Shakespeare gave birth to his dramatis personae from within his own vital being: not his intelligence, nor his moral piety, nor even his *feelings*, but from his life cells girt round with all the human functions and faculties. There is in literature the idea of creation, not of construction.[†] Creation embodies a mysterious, vital, self-oblivious order; construction willingly accepts the guiding hand of this order. The power of creation is in one respect less percipient than that of construction, in another respect more so. This is because the task of construction requires one, at each moment, to consciously exercise the authority of the self over inert materials; it is not so with creation. Rather, during creation, those inert materials seem endowed with consciousness by some novel principle, so that they fashion themselves by their own force—as though they are linked up with their own veins, letting the vital power flow easily through them.

We see how in a steam engine, one rotating wheel is linked to another so as to generate motion in various directions. In the same way, the wheel of my life revolves with the great wheel of the world; through the centre of that life-wheel, the world's motion is linked to literature, and literature acquires the eternal motion of wider existence. One person might push along the wheel of literature by hand; another might hitch a horse to it to make it speed; yet another might have succeeded in binding it to the wheel of life. It is by this last means that literature is invested with sustained motion.

Yet all these similes and metaphors seem like the play of fancy, not solid utterance. Solid utterance is that which can be tested by all and sundry. It has been observed earlier, almost in so many words, that these matters cannot be rendered solid enough to satisfy one.

I have myself experienced, over and over, what is probably familiar to everyone: when immersed in literary composition, one seems to achieve a kind of superconscious state, as though an inner self separate from my own has run off with the greater part of my consciousness, and is carrying out its task half unknown to me. That being seems to dissolve all the witting and unwitting experience I have gathered, the *Real* and the *Ideal* within me, my everyday self and my potential self, and to pour a drop of the admixture into the text. The point of essence at the centre of my life is a precious possession of all human existence; it is not merely an unknowable, unfamiliar, fragmentary part of myself. Hence that vital power, as enshrined in literature, can enter the hearts of all humankind for all time.

TRANSLATED BY SUKANTA CHAUDHURI

The Five Elements: A First Acquaintance

For ease of writing, let me call my five companions the five elements: *kshiti* [earth], *ap* [water], *tejas* [fire], *marut* [air], and *vyoma* [space].

A person has to be refashioned when given a made-up name. As with a sheath for a sword, it is impossible to find the right name for a person in the language. How, especially, is one to find five characters to fit the five elements to perfection?

I do not want to make them fit exactly, either. I am not appearing in court, after all. The only oath I have taken is as a writer at the reader's tribunal to tell the truth. But I shall make up the truth and tell it.

Let me now acquaint you with the five elements.

The Honourable Master Kshiti is the weightiest of us all. He holds firm, immovable opinions on most matters. He considers to be real whatever, and only what, he perceives directly in a definite form and can make use of as and when needed. If there is a truth beyond that, he has no respect for it, nor does he wish to retain any ties with it. He says that it is hard enough to bear the burden of necessary knowledge. The burden is ever increasing, and learning is ever becoming more difficult. In earlier times, when knowledge had not accumulated in so many strata, when whatever man was obliged to learn was quite paltry, there was free time for amateur study. But there is no such free time any more. It does no harm to deck up a little child in fancy clothes and ornaments: he has no business to attend to beyond eating and sleeping. But would it do to decorate an adult with ankle-bells, bangles, and a peacock-plume head-dress? He has to earn a living and move around and about. He needs must tuck in his dhoti, put on a helmet, and move forward briskly. That is why civilisation is shedding its ornaments every day. That is what progress means: the gradual accumulation of essentials and eschewal of the redundant.

Mistress Ap (whom we shall henceforward call Srotaswini†) cannot

Rabindranath Tagore: 'Group of five figures'.
By courtesy of Rabindra Bhavan, Shantiniketan.

give any cogent reply to this argument of Kshiti's. She simply keeps saying, in mellifluous voice and graceful manner, 'No, no, this can never be true. I can't accept it from my heart, it can never quite be true.' Again and again, it is 'No, no, it isn't so, it isn't so.' She has no arguments to back her: only a liquid musical sound, an entreaty, the movement of an undulating neck: 'No, no, it isn't so, it isn't so. I love what's redundant, so even the redundant is essential. Very often the redundant is of no use to us—it simply arouses our affection, our love, our compassion, our desire for self-sacrifice: is there no need for such love in this world?' Master Kshiti almost thaws under this torrent of entreaties from Mistress Srotaswini, although he is invincible to any argument.

Mistress Tejas (henceforth given the name Dipti[†]) flashes almost like an unsheathed sword and, in a beautifully sharp-edged voice, tells Kshiti: 'Oh, indeed! You think you're the only ones who carry out the world's work? What you want to lop off as redundant for your tasks may well be essential to ours. You want to rid your conduct, your speech, your beliefs, your education, and your bodies of anything and everything that is ornamental, because the push and jostle of civilisation leaves so little space and time. But when those ornaments are cast off, *our* perennial tasks almost come to a standstill. We have to save up so many odds and ends, this and that, sweet nothings, civilities, words, tales, sentiments, manners, bits of free time to keep up the housework of the world. We smile sweetly, speak modestly, work bashfully, spend much time dressing as befits each occasion; that's why we can do the work of your mothers and your wives with such ease. If everything but the most essential knowledge were indeed chased away by civilisation, I'd like to see just once what fate befalls our guardianless children and such an utterly helpless and foolish group of people as men!'

Master Vayu (let us call him Samir[†]) laughed all this off at first. He said, 'Forget about Kshiti: whenever he tries to move back, turn sideways, reposition himself to inspect some truth from different viewpoints, there's such an earthquake in the inert territory of his mind that the poor fellow's carefully-built concrete opinions crack and collapse. So he says that everything from gods to insects originates in the ground, because to recognise anything as existing away from the ground, one has to travel far beyond it. He needs to understand that the human world isn't primarily about the relation between man and inanimate things; the true bond of the human world is the bond between one human being and another. So however much you may learn of the science of material things, that doesn't help at all in learning how to deal with people. But the things that adorn our lives, things that are charming or poetic—it's those that set up true bonds between people, remove the obstacles in one another's paths, heal the wounds of one another's hearts, widen our vision, and extend our lives beyond earth to heaven.'

Master Byom closed his eyes for a while and said: 'If you're talking of human beings, whatever's unnecessary is most necessary for them. Every day man detests whatever makes for convenience, whatever meets his needs, whatever fills the stomach. That's why the sages of India repudiated hunger and thirst, cold and heat altogether, and preached the freedom of humanity. It's demeaning for the living soul to admit that anything external should be indispensable. If a civilisation enthrones the indispensable as king, with no emperor superior to it, it can't be called the best kind of civilisation.'

No one ever pays attention to what Byom says. Although Srotaswini appears to hear him out seriously lest he feel hurt, secretly she says to herself, 'Poor crazy fellow!' and feels sorry for him. But Dipti cannot stand him. She gets restless and seeks to change the subject midway. It is as if Dipti harbours an intense dislike for him because she cannot fully understand what he says.

However, I never dismiss Byom's words altogether. I said to him, 'Science wants to do for all and sundry what the sages did individually for themselves through hard penance. Science aims to dispel hunger and thirst, heat and cold, and the myriad tyrannies of matter over mankind. Instead of running away from material things and seeking the liberation of humanity in a forest hermitage, if one can enslave the material and make it one's servant, anointing man himself as king in this palace of the natural world, man is no longer demeaned. So, to be free of material bonds and attain to an independent, spiritually active civilisation, it's absolutely necessary to go through a stage of prolonged scientific endeavour.'

Kshiti considers it utterly superfluous to refute his opponent's arguments. Byom, on his part, says something and then keeps mum: no matter what anyone may say thereafter, they cannot break his ponderous silence. My words, too, did not affect him. Kshiti remained immobile where he was; Byom, too, remained ensconced behind his copious facial hair and his inviolable dignity.

So here am I and my Club of Five Elements. One morning, Mistress Dipti asked me: 'Why don't you ever keep a diary?'

Women have a number of unfounded beliefs in their heads; among these was Mistress Dipti's notion that I was not a mere nobody. Needless to say, I did not try very hard to dispel this belief of hers.

Samir slapped me expansively on the back and said, 'Do write one, dear fellow!'

Kshiti and Byom held their tongues.

I said, 'There's a grave pitfall in writing a diary.'

Dipti said impatiently, 'Never mind, just write one.'

Srotaswini said gently, 'What pitfall? Let's hear it.'

I said, 'A diary's just a make-believe life, but once composed, it cannot but exert some control over one's real life. As it is, there are a thousand parts to a single person, and it's a hard business to control them all and live from day to day; to fashion a make-believe counterpart to it from outside with one's own hand only compounds the ordeal.'

Byom spoke up all of a sudden: 'That's precisely why wise men forbid all actions—because each action is itself a creation. As soon as you create an action, it becomes immortal and sticks to you. The more we go on thinking and experiencing, the more we go on fragmenting ourselves. If you want the unadulterated soul, you must eschew all thought, all belief, all tasks.'

Ignoring Byom's remark, I said, 'I don't want to break myself up into pieces. There's a man within who keeps sticking a variety of thoughts and actions onto worldly existence every day and building up a life by some undiscovered law. If I begin writing a diary alongside it, that would be to demolish him and build another man, erect another life.'

Kshiti laughed and said, 'I still can't understand why you call a diary a second life.'

I said, 'My point is this: Life's tracing out a path along one trajectory; if you take your pen and keep tracing another such line beside it, a situation may arise where it's hard to tell whether your pen traces a line alongside your life, or your life proceeds along the line of your pen. It becomes harder and harder to tell which line is the original and which is the copy. Life's course is inherently mysterious: it has many self-refutations, many contradictions, many inconsistencies between precedent and consequence—but the pen, by its nature, wants to follow a well-defined route; it can only draw an approximate line after resolving all contradictions and smoothing out all inconsistencies. When it sees an event, it can't but arrive at its logical conclusion. So its line runs effortlessly towards its own structured conclusion, and tries to make life merge with it and follow the same path.'

Noticing my anxiety to explain the matter properly, Srotaswini compassionately said, 'I see what you want to say. Normally, it's our Great Being who sits in his top-secret workshop and fashions our lives according to some wonderful law; but when one tries to write a diary, it's as though two people are given the responsibility of constructing a life. So the diary partly follows the life, and the life partly follows the diary.'

Srotaswini listens to every word so patiently, silently, and attentively that she seems to be trying very carefully to comprehend what I say—but all of a sudden, one discovers that she has understood my point a long time back.

'That's indeed so,' I said.

'What's wrong with that?' asked Dipti.

I said, 'Anyone who's suffered in this way would know. A person who trades in literature will understand my words. A trader in literature has to draw many different moods and characters out of his inner being. Just as a good gardener breeds different varieties of flowers to order from a single species, crossing them in various ways by special techniques—one variety may have large leaves, another multiple colours, a third a lovely fragrance, yet another sweet fruit—likewise a literature-merchant grows a variety of produce out of his own solitary mind. He applies the heat of imagination to different moods and presents each of them in a distinct, complete form. He separates out the moods, the memories, the impulses of temperament that perform their due function in the ordinary person's mind and then wither in due course or turn to something else, and imbues them with permanent form and beauty. As soon as he embodies them properly with form, they come to be immortal. In this way, a colony of autonomous individuals gradually grows within the literature-merchant's mind. His life loses its integrity: he soon comes to be divided into a hundred parts. The bands of his eternalised, avid feelings stretch their hands across the universe. They're curious about all matters. The mysteries of the universe lure them in ten different directions. Beauty plays its flute and binds them in the toils of feeling and apprehension.† They make sorrow their playmate, they even seek a taste of death. Like newly-aware infants, they touch, smell, taste everything and refuse to obey any strictures. They light a lot of wicks together in a single lamp: an entire life burns up at once in a raging fire. So many living growths in a single human nature become cause for great conflict and disorder.'

Srotaswini asked a little dejectedly, 'Can't he find any happiness in expressing himself in such varied and distinct ways?'

I said, 'There's a great joy in creation, but no one can be engaged in creating all the time: there are limits to one's powers, and one has to live in this world and pursue one's daily life. This pursuit of daily life is very troublesome for such a person, who's continually warmed the heart with imagination, like a brooding bird, until it's intolerant of everything. A bamboo flute with seven holes is good as a musical instrument—it resonates at a breath; but a sturdy unpierced bamboo stick is best for negotiating the roads of daily life, because we can rely on it completely.'

Samir said, 'Unfortunately, a human being can't be segregated by function like a piece of bamboo: when playing music, a human flute has to be a flute, and when walking down the road one needs must be a walking-stick. But, my dear friends, you're lucky people: some of you are flutes and some are sticks; I, on the other hand, am a mere breath. I have all the internal ingredients of music within me; I only lack an instrument through whose external shape they can be sounded as a ragini.'

Dipti said, 'Many objects of our human existence go waste. So many thoughts, feelings, events raise big waves of happiness and sorrow and sway me every day in passing; if I could arrest them in writing, I'd feel that much of my life remained within my grasp. Whether it's happiness or sorrow, I don't like to give up all control over anything.'

I had much to say on this subject, but I noticed Srotaswini hesitantly trying to say something: if I began lecturing at this point, she would immediately give up her own turn. I remained silent. After a pause, she said, 'I don't know, my friends: I find what you've just said rather more objectionable than anything else. If every day, we were to record in writing what we feel that day, its proper proportions would be lost. Many of our joys and sorrows, annoyances and misgivings suddenly loom large for trifling reasons. What we've put up with unflinchingly for a long time may become absolutely unbearable one day; I may one day find offensive what isn't really an offence; for some trivial reason, a day's sadness may appear to me more serious than many greater sorrows; we may often judge others unjustly because we're in a bad mood for some reason. Out of all this, whatever is unjustified is erased from our minds over time; the excesses of life are gradually removed and the median remains: that is my true selfhood. Besides, many things turn and pass and disappear within our minds in half-formed shape; if they're all made explicit, they sully the fineness of the mind. By keeping a diary, we artificially enlarge all the trivialities of life; and in trying to force many tender unformed ideas into full bloom, we tear them or deform them.'

Srotaswini suddenly realised that she had been making her point for quite some time, and with some fervour. She instantly blushed to the roots of her ears, turned her face away a little, and said, 'I don't know—I can't quite tell; who knows whether I've got it right?'

Dipti never hesitates for a moment in any matter. Seeing that she was about to make a forceful reply, I said, 'You've got it quite right. I was going to say the same thing, but I doubt whether I could have said it so well. Mistress Dipti should remember this: if you want to grow bigger, you have to curtail something. If you want to earn, you have to spend. We can progress only by forgetting, jettisoning, giving away a lot from our lives. What's the good of hoisting every trivial item onto one's head, stuffing every broken bit into one's bundle—dragging every day, every moment of one's life behind oneself? A person who hurls himself into an embrace with every word, every feeling, every incident is unfortunate indeed.'

Dipti gave an ironic smile, joined her hands in mock apology, and said, 'I'm sorry I asked you to write a diary: I'll never do such a thing again.'

Agitated, Samir said, 'You mustn't say that! In this world, it's a great blunder to confess to one's misdemeanours. We think the judge will view our crime leniently if we confess to it, but that's not so. The pleasure of judging and censuring another person is a rare pleasure; however much you may exaggerate your crime in recounting it, a harsh judge derives that much more pleasure from seizing upon it. I was wondering which path to follow; now I've decided I'm going to write a diary.'

I said, 'I'm ready to do so as well. But I'm not going to write about myself. I'll write about things that pertain to all of us. All these things that we discuss every day . . .'

Srotaswini looked somewhat alarmed. Samir said with joined hands, 'Please, I implore you: if all our words are to be put down in writing, I'll learn up words at home and then come and say them here; if I suddenly forget them midway, I'll have to go home, refresh my memory, and then come back. The outcome will be less talk and more labour. If you're going to write down the very exact truth, I'll cross my name off your list of companions and go away.'

'No, no,' I said. 'I'll honour my friend's request rather than the demands of truth. None of you need worry: I'll make up words and put them in your mouths.'

'That's even worse,' said Kshiti, opening his large eyes very wide. 'If you lay hold of a pen, I can already see you putting every possible false argument in my mouth, while you issue irrefutable replies to them from yours.'

I said, 'When writing, one can't but take revenge on somebody who has defeated one in verbal argument. Let me tell you at the very outset: I'm now going to pay you back for all the pain and defeats I've suffered at your hands.'

The eternally tolerant Kshiti contentedly said, 'Let it be so.'

Byom said nothing, but gave a slight brief smile. I have not yet been able to fathom its deeper significance.

TRANSLATED BY TISTA BAGCHI

The Five Elements: Prose and Verse

I had been saying, 'The sound of a flute or the light of the full moon, say the poets, awakens memories in the heart. But we can't tell what they are memories of. There's no reason why, of all things, I should call something that doesn't have a definite form a memory—why, indeed, I shouldn't call it a forgetting. It's just that it sounds odd to say "Forgettings arise." Yet this statement isn't altogether unfounded. Sometimes the countless memories of a past life, which have lost their distinctness and become fused, which can no longer be separately identified, which sleep silently like a sea of oblivion around the landmass of our conscious mind, are agitated and swayed in unison at the rising of the moon or the southern breeze. Our conscious mind then feels the impact of those waves of forgetting; we apprehend their mysterious deeper existence, and hear the concerted wailing of that immense forgotten vastness.'

Unable to control his laughter at my sudden flow of sentiment, Master Kshiti said, 'O brother, what are you doing? Stop before it's too late. It's nice to hear poetry only when it's in metre; that, too, not always. If the five of you start mixing poetry into simple prose, it turns unfit for everyday use. One might add water to milk; if you add milk to water, it can't be used for bathing and drinking. If some prose is mixed in with poetry, it becomes digestible for prosaic people like us; but poetising in prose is quite unacceptable.'

That was that. No more words from the heart. Friend Kshiti uprooted my new shoot of sentiment of an autumn morning with one jab of his sharp trowel. A person is not left quite so helpless by a counter-opinion on a point of argument, but one feels enfeebled when someone cuts short an expression of sentiment. This is because expressions of sentiment rely solely on a sympathetic ear. If the hearer exclaims, 'What folly!', no repartee can be found in any treatise of logical argumentation.

For this reason, when embarking on an expression of sentiment, ancient artistes would begin by imploring the audience for their kind attention. They would say: Learned connoisseurs can strain out the cream from the water, as swans are said to do. They would admit their own fallibility and express complete faith in their hearers' discernment. Occasionally, someone like Bhavabhuti† would try to impress the assembly by exquisite self-aggrandisement from the very beginning; yet after all this, they would return home and say in self-deprecation: 'Hail to the land where glass and gems sell for the same price!' They would pray to their god: 'O Four-Faced One,† I can bear whatever other punishment you lay down for my sins; but do not, do not, do not destine me to serve rasa† to those without a taste for it.' There is indeed no punishment like it. It would be too much to demand of the god that there should be no uncultivated people in the world: the population of the world would then dwindle to insignificance. Most of the world's tasks are accomplished by people not interested in rasa: they are indispensable to human society. Without them, meetings would be adjourned, committees would not function, newspapers would be silent, and the quota allotted to criticism† remain utterly unfilled; so I have due respect for such people. But just because oil flows copiously when mustard seeds are fed into the oil-press, one can't expect to throw in flowers and get nectar out of it. Therefore, O Four-Faced One, preserve the oil-press in the workaday world to eternity, but pray do not feed it with flowers, or the hearts of discerning folk.

Mistress Srotaswini's tender heart always favours the distressed. Somewhat pained at my discomfiture, she said, 'Why, are prose and verse really so far apart?'

I said, 'Poetry is like the private inner quarters† of a house, prose like the outer rooms where outsiders may enter. Both have their respective areas defined. If a feeble woman moves about outside, she wouldn't necessarily land in danger. But if some boorish person does humiliate her, she has no other weapon besides weeping. That's why the inner quarters are her safe haven. Metrical verse is that inner refuge of poetry. No one dares to attack it abruptly through the high walls of metre. It's fashioned an insurmountable yet aesthetically pleasing boundary for itself, independent of everybody's everyday language. If I could set up my heart's sentiment within those borders, no lord of the earth, let alone Kshiti himself, would have the gall to enter and make fun of it.'

Byom drew the hookah stem out of his mouth and said with eyes closed, 'I believe in singleness. All our needs could have been met by prose alone, but poetry has intruded and brought an unnecessary rift into our mental realm: it has given rise to a separate race called poets. When common property is entrusted to a particular community, they acquire a vested interest in making it inaccessible to everybody else. Poets, too, have built an insurmountable barrier all around feelings and sentiments, and fashioned an artificial substance called the poetical. A deluded public finds no place to contain their amazement. Their habits have become so perverted that, without the hammer blows of metre and rhyme, their minds are never roused to consciousness: sentiment has to discard the garb of natural, straightforward language and put on a motley disguise. It could have met with no greater indignity. It's said that poetry is a modern creation; that's why it preens its plumage and struts about continually like an upstart Nawab.† I can't stand it!'

Having said this, Byom began puffing at his hookah once more.

Mistress Dipti cast a scornful glance at Byom and said, 'Science has put forward a theory called natural selection. The law of natural selection holds not just among animals but among human creations as well. It's by virtue of natural selection that the peahen hasn't needed to have plumage, while the peacock's train has grown longer and longer. The plumage of poetry is also the outcome of such natural selection, not the conspiracy of poets. Is there any country, from the primitive to the civilised, where poetry hasn't flowered in metre?'

The Honourable Master Samir had sat listening all this while with a little smile on his face. When Dipti joined in our discussion, an idea cropped up in his head. He came out with an outrageous statement. 'Artifice,' he said, 'is the greatest achievement of humankind. None other than human beings have the right to be artificial. A tree doesn't have to prepare its own leaves; the sky doesn't have to construct its own blue colour; Nature paints the peacock's plumage with her own hands. The Creator has made humankind alone His apprentice in His work of creation, and assigned small tasks of creation to humans. The more proficiency one has shown in that work, the greater one's acclaim. Poetry is indeed more artificial than prose. It has more of human creation in it; it calls for more colour, more care. In poetry there's more of the skilled handiwork of the Vishvakarma† who dwells in our minds, who sits in a secluded workshop within us and is perpetually engaged in a variety of projects, configurations, endeavours, expressions. That's his chief glory. Natural language belongs with the rippling sound of water and the rustling of leaves; but where there's a mind, there is carefully composed artificial language.'

Srotaswini heard Samir through like an attentive student. A new light seemed to fall on her beautiful, gentle face. Without hesitating to express an opinion as she normally would, she began straightaway: 'Samir's words have inspired an idea in me; I don't know whether I'll be able to state it clearly. The aspect of creation that relates to our hearts—that's to say, which doesn't merely impart knowledge to the mind but evokes sentiments in the heart, like the beauty of a flower or the loftiness of a mountain—calls for so much play of skill, so much splashing of colour, so much preparation. Each petal of the flower has had to be fashioned carefully to make it shapely and symmetrical, and stood on its stalk at a graceful angle; the mountain has had to be adorned with an eternal crown of snow and set against the blue sky with such grandeur; so many brush strokes of different colours have had to be traced on the canvas of a sunset over the western seashore. It's taken so much decoration, so many colours, so many moods and manners to appease our puny human minds. God Himself has had to exercise skill wherever He's manifested love, beauty, and magnanimity in His creation. He too has had to arrange sound and rhythm, colour and fragrance with great care. He's employed so many alliterations of petals, so to speak, in the flowers that he has made bloom in the forest; and science is counting the feet and syllables of the well-defined, controlled metre he has had to compose so that a single star may shine on the canvas of the sky. To express their feelings, human beings, too, have to resort to various devices: music, rhythm, beauty have to be infused into words before the heart's thoughts can enter other hearts. If this is to be called artifice, then the whole of universal creation is artificial.'

Having said this, Srotaswini glanced at me as though imploring me for help. Her eyes seemed to say, 'I've been rambling on about heaven knows what: would you articulate all this a little more clearly for me, please?' But just then Byom said, 'There is indeed a view that universal creation is artificial. It's very hard to disprove that what Srotaswini has described as the expression of feeling—scenes, sounds, scents, and so on—is mere illusion, the artificial creation of our minds.'

Kshiti burst out in indignation, 'All of you are talking irrelevantly. The question was this: whether verse is really needed for the expression of ideas. Taking off from there, you've crossed the seas and landed in the quicksand with your theories of creation, destruction, and illusion. I hold that metrical verse wasn't created for the expression of ideas. Just as little children like verses not because of their beauty of thought but simply because of their rhythmically arranged sounds, in our primitive stage the mere resonance of meaningless words sounded pleasant to our ears. That's why our earliest poetising consists of meaningless rhymes. As both individuals and humankind advance, they grow increasingly dissatisfied if meaning is not added to metre. But even after reaching adulthood, we retain a part of the child in one or two shadowy recesses within ourselves; a love for resonant sound and metre is part of the nature of that secret child. Our adult part seeks meaning and ideas; our childish part wants sound and rhythm.'

Dipti arched her neck and said, 'Thank goodness not every bit of us becomes adult! I thank man's childish self from my heart: whatever sweetness the world has is owing to its virtue.'

Samir said, 'A person who's matured completely into an adult is the world's arch-precocious child. He doesn't approve of any kind of sport or childishness. Our modern Hindu community is the most over-precocious community in the world; it flaunts its precocity to excess, yet it remains immature in all kinds of matters. It's very hard for a precocious child and a precocious community to rise in life, because they have no modesty in them. But this is my *private* view—please make sure it doesn't become public. People have become rather irritable these days.'

I said, 'When steamrollers are brought in to repair the city roads, they put up a wooden sign saying: "Machinery in operation! Caution!" I'm cautioning Kshiti in advance: I'm going to set the machinery working. He fears steam-engines the most, but I find it easier to travel when driven by the steam of the imagination. I shall wander into irrelevance once again in talking about prose and verse. Listen on at your own risk.

'Motion operates according to a very precise law. A pendulum swings with a regular oscillation. When a person walks, his feet rise and fall at a measured rate, and the rest of his body moves to this beat and brings harmony into his movements. There's an enormous rhythm in the waves of the sea. The earth too revolves around the sun to a cosmic beat . . .'

The honourable Byom interrupted me all of a sudden and began to speak: 'Only stasis is truly independent: it presides in its unshakable dignity, while motion has to regulate itself at every step. Yet there's a misconception among the populace that motion is the true embodiment of freedom, while stasis is bondage. This is because desire is the only motion of the mind, and naïve people call freedom what is simply motion according to one's desire. But our learned men knew that desire is the cause of all our movements, and the root of all our bonds. That's why to gain freedom—that's to say, supreme stasis—they prescribed the elimination of desire at its very root, and why *yoga-sadhana*, the attainment of bliss through meditation, consists in halting all movement of body and mind.'

Samir laid a hand on Byom's back and said with a laugh, 'When a person has raised a particular topic, interrupting him midway is called *golayog-sadhana*—the attainment of confusion.'

I said, 'It can't be unknown to the scientifically minded Kshiti that there's a close kinship between one movement and another, one vibration and another. When you strike a string tuned to the note *do*, another string tuned to the note *fa* starts vibrating as well. A similar tie of kinship exists between all kinds of waves such as light waves, thermal waves, sound waves, neural impulses. Our consciousness too is an undulatory, vibratory state. That's why it's connected to the varied vibrations of the universe. Sounds come and set its nerves swaying; light rays come and strike at its nerve cords with ethereal fingers. Its ever-vibrating neural network keeps it awake by binding it through many links to the rhythms of all the vibrations of the universe.

'The inherent disposition of the heart—what's called *emotion* in English—is the outpouring of our heart, that's to say, motion. Other vibrations of the universe have a profound unity with this as well. It has a vibratory connection, a consonance, with light, with colour, with sound.

'That's why music can touch our hearts so immediately: the two enter into accord without delay. As the tempest and the ocean rage together, an intimate conflict is sustained between music and the soul.

'The reason is that music transmits its vibrations and arouses our entire inner being. It fills our soul with an indefinable emotion. It makes the mind abstracted, draws it out of itself. Many poets call this extraordinary feeling a longing for the eternal. I too have sometimes experienced this kind of feeling and may have employed this kind of language as well. Not only music: the light of the setting sun in the evening sky, too, has extended the heartbeat of the limitless universe into my inner soul. The ineffable, lofty music sounded there has no connection with my everyday joys and sorrows; it's the Sama-Vedic chant of the entire firmament as it circles the shrine of the Lord of the World. Not just music and the sunset: when a love agitates our entire being, that also detaches us from the petty ties of everyday existence and links us to eternity. It assumes the form of a great worship; it rends the rocky barriers of space and time and flows like a spring towards the eternal.

'In this way, the intense vibration connects us to the vibrations of the world. Just as soldiers in a large army acquire fury of passion from one another and become one single soul, likewise when the tremor of the world enters our hearts through the medium of beauty, we walk in step with the universe—we are united with every vibrating atom in the cosmos and propelled towards the eternal with irresistible momentum.

'Poets have tried to express this feeling in many languages and through many devices, and many people haven't been able to understand them at all: they've simply thought of it as a poetic mist.

'This is because language has no direct connection with the heart: it must pass through the brain in order to enter the inner recesses. It's a mere messenger—it has no right of entry into the private chambers of the heart; it can only leave its message in the outer hall of the general assembly. It takes quite a while to understand it, to make sense of it. But music embraces the heart at the first signal.

'For this reason, poets employ a kind of music along with language. That opens the doors of the heart with its magic touch. When the heart is spontaneously aroused through rhythm and through tone, the task of language is made much easier. When a flute is playing in the distance, when a flower-garden has bloomed before one's eyes, words of love are easily understood. Nothing can instantaneously introduce the heart to ideas and sentiments in the way beauty can.

'Tune and beat, rhythm and tone are two different aspects of music. The Greeks in their time talked of something called 'the music of the spheres'; Shakespeare mentions it too. I've already spoken of the reason behind this: each motion has a close connection with other motions. The moon and sun, planets and stars are dancing in rhythm through the limitless skies. One can't quite hear their great cosmic music: rather, one can see it. Rhythm is another form taken by music. In poetry, this rhythm and tone come together to vibrate and give life to sentiment; they turn even external language into the heart's precious wealth. If there's anything artificial, it's language: beauty isn't artificial. Language belongs to mankind, beauty to the entire world and to the world's Creator.'

Her face animated with joy, Mistress Srotaswini said, 'In drama, a number of ingredients that arouse our hearts are brought together. Music, lighting, background scenery, attractive costumes, and props all strike and excite our minds from different directions; through all these, a continuous stream of feeling keeps taking various forms and assuming the shape of various functions. Our minds surrender helplessly to the dramatic flow and are swiftly washed away. The theatre shows how closely con-nected are the various *arts*: music, literature, painting, and dramatic art come together there to serve a common purpose. Perhaps one can't quite see this anywhere else.'

Translated by Tista Bagchi

The Five Elements: The Significance of a Poem

Srotaswini said to me, 'I want to hear you recite the poem you've written about the encounter between Kacha and Devyani.'[†]

This made me feel a little proud; but Madhusudana the Pride-Destroyer[†] was alert the while, so Dipti exclaimed impatiently, 'Don't be offended, but I haven't been able to find any significance or purpose in that poem. That piece of yours hasn't turned out well.'

I remained silent; secretly I said to myself, if this opinion had been expressed a little more modestly, it wouldn't have greatly harmed the world or impaired the truth. It's no marvel for a piece of writing to have flaws; nor is it impossible for the reader's poetic sensibilities to be wanting. Aloud, I said, 'Though a writer might often have a fixed opinion about his own writing, there's ample evidence in history that it may be mistaken. There's also no dearth of evidence that critics aren't always entirely unmistaken either. Therefore, only this can be said for certain: This piece of mine isn't to your liking. That's doubtless my misfortune; it might be yours as well.'

Dipti said briefly and sternly, 'That may be so.' She then drew a book towards her and started reading.

After this, Strotaswini did not request me a second time to read out that poem.

Byom looked out of the window and seemed to address some imaginary man in the sky as he said, 'Talking about significance, I've drawn a significance from this recent poem of yours.'

Kshiti said, 'Tell us first what it's about. For fear of the poet's wrath, I've been hiding the fact that I haven't read the poem; now I'm forced to reveal it.'

Byom said, 'The gods sent Kacha, the son of Vrihaspati,[†] to the hermitage of Shukracharya, the teacher of the demons, to learn the art of *sanjivani*, reviving the dead. There Kacha entertained Devyani, Shukra's daughter, with dance and music for a thousand years to acquire the art. Finally, when the time came to bid farewell, Devyani declared her love for him and asked him not to leave the hermitage. Despite his feelings for Devyani, Kacha disregarded her bidding and returned to the abode of the gods. This is the story. It departs a little from the *Mahabharata*, but only a little.'

Kshiti said with a rather pained expression, 'The story may not be more than twelve hands long, but I fear it may bear an exegesis of thirteen hands.'†

Byom turned a deaf ear to Kshiti and said, 'The tale concerns the body and the soul.'

Everyone was alarmed on hearing this.

Kshiti said, 'I'm off this very minute while my body and soul are still intact.'

Samir pulled him back by his garment with both hands and said, 'Where are you off to, deserting us in time of danger?'

Byom said, 'The living being has come from heaven to the hermitage of this world. It derives education from the joys and sorrows, the assets and liabilities of this world. As long as it remains a pupil it has to keep this daughter of the hermitage, the body, duly pleased. It knows the delightful art of pleasing. It plays such heavenly music on the veena of the bodily senses that the mirage of a celestial garden of beauty spreads across the earth; all sounds, scents, and sensations leave off the mechanical functions of inert matter and begin to vibrate in an exquisite celestial dance.'

As he spoke, the dreamy vacant-eyed Byom grew animated. He sat up straight in his chair and said, 'If you look at it this way, you'll find an eternal drama of love being enacted in each human being. Watch how the living being drives his foolish, innocent, dependent companion wild. He awakens a desire in every atom of the body—a desire that can't be satisfied by corporeal means. Eyesight can't fathom the beauty he brings before the eyes, and so she says,

> Ever since birth, your face have I descried;
> Yet the eye's unsatisfied.

The ears can't encompass the music that he brings to the ears, and so she says wistfully,

> Your honeyed utterance entered at my ear;
> Yet I seemed not to hear.†

On the other hand, this simple-minded companion, glowing with vitality, also throws out a thousand tendrils like a creeper, enthralling and overwhelming the living being in a soft embrace, warm with love; she gradually charms him; she stays beside him like his shadow and ministers to him with all kinds of things in untiring care; she always keeps her eyes, ears, and limbs alert so that he may not feel his exile to be exile, that there may be nothing lacking in her hospitality. After all this love, the living being nonetheless leaves this eternally loyal, unwaveringly faithful creeper of a body lying in the dust and departs. He says, "My dear, I love you like myself; yet I'll leave you with no more than a sigh." The body then clutches his feet and says, "Dear friend, if you're finally going to fling me in the dust like a fistful of dust and leave, why then did you exalt me by your love all this while? Alas, I am not worthy of you; why, then, did you come on your tryst across the boundless seas in the mysterious dark night to this, my secret temple of gold lit by life's lamp? By what magic power did I bewitch you?" No one knows where the stranger goes without replying to these plaintive questions. In which love poem is such a poignant scene of separation to be found—such an end to the love ties of a lifetime, such a day of farewell before the journey to Mathura,† that last dialogue between the body and the lord of the body?'

Fearing an impending witticism from Kshiti, judging from the expression on his face, Byom said, 'You don't consider this to be love; you think I'm simply speaking in metaphors. It's not so. This is the very first instance of love in the world; and just as the very first love of one's life is usually the most violent, the very first love of the world is also simple and yet powerful. When this original love, this love of the body first appeared in the world, the earth had not yet been divided between land and water. There was no poet present on that day, no historian had yet been born; but it was first announced that day, on this watery, muddy, unformed earth, that the world isn't merely a mechanical world: an ineffable, joyful, painful power of intent called love is raising a lotus-bed out of the mud, and in the devotee's esteem, Lakshmi,† the embodiment of beauty, and Sarasvati,† the embodiment of feeling and idea, are enthroned today on that lotus-bed.'

Kshiti said, 'I'm thrilled to hear that there's such a great poetic enactment going on within each one of us; but it must be admitted that the fickle-minded soul's treatment of the simple-minded body is far from satisfactory. I earnestly hope that my own soul stays on for some length of time in the hermitage of Devyani the body without displaying such inconstancy. May all of you bless me to that end.'

Samir said, 'Brother Byom, we never heard anything contrary to the shastras[†] from you. Why are you speaking like an alien Christian today? That the living soul is sent to the temporal world from heaven, finds the company of the body, and attains its end through joys and sorrows—all this doesn't match with your earlier opinions.'

Byom said, 'Don't try to match opinions in these matters. I don't differ from any opinion whatsoever in these fundamental matters. In the business of living, every community gathers capital in the currency of its own state; the point to see is whether their business flourishes or not. Life goes on beautifully if one takes as one's stock-in-trade the view that the living being has been sent to the school of the world to be educated through joys and sorrows, liabilities and assets; in my view, therefore, this piece of currency can't be counterfeit. Again, when the opportunity arises in due course, I'll demonstrate that the banknote with which I've ventured to trade in my life is valid at the bank of the world's Creator.'

Kshiti said plaintively, 'Please, my friend! Hearing you talk about love was hard enough; if you now start offloading your views about trade, I'll have to offload myself from here as well: I'm feeling quite faint as it is. If I'm allowed the opportunity, I could also tell you about a certain significance.'

Byom leaned back in his chair and put his feet up on the window sill. Kshiti said, 'I find the essence of *evolutionary theory* implicit in this poem. The art of reviving the dead signifies the art of survival. It's evident in the world that someone has been exercising that art every day, for not just a thousand but a million years. However, he's evinced only fleeting love for the living beings on which he's practised his art. As soon as a particular chapter is finished, the heartless lover, the transitory guest ruthlessly leaves it to destruction and departs. The dirges of these cruel farewells are engraved in fossil rock in layer after layer of the earth.'

No sooner had Kshiti finished than Dipti spoke up impatiently: 'If all of you keep extracting significances like this, there can be no end. A fire burning up all the wood and disappearing, a butterfly breaking out of its chrysalis and escaping, the withering of a flower and emergence of the fruit, the bursting of a new shoot out of a seed—one can collect heaps of such significances!'

Byom began to say solemnly, 'That's quite true. Those are not significances, only examples. The real truth is this: We cannot walk in the material world without using at least two legs. When the left leg's anchored behind, the right leg moves forward; then, when the right leg's anchored forward, the left leg frees itself and moves ahead. Now we bind ourselves down, and the very next moment we free ourselves. We must both love and break free of that love: that's the greatest sorrow in the living world, and it's through this great sorrow that we have to move ahead. This holds for society as well. When in the course of time a new law becomes old custom and ties us down to a particular point, social revolution comes to free us by uprooting it. We have to lift up the foot that we put down immediately thereafter, else we cannot walk: it's God's intent that every step forward should be accompanied by the pain of separation.'

Samir said, 'None of you has mentioned the curse at the end of the story. When Kacha completed his education and left, sundering his ties of love with Devyani, she put a curse on him, saying, "You shall be able to teach others the skill that you have acquired, but not use it yourself." I've drawn a significance from this, curse and all: I can tell you if you have the patience.'

Kshiti said, 'We can't tell beforehand whether we'll have the patience. A promise made might not be kept after all. Why don't you start off? If our response arouses your compassion, all you have to do is stop.'

Samir said, 'Let's call the art of living life well the art of *sanjivani*. Let's suppose that a poet has come into the world to learn this art and impart it to others. He charms the world by his inborn heaven-gifted powers and acquires that art from it. It's not that he doesn't come to love the world; but when the world tells him, "Surrender to me", he says, "If I surrender, if I'm drawn into your whirlpool, I shan't be able to impart this art of *sanjivani*; I'll have to keep myself detached even when I'm in the world, amongst everyone." The world then curses him, saying, "You shall be able to impart to others the art that you have acquired from me, but not use it yourself." Because this curse of the world remains, one often sees a master's teachings being of use to the disciple, but the master remaining as inept as a child in implementing that worldly knowledge in his own life. This is because if one learns the art in a detached manner from outside, one might acquire the art well; but unless one remains immersed in its practice, one can't learn how to apply it. That's why in ancient times the brahman would be a minister, but it was the kshatriya king who implemented his counsel in practice. Had the brahman been put on the throne, he'd have been at sea, and brought the kingdom to ruin as well.

'The issues you have raised are too commonplace. Suppose one were to say, "The significance of the *Ramayana* is that many people suffer by being born into royal families," or "The significance of *Abhijnanashakuntalam* is that, given the appropriate circumstances, it isn't impossible for mutual love to awaken in the hearts of a woman and a man," that couldn't be called a novel lesson or stirring news.'

Srotaswini said somewhat hesitantly, 'But I feel that poetry is about such ordinary matters. Despite their royal birth, despite every prospect of happiness, Ram and Sita were pursued all their lives by immense suffering from one crisis to another, as a hunter pursues his prey; this old, sorrowful, all too credible tale of human fate, the familiar lot of humankind, is what has captured and moved the readers' minds. There is indeed no novel lesson or stirring news to be derived from the spectacle of Shakuntala's love; only this very old and ordinary notion that love comes unawares with irresistible force, in a fortunate or unfortunate moment, and unites the hearts of woman and man in a firm bond; the general populace have enjoyed the story precisely because of this very ordinary notion in it. Some may say, "The special meaning of the disrobing of Draupadi† is that death keeps tugging at the robes of this earth, covered with animals and plants, but by God's blessing there's never any end to her robes; she remains clad in beautiful new living robes for ever." But in the Sabha Parva,† when our blood boiled in our hearts, and finally tears filled our eyes at the god's mercy towards the beleaguered devotee, was it because of that special new meaning? Or was it because of the very natural, commonplace old matter of a humiliated woman's shame and the amelioration of that shame? In the dialogue between Kacha and Devyani, too, there's a very old and commonplace tale of sorrow; those who consider it trivial, and instead privilege some special inner meaning, lack a poetic sensibility.'

Samir laughed and said to me, 'Mistress Srotaswini has banished us from all claim to a poetic sensibility. Let's now hear what the poet himself opines.'

Highly embarrassed and apologetic, Srotaswini repeatedly protested against this accusation.

I said, 'I can say this much: When I sat down to write the poem I had no meaning whatsoever in my head; thanks to you, I now see that the poem wasn't quite meaningless after all—no dictionary can encompass all its meanings. There's a virtue in poetry, in that the poet's creativity arouses the reader's creativity; people then proceed to evoke beauty, or morality, or abstraction from it according to their inclinations. It's like lighting fireworks: poetry is the igniting flame and the readers' minds are fireworks of different kinds. On catching fire, some fly off at once into the sky like rockets, some effervesce like squibs, some make noises like firecrackers. Even so, I don't see any overall conflict of opinion between

Mistress Srotaswini and myself. Many people say that the pit is the most important part of the fruit, and this can be proved by scientific arguments. Yet many connoisseurs[†] eat the flesh of the fruit and throw the pit away. Likewise, even if a poem carries a specific moral, no one can blame a connoisseur of poetry if he accepts the juicy poetic part of it and discards the moral. As for those who eagerly seek to extract the moral alone, I wish them success and happiness. No one can be made to derive pleasure by force. Some people extract a dye from the kusumbha flower; others press oil from its seed; yet others gaze at its beauty with rapt eyes. Some people extract history out of poetry; others unearth philosophy in it; others discover morality or worldly wisdom; while yet others can extract nothing but poetry from it. Each person can return content with what each has found. I see no need for any conflict with anyone, nor will it yield any good.'

TRANSLATED BY TISTA BAGCHI,
VERSE TRANSLATED BY SUKANTA CHAUDHURI

The Five Elements: Lucidity

Srotaswini mentioned a certain famous English poet and said, 'I don't know why, but his works don't appeal to me.'

Dipti seconded Srotaswini's opinion even more vehemently.

Samir never openly objects to women's remarks if he can help it. He therefore smiled a little and said with some hesitation, 'But a number of eminent critics accord him a very high place.'

Dipti said, 'To properly understand that fire burns, you don't need a critic: you can test it even with the tip of the little finger of your left hand. If I can't grasp the goodness of a good poem just as easily, I don't see that reading a criticism of it will help.'

Samir knew that fire had the power to burn, so he remained silent; but poor Byom had no notion of such matters, so he loudly began to soliloquise.

He said, 'The human mind moves ahead of humankind itself: often it can't be reached by anyone . . .'

Kshiti interrupted him: 'In the Treta† age, Hanuman's 800-mile-long tail would extend far beyond the venerable Hanumanji himself; if the tip of his tail had been attacked by lice, he'd have had to start a mail rider service to scratch it. The human mind extends even farther than Hanuman's tail, and so no long arm except the critic's mail-horse can reach where the mind reaches at times. The difference between a mind and a tail is that the mind moves on ahead and the tail drags along behind. That's why the world looks down so much upon tails and holds the mind in such high esteem.'

When Kshiti had finished, Byom began again: 'The aim of science is to know, and the aim of philosophy is to understand, but things have come to such a pass that to know science and to understand philosophy have become harder than to know and to understand everything else. So many schools, so many tomes, so much preparation were needed to accomplish this. The aim of literature is to impart pleasure, but it isn't very easy to partake of that pleasure either: that, too, asks for kinds of training and support. That's why I was saying that the mind advances so far ahead in a trice that one has to raise a flight of steps to reach it. If someone digs in his heels and says, "What can't be known without training isn't science; what can't be understood without effort isn't philosophy; and what doesn't impart pleasure without striving isn't literature," he'll have to lag far behind with nothing but Khana's† sayings, proverbs, and panchalis.'

Samir said, 'Anything becomes more difficult as men handle it. Savages find it exciting to yell just anyhow; but we are so ill-starred that we can't be happy unless we hear music, which needs special practice and training. Worse still, just as to make good music needs training, so does the appreciation of good music. The upshot is that what was once common property gradually accrues only to the initiated. Everyone can yell, and the vulgar enjoy stimulation from yelling; but not everyone can make music, and not everyone finds pleasure in it either. Thus the more society advances, the more it creates two communities: the 'cans' and the 'cannots', the connoisseurs and the philistines.'

Kshiti said, 'The human being, poor creature, has been made in such a way that the more we seek a simple means, the more we get tangled in complexities. We fashion machines in order to work more easily, but the machine itself is an exceedingly complicated affair; we create science in order to systematise all natural knowledge easily, but to master science is itself a difficult task. Laws were decreed to find an easy way to judge matters truly, but now long-lived people have to devote three-quarters of their lives simply to understand the law. Money was created to make transactions easier, but now money has become such a problem that no one can resolve it. In their efforts to make everything easier, people have made their knowledge, their interactions, even their eating and merry-making impossibly complex.'

Srotaswini said, 'In keeping with this, poetry too has become difficult. People are now very clearly divided into two groups. A few are wealthy and many are poor; a few are accomplished while many more lack parts; so also, nowadays poetry isn't for the masses but for special people. I understand all this. But the point is, the specific poem in whose context we've raised this issue isn't difficult in any respect: it contains nothing that even people like us can't grasp; it's perfectly simple. If it doesn't appeal to us, it's not because we can't understand it.'

Kshiti and Samir showed no desire to say anything further. But Byom continued unfazed: 'It isn't necessarily the case that something that's simple is easy to understand. Often it's particularly difficult, because it doesn't adopt any shoddy ploy to make itself understood, but simply stands quietly by. If one passes it by without comprehending, it doesn't use any artifice to call one back. The principal virtue of lucidity is that it establishes a direct connection with the mind: it has no intermediary. But to minds that can't accept anything without the help of an intermediary, minds that have to be attracted by enticements, lucidity is very abstruse indeed. The clay water-carrier fashioned by the artisan of Krishnanagar,[†] with his painted colours, his water-skin and his exaggerated posture, can make his way at once into our minds because of our conditioning to its sensory appeal. But a Grecian sculpture has no colouring or posturing: it is lucid and devoid of all contrivance. That doesn't make it easy to comprehend. It needs to have greater inner content precisely because it doesn't resort to petty external artifices.'

Dipti said with considerable irritation, 'Forget about your Grecian sculpture! I've heard a lot on the subject, and will have to hear a lot more if I stay alive. The problem with a good thing is that it's forced to remain in the public eye; everyone talks about it; it has no veil, no privacy; no one has to discover it, understand it, or even look at it properly with open eyes any more, only to hear and utter platitudes about it. Just as the sun ought to be clouded over sometimes so that the glory of the cloud-free sun can be appreciated, I feel that a veil of neglect should be cast from time to time on the wonders of the world. It would be good if it were sometimes the fashion to denigrate Greek sculpture; it ought to be publicly demonstrated sometimes that Chanakya[†] is a greater poet than Kalidasa. It becomes unbearable otherwise. But that's beside the point. What I want to say is, one should keep in mind that poverty of thought and barbarity of custom can often be mistaken for simplicity; the lack of expressive power is often held to stem from an excess of ideas.'

I said, 'Simplicity in the arts accompanies mental elevation of a high order. Barbarism is not simplicity. Barbarism has too much pomp and splendour; civilisation is relatively unembellished. Too many embellishments attract our eyes but repel our minds. In our Bengali language, whether in the newspapers or in high literature, one finds a lack of simplicity and restraint. Everyone loves to shout and posture to excess; no one's inclined to tell the plain truth clearly, without embellishment. This is because we still have a primeval barbarism within us: when truth comes in lucid guise, we can't recognise its depth and its greatness. Unless the beauty of feeling comes laden with artificial adornments and excesses of every sort, its value is diminished for us.'

Samir said, 'Restraint is a major characteristic of civility. Gentlefolk don't proclaim their existence blatantly by any obtrusive excess; they preserve their dignity with modesty and restraint. Quite often, pomp and posturing prove more attractive to common people than restrained, self-possessed civility. That's not the misfortune of the civilly disposed but of the general populace. Restraint in literature and in social mores is a sign of advancement: it's the effort to attract attention through excesses that's barbaric.'

I said, 'Forgive me for using a word or two of English. As among gentlefolk, so also in civilised literature, there's *manner* but no *mannerism.* Good literature doubtless has a distinctive form and nature, but it's so graceful and restrained that the peculiarities of its form and nature are not what capture the eye. It has in it a conception, a subtle influence, but no novel mannerism. In the absence of any upheaval, even the fullness of perfection can often escape people's attention; and in the absence of that fullness, people might be swayed by a mere upheaval. But no one should mistakenly conclude from this that the simplicity of perfect fullness is easy to comprehend, while shallow posturing is abstruse.'

Turning to Srotaswini, I said, 'It's often difficult to appreciate lucid literature of a high order for this reason, that although the mind grasps it, it doesn't keep trying to make itself understood.'

Dipti said, 'My homage to you! We've learnt enough of a lesson today. Never again shall we reveal our barbarism by expressing our views on high literature to such high pundits.'

Srotaswini again mentioned that English poet and said, 'However much you may argue and abuse me, I still don't like his poetry at all.'

TRANSLATED BY TISTA BAGCHI

The Five Elements: Mirth

In this essay and the next, the following terms have been used to render the chief Bengali words signifying humour, laughter, or the comical: koutuk, *the comical;* koutukhasya, *mirth;* hasyaras, *(the rasa of) humour;* hasya, *laughter;* amod, *amusement, fun.*

A man is going down the street this winter morning, peddling date-palm juice. The hazy dawn mist has cleared, and the morning has grown pleasurably warm in the early sunshine. Samir is sipping tea, Kshiti is reading the newspaper, and Byom has just arrived with a garish blue and green woollen scarf wrapped round his head and an incongruously thick walking stick in hand.

Standing at the door nearby with their arms round each other's waists, Srotaswini and Dipti were going into splits of laughter over some joke. Kshiti and Samir were of the opinion that the outlandish blue-and-green-wool-clad, contented, complacent figure of Byom was the cause of their laughter.

Finally, even the absent-minded Byom was attracted by the laughter. He turned his chair slightly towards us and said, 'From afar, a man might be deluded into thinking that those two friends are laughing over something humorous. That, however, would be an illusion. A partial Creator has not endowed men with the ability to laugh without reason, but *deva na jananti kuto manushyah* [not even the gods know, let alone men]† what makes women laugh. A flintstone has no natural lustre; when suitably struck, it emits a few sparks with much noise, whereas a gem scatters light on its own, without waiting for due occasion. Women know how to weep for little reason, and can laugh for none at all: the strict law of the world, that there can be no effect without a cause, holds only for men.'

Samir replenished his empty cup and said, 'I find not just women's laughter but humour itself a little illogical. It's easy to grasp that we weep out of sorrow and laugh out of joy. But why do we laugh at the comical? The comical isn't quite the same as the joyful, after all. When a fat man breaks his chair and falls, we can't say it gives us cause for joy, but it's a proven fact that it gives cause for laughter. If one thinks about it, there's reason here for wonder.'

Kshiti said, 'Spare us, brother! There are enough matters in the world to wonder at without thinking; exhaust those first and start thinking afterwards. There was this madman who first swept his courtyard thoroughly with a broom to free it of dust; not satisfied with this, he then began digging it up with a spade. He thought he could sweep the whole dusty earth away into the sky and get a nice clean courtyard; needless to say, he didn't succeed, for all his perseverance. Brother Samir, if you not only sweep away the upper layers of the wondrous but then begin to think and wonder, your friends must take leave of you. They say *Kalohyayam niravadhih* [Time is eternal],† but we don't have eternal time on our hands.'

Samir laughed and said, 'Brother Kshiti, you've been thinking more than I have. With much thought, one might conceive of you as a great wonder of creation, but you must have thought harder still to think of comparing me with your ideal courtyard-sweeping being.'

Kshiti said, 'Forgive me, brother: it's because you're such an old friend that I felt so apprehensive. Never mind. The question before us is, why do we laugh at the comical? That's indeed very curious. But the next question is, why do we laugh at all, for whatever reason? As soon as something pleasing appears before us, a weird sound rises from our throats and we bare our front teeth, distorting our facial muscles: for a civilised creature like man, isn't such an uninhibited, incongruous act more than a trifle odd and demeaning? The elite of Europe are ashamed to show signs of fear or sorrow; we Orientals consider the public expression of mirth to indicate a gross lack of restraint.'

Interrupting Kshiti, Samir said, 'That's because we think it to be quite illogical to feel amused at the comical: it befits only a child. That's why every adult among us considers the rasa of humour to be vulgar. I once heard a song about how Lord Krishna, waking up one morning, went to Radha's hut, hookah in hand, to ask for a light. This made all the hearers laugh. The picture of Lord Krishna with hookah in hand is neither beautiful nor pleasing. Isn't it strange and illogical that we should nonetheless laugh and be amused? That's why our wise men don't condone such frivolity. It seems to be largely a corporeal process, a mere excitement of the nerves. It has nothing to do with our sense of beauty, our intelligence, or even our self-interest. Such an irresistible defeat of the intelligence, such an utter loss of balance, so fitfully and on such trivial pretext, is undoubtedly shameful for a thinking being.'

Kshiti thought for a while and said, 'That's true. You might know of this poem by some anonymous poet:

> I was thirsty and asked for a pitcher of water;
> You quickly brought me half a wood-apple.

If someone rushes up with half a wood-apple when a thirsty man's asking for water, there's no lawful or logical reason why a third person should feel amused. When the thirsty man is brought the pitcher of water he'd asked for, we feel a sympathetic pleasure; but I don't know what impulse makes us feel amused when he's brought half a wood-apple. Since there's a difference of category between pleasure and amusement, their means of expression ought to have been different. But such is Nature's housekeeping: wasteful spending in some areas and stinting on essentials in others. The same act of laughter shouldn't have been made to serve the needs of both pleasure and mirth.'

Byom said, 'Nature's being unjustly slandered. We smile out of pleasure, but we laugh out loud in mirth. We may compare light and lightning in the natural world. One's steady and generated by harmonic movement; the other's sudden, and created by collision. I feel that once we know the varying reasons why light and lightning are generated in the same *ether*, the reason why we smile for pleasure and laugh in mirth will emerge by analogy.'

Ignoring Byom altogether, Samir said, 'Amusement and mirth are not exactly happiness: rather, they're mild degrees of pain or sadness. We may well feel some pleasure when sadness or pain impinges on our consciousness in small measure. We eat meals prepared by the cook at fixed times each day without hardship; we don't consider this amusing. But we're amused when, on a day's picnic, we break rules, undergo hardship, and eat possibly inedible food at the wrong time. In our amusements, the small measure in which we voluntarily evoke disquiet and privation excites our sensibility.

'Mirth, too, is a kind of pleasurable pain. When Lord Krishna is shown in front of Radha's hut with hookah in hand, this strikes abruptly at our traditional conception of him. That blow gives us a little pain, but so regulated as to yield more of pleasure by stimulating our sensibility. Once this limit is exceeded even slightly, the humour turns into genuine pain. If some humour-afflicted young man were suddenly to sing about Krishna thirsting for tobacco in the middle of a genuinely devotional kirtan,[†] that wouldn't cause mirth; the blow would be so harsh as to materialise immediately as clenched fists showered on the joker's back. In my view, mirth is an oppression of the sensibility, and so is amusement. That's why true joy is expressed in a smile, and amusement or mirth in laughter: it's as though the laughter's noisily thrust upwards by the shock of a sudden swift blow.'

Kshiti said, 'When people like you can attach an analogy of your choice to a theory of your choice, you're so overjoyed that you lose all sense of reality. We all know that comical things don't only make us laugh out loud: they can make us smile and sometimes even laugh inwardly. But that's beside the point. The real point is that the comical excites our minds, and mild exciting of the mind is pleasurable to us. A logical order reigns both within us and outside: everything's habitual and predictable. When our mind travels smoothly across this level ground of logic and order, it doesn't register on us in a conscious way. But if, amidst this measured predictability, an incongruous element is introduced all of a sudden, the flow of our consciousness encounters a sudden barrier and is stirred up in uncontrollable waves of laughter. This barrier is not one of pleasure, or beauty, or benefit, but not of great sorrow either; we therefore feel amused at such pure, unalloyed stimulation by the comical.'

I said, 'Any feeling is pleasurable if there's no fear of great suffering or harm to oneself associated with it. Even fear can hold pleasure if there's no real cause for fear. Children love listening to ghost stories, because the stimulation generated by the fluttering of the heart affords pleasure. We're saddened by Rama's sorrow on losing Sita in the *Ramayana*; Othello's unfounded jealousy upsets us; we're pained by the mental suffering of the demented Lear, his heart pierced by his daughters' ingratitude; but all those works would have seemed worthless to us if they hadn't afforded pain by the evocation of sorrow and suffering. Indeed, we tend to value poems of sorrow over poems of joy, because feelings of sorrow stimulate our minds more. The comical strikes a sudden blow to the mind and arouses our customary faculties. That's why a lot of fun-loving people view a sudden physical blow as a joke; many people use terms of abuse as expressions of humour; the ladies of Bengal have agreed to find humour of a sort in boxing a bridegroom's ears or inflicting other deft tortures in the bridal chamber; making a cracker go off suddenly with a bang is a feature of festivities in our land; and we commonly inspire devotion by driving ourselves crazy, like a swarm of bees smoked out of a beehive, with the deafening noise of drums and cymbals.'

'Calm yourselves, my friends,' said Kshiti: 'The matter's more or less settled. You've exceeded what little affliction causes pleasure; the pain's growing more and more acute. We've come to understand quite well that the laughter of *comedy* and the tears of *tragedy* depend on varying degrees of sadness.'

Byom said, 'Just as snow glitters when the first sunshine falls on it, but begins to melt when it gets hotter. Name a few farces and *tragedies*, and I'll demonstrate on their basis that—'

Just then, Dipti and Srotaswini came over to us, still laughing.

Dipti said, 'What did you set out to prove?'

Kshiti said, 'We were proving that the two of you were laughing all this while for no reason.'

On hearing this, Dipti looked at Srotaswini; Srotaswini looked at Dipti; and they both again burst into laughter.

'I was going to demonstrate,' said Byom, 'that in *comedy* we laugh at the mild suffering of other people, and in *tragedy* we weep at their greater suffering.'

The house filled yet again with Dipti and Srotaswini's laughter in sweet unison. Wagging their fingers at each other for laughing without reason, the two friends left the room coyly, still laughing.

The male members of the gathering remained smilingly silent, wondering at the sight of such unprovoked bursts of laughter. Only Samir said, 'Byom, it's quite late in the morning. I don't foresee any damage to your health if you take off your multicoloured serpentine coils.'

Kshiti picked up Byom's walking stick, inspected it for some time, and said, 'Byom, is this bludgeon of yours a matter of *comedy* or an implement of *tragedy*?'

TRANSLATED BY TISTA BAGCHI

The Five Elements: The Measure of Mirth

Having read about our discourse on mirth in the other day's diary, Mistress Dipti has written us the following note:

'One morning, Srotaswini and I laughed together. Blessed be that morning, and blessed the laughter of two women friends! Since the world was created, many women have shown such playfulness, and its effects have been perpetuated in history in many forms, good and bad. A woman's laughter may be without cause, but it is reported to have been the cause of many compositions in many metres—the mandakranta, the upendravajra, even the shardulavikririta† —and many tercets, quatrains, and sonnets. Woman laughs without reason by her frivolous nature; many men see this and weep without reason, others sit down to make words rhyme, and yet others proceed to hang themselves. But now I see that women's laughter can make new *philosophy* flower in an old *philosopher*'s brain. To tell you the truth, we prefer the three earlier states to philosophical analysis.'

Mistress Dipti thus dismisses as illogical and inconclusive the conclusion we had reached that day on laughter.

The first thing I have to say is this: Mistress Dipti should not be vexed at the paucity of reason in our theorising that day. The failure of a clever man's intelligence is one of the calamities brought about by womanly laughter. Given the state of mind in which our *philosophy* turned to delirium, we could have written poetry had we so wished, and hanging ourselves might not have been impossible either.

My second point is: Just as they had not imagined that we would draw theory from their mirth, we too had not imagined that they would try to extract reason from our theorising.

After a lifetime's search for truth, Newton said, 'I have merely gathered pebbles by the vast ocean of knowledge.' We four witty souls do not hope to gather even pebbles during our ephemeral conversations—we only build sandcastles. Our objective is to gain a breath of fresh sea air from the ocean of knowledge, on the pretext of this game. We do not bring back gems, but we bring back a measure of good health; it matters to no one whether the sandcastles stand or crumble.

I do not believe that good health is any less precious than gems. Gems often prove to be fake, but good health cannot be other than itself. One might doubt whether we, the five spooks† of our Circle of the Five Elements, have so far drawn a single conclusion worth even a dummy cowrie-shell;† but there is no doubt that, whenever we have met, although we have returned empty-handed, the blood has flowed vigorously through our minds and we have felt happy and healthy.

Not an ounce of produce grows on the Calcutta Maidan;† but all that land is not going waste. Our Meeting of the Five Elements is our Maidan: we come here to gather not the produce of truth but the joy of truth.

Hence no harm results even if nothing is fully resolved in our meetings; we can do with even a fraction of the truth. Our aim is to walk lightly over the fields of truth without ploughing them too deeply.

The matter might be clarified by a different analogy. When we are ill, the doctor's medicine cures us, but our kinsperson's ministrations soothe us. The far-reaching conclusions in some German theorist's book might be called medicinal pills but not mental comforts. The way we debate about truth at the meetings of the Five Elements may not be thought of as curing illness, but it can be called ministering to the sick.

I shall not use any more analogies. The main point is, none of the issues that we four clever fellows had raised about laughter provides the last word on the subject. Had we sought the last word, we would have violated the chief rule of our conversational meetings.

A principal rule in such meetings is to proceed swiftly and with ease—that is, to pace around mentally. If we did not have feet, if our legs were like two pointed rods, it would be easy to dig ourselves deeply into the ground, but not to move even a single step forward. In our dialogic society, if we tried to probe every part of every statement to its depth, we would become so helplessly stuck in one place that we would not be able to move. Sometimes it so happens that we suddenly step into mud: we are mired up to the knees, and find it impossible to walk. There are matters where one has to probe the depths at every step; in conversation, it is advisable not to set foot in those uncertain, suspect areas. Such terrain is not

Rabindranath Tagore: 'Laughing heads'.

By courtesy of Rabindra Bhavan, Shantiniketan.

suitable for travellers seeking a change of air; it is meant for those who live by agriculture.

Broadly speaking, we raised the following question that day. Just as there are tears of sorrow, there are also smiles of happiness; but where did mirthful laughter come in? Mirth is a somewhat mysterious thing. Beasts, too, feel joy and sorrow, but not mirth. All the rasas cited in the rhetorical texts occur in the unformed, inarticulate literature of animals, except for the rasa of humour.[†] Perhaps one finds some trace of this rasa in the nature of the ape; but apes resemble humans in many other respects as well.

What is incongruous ought to arouse sadness in man; there is no reason why it should arouse laughter. If someone falls down while trying to sit down on a chair that isn't there, there is no logical reason why it should give the spectators pleasure. Not only in this example, but in anything comical, there is an element that should provoke sadness instead of pleasure.

In our discussion that day, we had suggested a reason for this. We said that comic laughter and the laughter of amusement or fun are of the same kind: both have a certain forcefulness. So we suspected that fun and humour might have a certain similarity in their nature. If that is unearthed, the mystery of mirth might be solved.

There is a difference between amusement or fun and ordinary happiness. Fun cannot be experienced without the slight distress caused by breaking rules. Fun is not subject to normal everyday rules: it is occasional and intermittent, and requires effort. The excitement generated by friction between the distress and the effort is the main ingredient of fun.

We said that the comical too carries a certain distress caused by the breaking of rules. The sudden blow of pleasurable excitement makes us laugh out aloud so long as that distress does not exceed a certain limit. What is coherent is governed by everyday rules; a momentary violation of rules is incongruous. When something happens as it ought, it does not stir us. If it suddenly fails to happen or happens otherwise, our minds derive pleasure from a special sensation aroused by that unexpected mild blow, and we laugh out aloud.

That day, we had gone so far and not much further. That does not mean one cannot go further. There is more to say on this.

Mistress Dipti has argued: If this conclusion reached by four learned men is correct, we should want to laugh, or at least feel a pleasurable excitement, if we suddenly stumbled while walking, or smelt a slight but foul odour while passing down the street.

This question does not refute our arguments; it merely limits them. It shows that mirthful excitement does not arise from any distress. It becomes necessary to see what is special to the stimulus of mirth.

In inanimate nature, there is neither a rasa of sadness nor one of laughter. If a large boulder crushes a smaller one even to powder, it does not bring tears to our eyes; when we suddenly see an incongruous hillock in the middle of a plain, it does not drive us to laughter. One sometimes finds unexpected incongruities among rivers and springs, mountains and seas; these might create obstacles, frustration, hardship, but they never arouse mirth. Purely inanimate substances cannot evoke our laughter; only irrational happenings among animate beings.

It is hard to say exactly why this is so, but there is no harm in discussing it.

In our language there is a connection in meaning between the terms *koutuk* [the comical] and *koutuhal* [curiosity]. In many places in Sanskrit literature, they are used interchangeably with the same meaning. We gather from this that there is a special relation between curiosity and humour.

A primary feature of curiosity is the desire for novelty; novelty is a major ingredient of humour too. The absolute, unadulterated novelty found in the incongruous is absent in the expected and consistent.

True incongruity, however, involves the power of will, which inanimate entities do not have. If I encounter a foul smell while walking down a clean path, I know this is caused by something putrid close by. This does not violate any rule; it is expected. Whatever happens in inanimate nature, for whatever reason, could not have happened otherwise.

But if, while walking along the street, I suddenly see a decorous elderly person dancing a jig, that strikes me as truly incongruous, because it is not determined by inviolable law. We simply cannot expect such behaviour of the elderly person, since he is endowed with free will: he is dancing voluntarily and need not have danced if he had so wished. Nothing, we hold, can be effected by an inanimate object of its own free will; hence nothing can be incongruous or comical about it. This is why a sudden-stumble or a foul smell does not evoke laughter. If a teaspoon accidentally falls out of a teacup into an ink-pot, this is not comical vis-à-vis the teaspoon, since it cannot but obey the law of gravity. But if an absent-minded writer dips his teaspoon into his ink-pot and tries to sip tea from it, that is a comical matter. There is no moral principle in inanimate things; there is likewise no incongruity. The proper and the prohibited, the harmonious and the incongruous, can be distinguished only when the substance of the mind comes in to create alternative possibilities.

Curiosity is often cruel: there is cruelty in humour too. It is reported that Siraj-ud-Daulah† used to tie two men together by their beards and put snuff up their nostrils; when they both started to sneeze, he would feel amused. Where does the incongruity lie in this? It is only to be expected that one would sneeze if snuff were put into one's nostrils. But here too there is incongruity between intention and circumstance. The persons being plied with snuff do not want to sneeze, because it will cause a painful tug on their beards; yet they are compelled to sneeze.

There is cruelty in such incongruities between intention and circumstance, between ends and means, between words and deeds. Often we laugh about a person who finds his own predicament no laughing matter. This is why Byom said at our last meeting that *comedy* and *tragedy* merely represent different degrees of distress. The small measure of cruelty expressed in *comedy* makes us laugh, while its greater extent in *tragedy* brings tears to our eyes. The way in which many Titanias† offer themselves to asses under a profound spell can be occasion for heart-rending grief, depending on the intensity and the people involved.

Incongruity is the subject of both *comedy* and *tragedy*. *Comedy*, too, reveals a discrepancy between intention and circumstance. Falstaff set out confidently in amorous desire for the merry wives of Windsor, but retreated in the greatest ignominy. When Rama, having slain Ravana and fulfilled his vowed term of forest exile, had returned to his kingdom and attained the summit of conjugal bliss, there was a bolt from the blue: he was compelled to banish the pregnant Sita to the forest. In both instances, there is a discrepancy between expectation and result, intention and circumstance. Hence we see that there are two classes of discrepancy: one is comic, the other deplorable. I would put the vexing, the astonishing, the enraging in the latter class.

That is to say, we experience the comical only when incongruity strikes at the superficial level of our minds; when it strikes at a deeper level, we feel sadness. When a hunter, after taking long and careful aim, shoots at a distant white object thinking it to be a swan but, on approaching it, finds a piece of white cloth, we feel like laughing at his disappointment. But when someone, intently and laboriously all life long, pursues what he conceives to be his life's greatest goals, finally succeeds and holds it in his hand only to find it is a mere sham, our hearts are pained by his despair.

When people die in hordes during a famine, no one finds it a farcical matter. But we can easily imagine that this might be a highly comic scene for a humour-loving devil: he may glance laughingly at all those emaciated beings possessed of immortal souls and say: 'See, your six systems of philosophy,† your poetry of Kalidasa, your 330 million gods† are all around you: you lack nothing but two lowly fistfuls of rice, and simply because of that your immortal souls, your world-conquering humanity are fluttering at your throats, waiting to fly out of your mouths!'

The broad point is this: As the degree of incongruity rises, surprise gradually turns to laughter and laughter to tears.

TRANSLATED BY TISTA BAGCHI

The Five Elements: *A Novel* Ramayana

There was an auspicious function at home; so, late in the afternoon, a shehnai ensemble had been playing the raga Barawaan from a nearby raised platform. Byom sat for a long while with his eyes closed, then suddenly opened his eyes and began to speak:

'There's a pervasive sense of bereavement in these native raginis† of ours: the notes seem to weep and say, nothing lasts in this world. For the dweller in this world, it's neither new nor pleasant to be told that everything in the world is transient. It's an immutable, harsh truth; but why is it so appealing when heard from the flute? It's because the flute articulates this starkest truth on earth in the sweetest way—so that death seems intensely sad but also beautiful, like this ragini. By some magic spell, the tune lightens the heaviest inert rock weighing upon the bosom of the universe. The pain that would have rung out as a scream or burst out as tears had it issued from a person's heart—the flute is giving voice to it, as if from the lips of the universe, to create this intensely plaintive yet infinitely consoling ragini.'

Dipti and Srotaswini had just finished attending to the guests, and come and sat down, when they heard Byom's discourse upon death marring this auspicious day; highly irritated, they got up and left. Not registering their irritation, Byom continued unmoved and unsubdued. We were enjoying the shehnai ensemble: we were not in a mood to argue with him too much that day.

'Listening to this flute music today,' said Byom, 'something comes specially to mind. Every poem has a special rasa—what our texts on poetics have classified under distinct heads such as the primal or erotic (*adi*),† the sorrowful (*karuna*), the peaceful (*shanti*). It strikes me that if universal creation is viewed as a poem, its principal rasa is the rasa of death:† it's death that has endowed the world with true poetic quality. If there had been no death, if everything had stood intact in its place forever, the universe would have been very narrow, very stark, very enclosed, like an enduring mausoleum. It would have been hard for living beings to bear the everlasting burden of this eternal immobility. Death has always lightened this terrible burden of existence, and has given the universe a boundless space to roam in. In the direction of death lies the infinitude of the universe. All poetry, all music, all religious doctrines, all unfulfilled desires fly towards that infinite realm of mystery, like birds crossing the seas in search of a nest. As it is, whatever's visible, whatever's extant affects us powerfully; if in addition it were to be permanent, there would be no end to its sole and exclusive tyranny: how could one have appealed against it? Who could have indicated that there's an infinitude beyond it? How would this world have borne the burden of eternity if death hadn't forever carried along the eternal in its own everlasting flow?'

Samir said, 'If one didn't have to die, there would be no value accorded to staying alive. A person whom the whole world disdains is still endowed with the glory of being alive, precisely because there is death.'

Kshiti said, 'I'm not too worried about that. In my opinion, the greatest worry would be that we couldn't draw a period to any matter in the absence of death. In that case, if Byom were to start a discourse on Advaita philosophy,† nobody would be able to fold his hands imploringly and say: "Dear brother, there's no time, please stop." Without death, there would be no end to opportunity. At least nowadays, people begin their education at seven or eight, pass out of college or simply fail by the time they're twenty-five, and quit in relief. In the situation we're considering, there would be no reason to start or to finish at any particular age. All commas, semi-colons, and periods would be eliminated from our activities and our lives.'

Not paying much attention to all this, Byom persisted with his own line of thought: 'Death alone is eternal in the world; that's why we've located all our eternal hopes and desires in death itself. Our paradise, our virtue, our immortality all reside there. We make over to death all things so dear to us that we can't even imagine their destruction, and wait out our lives to attain them. There's no judgement in this world; true justice is obtained only after death. Ardent desire is frustrated in this world; success dwells at the foot of death's wishing tree.† In all other directions, the hard, gross mass of materiality thwarts our ideals and disproves our immortality and infiniteness; only at the bounds of the universe, where death resides and everything ends, there is no barrier to our strongest, best-loved desires, our purest, loveliest imaginings. Our Shiva dwells in the cremation ground:† our highest ideal of good is in the abode of death.'

Winding up the raga Multan-Barawaan, the shehnai ensemble began to play the raga Purvi† in the golden dusk of sunset. Samir said, 'These notes are bringing back to the world of men the eternally tear-laden treasures of the heart, the hopes and wishes that man had banished beyond the borders of death. Literature, music, all the arts recall the enduring substance of the human heart from the realm of the afterlife and establish it in the middle of this life. They say: We must make this earth a paradise, reality beautiful, this momentary life immortal. Death has made manifest the infinite form and beauty of the universe and bound it by a marriage-bond to a profound mystery on an eternal bridal bed: the fragrance and music of eternal beauty waft to us through a secret window of that closed bridal chamber. So too, in our burdened, distracted daily lives, the rasas of literature and art unite the manifest with the implicit, the transient with the eternal, the trivial with the beautiful, our little personal joys and sorrows with the great raginis pervading the world. The question is whether we should recall all love from the world and consign it to the realm of death, or whether we should retain it in the world. Our ancient doctrine of asceticism says, "The place of true love is in the afterlife." Modern literature and art say, "We are showing its place to be in this very world." '

Kshiti said, 'I want to wind up this meeting by telling the tale of a novel *Ramayana*† in this context.

'King Rama—that's to say, man—had saved Sita, alias love, from various demons, and was living with her in great bliss in his city of Ayodhya. All of a sudden, some religious doctrines ganged up and spread slander against this love. They said: She has lived with something impermanent under the same roof, so she must be cast out. Who was there to prove that, although she had been locked up in the chamber of the impermanent, in actuality no blemish had been able to touch this princess of divine lineage? One could put her through ordeal by fire; it had been done, but instead of destroying her, Agni, the fire, had only brightened her the more! Nonetheless, because of the wagging of doctrinaire tongues, this king finally banished love to the shores of the dark river of death. Since then this deserted woman has remained in the refuge of the great poet and his disciples and given birth to Kusha and Lava, the twin brothers poetry and fine art. The same two children have learned music from the poet and come today to sing the praises of their abandoned mother at the royal court. The love-reft king's heart is agitated, and his eyes fill with tears on hearing the music of these young singers. Uttarakanda,† the final canto, hasn't yet been concluded. Let's see who triumphs: the ancient ascetic doctrine of renunciation or the two immortal children singing the tale of beneficent love.'

TRANSLATED BY TISTA BAGCHI

The Theatre

There is a description of the stage in Bharata's[†] *Natyashastra.* One finds no mention there of scenery. I do not feel it to have been a great loss.

The muse rules in full splendour where she rules alone. If she has to share the household with a co-wife, her stature is bound to be diminished, especially if the other wife's presence happens to be strong. If the entire *Ramayana* were to be sung from start to finish, the tune would have to be a steady monotonous drone all the time; the poor thing would never make it to the status of a raga. Poetry of a high order provides its own music according to its own laws; it scorns any outside musical aid. Music of a high order speaks according to its own rules. It does not look to a Kalidasa or a Milton to supply the words: it can do very well even with the trite scat of *tom-tana-nana.*[†] One might scramble up a sort of aesthetic jumble-sale by throwing together picture, music, and words, but that would be more in sport. It would be a fit thing for the market place, not for the place of honour at a royal pageant.

But it is true that poetry performed is somewhat less self-sustaining than poetry merely heard. It is written in such sort that it may fulfil its purpose only with outside assistance. That it awaits performance is a fact it must accept.

However, we do not admit this to be true. Just as a loyal wife desires none but her husband, so does good poetry wait for no one but the sensitive reader. We all play roles in our minds when we read literature. A poem whose beauty is not enhanced by that acting has never brought its author renown.

You may rather say that the art of acting is dependent on others for shelter. It is an orphan:[†] it sits waiting for a play, its eyes on the road. To display its splendour, it must rely on the graces of the play text.

An uxorious husband is an object of derision; so is a play which compromises itself in the interest of performance. A play-text should say to itself, 'If someone acts me, well and good; if not, it's acting's loss—it makes no difference to me.'

Rabindranath Tagore: 'Actors'.
By courtesy of Rabindra Bhavan, Shantiniketan.

Be that as it may, performance has to accept its subjection to poetry. That does not mean it has to wait on all the arts. If it wishes to preserve its dignity, let it accept that which is absolutely essential for its self-expression; it is demeaned by anything it adopts in excess of that.

It goes without saying that the words in a play are absolutely necessary for the actor. His laughter rests on the humorous dialogue the poet provides; only if the poet gives him an occasion for crying, can he cry himself and make the spectators shed tears with him. But why the scenery? It hangs behind the actor; it is mere painting, not something he brings into being. In my view, it betrays the actor's incapacity and timidity. This device by which he breeds illusions in the spectators and thus eases his own job is one he has scrounged from a painter.

Besides, is the spectator who has come to see you perform destitute of any resources of his own? Is he a child? Is he not to be relied on for anything? If that is the case, then you should not be selling him tickets even if he pays double the rate.

You are not in the courtroom that you have to swear to each word. Why go to such lengths to deceive those who have come to believe and to be entertained? They have not come leaving their imagination locked away at home. You will explain some, they will make out the rest—you have a bargain of that sort with them.

Dushyanta is standing behind a tree and overhearing Shakuntala's conversation with her friends. Very well. Speak the lines, savouring them to the full. Even if the entire tree-trunk is not before my eyes, I can assume it is there. I have that little bit of imagination. It is hard to make a vivid guess of every movement and every turn of voice in Dushyanta and Shakuntala, or Anasuya and Priyamvada;† so when I see them present before my eyes, my heart is infused with delight. But it does not take much to imagine a couple of trees or a cottage or a river. If you do not trust us even to do that, but resort to scenery, you are betraying an absolute lack of faith in us.

I like our jatra† for this very reason. Its performance does not maintain a strict distance between spectator and actor. They trust and help each other and the job is done well in a cordial setting. Assisted by performance, the poetry, which is the real thing, flows over the thrilled hearts of the spectators like a fountain. The gardener-woman† roams her barren garden all day in search of flowers—you do not need to cart whole trees on to the stage to demonstrate that: the entire garden should spontaneously spring to life in the gardener herself. Or else what is so special about her, and what is the purpose of having spectators sit there like wooden dummies?

If the poet of *Abhijnanashakuntalam* had to worry about stage scenery, he would have stopped the deer-chase on chariot in the first place. Of course he was a great poet, it is not as if his pen would have stopped with the chariot. But I would like to ask, why should the major element compromise itself for the sake of the minor? The imaginative viewer has a stage inside his heart, where there is no lack of room. The scene composes itself in that theatre at a magician's touch. That stage and scene are what the playwright aims at. No artificial stage or scene can serve a poet's imagination.

So when Dushyanta and the charioteer remain rooted in the same place and discuss the chariot's speed through description and gestures, the spectators easily infer the simple fact that the stage is cramped but the poetry is not. For the sake of the poetry, they happily forgive this other unavoidable limitation; and by spreading their imagination across that small space, they ennoble the stage. But if the poetry had to be pared down to suit the dimensions of the stage, who would have forgiven those wretched wooden planks?

It is because the play of Shakuntala did not count on any painted scene that it was able to create its own settings. It did not commission anyone to counterfeit Kanva's ashram,† the cloudy path out of heaven,† the sylvan retreat of Maricha:† it drew on itself for its own perfection. In the portrayal of character as well as mood, its sole resort was to the resources of poetry.

I have said in another essay† that Europeans cannot do without the truth of material fact. It is not enough for the imagination to delight their minds, it must make the imaginary simulate the actual and beguile them as it beguiles children. It is not enough to have the life-saving vishalyakarani† of poetry, one must have the whole Gandhamadan† of materiality along with it. These are fallen days;† one thus needs technology to haul in the Gandhamadan, and that does not come cheap. The fortunes wasted in Europe on such trifles are deep enough to absorb many towering Indian famines.

Ritual and work, pleasure and play—these are simple and natural in the East. At a banquet, we eat off plantain leaves, and this allows us to enjoy the purest pleasure of the feast—that is the pleasure of inviting the world without hindrance into one's own little room. Elaborate and excessive hospitality would have killed off the real thing.

The theatre we have fashioned in imitation of the West is a cumbrous and bloated object. It is hard to move, and impossible to take to the common people's door: in it, Lakshmi's owl† virtually obscures Sarasvati's lotus.† It calls for the capital of the rich more than the talent of the poet and artist. If the spectator is still untutored by European puerility and if the actor has faith in himself and in poetry, then it would be a work of Hindu charity if the actor's art were set free and restored to its glory by sweeping away the expensive rubbish that hems it in. It is time we rid ourselves of such crude European barbarisms as demanding that a garden must be presented by an exact painting or female roles acted by bona fide females.

On the whole one can say that overelaboration is a mark of incompetence. Naturalism enters art like a colourful glass-fly but sucks it dry from the inside like a borer beetle. Where indigestion has resulted in lack of appetite for real aesthetic nourishment, one sees an appalling increase of costly condiments, which keep piling up until they swamp the main rice course.

Translated by Swapan Chakravorty

Children's Rhymes

In this essay, the word commonly used by Rabindranath for a child is balak. *Its usual meaning is a boy, but it can be applied to children of either sex. As the observations obviously apply to girls and boys in equal measure, 'child' seemed the fittest rendering. But the pronoun 'he' has been used to remind the reader of the implicit gender bias of the diction. The word* shishu, *which covers children of both sexes, has also been used fairly often.*

The translations of the rhymes follow the versions quoted by Rabindranath. These often differ from variant versions that may sometimes be more current.

It hardly needs stressing that the translations of traditional rhymes are inadequate efforts. The sole purpose of these rough approximations is to illustrate Rabindranath's arguments. Much of the folk diction is patently untranslatable, especially the nonce-words and nonsense-words. More often than not, the rhyme pattern could not have been maintained without grossly impairing the simplicity of diction and easy flow of the verse. To preserve the latter was clearly the prime need.

For some time now, I have been collecting the rhymes current in Bengali by which women divert children. These rhymes may have a special value in determining the history of our language and our society; but to me, their simple natural poetic strain seems more worthy of regard.

I feel afraid to commence a critical essay by saying what I like or do not like. Expert critics consider such assertions to be conceited. I would humbly ask them to consider that this conceit does not amount to egotism, but rather the reverse. Worthy critics have a pair of scales at their disposal. They have worked out a fixed weight and a number of set formulations for literature: whatever composition is placed before them, they can confidently stamp it on the back with the appropriate number and seal.

But those who, from inability and inexperience, have not been equipped with this set of weights have to undertake criticism with nothing but their likes and dislikes to guide them. For such persons it would be audacious to proclaim their utterances on literature as gospel truth. Rather than declare what writings are good or bad, they should simply confess what writings they like or dislike.

If someone were to ask, 'Who wants to hear that?', I would reply that all humankind has been hearing such things through literature. The term 'criticism' is applied only to the criticism of literature; but in fact, most literature is the criticism of nature and human life. When a poet expresses his joy, sorrow, or wonder about nature, about humankind, or about events, and when he wishes to infuse that state of mind in others solely through emotion and writing skill, no one finds fault with him. The reader, too, then considers egotistically only whether his state of mind matches the poet's words. If the critic of poetry likewise eschews argument and classification, wishing to gift his readers only with the state of mind induced in him on reading the poem, he should not be held to blame.

This is particularly so in the present case, for what I am about to say cannot but contain an element of self-justification. It is impossible for me to dissociate my delight in savouring children's rhymes from my memories of childhood. The present author does not have the acumen to judge how much of the sweetness of these rhymes is owing to those memories and how much to the perennial principles of literature. I should admit this at the outset.

'The rain falls pitter-patter, the river is in flood'—in my childhood, this rhyme was like a magic chant to me, and I have yet to overcome that magic. I cannot rightly gauge the sweetness and aptness of the verses without recalling that spellbound state of mind. Nor can I otherwise explain why so many epics and lyrics, theories and precepts, so much human labour and sweating toil should be spent in vain and forgotten every day, while these inconsistent, meaningless, wilfully composed verses should flow for ever through popular memory.

There is a permanence about these rhymes. We do not know that any of them had a recognised author at a set point of time. No one has ever thought of asking on which date, computed by which era, each of them was composed. By this virtue of natural permanence, they are old even if composed today and new even if composed a thousand years ago.

If we consider the matter rightly, nothing is so old as a child. Adult human beings have changed in so many ways by accidents of place, time, upbringing, and custom; but the child remains as he was a hundred

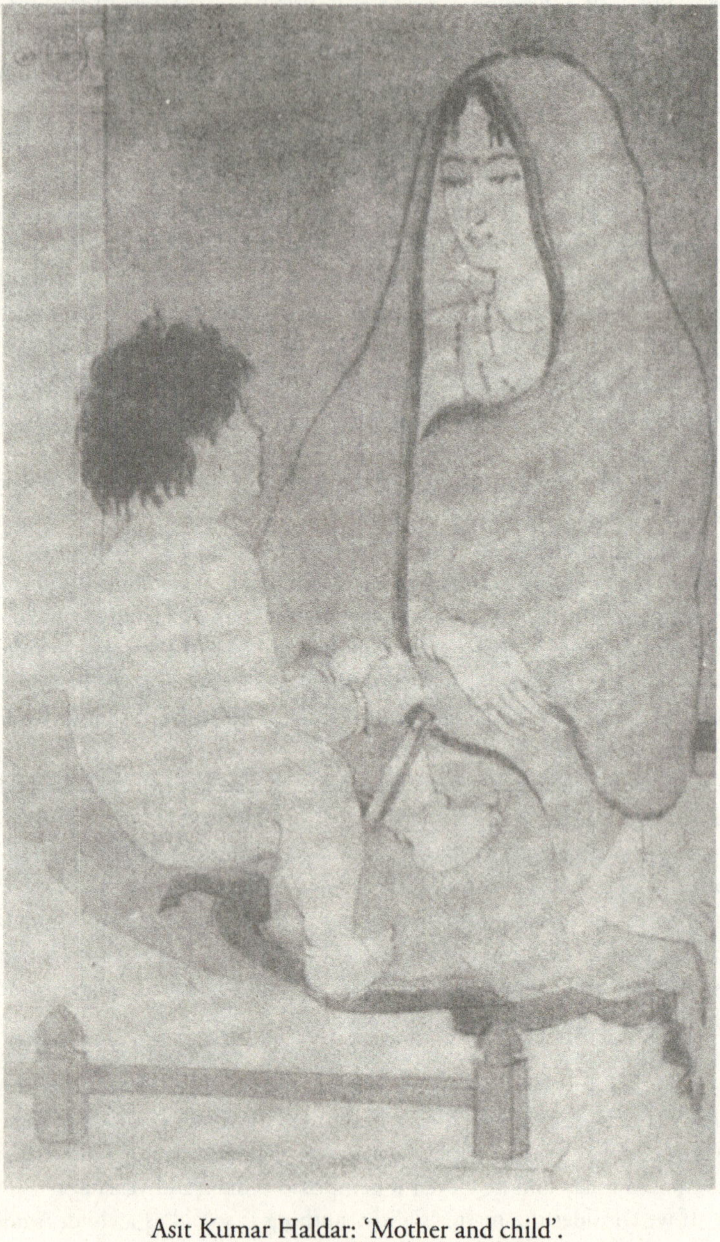

Asit Kumar Haldar: 'Mother and child'.

Illustration for the poem 'The Beginning', *The Crescent Moon.*

thousand years ago. That unchangeable antiquity is being reborn again and again in human homes in the shape of a child, yet it remains as young, as tender, as foolish, as sweet today as it was on that first day. The reason for that youthful permanence is that the child is nature's own creation. The adult, on the contrary, is largely a human creation. In the same way, these rhymes are children's literature: they have been born of themselves in the human mind.

The phrase 'born of themselves' is significant. In the normal way, echoes and reflections of the universe revolve in our minds in a scattered, disjointed manner. They take on various appearances and shift suddenly from one context to another. As in the atmosphere, roadside dust, flower-pollen, countless smells, assorted sounds, fallen leaves, water droplets, the vapours of the earth—all the ejected, whirling fragments of this turning, agitated universe—float and roam meaninglessly, so is it in our minds. There too, in the ceaseless stream of our consciousness, so many colours, scents, and sounds; so many vapours of the imagination, traces of thoughts, broken fragments of language—hundreds of fallen, forgotten, discarded components of our practical life—float about, unobserved and purposeless.

When one starts to think consciously with a specific objective in view, these shadowy mirages vanish in a moment: one's intellect and imagination take on an integrated purpose and begin to flow in a single direction. The substance one calls one's mind is so authoritarian that when it awakens and emerges into the light of day, the greater part of the world within and outside us is obscured under its influence: its own retinue of attendants fills all creation under its power, its law, and its bidding. Think about it: the call of birds in the sky, the sough of leaves, the babble of waters, the hubbub of human habitations—so many thousands of sounds, big and small, rising without end; so many waves and tremors, comings and goings, the restless playful flow of light and shade; yet only a small fraction of all this impinges on one's consciousness. This is chiefly because one's mind, like a fisherman, casts a net of integration and accepts only what it can gather at a single haul: everything else eludes it. When it sees, it does not properly hear; when it hears, it does not properly see; and when it thinks, it neither sees nor hears properly. It has the power to move all irrelevancies far away from the path of its set purpose. It is by this capacity that it can preserve its primacy in its own estimate amidst the infinite variety of the universe.

One reads in the Puranas[†] that in ancient times, certain great souls had the power to will their own deaths. One's mind has the power to will its own blindness and deafness; and because it must constantly exercise this power, the greater part of creation passes over the exterior of its consciousness from birth till death. It perceives only what it exerts itself specially to register, and what it shapes according to its own nature and requirement. It does not keep proper count of what is happening all around it, even within the province of the mind.

In one's normal state, sounds and shadows travel across one's mind's sky like dreams, as though divinely propelled on some unperceived wind, continually forming new clouds by their changes of shape and colour—sometimes joining, sometimes drifting apart. If they could leave an impress of their reflections on some canvas of the unconscious mind, we would find many resemblances to the rhymes we are discussing. These rhymes are mere shadows of the ever-changing sky within us, like the shadows cast by the play of clouds on the clear waters of a lake. That is why I said they are born of themselves.

Before citing a few such rhymes by way of example, I must ask pardon of my readers. First of all, how can the pen of a sober adult male, fearful of his dignity, bring out the sweet, simple, affectionate tone in which these rhymes have been uttered through the ages? My readers must mentally imbibe the soothing nectar of that melody from their own homes and their own childhood memories. There is no spell by which I can bring before them that love, that music, that lamplit evening image of beauty that has forever mingled intimately with these rhymes. I trust they contain their own spell.

Secondly, it does a certain violence to these domesticated, uncultured, non-Sanskritic† rhymes, devoid of all finery, to set them up in this way in the middle of a tightly planned essay in formal Bengali.† It is like making a housewife stand in a witness box at court. But there is no help for it. The court must function according to its own rules, and so must the essay. The cruelty is unavoidable.

Jamunabati, wise lady, tomorrow she'll be wed.
By the kaji trees to her father-in-law's she'll pass along the road.
I went to gather kaji flowers, and found a garland gay.
His hands ring, his feet ring, Sitaram's at play.
Dance, dance, Sitaram, swaying your hips.
I'll give you a basket full of sun-dried rice.
As he munched the sun-dried rice, his throat grew dry as wood.
There's no water here but only at Tripurni's ghat.

At Tripurni's ghat two fish have swum up to the shore—
The holy guru's taken one, but who has had the other?
I'll marry his sister with hibiscus flowers.
I went to gather hibiscus, and fell in a delay.
I'll marry his sister in the middle of the day.

The most partial critic must admit that there is no connected sequence of thought in all this. A number of detached pictures are set before us, linked by a very meagre contextual thread. There is no discrimination whatsoever. It is as though the rascally doorman at the lion-gate of poesy had stretched out his legs and gone to sleep in the sweet sunshine of a still autumn noon. The words and ideas declare no identity, profess no purpose; they simply step over his legs, or sometimes even box his ears with a light touch, and roam at their will through the sky-high magic palace of the imagination. If the doorman were suddenly to start up from his drowse, they would run away that instant in all directions, leaving no trace.

Whoever the wise lady Jamunabati might be, it is explicitly stated that tomorrow is the auspicious day of her wedding. It need not have been added straightaway that after the ceremony, she would travel in due course to her father-in-law's past the kaji trees; but at least it is not irrelevant. However, there is no sign of any preparation for the wedding, or the least interest in the matter on anyone's part. The realm of nursery rhymes is not that kind of regime. There anything might happen, or might not happen, so very readily that no one is worried or stirred to action on that score. Hence though Mistress Jamunabati's marriage has been arranged for the next day, that event is not given the least importance. Nor is anyone anxious to explain why, in that case, the subject needed to be raised at all.

Being a town dweller, I cannot tell what kind of flower a kaji flower might be; but I clearly sense that gathering this flower has nothing to do with the young woman's impending marriage. Nor can we offer the least explanation why in the middle of all this, Sitaram should suddenly start to dance, sounding the bangles on his arms and the anklets on his feet. The prospect of obtaining sun-dried rice might be a tempting motive; but that in turn leads us away from Sitaram's unforeseen dance to the landing jetty at Tripurni. It is not surprising that two fish should swim to shore in such a place; we may yet be astonished that though the identity of the man who takes one of the fish is left entirely dark, our poet should so firmly resolve to marry his sister. Yet he defies the customary rites of marriage by taking hibiscus flowers as sole and sufficient ingredient for the holy ceremony; and the hour he chooses is not considered auspicious by any almanac, new or old.

Such is the structure of the poem. If we had been entrusted with its composition, we would no doubt have fashioned its plot more skilfully. In the last chapter of the work, the Jamunabati of the start would have stood at Tripurni Ghat as the obscure sister of that unspecified man; and the gandharva marriage[†] conducted with hibiscus flowers at twelve noon sharp would have delighted all readers.

But in the child's nature, the power of the intellect is much feebler. Both the external world and his own imaginings strike him disjunctly, one after another. Any tie upon the mind is oppressive to him. It is hard for him to follow a matter through from beginning to end by a linked chain of cause and effect. He happily sits and builds sandcastles by the shores of both the external world and the world of his mind. Sand does not bind together, its structures do not last; but that very absence of cohesiveness makes it the ideal material for such childish edifices. It can be raised high in a trice, fistful by fistful; if not to one's liking, it can easily be remodelled; and if the playful creator grows tired of the exercise, he can flatten it to the ground with a single kick and go blithely home.

But where the building must be raised carefully, brick by brick, the builder has to proceed by rule from the outset. A child cannot proceed by rule: he has just arrived from a lawless heaven filled with the joy of the heart's desire. He has not grown accustomed like us to the prolonged slavery of rules; that is why, within the measure of his feeble strength, he builds sandcastles by the sea and versified pictures in his mind as his spirit leads him, imitating on earth the Deity's creative play throughout the universe. That is why in our shastras,[†] the works of God are continually compared to a child's play: they are similar in their element of wish-replete joy.

The verses quoted above do not have consistency, but they have pictures. The happenings on the road lined with kaji trees, the landing-ghat at Tripurni, or the woods full of hibiscus flowers are as fantastic and as truth-like as the dreams.

The reader should not question the alertness of my mind because I have talked about the truth of dreams. Many learned philosophers have dismissed the observed world as a dream; but no such philosopher has been able to dismiss dreams. He says there is no observable truth. What, then, is there? Dreams. We thus see that reality can readily be denied by powerful arguments, but there is no way of denying a dream. This holds good of sleeping as well as waking dreams. Even the acutest savant cannot disbelieve a dream while he is dreaming it. In the waking state, such persons question even probable truths; but when dreaming, they unquestioningly accept even the grossest impossibility. The attribute of credibility, which should be the foremost criterion of truth, is therefore present in dreams as in nothing else.

The reader will understand from this that to the ever-dreaming child, the dream-world of rhymes is more real than the observed world can ever be to us. That is why we often reject the truth as impossible, while children accept the impossible as true.

The rain falls pitter-patter, the river is in flood:
Shibu the Brahman's married, they've gifted him three brides.
One bride she cooks and serves, and one bride she eats,
And one bride to her father's house goes back without her meal.

Hearing this rhyme at this advanced age, I might well conclude that of Shibu's three brides, the second was the most astute. But I was once of an age when we did not have such powers of assessing character. At that time, these four lines were the *Meghadutam*† of my childhood. A dark overclouded rainy day and a choppy river would be imaged on the canvas of my mind. Next I would see two sailboats moored on a sandbank upon that river, and Shibu's newly-wed wives alighting from them to cook a meal on the sand. To tell the truth, I would consider Shibu's life a very happy one and rather yearn for it. Even the figure of his third lady wife stomping her way back to her father's in a temper could not impair this happy picture. In my innocence, I did not realise what a heart-rending calamity in Shibu's life was being indicated by this single line of verse. As I said some time ago, my mind was then bent towards creating pictures rather than analysing character. Now I realise that the stunned Shibu could not have viewed the departure of his youngest wife for her father's house as a very pleasing picture.

Was there ever such a person as this Brahman Shibu? There might have been. Some minute fragment of forgotten history might lie embedded in this rhyme. Another rhyme might contain another such fragment.

Here the Ganga, there the Ganga, in between the shoal—
And Shibu the merchant sits there in the middle.
Shibu went to his father-in-law's, they gave a stool to sit,
And of the finest shali grains, pressed-rice for him to eat.
No, no, not shali pressed-rice—puffed-rice from binni grains,
And yoghurt brought from Kagmari, and a bunch of fat plantains.

The indications are that Shibu the Brahman and Shibu the merchant must be one and the same person. They are both addicted to matrimony and apparently partial to food as well. Moreover, the chosen spot in the middle of the Ganga is eminently suitable for a young couple's first night together.

Readers will observe that, in the account of the refreshments served to Shibu the merchant, pressed-rice from shali paddy is first mentioned inadvertently, but corrected at once to 'puffed-rice from binni grains'. There seems to be no jot of doubt about the truth of the report. Yet the change is scarcely a substantial one; it does not materially enhance our sense of the family's hospitality towards their son-in-law. The poet seems more intent to preserve the truth than to defend the dignity of the in-laws. Yet we cannot really say that either. It is all like a dream. The pressed-rice of shali paddy seems to turn in an instant into puffed-rice of binni paddy. Probably no one can say when Shibu the Brahman has been transformed into Shibu the merchant by a similiar process.

We are told there are some fragmentary planets between Mars and Jupiter. Some say that a whole planet has broken into bits. In the same way, these rhymes seem to me like fragments of a universe. Many old histories, the detritus of old memories, lie scattered in them. No archaeologist can put them together again, but our imagination seeks distant yet intimate acquaintance with an antique, forgotten world through these fragments.

Needless to say, the child's imagination is not intent on building up any such historical unity. To him, everything exists in the present, and it is the present that is glorious. He wants only visual images; he does not want to blur those images with the vapours of tearful sentiment.

In the following rhyme, the disjunct images fly along like a flock of birds. One after another, each new flight excites the child's soul by a fresh, swift impact.

A flock of pouting pigeons are showing off their crests.
All the burra sahibs' wives have come to have their bathe.
A rohu and a katla fish have swum up to the bank;
When Dada[†] saw, he threw at them a pen he had in hand.
Two girls by the farther shore are sitting down to bathe,
Their bangles chime as they lift their hair and dry it with a shake.
Who's kept it? Who's kept it? Dada's kept it all.
Today Dada's throwing stones, tomorrow he'll be wed;
Underneath the bakul trees he'll pass along the road.
I went to gather bakul flowers, and found a garland gay.

The rainbow sounds its music, Sitanath's at play.
'I'll have some rice and dried peas, brother,' says Sitanath.
He munched his rice and dried peas, his throat grew dry as wood.
Wandering for water, he came to Chitpur field.
In Chitpur field the bright sand lies glittering all about.
The sun cracks his shining face, the blood trickles out.

None of these images takes hold of us, nor can we take hold of any. The crested pigeons, the burra sahibs' wives, the two floating fish, the two girls bathing across the river, Dada's wedding, Sitanath's gambols to the accompaniment of rainbow music, the parched flushed face among the hot noontide sand—all this is like a dream. The two girls who are sitting down to bathe, shaking out their hair to the chime of bangles, are palpably real as pictures but, in respect of relevance, an exquisite dream.

My readers must also remember that it is very hard to construct a dream. It may appear easy† enough at first sight to somehow scribble a nursery rhyme. But that somehowness is not easy to achieve. In all the world's work, we have grown so conditioned that it is simpler for us to achieve a laboured effect than a simple† one. Even where we do not call him in, labouredness thrusts his way like a busybody into all our tasks. And whatever idea he touches relinquishes its light cloudlike state: it crystallises and hardens, it can no longer fly through the air. That is why rhymes are very easy indeed for those to whom they are easy; for those to whom they are at all difficult, they are impossible. Whatever is most simple is most difficult; that is the chief characteristic of simple things.

The reader may also have noticed how this rhyme overlaps with the one previously quoted. Just as cloud blends into cloud, and dream into dream, these rhymes blend and twist into each other. No poet accuses another of theft on this score, and no critic alleges that the sentiment of the work has been impaired. These rhymes are truly the play of clouds in the mind's realm: they have no bounds or forms or proprietory rights, no connexion with the police or the law. Consider carefully the following rhyme, drawn from another source:

The janti tree on the other bank is full of janti fruit:
I've bit off a cow-janti's head, my heart goes pit-a-pat.
My breath comes heaving, my throat's as dry as wood.
To get to Hara-Gouri's field, how long upon the road?
Hara-Gouri's field is full of big ripe betel-leaves.
We bought and ate betel-and-lime, two sisters-in-law together,
But when we lost a betel, I went to tell Big Brother.
'Dada, Dada,' I called out: Dada was not at home.

'Subal, Subal,' I called out: Subal was at home.
Today is Subal's adhibas,† tomorrow his wedding day:
Through Dignagar with Subal I'll pass along the way.
All the girls of Dignagar are sitting down to bathe,
And as they sit, their thick long hair along their backs they spread.
They're shaking out the water from their sleek long hair:
The shell-bangles upon their arms like white clouds glow,
The golden chains around their throats like red blood flow.
About her form a striped sari swirls and falls around.
On either side a katla fish has swum up to the bank.
The holy guru's taken one, the parrot took the other.
It's the wedding of the parrot's mother:
Her red scarf glitters.
Peepal leaves and spice,
Gouri is the bride,
Naka is the groom.
Dham-kur-kur the drum beats, Charakdanga's his home.

If one looks for truth in these rhymes, one falls into a great quandary. In the first poem, we saw that Sitaram, a greedy boy fond of dancing, ate some sun-dried rice and went to quench his thirst at the landing-stage at Tripurni. In the second poem, it is a Sitanath that eats rice and dried peas and goes to look for water in Chitpur field. The third poem, however, presents neither Sitaram nor Sitanath but a hapless young wife whose husband's malicious-minded sister, having consumed janti fruit, goes thirsting to Hara-Gouri's field to have betel leaves, but then sets up a great clamour to tell her brother about her sister-in-law's trifling inadvertence.

Such are the disparities between the three pieces. Even within each piece, there is no perceptible sequence of events. Most of the stuff is patently made-up. But we see something else as well. When people make something up, they try to render it more credible than the truth by adducing a quantity of proof; here, however, there is nothing of the sort. What these verses tell us is neither true nor false, but something remote from either. The reference to Subal's marriage, for instance, does not strain one's belief; but it does not appear true either.

'Dada, Dada,' I called out; Dada was not at home.
'Subal, Subal,' I called out; Subal was at home.

As soon as the name Subal is uttered, the next line automatically slips out: 'Today is Subal's adhibas, tomorrow his wedding-day.' This too cannot provide a stable subject-matter; we soon pass on to the long-haired girls of Dignagar. Just so is it in a dream: one topic is created out of another by some fortuitous resemblance of words, or some other trifling unsubstantial link. A moment earlier, they had not been present even in potential; a moment later, they will again vanish casually from the realm of the possible.

Even if our readers take Subal's wedding as reflecting an actual event of that place and time, they will all agree that the parrot's mother being married in a red scarf cannot possibly be recorded in the history of the period. Although widow remarriage is customary among parrots, we have never heard of that community donning red scarfs. But those to whom these disjointed impossible happenings are presented rhythmically in a sweet voice neither believe nor disbelieve such stuff; they see picture after picture in the mind's eye—like a dream, like perceived reality.

Nor do children need much preparation to compose these pictures. I have earlier explained the reason for this: children are like gods in the power of their wish. A child can create readily according to his wish, as we cannot. Think about it: it is no easy matter to imagine a piece of cloth knotted at one end to be a human creature, complete with head, and nurse it like one's own child. If we are to imagine a figure to be a man, we needs must shape it like a man: to the extent that the imitation falls short, it impedes our imagination. We are governed by the tyrannous materiality of the external world; we cannot see things otherwise than as they appear to the eye. But the child takes what he sees as the pretext to construct things within his mind, according to his mind. He is not struck by any incongruity between the human form and a cloth toy. The form created by his wish shines before his eyes.

Nonetheless, the carelessly crafted pictures in these rhymes are not all generated by the child's natural creativity. In many places, they evince a clear definition of line that at once presents the briefly sketched scene even before our sceptical eyes.

These pictures are composed of a single line, a single word. Just as a match lights up at a single strike, an entire picture has to be awakened in the child's mind in a trice, by a single verbal stroke; it cannot be built up by accretion.

> In Chitpur field the bright sand lies glittering all about.

This single utterance brings a great barren field before our eyes in the glare of noonday.

> About her form a striped sari swirls and falls around.

The single verse images in a moment the way the stripes on the sari engird the slim erect form, like the currents of a whirlpool. Another version has

About her form a striped sari blows itself around.

This picture too is not unattractive.

Come, sleep, come, sleep, where the Bagdis† live.
The Bagdis' boy is sleeping, wrapped in a fishing-net.

Any reader can image from that last line how the Bagdi boy, having flung himself down somewhere, lies sound asleep under his wraps. There is no great expense of words: the one specific detail about the fishing-net brings the sleeping child vividly to our eyes.

Come, boys, come: we'll fish with rod and line.
A fish bone's stuck in my foot, let's ride a palanquin.
What does it have inside?
Six times eighty cowrie shells, we'll count them as we ride.
The water in this river is brimming clear and sweet.
The sand beside this river crumbles beneath the feet.
The sun cracks the moon-bright face, the blood trickles out.

Even if my readers reject as inconsequential the picture of counting out six times eighty cowries while riding in a palanquin, they cannot so dismiss the image in the last three lines. The river water brimming and the sand crumbling along it—what clearer, yet more brief and simple, picture could there be of a river among sandbanks?

That is one category of pictures evoked by these rhymes. There is another category, whereby an entire situation is evoked in our consciousness. Perhaps some trifling detail touches our hearts by bringing the whole of Bengali society and domesticity to life. Such trifling matters cannot enter so readily, smoothly, and unabashedly into great literary works; or if they do, they change of themselves into other forms, other sentiments.

Dada, Dada, in town you stay
And three rupees you earn as pay.
With holy beads your neck is hung,
Your bride's as fair as is the moon.
I beg of you, my big brother,
Bring me a bride, I'll play with her.

The brother does not earn very much; but for his little sister, it is enough. Citing the affluence those three rupees can ensure, the sister pleads:

I beg of you, my big brother,
Bring me a bride, I'll play with her.

The astute girl does not neglect to hold out enticements to her brother to achieve her own ends: 'Your bride's as fair as is the moon.' Although the doll she demands is quite costly for someone earning three rupees, we can rest assured that the plea was not in vain, and that not solely by virtue of brotherly affection.

Ulu ulu,† flower of madar,
The bridegroom's come from very far.
He's come to Bagnapara—look!
Elder wife, go start to cook,
Younger wife, go fetch water.
The water's full of streaks and scrawls.
Flowers are blooming, round like wheels.
I bring the flowers my greetings.
Spinach leaves and gram-flour dumplings.

The picture of a happy celebration, with village women eager at the impending arrival of a bridegroom, readily depicts itself here. And thereby, as if by some magic, the village pathways hedged with sheora trees, the woods, the ponds, the village wife with pitcher on hip, the scurrying housewives with their veils slipping from their heads—all these are awakened to life.

Nearly every minor utterance in every such rhyme affords us an image of Bengal life, the music of the countryside, the savour of our homes. But I hesitate to quote such instances at length, as *bhinnaruchirhi lokah* [people differ in taste].†

It does not matter if the picture is somewhat odd: that may indeed be an advantage, because the novelty has a greater impact on the mind. To the child, nothing is odd because nothing is impossible. He has not yet beaten his head against the wall marking the farthest limit of the possible, and come back frustrated. He holds that if some things are possible, everything is possible. If a particular thing is not odd, why should something else be? He says, 'I believe implicitly in a one-headed man, because I have seen him; I don't want to raise questions about a two-headed man either, because I see him just as clearly in my mind; and a headless man is equally true for me, because he does not lie beyond my apprehension.' There is a story about a man who enters a company and says, 'I saw something wonderful today. A man had his head sliced off in a quarrel, but he nonetheless walked ten steps.' Everyone was amazed: 'What's that you're saying? He walked ten steps!' But a woman among them said, 'There's nothing wonderful about his walking ten steps. The wonderful thing was that he could walk a single step.'

In a work of creation too, the wonder lies in the first step. That something has been created is the first and greatest cause for amazement; not so amazing that something else should follow. The child is looking at that first wonder for the first time. He sees as soon as he opens his eyes that there are many things around him; he does not find it impossible that there should be many more. That is why in the land of nursery rhymes, there are no boundary disputes between the possible and the impossible.

Come, parrot, come.
Load your boat and come.
The bowal fish has taken the boat,
The otter dances at such sport.
Turn, otter, turn your glance:
Come and see my Khoka† dance.

First of all, no boy since his father's days has ever seen a parrot riding a boat. Nor indeed has the father; but the fun lies chiefly in the unprecedented nature of the sight. And that fun increases when a corpulent bowal fish suddenly rises from the water's depths and carries the boat away without warning, leaving the angry and excited bird shrilly voicing its protest, puffing out its feathers and beating its wings. Equally remarkable is the otter's sudden saltatory urge on seeing the poor parrot's plight and the aquatic creature's ill-mannered ways. Finally, there is immense delight in exhorting the heartlessly capering otter to leave off its own dance and turn to see the little boy's. Just as, on hearing a pleasing beat, one wants to make up a song to that rhythm and sing it, so too, on seeing these verbal pictures, one wants to translate them into visual ones and draw the resultant forms. But alas! to preserve the appeal of such pictures, drawing them in all their conviction, childlike simplicity, shining freshness, and easy realisation of the impossible would call for an artist rare in our land and, no doubt, everywhere.

Beside the Creamy River my Khoka's gone to fish.
The toad has snatched his angling-rod, the kite has snatched his fish.
The bird I call my Khoka, by what lake does he roam?
But when I call out 'Khoka', he flies back to my home.

Can the mind be satisfied till it has depicted with brush and paint the straits that Khoka landed in when he went to fish by the Creamy River? Needless to say, Khoka Babu knows the geography of that river much better than we do. But wherever it may be, it is diverting enough that he should sit angling on its bank with patient sage-like dignity, wielding a rod four times as big as himself. When, moreover, a grotesque toad raises its protruding eyes from the water and seizes the rod, and a kite from landward swoops on the fish, the Babu's vexed, startled, beleaguered expression—now leaning back to clutch the rod with all his might, now throwing his arms up at the flying thief—has long awaited a skilled and sympathetic artist to represent it.

The image of Khoka as a bird is just as pictorial in scope. We see a vast lake before us: we cannot clearly make out its farther shore. On this side, to one corner, there is a clump of tall grass, cane bushes, and taro plants; on the water, a tangle of moss and nal flowers; and in the midst of this, Khoka Babu is grazing intently with drawn wings and lowered head, in company with certain long-billed, long-legged, grave, contemplative herons and cranes. It makes for a pleasing scene. Not far from the lake, adjoining the submerged, ripening late-monsoon paddy fields, there stands a cottage. From its courtyard, her left hand resting on a bamboo fence, the mother extends her right hand towards the lake and calls to her Khoka Babu in the declining afternoon sun. From beside the fence, a tethered cow, just back from grazing, also looks out with mild curiosity; and Khoka Babu himself, replete from feeding, looks up from the nal plants and moss, startled by his mother's call, and prepares to fly home. That is another beautiful scene. And there is a third scene where the bird flies to his mother's breast, hides his face in her shoulder and almost envelops her in his two wings; while the steady-gazing mother enwraps him in her arms, tender wings and all, and holds him to her breast in a tie of deep affection. That too is beautiful.

When astronomers observe the Milky Way, they see how at certain points of that vaporous stellar mass, the vapour seems to be solidifying and making ready to transform itself into a star. So also in the galaxy of our children's rhymes, certain half-formed poetic shapes may suddenly be observed here and there. There is nothing complex about these newly created orbs of the imagination: they are still imperfectly solid, like the infant earth in its first age. Let me cite one such piece.

'Here is good sport, my friend, a good game to play:
Show me four things that are black, with you I'll go away.'
—'The crow's black, the koel's† black, in black the drongo's clad.
But blacker than all these, my girl, the hair upon your head.'

'Here is good sport, my friend, a good game to play:
Show me four things that are white, with you I'll go away.'
—'The heron's white, and cloth is white, the swan is white as well,
But whiter than all these, my girl, your bangles made of shell.'†

'Here is good sport, my friend, a good game to play:
Show me four things that are red, with you I'll go away.'
—'Oleander's red, the safflower red, red the hibiscus flower,
But redder than all these, my girl, the reddle on your brow.'[†]

'Here is good sport, my friend, a good game to play:
Show me now four bitter things, with you I'll go away.'
—'Bitter the neem, the makal fruit, bitter nisunda leaves,
But bitterer than these, my girl, to live with your co-wives.'[†]

'Here is good sport, my friend, a good game to play:
Show me four things that are cold, with you I'll go away.'
—'The water's cold, the earth is cold, and cold the palm-leaf mat,
But colder than all these, my girl, the cold within your heart.'[†]

Since the start of poetic creation, the race of poets, in various languages and varied metres, has been singing hymns in praise of women; but few poems afford such a simple artless idea and simple artless picture as this. There is also a little unwitting humour. Sita's vow regarding the bow,[†] and Draupadi's regarding the feat of marksmanship,[†] were manifestly stern resolutions; this artless young woman's vow seems undemanding by comparison. There are so many black, white, red, and sweet things[†] in this world: fortunate is the man who can win such a partner by adducing only four of each. Of course, in this final phase of the degenerate Kali Yuga,[†] all males have struck good fortune. They need not break a bow in two, nor hit some difficult target, nor triumph in a battle of wits. Instead, it is they who demand Company bonds[†] as a precondition of marriage, and do not feel the least shame about this cowardly vileness. Far better the brief and simple test by which the hero of our rhyme obtains his bride. Although the poem does not announce the final results, we may assume that he won full marks, as of the four answers offered in each stanza, the last one was eminently satisfactory. As the examining mistress was present in person before his eyes, he could not have found it hard to locate the answers: it must have been rather like copying from an open textbook. But I do not wish to express futile envy on that score. If the examiner was satisfied, we have nothing more to say.

In the very first line, the lady says,

Here is good sport, my friend, a good game to play.

This makes us deduce that the examination had commenced earlier; the candidate has already provided such ideal and delightful answers that the lady is moved to question further. Indeed there can be no such sport.

Be that as it may, if we had been entrusted with composing the rhyme, we would probably have devised an elaborate introduction: we would not have plunged in abruptly halfway in this manner. We would first have described an examination room: if not quite like the Senate Hall,† at least like the Eden Gardens.† We would have added a dash of moonlight, a south breeze, and the call of koels to embellish the scene. We would have provided all kinds of ingredients; but we could not, in our elegant multi-coloured metrical toils, have so bound for ever that comely maiden whose hair is blacker than the drongo, bangles whiter than the swan, the vermillion in her hair redder than the safflower, embrace sweeter than children's speech, and heart more soothing than cool water—the maiden who, on being paid a few trifling compliments, surrenders herself with simple faith and ready joy.

Not these verses alone: if we were so commissioned, we could totally revise most of these rhymes and make them worthy of new editions; we might even build nests in them for universal morality and universally obscure theories to lodge in. At the very least, we could elevate them to our current level of education and social evolution. Think about it: if we ever wished to invite the moon as a guest to the refined society of our time, would we do so with the following paltry enticements?

Come, Uncle Moon, touch my little one's forehead:
Come, Moon, come and touch my moon's forehead.
    Slice my fish, I'll give you the head.
    Thresh my rice, I'll give you the skins.†
    I'll give you milk from a black cow,
    And a bowl to hold the milk too.
Come, Moon, come and touch my moon's forehead

What moon is this? The simple moon of the Bengali homestead—the universal Uncle Moon of our juvenile community, eldest of all. With his familiar, affectionately smiling face, he peeps through the gaps in the wind-tossed bamboo grove near our rustic cottages to see the naked child play in the courtyard dust. He is our village kinsman. Or else who could have dared to tempt such a celebrity—whose sign is the hare, who is wreathed with cold light, who spends the year in the private chambers of twenty-seven stellar beauties,† who day and night holds all heaven's ambrosia in his inviolate silver vessel—with the prospect of fish-heads, rice-skins, a black cow's milk and a drinking-bowl? We would have sat down instead to list such rare items as the nectar of the parijat flower,† the scent of the tuberose, the song of the cuckoo, the smile of union, the heart's hope, the eye's yearning, the new bride's bashfulness—and yet the moon would have remained where it was. The people in the rhymes, on the contrary, would not dare hold out empty promises to the moon of the rhyme: they would not hold it impossible that the moon should descend to earth to touch a little boy's forehead. They were not of such an utterly sceptical, faithless, atheistical bent of mind. Hence they could not, out of poetic ardour, commit themselves to anything much beyond the ready stock in their storehouses and treasuries. Our Uncle Moon of Bengal, hearing a thousand invitations in sweet voices rise from a thousand cottages of Bengal, would have laughed quietly to himself, saying neither 'Yes' nor 'No'. He would have behaved as though some day or other, as he set out from the eastern horizon, he would stop on the way without reason or announcement, to come and stand under our eaves with his full, smiling, humorous face.

I have said earlier that these rhymes are like broken fragments of an entire universe. A variety of forgotten joys and sorrows, scattered in a hundred directions, have come to rest in them. It is like the footprints left in mud by extinct birds on the ancient ocean shore of the antique earth: with the passage of time, the slime with its imprints has turned to stone. Those imprints were left of themselves and preserved of themselves: no one carved them with an implement, no one gathered them up with care. So is it with these rhymes: many smiles and tears of many days have been etched on them of their own accord; many heartaches lie bound up in their broken rhythms. A piece of the human mind, from who knows how long ago, has come floating down the sea of time to be cast up on this far shore of the present; and no sooner come to rest against our minds than all their forgotten pain been nurtured to tearful vitality by the warmth of life.

> 'It's dark upon the other shore:
> *Jham, jham,* the raindrops pour.
> On this bank the chilli bush is hung with chillis red.
> O my worthy brother, my heart begins to ache.'
> —'Stay in tears and sorrow this month, O sister mine.
> Next month I'll come to take you in a palanquin so fine.'
> —'My bones are dry and frizzled, my flesh is taut as ropes.
> Come, let me rather plunge into the river's deeps.'

In what age, from what secret corner of a household did this inward pain break out—this pent-up flood of tears, rending the soft heart of a nameless, renownless, forgotten new bride? How many such unbearable griefs lose themselves on the winds like unperceived sighs, leaving no trace behind! This one, somehow, has been preserved in a rhyme.

> It's dark upon the other shore:
> *Jham, jham,* the raindrops pour.

On such a day, the mind cannot help being melancholy. It has always been so. The great poet of the court at Ujjayini† said the same thing long ago:

> *Meghaloke bhavati sukhinopyanyathabrittichetah*
> *. . . kim punardursamsthe.*

[The sight of rain-clouds makes even happy hearts restless; . . . what then of the parted one.]

What Kalidas indicated with a brief sigh cries out from a sundered heart in this rhyme:

> O my worthy brother, my heart begins to ache. . . .
> My bones are dry and frizzled, my flesh is taut as ropes,
> Come, you river water, I'll plunge into your deeps.

Who can bring out the full burden of the moving tale, the intolerable sequence of sorrows contained in these lines? How much did she have to bear—day after day, night after night, minute after minute? Suddenly one day her brother, the intimate sharer of her sorrows in her paternal home, comes to ask after her at that alien house, devoid of pleasure and of memories of love. The tears stored in the hidden layers of the heart cannot be held back any more. The yearning, intractable heart will not be restrained a moment longer, as she recalls their old home, their games, their father and mother, their happy childhood. A month's delay seems intolerable—specially on a day when the river's farther shore is dark with clouds, and the rain pours down. She longs to quench the flaming agony within her bones by plunging into that cold deep river, full to the brim, dark with the shadow of clouds, resounding with the fall of the rain.

There is a grammatical error in the poem which the alert guardians of the Bengali language may be so good as to pardon or even, conceivably, to shed a tear over. The nameless young woman revealed immeasurable ignorance by addressing her brother as 'worthy' in the feminine gender, *gunabati.* The hapless girl did not dream that along with her single heart-rending cry, this solecism too would be preserved forever in the world. Had she known, she would have died of shame. It may not be a grave error; she might even have been speaking to a sister. I hope even those persons who have recently undertaken to preserve the purity of the Bengali language by sacrificing traditional idioms and old beauties of speech sometimes, forgetting themselves in an affectionate impulse, flout grammar to address a sister as a brother (*bhai*); they may not even rush to correct the error if someone in the position of a wife lovingly calls them *bhai.*

There is a hard, hidden sorrow in the Bengali psyche: sending the daughter to her in-laws' house. The immature, inexperienced, undiscerning girl must go to a strange house: this endows her face with an anxious, sorrowing look expressive of all Bengal. That sad, tender affection has been apotheosised in Bengal's autumn festival. This festival has been set up in the midst of our heart, like a tree putting forth its shady foliage, by drawing forth our homely affection and homely grief, the lasting sorrow of Bengali domesticity. In this festival, the Bengali worships both the mother goddess and the maiden goddess.† The Agamani† and Bijaya songs† are the music of the maternal heart of Bengal. We can therefore readily expect that in our rhymes too, this heart's grief of maternal Bengal will find expression in many forms.

> Today is Durga's adhibas, tomorrow she'll be spoused.
> The world will weep as Durga goes to her father-in-law's house.
> The mother weeps, the mother weeps, upon the dust outstretched,
> The mother who has given her a gold and coral chain.
> The father weeps, the father weeps, sitting in his state,
> The father who has given her a chest stuffed full of coins.
> The masi† weeps, the masi weeps, sitting in the kitchen,
> The masi who has given her rice on a stone platter.
> The pisi† weeps, the pisi weeps, sitting in the dairy,
> The pisi who has given her milk in a brimming bowl.
> The brother weeps, the brother weeps, by her anchal drawing her back,
> The brother who has given her saris to fill her rack.
> The sister weeps, the sister weeps, clutching the leg of her bed,
> The sister who . . .

At the risk of offending my readers, I must here say a word or two before completing the rhyme. The previous behaviour of this sister, who now clutches the bed as she weeps, is not to be emulated by the daughters of gentlefolk. It would be best if sisters never quarrelled, yet they commonly do. Even so, they should not use language that I hesitate to utter in respectable society. Yet I cannot dispense with the line; for although it contains some vulgarity of diction, it contains much more of the pure rasa of sorrow. To use a paraphrase, one might say that this weeping girl had once, in an altercation, called her sibling a husband-devourer. Rewording this allegation more mildly, we have completed the verse as follows:

> The sister weeps, the sister weeps, clutching the leg of her bed,
> The sister who has called her names, as her husband's eater-up.

The mother has given jewellery, the father money, the mother's sister rice, the father's sister milk, the brother clothes. We might have hoped that in such a loving family, the sister too would have made an affectionate gesture at par with the rest. But the last verse is like a blow to the heart: it brings tears to our eyes. The parents' parting tears are congruous with their previous love: it is no more than expected. But at this moment of separation, the tears of this sister, who had continually quarrelled with the bride and called her unrepeatable names, are the most moving of all. Now, suddenly, it is revealed how a tender affection was forming secretly beneath all such conflicts: the unsuspected love strikes her today with fierce remorse. She begins to weep, clutching the leg of the bed where the two had lain together in their infancy: this bedroom was the scene of all their bickerings and all their play. Now that they must part, this grieving girl comes to that bedroom to shed secret, solitary tears of distress: the clear stream of that deep wellspring of love cleanses white her words of abuse.

In these rhymes, a whole chapter of joy or sorrow lies hidden in a single verse, a single word. The rhyme I shall now quote expresses in two of its lines a history of the perennial grief of all mothers of Bengal, from the earliest days to this.

> Rock, rock, rock.
> Comb her pretty locks.
> The bridegroom will be here today,
> And quickly take her right away.
> What cause have you to weep?
> Think of yourself: whose house is it you keep?

Even when rocking an infant daughter in her cradle, the far-seeing mother thinks automatically of the parting to come, and her eyes fill with tears. The only consolation is that it has always been so. You too once made your mother weep as you came away to a stranger's house. Today, as you go about your family life, the wounding pain of that wrench has healed. So will your daughter leave you in due course, and that grief too will not last long in this world.

We find many pictures and many accounts of Putu's[†] journey to her in-laws' house. The matter is continually in mind.

Putu's off to her father-in-law's: who'll go with her as guard?
The tom cat in the corner is girded and prepared.
I'll give mango and jackfruit groves to shade her from the sun,
And four strong men I'll give her to bear her palanquin,
Pressed-rice of the finest grain upon the way to eat,
Four handmaids too I'll give her to oil and press her feet,
And sugared rice from urki grains, her mother-in-law to greet.

The last verse indicates how even in those times, the great worry about pleasing the mother-in-law was present in full measure. If we are to believe that this difficult goal was attained simply with the aforesaid sugared rice, then many mothers of present-day daughters will no doubt sigh for that golden age. Today, the bride's father cannot forget in his lifetime how one has to divert the mother-in-law's displeasure.

Parting with the daughter is not the only cause of grief; another is her marriage to an unworthy husband. Yet all too often, parents and relatives knowingly make over a helpless girl to such a groom with an eye to self-interest, or gain, or social esteem. Society sometimes proclaims the pain of that iniquity: the rhymes testify to it. But readers must remember that everything the rhymes say is in fragmentary form—a medley of the comic, the tearful and the grotesque.

Come and see the cuckoo dance
On the pomegranate branch:
Tak-duma-dum go the drums.
Don't you know my face?
Go fetch me a plate of rice.
Annapurna, milk-and-cream,
Is going to another's home.
Another's son has slapped her face:
She goes crying to her uncle's place.
Uncle gets her an old groom.
—'Uncle, uncle, I beg you,
Take me to my mother's home.'
The mother gives a thin shell-bangle,
The father gives a sari,
The brother gives a thwack and push—
'Go back to where you're married.'

The law of the Englishman did not run in those times. In other words, the policeman was not entrusted with restoring marital rights. Hence the family had to take the initiative in the matter, as simply and briefly as possible. In my humble judgment, this domestic law for the discipline of wives worked better than police law; the brother's stick was preferable to the constable's baton. Today we have learnt to go to court to fetch back a wife from her father's house; tomorrow, we may need to petition the Presidency Magistrate to coax her out of a fit of sulks. But by whatever law, ancient or modern, there can scarcely be a more unnatural, barbarous cruelty on earth than to bind a helpless girl to an unworthy man by sheer brute force.

Society forgets the parents' crime in this respect; but it holds an aged bridegroom in despise. Hence the full wrath of society is vented upon the latter through piercing satire.

Chop down the palm, to the Bose's home Gouri has come as wife.
What can I do if your husband's old? That's your lot in life.
I spent my coins on shell-bangles and jewels for the ear,
And on the wedding-day I find an old man with a beard.
Father, mother, uncle—had you no eyes to see,
To find a smoking gaffer and marry him to me?
The gaffer puts his hookah by, and starts to cough as if he'll die.
I prod him and I shake him—he looks as though he's dead,
But when I go to drain the rice, he starts to dance instead.

Can anything be more mortifying to an old man?

It remains to talk about the emperor of the Bengali home, youngest in age but greatest in power, the magnanimous Khoka or Khuku.†

The *Rig Veda*† was put together in ancient times out of hymns to Indra, Chandra, and Varuna. These rhymes have a similar origin, from the hymns of the maternal heart to its twin gods, Khoka and Putu. Both sets of texts are of venerable ancestry: for the antiquity of the rhymes is not a chronological antiquity; they are naturally ancient. By their primal simplicity, they are earliest among the compositions of man. Even amidst the fierce cloudless midday sun of this nineteenth century, they preserve the first blush of sunrise in the human heart.

The loving ballads and hymns to infancy that make up this ever-ancient New Veda are of illimitable variety, beauty, and joyful impulse. The devoted women worshippers have set up countless images of the one goddess Khuku in new loving moulds. Sometimes she is a bird, sometimes the moon, sometimes a jewel, sometimes a flowering copse.

I'll go to the woods with my precious—what will I eat while there?
I'll sit alone beside my moon and see her face so fair.

Nothing is so discomposing as love. It has pervaded the beginning, middle, and end of creation since the origins of time, yet it wishes to transgress every one of creation's rules. It is like a soaring bird in the iron cage of creation. Despite a hundred thousand buffets, censures, prohibitions, and impediments, it cannot rid itself of the belief that it can readily flout all laws. In its heart, it knows it can fly; so it continually forgets about the iron bars around it. There is no need whatsoever to go to the woods with one's precious; it would be convenient for everybody to remain at home. One can indeed obtain a certain privacy in the woods, but very little else; in fact, the speaker herself admits the possible dearth of nourishment. Yet love insists on saying, 'You think I can't do it?' Such unabashed audacity can derange even mature men of judgment like us. 'Indeed,' we say, 'why shouldn't it be possible?' If a narrow-minded materialistic sceptic should ask, 'What will you eat there?', the undaunted reply comes: 'I'll sit alone beside my moon and see her face so fair.' And we at once agree that this is the right answer. What from anybody else would have been a profound self-evident falsehood, a lunatic hyperbole, becomes proven, indisputable truth from the lips of love.

Another virtue of love is that it turns one thing into another: it does not want to recognise the difference between substances. The reader has already had evidence of this. We have seen how in one rhyme, a Khoka is suddenly classified among the birds without any preamble; no zoologist protests at this. The very next moment, when the same Khoka is made close kin to the moon, no astronomer dares demur. But the wilfulness of love is best expressed when it sets up an elaborate edifice of reason only to stamp it contemptuously to the earth at last. An example follows.

Where shall I find such a moon, my love?
Not an earthen moon that I can shape,
Not a moon on a tree that I can pluck—
Where shall I find a moon like you?
Of all the moons you are the best.
Sleep, my darling, sleep at rest.

The moon is beyond reach; it is not made of earth; it is not a fruit growing on a tree. All this is entirely true, incontrovertible, and novel: there is no flaw in the argument anywhere. But if after all this, we tell Khoka that he is indeed a moon, the best of all moons—why then, an earthen moon is possible too, and one growing on a tree should not surprise us either. There was no need for the initial show of rationality.

It may not be irrelevant to raise another issue at this point. The high degree of irrationality that we see in women is not a sign of foolishness. They dwell in a world dominated by love. Love is a celestial being. 'Why should anything else be more important than me?' he says. 'Why shouldn't all the laws of the universe cease their obstruction because I wish it?' He dreams that he is still in heaven. Alas, what is so utterly irrational on this lowly earth as heaven? Nonetheless, whatever little of heaven there might be on earth is held down here, against the current of all rule and logic, by the combined efforts of women, children, lovers, and contemplative men. They often forget that this earth is the earth; thanks to that error, heaven sometimes descends to earth.

Just as love can erase distinctions, fusing moon, flower, boy, and bird in an instant, it can contrarily draw distinctions where there are none, impart form to that which has no form.

No zoologist to the present day has classified sleep as a mammal or any other category of animal life. But because sleep descends to Khoka's eyes, it is touched by the creative hand of love and turned into a human being.

The market's sleep, the ghat's sleep, down every road is cried:
I've bought some sleep for four coins—come to my darling's eyes.

It is late at night. There is no one about in the market place or at the landing-jetty. The sleep belonging to those places is therefore wandering shelterless in the dark, looking for people. That may be why it was so cheaply bought: for at current wage levels, four paltry coins for a whole night's sleep is nothing.

We are told that the Greek poets, as well as Michael Madhusudan Datta,† have described sleep as a specific human female; but to consider dance as a specific substance is possible only in these rhymes of ours.

Dance, dance, dance.
Pakur fruit and banyan in a bunch.
The ox ate the cheena grain, the goat ate the paddy.
Go and buy some dance, to give my little laddy.

Not only that: to see this dance as separately and autonomously present in each of Khoka's limbs is possible not by the scientist's telescope or microscope, but only through the lenses of love.

Dance of the hands, dance of the feet, dance of a pretty mouth,
Dance of two little eyes, dance of two fuzzy brows,
Dance of a nose like a flute, dance of a bending waist—
What other dance can there be?
After many labours my darling's come to me.

Love sometimes sees many as one, sometimes one as many; sometimes great things as trifling, sometimes trifling things as great. 'Dance, my darling, dance: let me see the dance.' 'The dance'—as though it can be isolated from the darling performing it and seen as a distinct substance, a loved object in itself. 'Khoka'll go walkies where the oilwomen live.' If the phrase had been 'go for a walk' (*beraite*) instead of 'go walkies' (*beru karte*), the conventional dignity of the language would have been preserved, but the dignity of Khoka Babu's expedition would have diminished. All the world goes for a walk; only Khoka Babu goes walkies. It reveals his walk to be a very special, very lovable phenomenon.

Khoka's back from walking,
Cool some milk to give him.
The bowl of milk is very hot:
Angry Khoka starts to shout.
Khoka'll go to ride a boat,
Red booties upon his feet.

Khoka Babu's tantrum over a bowl of milk at the end of his travels is no doubt a domestic catastrophe; his desire to go on a boat is also worthy of documentation; but I would exhort my readers to pay special attention to the last line. If we buy knee-length boots from the leading English shop and stomp about in them, people would still call them nothing other than boots or shoes (*juta* or *juti*). But Khoka Babu's tiny inexpensive red footwear with little bells attached, adorning a pair of soft tiny feet, are booties (*jutua*). Clearly, the respect commanded by a pair of shoes is largely determined by the feet that wear them; their value by any other criterion is irrelevant.

There is one last matter to observe. Human beings worship the divine only where they feel deep love and genuine affection. We perceive the deity when we love humanity. Think of those words,

I'll sit alone beside my moon and see her face so fair.

This is the contemplation of the divine. What is there in a child's small face to make one seek the solitude of the woods in order to gaze at it, perceive it fully and perfectly—to make one feel that everything in the world, every daily task, diverts the mind from this store of joy? The ancient yogis, in their lust for ambrosial immortality, would relinquish food and drink and seek unbroken peace in the forest. The mother has found that ambrosia, hard-won even by the gods, in her child's face; that is why this hymn rises from the prayer temple of her heart:

I'll go to the woods with my precious—what will I eat while there?
I'll sit alone beside my moon and see her face so fair.

That is why we find that in these rhymes, the mother often confuses her own offspring with Devaki's.† In other lands, such confusion between gods and men would have been considered blasphemous. But in my judgment, if the deity is kept remote and distinct from the highest, sweetest, deepest human relationships, it demeans humanity yet does not honour divinity either. In our rhymes, the earthly child and the heavenly image of a god can merge at any time, and that too very readily and casually. Such an icon does not require a separate backdrop† to set it off. Before the odd, incongruous, purportless backdrop to the image of the child-as-god, the god of heaven comes unobserved to stand in his own entity, merged with the child.

Khoka'll go walkies where the oilwomen live.
The oilwomen start brawling, 'Is that the butter-thief?'
He's broken the pot and stolen the butter†—now he'll be scarce to see.
I'll snatch his flute if I catch him under the kadam tree.

Our little Khoka Babu has suddenly imported the flute of Vrindavan† into the quarter where the oilwomen live. Only those whose ears have conveyed the music to their hearts could have told when it happened.

I have compared the children's rhyme to a cloud. Both are changeable in form, tinged with many colours, floating freely upon the wind. They seem devoid of significance. Children's rhymes lie beyond aesthetics, just as the science of clouds cannot be properly formulated. Yet these two peculiar irregulous substances—one in the physical universe, the other in the human—have performed crucial functions through all time. The clouds descend as rain to give life to the child-crops, while the rhymes, condensing into a stream of love, make the child-mind fertile by the showers of the imagination. The light unbound cloud is fit to benefit the world by virtue of its very lightness and freedom from bonds. So also have the rhymes delighted children through the ages by their lightness, their lack of any binding signification, and their variety of pictorial effect. They have not been composed by book according to any principle of child psychology.

Translated by Sukanta Chaudhuri

Rural Literature

(PART)

One day towards the end of Shravan,† I was travelling by boat between Pabna† and Rajshahi.† The fields and landing stages were all submerged in water. Little villages stood out here and there, like the floating nests of aquatic animals. There was no coast-line to be seen—only water lapping all around. Just before sunset, ten or twelve men were seen approaching in a dinghy. They were singing at the top of their voices and splashing along swiftly through the water, rowing in time to the beat with bamboo stakes instead of oars. I pricked up my ears to listen to the song, and finally made out the following refrain, sung over and over:

> Young woman, why be you unhappy?
> From Pabna I'll bring you a motari† worth a whole rupee.

Any reader might doubt whether the song was appropriate to the scene—when the sun was setting silently over the monsoon floods—but in these two lines of song, all the villages seemed to speak out from amidst that mossy waste of water. I suddenly realised that a young woman can display her sulks here as well—beside these cattlesheds, in the shadow of these jujube trees—and her sidelong frowns of annoyance inspire the rural bard to send his songs resounding in music and in rhythm, across the fields and the river banks, over land and over water.

Of all the undesirable events in the world, the indifference of a young woman's heart is the foremost. To appease this angry planet, poets are ready to compose verse, and the hapless scorned ones even prepared to lay down their lives. However, when I heard 'From Pabna, I'll bring you a motari worth a whole rupee'—for a moment, at least, I felt greatly relieved in mind. I do not know exactly what a motari is, but the poet has left no doubt that it is worth no more than a rupee. The pangs of earthly life become relatively bearable when one contemplates that in one corner of the world, in Pabna district, there is a place where one need not work miracles to placate a displeased lady love: where one need not travel farther than Pabna, or fetch back anything rarer than a motari. In such a situation, poets of the first order such as Kalidasa† and Bhavabhuti† would have unhesitatingly bid for the golden lotus of Manas Sarovar,† a star from the sky, or the parijat flower† of the celestial garden. And young women of the first order in the kingdom of Ujjayini† would not but have been mollified at the mere proposal of such difficult feats, set to the shikharini or the mandakranta metre.†

By reading poetry, at least, one gets such a mistaken impression. Unbelieving people who live by prose cannot place so much trust in poetising. When asked whether a flock of sheep can be killed solely by incantation, Voltaire says they can, but there must be enough arsenic along with it. A sulking maiden may be satisfied by a bid to fetch a star from the sky or a parijat flower from the celestial garden, or to lay down one's life; but in most cases, an armlet or an anklet is needed as well.The poet suppresses this fact.He wants to prove that incantation alone can do the job, by the power of rhythm and sentiment: ornaments may be needed, but only poetic ornaments. In this respect, the townswomen of Pabna regard the trappings of poetry as redundant; and the rustic poet, smitten for good by their charms, eschews incantations and, without wasting any time, proceeds straight to the subject of a motari worth a whole rupee.

Nonetheless, there has to be a rhythm and a tune. This is needed even beside this lake in Pabna District, in this little corner of the world.This raises the value of that motari to much more than a rupee. The motari is alchemised, as it were, by the philosopher's stone of rasa and sentiment. The harsh impoverishment that invades these lines if uttered in everyday prose, not set to a tune, is instantly removed by rhythm and music. The film of sentiment shields those few brief words from the dust of everyday life.

For human beings, this serves a special need. We wish to adorn with rhythm and tempo the everyday affairs by which we are closely surrounded, and view them in the steady beautiful light of poetic sentiment.

This is why, just as farming and ferrying are carried on in human settlements, just as ploughshares are being forged at the blacksmith's, dhenkis† at the carpenter's, and one-rupee motaris at the goldsmith's, the manufacture of literature is also going on—behind them, alongside them, without pause. Literature tries to thread together and prepare for eternity what is being accomplished in dispersed, isolated, fragmentary form each day. The multifarious tasks of everyday life go on in the village; through their interstices, a musical tune is constantly striving to break forth.

When one hears the call of wild ducks as one travels along the Padma, no one can mistake it for the koel's song. It hits no musical notes—fourths or fifths, flats or sharps—with any degree of precision; nonetheless, it would not be a mistake to call it the music of the Padma-front. This is because, whether musical or not, the joyful clamour of countless creatures' delight in life rings upon the clear river breeze in the winter sun.

In rural lore, too, there is that note of joy, whether or not there is too much music of the imagination. The poet who makes music, in rhythm and beat, out of the everyday life of village people, gives voice to the spirit of the entire countryside. Like the music of the wild duck beside the Padma, it does not wait to achieve flawless tune and beat. The poet of the *Meghadutam*† has ventured as far as the celestial city of Alaka,† he is a poet of the royal court of Ujjayini—while the unknown poet of our song has not proceeded beyond Pabna even when in dire straits. Had he succeeded, the people of his village would have ostracised him. It is the limitations of his imagination that enable him to form a bond with his neighbours. That is why the soul of an entire settlement, not merely of a solitary imaginative poet, has found strident voice in his song.

Therefore, in order to accept as poetry the literature that is continually swaying the hearts of country folk in Bengal in the form of verse, songs, and tales, one has to link every village, every settlement with it in one's mind. It is these that imbue its broken metre and imperfect rhyme with meaning and with life. Rural literature relies on images and memories of the countryside of Bengal; this is why it holds a special appeal for the Bengali. When the mendicant Vaishnavi† calls out 'Hail to Radha' and enters the women's quarters to sing for alms, the mistress of the house and her veiled daughters-in-law come out expectantly to listen to her. What children and adolescents have been clamouring to hear for hundreds of years, on moonlit and starlit nights, from the aged grandmother steeped in tales, songs, and verse, is of deep and enduring appeal to the Bengali reader.

As the roots of a tree are tied to the ground while its top extends towards the sky, the base of literature stays largely concealed and entangled in the soil of the homeland. It is rural, local, in a special and restricted sense. It is enjoyable and accessible to the common people of the countryside alone: outsiders have no right of access. The part of literature that is universal stands on this lowly, regional subsoil. Thus there is a perpetual link between the so-called low and high literatures. The roots beneath the soil cannot bear comparison with the flowers, fruit, leaves, and branches reaching towards the sky; but to the scholarly eye, their resemblance and affinity is indelible.

This connexion between the upper and the lower parts is clearly visible in early Bengali literature. The poet of the *Annadamangal*,† like the Kabikankan,† frequented the royal courts† and the salons of the rich; they were both learned, and proficient in Sanskrit poetry; yet they were unable to leave the common regional literature too far behind. There is little difference between the narratives of the *Annadamangal* and the *Kumarasambhavam*;† but the *Annadamangal* has not been fashioned after the *Kumarasambhavam*. Its deities are the rustic Hara and Gauri† of Bengal. The *Kabikankan-Chandi*,† the *Dharmamangal*,† the *Manasar Bhasan*,† the narrative of Satyapir† are all based on rural tales. Only through acquaintance with those rural narrative poems can one come to know the narrative verse of Bharatchandra or Mukundaram. The metre, the rhyme and the poetic skills to be found in the courtly poetry are undoubtedly well executed, but these works are no different in essence from the rural verses.

I cannot tell for certain whether the verses that I have collected are old or new. But verses of this kind do not age a great deal in a century or two. The verses that the village poet composed fifty years ago can, in one sense, be thought contemporaneous with Mukundaram's, because time's stream cannot dash with much force against the hidden heart of village life. The rural way of life, and the literature that accompanies it, continue unchanged over a long period of time.

Only very recently has the modern age, like the young son-in-law from afar, made inroads with its modern ways into the inner quarters of the village. Within the village, too, the hand of change has become evident. That is why those who have undertaken to collect rural verses write to me as follows:

One cannot expect to hear such verses from today's women, except elderly ones. Most of them do not know these verses, and have no interest in learning them. There are very few older women still around. Even among them, many do not know such things: one or two might do so, but not all. To collect five such ballads, therefore, one needs have recourse to five elderly women from five different villages. Occasionally one sees one or two traditional mendicant Vaishnavis of this region recite such ballads as they beg. Their verses are all about the love between

Radha and Krishna. But such Vaishnavis are rare, and a number of them sing the same kind of ballads. Hence to collect more than one new ballad, one needs the assistance of a relatively large number of Vaishnavis. Thanks to our fertile green motherland, however, it is not unusual to hear 'Hail to Radha' from at least one or two new Vaishnavis from far away every week.

Earlier, these rural verses would be broadcast orally in the women's quarters by mendicant women and by grandmothers, to quench the literary thirst of even well-born rural women. Now a number of them have learnt to read: the literature of the Bengali printing press has reached them. I imagine the rural verses have been relegated to the lower strata of society.

The subjects of the verses can be roughly divided into two groups: those relating to Hara and Gauri, and those relating to Krishna and Radha. The tales of Hara and Gauri give voice to the Bengali's household concerns; those relating to Krishna and Radha, to the Bengali's sentiments. On the one hand, the socially sanctioned conjugal bond; on the other, a love that transcends social sanctions.

The conjugal relationship is marred by an obstacle: poverty. The tales about Hara and Gauri rise in waves from many different directions as they surround and wash against that rock of poverty. Sometimes the affection of the parents-in-law strikes against that rock; at other times, the love between man and woman is thwarted by it.

The poetic heart of Bengal has elevated this poverty to a lofty and divine level. Divesting poverty of its lowliness through renunciation and self-oblivion, the poet has portrayed it as far greater than wealth. For a poor community, there is no happier ideal than Bholanath's[†] assumption of poverty as though it were a bodily adornment. One who says 'I have no worldly means' is truly needy. What need does one have if one can say 'I have no need'? Truly his ideal is Shiva.

Unlike in other countries, wealth has no special status in India—or at least it had none in earlier times. It is not uncommon in our land for a lineage or household that commands high honour and respect to have no wealth. This is why rich families and poor are being linked in marriage all the time.

But whatever the social ideal may be, wealth has an inherent intoxicating power. In the pride of wealth, the rich person looks pityingly on the poor. Where there is no difference in social status, a difference in wealth enters and sparks off a conflict. Such a situation can cause a crisis in conjugal life. It is only natural that when the wealthy father-in-law holds his needy son-in-law in contempt, or a rich man's daughter grows impatient with her indigent husband and her own ill luck, the order of the household is shaken.

The tales of Hara and Gauri recount how this planetary crisis of conjugality can be dissipated. The unfailing devotion of the chaste wife is one of its ingredients. Another is the dispelling of the abjection of poverty, the singing of its praises. Although he is poor, Umapati is not to be slighted.† The wife of this wanderer in cremation grounds is more honoured in her husband than Indrani, the consort of Indra, king of heaven.

Another great vitiator of conjugal ties is the husband's old age and bad looks. That too has been overcome in the relationship between Hara and Gauri. When Menaka† laments on seeing her aged son-in-law at the wedding, the old man's good looks and youthfulness, his sumptuous robes and jewellery are miraculously revealed. Every aged husband has such extra-human good looks and youthfulness, but subject to his wife's true love and devotion. The mendicant, the bard, and the village singer pass from door to door, invoking that devotion over and over in their tales of Hara and Gauri.

The poetic genius of the village does not stop here. It makes Shiva crazed with addiction to hemp, cannabis, and the like. Not only that: it declares his weakness for savage tribal women. Such is the fate that befalls the ascetic lord in Kalidasa,† who is like a calm sea or an unwavering lamp-flame, on coming to the countryside of Bengal.

The broader point, however, is that the tales of Hara and Gauri narrate the triumph of conjugal ties over all hurdles, big and small. In the lore of Hara and Gauri, a vivid ideal of womanhood has been constructed as the core of the extended family, on which our community life is based. Whether the husband is needy, poor, elderly, or ugly, the wife is resplendent in good looks and youth, devotion and love, mercy and patience, energy and honour. The wife alone is the wealth of the poor, the Annapurna† who feeds the beggar, the Lakshmi† who guards the honour of the barren homestead.

As the ballads of Hara and Gauri are about the community, the ballads of Radha and Krishna are about beauty. We discount the spiritual doctrine they contain: when doctrine adopts the disguise of allegory to attract the attention of common people, it conceals its own doctrinal nature. It wins the hearts of common people by virtue of its external guise. There is something in the allegory of Radha and Krishna that, in Bengal, is palatable to the Vaishnava and the non-Vaishnava,† the spiritually experienced and the inexperienced alike. That is why it has spread far and wide through verse and song, jatra† and kathakata.†

The romantic attraction between man and woman through beauty is recounted in the literature of all countries. The ties of social duty cannot fully contain it. Its rule extends beyond the community. The five-darted god ranges everywhere; and spring—that is all the youth and the beauty of the world—is his constant companion.

Through the ages and across the lands, man has felt and described as a spiritual allegory this enthralling power of love between man and woman—the power whereby in a moment, sweetly and brightly, it links and orders around itself the sun, moon and stars, the flowering forests, the rivers and streams. By its sudden ineffable manifestation, the power of love brings complete fulfilment to a disjoint, dispersed, neglected cosmos in the twinkling of an eye. The Song of Solomon,† the poetry of Hafiz† and the lyrics of the Vaishnava poets bear evidence to this. There is such a vast universality in the love of two human beings that spiritual thinkers feel its full significance is not confined to those two alone: it suggests the eternal relationship and limitless longing between the world and its Lord.

There is no other comparable material for poetry. It is at once beautiful and vast, intimate and world-encompassing, commonplace and ineffable. Although, for lack of free mixing and independent choice of partners, this love exists in humiliation and secrecy in Indian society, the poets of Bharatavarsha† have invoked it in their poetry by various ploys and devices. Without openly demeaning society, they have established poetry outside of it. The dewy young Shakuntala, amid a grove of nabamallika plants with their spouses, the lordly mango trees, in the hermit's retreat on the banks of the river Malini, is the imaginative dream of a poet imprisoned in society. The love between Dushyanta and Shakuntala transcends society; it even defies society. Pururava's† fury of love tore social constraints to shreds and went on the rampage among the rivers, hills, and forests like a wild elephant in frenzy. The *Meghadutam* is a poem about lovers' separation. It is as though, when separated by a slight loosening of the taut bonds of conjugality, people find anew the leisure to love on their own. The heart's forceful ardour finds space to flow freely where a distance opens up between woman and man. If the maiden Gauri in the *Kumarasambhavam* had not, defying social convention, ministered all alone to Mahadeva† in the mountain-forest retreat, how would such incomparable poetry as the third canto† have been created? On one side, the quivering Uma, adorned with the flowers of spring and lissom as the rain-tree; on the other, the still, fathomlessly reposeful heart, expansive as the sea, of the meditating Mahadeva. Where would such grand opportunity for all-conquering love be found within the immuring laws of a human community?

Be that as it may, man-made society is not entirely contented with itself. Man cannot help installing at least within the realm of the mind, and enjoying if only in imagination, the power of beauty and love that draws society out of itself. Even if it is thwarted in worldly interaction, it pursues this goal with doubled intensity in spiritual sentiment. That is the main reason why Vaishnava songs have spread so swiftly across India. Vaishnava songs are songs of freedom. They do not recognise caste or lineage. Yet this freedom is ordered by the bonds of beauty and of the heart: it is not the mere frenzied wildness of blind sensuality.

As the tales of Hara and Gauri depict certain obstacles in conjugal ties, the flow of love in the Vaishnava lyrics presents a single great obstacle: that is society. It has in itself the strength of a thousand men. In Vaishnava lyric poetry, waves of love break all around that social barrier. Not just that: Vaishnava poetics accords a special glory to extramarital love.† It goes without saying that this glory is not by the valuation of social directives: it is purely a valuation of love. The tremendous strength of love, its abstruse enigma, its freedom from bonds, a great apprehension that transcends society and worldly life, place, time and company, reason and argument, cause and effect—all this is made manifest by the self-oblivion, oblivion of the world, complete indifference to censure, fear, shame and punishment, and indifference also to the rigid prescriptions of family and community life, that are expressed in these lyrics. This is why the Vaishnava poets have set up the love they depict on the sky-high summit of universal opprobrium, and anointed it there. If this all-destroying, all-sacrificing love that defies every constraint cannot be taken in a spiritual sense, it does no harm as poetry, but it can cause harm as a social principle.

The dissemination of such love-songs may appear to be dangerous for common people and detrimental to society. But in effect this is not entirely so. Society cannot altogether eradicate the vagaries of human nature. It expresses itself variously in deeds, in words, in imaginings. When deterred from one side, it flows out through another. The danger to society, in fact, lies in trying to block human nature unduly from all sides. Rather it is when, in such a situation, those arrested propensities find vent in some form that the danger grows somewhat less. There is no socially sanctioned public space for unconstrained love in our land; our front doors are firmly shut against it; yet even after it is buried under the weight of scripture, it enters at midnight through holes in the closed door and roams as a ghost with doubled energy among human habitation. Hence it is specially in our society that such smirched, dishonourable love is liable to find a secret place for itself in the natural course of things. By channelling the deep, irrepressible emotion of that unfettered love into the spiritual domain of beauty, the Vaishnava poets have to a great extent diverted its course from a worldly path into a mental one; they have arranged for that ever-hungry spectre of our society to be appeased with a pinda at holy Gaya.[†] They have practised various alchemies of metrically arranged imagination in an effort to transform desire into love. We cannot say that sensual perversion finds no place anywhere in their creations. But just as many putrid and decomposing substances get purified in a large, swift-flowing river, all such perversions are easily rectified and carried along in the flow of beauty and feeling. Rather, the poet of *Bidya-Sundar*[†] is a true offender against society. He has laughingly dug a tunnel[†] underneath the palace of society. The holy sunlight and fresh air find no entry into that tunnel. Why, despite this, are the poem and jatra of *Bidya-Sundar* so popular in our land? They are human nature's deft way of mocking a repressive, rigid society. This poet has branded on society's back what the Vaishnava poet had beautifully painted onto the Milky Way of sentiment:[†] whoever sees it derives amusement from it.

Be that as it may, our rural literature is largely composed around Hara–Gauri and Radha–Krishna. Out of this, the tales of Hara and Gauri are tales of our household. They express a trenchant theme of our Bengal through these tales. A daughter is a major burden of one's household. No responsibility is comparable to that of marrying off a daughter: *Kanya-pitritvam khalu nama kashtam* [Being the father of a daughter is indeed misery.][†] We are compelled to marry her off within a prescribed age and a limited social group. Because of this artificial compulsion, a bridegroom's social value rises steeply: he no longer needs much by way of looks, talents, wealth, or abilities. To give one's daughter in marriage to an unsuitable bridegroom is a common mishap in our society. Household after household constantly suffers anxiety, regret, tears, disputes with the son-in-law's family, the cruel pain endured by the girl caught between her parents and her in-laws. We seek to hold together both near and distant relatives, even merely nominal relatives, in the extended family; only the daughter has to be jettisoned. A society where children and all other relatives, except husband and wife, move away on their own cannot imagine this unbearable suffering of ours. It is the sole parting admitted into our basically cohesive family life. Hence the same wound is touched time and again. The tales of Hara and Gauri are the tales of that pre-eminent sorrow of the extended family of Bengal. On the seventh autumnal lunar day the mendicant's bride, daughter of all Bengal, comes to her maternal home; and when that Annapurna of the mendicant's household returns to her husband's house on Vijaya, the tenth lunar day, the eyes of all Bengal fill with tears.

TRANSLATED BY TISTA BAGCHI

World Literature

Whatever faculties we have within us exist for the sole purpose of forging bonds with others. We are true and we achieve truth only through such bonds. Otherwise, there is no sense in saying 'I am' or 'something is'.

Our bonds with truth in this world are of three kinds—the bonds of reason, of necessity, and of joy.

Of these, the bond of reason may be described as a kind of contest. It is like the bond between the hunter and his prey. Reason builds a dock, makes truth stand in it like a defendant, and cross-examines it till it is forced to yield its secrets bit by bit. That is why reason cannot help feeling a self-conceit with respect to truth. It senses its own power in proportion to its knowledge of truth.

Next comes the bond of necessity. The bond of necessity, that is of work, engenders a collaboration between human power and truth. Enforced by need, this bond draws truth closer to us. Yet there remains a distance. Just as the English trader had once secured his aims by bowing to the Nawab and offering him gifts, but, his mission accomplished, eventually ascended the throne himself, so also we think we have gained the empery of the world when we have used truth to material advantage to achieve our purpose. We then boast that nature is our waiting woman; water, air, and fire, our unpaid servants.

Finally, the bond of joy. The bond of beauty or joy erases all distance: there is no more self-conceit; we do not hesitate to surrender ourselves to the small and the weak. The king of Mathura then has to do all he can to hide his royal dignity from the milkmaid of Vrindavan.† Where we are linked by the bond of joy, we feel the power of neither reason nor work: we feel exclusively our own selves; no concealment or calculation comes in the way.

In sum, the bond between truth and human reason is our school, the bond of necessity our workplace, and the bond of joy our home. We do not carry our entire selves to school, nor do we yield ourselves entirely to the workplace; it is at home that we are relieved to let go of our whole selves without restraint. The school is unembellished, the workplace unfurbished, but the home is variously adorned.

What is this bond of joy? It is nothing but knowing others as our own, and our selves as other. Once that knowledge is achieved, we have no more questions. We never ask, 'Why do I love myself?' The very sense of my own being gives me joy. When we feel the same sense of being about someone else, there is no need to ask why I like that person.

Yajnavalkya had told Gargi:†

Na va are putrasya kamaya putrah priyo bhavati atmanastu kamaya putrah priyo bhavati.
Na va are vittasya kamaya vittam priyam bhavati atmanastu kamaya vittam priyam bhavati.

I love my son not because I desire him, but because I desire the Self. I love wealth not because I covet it, but because I desire the Self. [And so on.]

It means that I desire that in which I realise my own self more comprehensively. The son fills a certain lack in me, that is, I find myself in greater measure in my son. It is as if in him 'I' becomes 'more than I'. That is why he is *atmiya* to my self: he makes my *atman*† true even outside of me. The truth that I apprehend in myself with immense certainty, and that thereby begets love in me, is the same truth that I apprehend with equal certainty in my son, thereby enhancing the same love. Hence if you want to know what a man is, you must know what he loves. It shows in which objects of the universe he finds his own self, how far he has been able to disperse his own being. Where I do not feel love, my soul has reached its limits.

A child is thrilled when it sees light or spots a moving object: it laughs, it gurgles. In this light and movement, it finds its own consciousness in greater measure—that is the reason for its delight.

But when its consciousness reaches beyond sensory apprehension to the various levels of the heart and the mind, that mild stir is no longer enough to cause delight. Not that it feels no joy at all, but it feels less of it.

Likewise, as a human soul develops, it desires to feel the truth of its own being in a larger way.

To begin with, one can apprehend one's innermost spirit in the outside world most readily and comprehensively in other human beings. It is natural that through sight, hearing, and thought, through the play of the imagination and the attachments of the heart, one should be able to recoup oneself roundly in humanity. That is why one's being is filled to the brim by knowing, befriending, and serving fellow humans. That is why, in every land and age, one is considered great in proportion to the number of souls in which one has merged one's own in order to realise and express oneself. Such a person is indeed a *mahatman*, a great soul. My soul finds fulfilment in all humanity—one who has not realised this even a little, by some means or other, has been deprived of a fair share of human nature. To know the soul as confined to itself is to know it only in a depleted sense.

The human soul has a natural disposition to know itself among others. Self-interest is a great obstacle to this end and so is vanity. Many such worldly impediments break up our souls' natural drift, preventing an unimpeded view of the consummate beauty of human nature.

I know that some will argue, why should the human soul's natural inclinations suffer such ill-use in the world? Why should you not regard self-interest and vanity, things you dismiss as impediments, as part of our natural disposition?

As a matter of fact, many do say such things. That is because the impediments to human nature strike our eyes more than the nature itself. When a man first learns to ride a bicycle, he is destined to fall more often than to move. If someone then says that the man is rehearsing the fall rather than the ride, it is pointless arguing with him. Vanity and self-interest jostle us at every step. But if we fail to see the human effort to preserve our deepest disposition—that is, the effort to unite with all others—if we insist that the fall is the more natural function, that would merely be cavilling.

In fact, the impediments are necessary to learn that what is natural for us is indeed our nature and to make that nature exert itself to the full. That is how our nature knows itself with heightened self-awareness: the fuller the awareness, the deeper its joy. It is thus with every other thing.

Take, for instance, our reason. To determine causal relations is part of its nature. As long as it does so easily among self-evident things, it cannot fully perceive itself. But the causal links of the universe are buried in such obscurity that reason has to labour incessantly to unearth them. This effort to overcome obstacles makes reason apprehend itself most intensely in science and philosophy, and it is this effort that enhances its glory. In fact, if we consider it well, science and philosophy are nothing but the self-realisation of reason in the object. Wherever it perceives its distinctive rationale, it sees that object and itself together. This is what we call understanding. Reason finds joy in this way of seeing. Otherwise, human beings need not have been so happy on discovering that the apple falls to the ground for the same cause as makes the sun attract the earth. If the sun pulls the earth, what is in it for me? This, that I can comprehend the universal phenomenon within my reason, I can apprehend my reason in all things. From the speck of dust to the sun, the moon, and the stars—everything can thus unite with my reason. In this way, the inexhaustible mystery of the universe is drawing human reason into the open to reveal it more fully to human beings and returning it to them after uniting it with all creation. Knowledge is this union of reason with the universe, and it is in this union that our rationality finds joy.

Likewise, it is the nature of the human soul to seek a union of its particular humanness with all humanity: in this lies its true joy. It has constantly to battle hostility and obstruction both outside and within in order to realise this nature with total awareness. That is why self-interest is so potent, vanity so stubborn, the way of the world so difficult. There is great joy when human nature shines in full splendour through these obstacles to express itself forcefully. It is our own enhanced selves that we then discover.

It is for this reason that we wish to read the biographies of great men. In their characters we see our own impeded and obscured nature freed and extended. When reading history, we enjoy descrying our own natures in various people in varying shapes and measures in different countries, periods, and events. Whether I clearly understand it or not, my mind begins to recognise that I am one by embracing all humanity. The more I apprehend that unity, the greater my good and my joy.

In biography and history, however, we do not have a clear view of the whole picture. That too reaches us dimmed by many impediments and doubts. The image of humanity we glimpse even then is certainly a lofty one; but our minds strive to refashion that image after our heart's desire and capture it in language for all time. It is as if that alone can make the image exclusively mine. It becomes the possession of the human heart when I can express my love in it through graceful language and formal skill. It is no longer lost in the world's ebb and flow.

In this manner, all that is exquisitely expressed in the outside world, be it the glow of sunrise or a noble soul's radiance or my own heart's passions—everything that excites the heart from moment to moment—

the heart entwines with one of its own creations and clings to it as its own. Every such occasion is a means for it to express itself in a distinctive way.

Human self-expression in the world follows two broad courses. One is work, the other literature. The two courses run parallel. Human beings have poured themselves into the compositions of their work and their thoughts. These two streams complement each other. We must read history and literature to know humanity as revealed in these two currents.

In the field of work, human beings have built homes, societies, political and religious communities with all the strength and experience of body, mind, and heart. All they have known, achieved and desired is expressed in these constructions. Human nature, thus intertwined with the world, has taken various forms and installed itself in the midst of all things. What was inchoate in the realm of ideas assumes concrete form in the world; what was feeble within the one assumes a larger, organic unity among the many. It is increasingly impossible for an individual to achieve clear and full expression except through the home, society, polity, and religious community fashioned by many people through many years. All this has become the means for humanity to reveal itself to itself. Otherwise, we would not call it civilisation, that is, total humanness. Whether in the polity or in society, we are uncivilised in respects where each of us is totally autonomous, where the one is isolated from the rest. For this reason, when society or the polity is hurt, the blow is felt by the extended body of each individual; if a society grows parochial in any respect, the development of each individual self is impeded. One can express one's humanness unreservedly in so far as these structures set up by human beings are open and free. The more the inhibition, the more one lacks expression and remains impoverished, because the world exists to express what is human by means of work, and expression alone brings joy.

But although human beings express themselves through work, such expression is not, in this case, the primary goal: it is an offshoot. The housewife expresses herself in household work, but that is not the purpose uppermost in her mind. Through domestic chores she fulfils various intentions: those intentions reflect off her work and reveal her nature.

But there are times when one wishes primarily to express onself. For instance, when there is a wedding in the house, people are busy making sure that all the work is done well, but, at the same time, they feel the need to proclaim their feelings. On that day, the members of the family cannot help declaring the well-being and happiness of their home to everyone. How do they declare it? The flute is played, lamps are lit, the house is decorated with garlands. Through the beauty of sound, fragrance, and spectacle, through all the radiance, the heart spreads itself like a fountain in a hundred streams in all directions. Thus, by various suggestions, it arouses its own joy in other hearts so as to make that joy true amidst them all.

The mother cannot help caring for the infant in her arms. But that is not all: mother love seeks expression surpassing the demands of care and without apparent cause. It wells up from within in various kinds of play, endearments, and words. Decking the child in many colours and ornaments, such love cannot help spreading wealth through extravagance and sweetness through beauty, quite without need.

It is clear from all this that such is the nature of one's heart. It seeks to join its own emotions to the world outside. Incomplete in itself, it is relieved if it can somehow turn its inner truth into the truth of the world. To the heart, its abode is never just a fabric of brick and timber; it paints its dwelling in its own colours and makes it a home. To the heart, the land that it inhabits is not made up simply of earth, water, and sky. It is happy only when that land unveils for it the maternal, life-fostering aspect of the divine: otherwise the heart cannot view itself in the outside world. Failing this, it becomes indifferent; and for the heart, indifference is death.

By such means, the heart continually establishes affective bonds with truth. Where there are affective ties, there is an exchange. The mistress of one's heart's abode is a proud housewife: her pride is hurt when she cannot send back a gift to match the one her kin, the world, sends her. To express good kinship, she has to create with such ingredients as word and sound, the brush and the chisel, and thus embellish her gift-basket. If some need of her own is served in the process, well and good; but often she is willing to express herself at the expense of her needs. She is eager to proclaim herself even if that makes her bankrupt. Expression is the prodigal wing of human nature: it drives reason, the parsimonious steward, to strike its forehead in repeated despair.

The heart asks, 'How can I be as true outside as I am within? Where in the world will I find the right resource and scope?' It continually wails, 'I cannot reveal my own self, I cannot install myself in the outside world.' When the rich man feels his own wealth in his heart, he can exhaust Kuber's† riches in trying to express it to the world. When the lover feels true love in his heart, he can sacrifice wealth, honour, and life in an instant to express that love, that is to make it true in the outside world. The heart never loses its intense eagerness to make the inward into the outward and the outward into the inward in this way. There is a lyric by Balaram Das† which says:

> You were in my heart, who has brought you out in the open?

It is as if the beloved object were an object within the lover's heart. Someone has drawn it out of doors, so the lover is longing to fetch it back inside again. There is the opposite situation as well. When the heart fails to perceive its desires and passions in the external world, it tries hard to fashion their image with its own hands out of various ingredients. In this way, the heart's longing to make the world its own and itself the world's is constantly at work. To express oneself in the outside world is part of this process. That is why when it comes to expression, the heart makes one agree to lose everything one has.

When a barbarian army marches to battle, victory over the enemy is not its sole concern. It manifests its inner violence in external guise by putting on warpaint, sounding drums and war cries, and dancing a wild war dance. It is as though its belligerence is not complete without all this. Violence secures its practical goal through battle, and slakes its desire for self-expression through such superfluous claptrap.

Western warfare of the present day has not rid itself totally of drums and music, or of dress and trappings, as expressions of bellicose passion. However, strategic wisdom is more crucial in modern battles: they are progressively moving away from the human heart's habitual nature. The band of dervishes† who attacked the British army in Egypt did not lay down their lives just to win a battle. They died to the last man to express the fiery zeal of their hearts. Those who fight only to win will never act in such an uncalled-for manner. The human heart expresses itself even at the cost of suicide: can one imagine a greater waste?

Take the instance of worship. It is different for the devout and the clever. The clever one thinks, 'My worship will obtain my salvation.' The devout says, 'My devotion is imperfect without worship; whether it profits me or not, worship brings my heart's devotion out into the world where it finds its full and secure dwelling.' In this way, devotion achieves its own fulfilment by expressing itself in worship. To the clever, worship is laying out money at interest; to the devout, it is idle expense. For when the heart expresses itself, it cares nothing for loss.

One's heart is a willing captive to whatever in the universe displays this quality, which is also its own: it does not then raise a single question. This thriftless excess in the world constitutes beauty. We glimpse the presence of the heart's creed in the wide world when the flower shows no hurry to turn into seed, but surpasses necessity and blooms in beauty; when the cloud does not rush through its chore and dissolve into rain, but tarries to hold our eyes in thrall with uncalled-for bursts of colour; when the trees do not stretch scrawny branches like gaunt beggars for the sun and rain, but shower a wealth of green splendour on the brides of the heavens;† when the sea is not just a giant clearing-house for dispersing water around the globe in the form of clouds, but is awesome with the unfathomed dread of its liquid blue; when the mountain is not content merely to supply the earth with water from its rivers but keeps the force of the terrific motionless across the skies, like destruction's lord stilled in meditation. Reason, that is forever old, shakes its head and asks, 'Why such a waste of needless effort all over the world?' The heart, that is forever young, answers, 'Only to beguile me: I see no other reason.' The heart knows that all through the world there is one heart that continually expresses itself. Otherwise why should there be so much beauty and music, so many gestures, shadows, and hints, and such adornments throughout creation? The heart is not blandished by the trafficker's thrift; that is why in water, earth, and sky, there is such superfluous effort to hide necessity at every step. If the world were not replete with rasa, we would have remained small and demeaned: the heart would perpetually have complained that it was uninvited to the festival of the world. But the whole world, brimful of rasa despite its countless chores, gives the heart this honeyed message, 'I want you. I want you in various forms. I want you in laughter and tears, in fear and faith, in sorrow and strength.'

In the world itself, we see two processes at work: the expression of function and the expression of idea. It is beyond our powers to observe and comprehend fully that which is expressed through functions. Our learning cannot encompass the immeasurable potency of knowledge that it contains.

But the expression of idea is unmediated expression. A thing of beauty is simply beautiful. The great has greatness. The fearsome inspires dread. The world's rasa enters one's heart directly and draws the rasa within it out into the world. Whatever hide-and-seek, whatever the hindrance in this meeting, ultimately there is nothing in it other than expression and union.

We thus see a likeness between the universe and the human world. The divine as truth and knowledge is expressed through the world's functioning, and its joyous form is perceived through its various rasas. It is hard to acquaint oneself thoroughly with the divine-as-knowledge through the world's functions; but there is no difficulty in apprehending the divine-as-joy through rasa, because through rasa He directly manifests Himself.

In the human world too, the power of knowledge is busy at work, and the power of joy is creating rasa. In work lies our faculty of self-preservation; in rasa, our faculty for self-expression. Self-preservation is necessary, but self-expression surpasses necessity.

Necessity impedes expression and expression impedes necessity: we have already seen that in the instance of warfare. Self-interest dislikes extravagance, whereas joy declares itself in prodigality. Hence, in the world of self-interest, such as at the office, the less we express ourselves the more we are esteemed; while at a joyous celebration, the festivities shine brighter the more we forget self-interest.

That is why self-expression finds no hindrance in literature. It dwells far from self-interest. There sorrow draws a film of tears over our hearts, but does not invade our homes; fear sways our minds, but does not hurt our bodies; pleasure makes our hearts quiver at its touch, but does not provoke and inflame our lust. Human beings continue to fashion a necessity-free realm of literature right alongside their world of necessity. In the former they can, without doing themselves any material damage, delight in apprehending their own nature variously through various rasas; they can view an unimpeded expression of their selves. In that realm there is no obligation—there is only joy; no beadle and bailiff, only the great king himself.

So what does literature acquaint us with? With humanity's wealth and abundance, which overflows all its material needs and is not exhausted within its mundane limits.

Hence I wrote in an earlier essay[†] that although eating involves a universal rasa, equally familiar to young and old, it is a minor presence in literature outside farcical comedy, because it never exceeds the satisfaction of the meal. Once the stomach is full, we dismiss it with the spot-fee of a resounding 'ah'; we do not invite it to the portals of literature for an honorarium. But the rasas that overspill the pots in our pantry course through literature in a purling flood. Since practical work cannot exhaust them, the human heart, impelled by that flood-tide, finds relief when it can express them in literature.

In such abundance lies the real expression of humanity. It is true that human beings are fond of eating, but true above all that they are heroic. Who can contain the powerful impulse of this truth? Like the Bhagirathi,[†] it flows right into the sea—crushing rocks, sweeping away Airavat,[†] slaking the thirst of town, country, and farmland. Human heroism rises above the world after finishing all the world's work.

In this way, whatever in human life is noble and timeless, whatever transcends human need and work, yields itself naturally to literature and automatically fashions humanity's greater image.

There is one other factor. What we see in the world we see dispersed—a glimpse now and a glimpse then, a little here and a little there; we see an object mingled with ten others. These gaps and admixtures disappear in literature. There all the light is focused on what is being expressed, we are allowed to see nothing else for the moment. Various devices are employed to create a space where that object alone may shine.

Naturally, we will not put something there that would not accord with such intense individuality, such sharp light. That would merely embarrass the unworthy. The glutton is not so visible under the cover of the world's ways; he becomes ridiculous when viewed in focused light on the literary stage.[†] Hence it is natural for human beings to establish in literature the expression that is not trite, that the heart accepts without demur as truly representing its compassion and courage, its fury or calm—that can stand within the pale of proficient art yet withstand, with head held high, the unblinking gaze of abiding time; with any other kind of material, the incongruity jars on us. Our minds rebel at the sight of anyone but the king on the throne.

But not everyone is capable of high-minded discernment, and not every society is great. There are times when petty, passing infatuations diminish human beings. The distorted mirror of such times magnifies the trivial; their literature exalts human pettiness and brazenly highlights its own blemishes. Then virtuosity displaces art, vanity passes for glory, and Kipling takes Tennyson's seat.

But great time[†] lies in wait, and it sifts everything. Whatever is small and worn-out slips through the sieve to blend with the dust. Among different ages and people, only those things survive in which all human beings can discover themselves. The things that pass this test are the permanent and universal human treasures.

Through this process of making and breaking, a timeless ideal of human nature and expression gathers of itself in literature. That ideal stays at the helm to guide the literature of a new age. To judge literature by that ideal is to draw on the support of humankind's collective wisdom.

It is now time to make my main point. It is that literature is not viewed in its true light if we see it confined to a particular space and time. If we realise that universal humanity expresses itself in literature, we shall be able to discern what is worth viewing in the latter. No literary work has succeeded unless its author has become the mere means of composition. A work is admitted to the ranks of literature only when the author has realised the ideas of the human race in his own thoughts and expressed humanity's pain in his writing. We have to regard literature as a temple being built by the master mason, universal man; writers from various countries and periods are working under him as labourers. None of us has the *plan* of the entire building; but the defective parts are dismantled again and again, and every worker has to conform to that invisible *plan* by exercising his natural talent and blending his composition with the total design. This is what brings out his artistic prowess; this is why no one pays him a common labourer's wages but honours him as a master builder.

Comparative Literature is the English title you have given to the subject I have been asked to discuss. In Bengali, I shall call it World Literature.

If we are to understand what people are saying through their work, or what their purpose and endeavour are, we have to follow the course of human intention through all history. The reign of Akbar, the history of Gujarat, the character of Elizabeth—viewing history in such isolated fragments merely satisfies our curiosity about facts. But he who knows that Akbar and Elizabeth are mere vehicles, that throughout history humankind continually tries to fulfil its deepest desire through diverse endeavours, errors, and restitutions; that it strives to emancipate itself by joining in expansive ties with all others in every direction; that the ideal of self-government struggles to realise itself in monarchies and thereafter in democracies; that human beings make and unmake themselves to seek expression and to realise their individual beings in and through the collective being of humankind—such a person seeks in history not an individual but the ever-active intention of the timelessly human. Such a one returns home after viewing not just the pilgrims but the very deity they come to worship from all parts of the world.

Likewise, the thing truly worth seeing in world literature is the way human beings express their joy in literature and the abiding form in which the human soul wishes to reveal itself through the diversity of this expression. We need to enter the world of literature to learn whether the human soul is best pleased to declare itself as sufferer or epicure or ascetic, and how far human kinship has been rendered true in the world—that is how far truth has become a human possession. It will not do to know of literature as artifice: it is an organic world. Its mystery is not any individual's private possession. Its creation is a continuous process like the material world's; and yet in the heart of this unfinished creation, an ideal conclusion dwells immovably.

The mass of matter at the sun's core is forming itself in many ways, both solid and liquid. We cannot see the process, but the surrounding ring of light ceaselessly expresses the sun to the world. It is thus that the sun gifts itself to the world and links itself to all else. If we could make humanity the object of such an integral view, we would see it like the sun. We would see that the mass of matter was gradually forming itself into layers, and around it, perpetually, a luminous ring of expresion spreading itself joyously in every direction. Look at literature as this ring of light, made of language, encircling humanity. Here there are storms of light, the wellsprings of radiance, the collision of radiant vapours.

As you walk through human habitations, you see that people have no leisure—the grocer minds his shop, the blacksmith hammers iron, the labourer carries loads, the trader checks his ledger. At the same time, something remains invisible. See it in your mind's eye: on either side of this road, among the houses, shops, and alleyways, the flood of rasa is spreading itself in so many streams and furrows over so much that is bleak, straitened, and impoverished; the *Ramayana* and the *Mahabharata*, stories and fables, kirtan† and panchali† are portioning out the nectar of the universal human soul to each man and woman day and night; Rama and Lakshmana are drawing up to stand behind the trivial labours of humble folk; the compassionate breeze of Panchavati† is blowing through dark tenements; the human heart's creations and expressions are enclasping the privations and stringencies of the labouring world with hands decked in bracelets of beauty and benediction. This is how we must see the whole of literature surrounding the whole of humanity. We need to see that the material being of the human race has extended itself far in every direction through the agency of its conceptual being. The rain that falls upon humankind is girt by many showers of verse and music, many *Meghadutams*† and Vidyapatis;† the joys and sorrows of its small abode swell with the joys and sorrows of the Chandra and Surya kings.† The sorrows of the Mountain King's daughter† float around the daughter of a humble home; the poor man's suffering is enlarged in the glory of the poor god on Mount Kailas.† By this continuous diffusion of the self, humankind seems to exceed and enhance its being continually in the outside world.

Although constricted by its situation, humankind is extending itself through the creation of feelings and ideas. Literature is this second world around the material one.

Do not so much as imagine that I would guide your way through world literature. We must all cut our paths through it as best we can. I simply wished to say that just as the world is not my ploughland added to yours and to someone else's—to see the world in this light is to take a rustic view—so also, literature is not my writing added to yours and to someone else's. We usually regard literature in this rustic light. It is time we pledged that our goal is to view universal humanity in universal literature by freeing ourselves from rustic uncatholicity; that we shall recognise a totality in each particular author's work, and that in this totality we shall perceive the interrelations among all human efforts at expression.

TRANSLATED BY SWAPAN CHAKRAVORTY

Literary Creation

In this essay, Rabindranath repeatedly uses the word bhab *(Sanskrit* bhava*). In the present context, 'idea' is usually the fittest rendering; but occasionally, the other implications of the word, as explained on p. xii above, may also play a part.*

Just as grains of sugar collect around a string, so do isolated ideas in our minds crystallise and try to acquire a shape the moment they find a connecting thread. Our thoughts seem constantly to strive to pass from obscurity to clarity, from isolation to union. Even in dreams, various thoughts instantly crowd round and take shape as soon as they find a lead. It is as if inchoate thoughts haunt our minds like spectres in sleep and wake, waiting for an opportunity to assume form. The day belongs to work: it is under the strict surveillance of reason, which does not allow idle crowds in the workplace to waste our time. Under its rule, our thoughts are compelled to cling to the thread of work and to express themselves coherently. During our quiet moments of leisure, the process begins again. Perhaps the scent of a flower provides a pretext—memories of days long past flock round it in no time. When a statement takes form, there is no telling how many more will have resort to it to define themselves, one after the other. They are all trying to grow into something in one way or another—nothing more. There is no end to this effort in the realm of thought.

Once the effort to come into being succeeds, there begins the effort to survive. In the due season, jackfruit in plenty jostle on the branches. But the fruits on the smaller branches, dangling from thin stalks, scarcely begin to sport their jackfruitness before disappearing among the unmanifest.

Our thoughts share the same lot. The ones that somehow cluster around a lasting thread grow to full maturity; their cells fill out in due order, and their being achieves its purpose. Those that barely have space to blossom soon make their exit in contorted disorderly guise.

There are trees from which the blossoms fall off as soon as they appear; they do not survive to grow into fruit. Likewise, there are minds in which thoughts come and go incessantly, without finding scope to mature into ideas. But a thinker's consciousness has the moisture and the heat for thoughts to grow into ideas. Of course there are many that fall off, but also many that reach fruition.

The fruits that mature plead that they cannot remain tied down to the branch. 'We must mellow and leave the tree and venture forth,' they say, 'filled with juice, flushed with colour, heady with fragrance, hardened in the seed. We are not fulfilled until we fall the right way on the soil below.' The thoughts that turn into ideas in the thinker's mind have the same plea. They say, 'Now that we have had the chance to take form, we must go out and enact the sport of new birth and eternal life on the soil of the universal human mind.' Human thoughts are gratified if they get these three opportunities: to blossom, to mature, and to go forth in search of the right soil. Thoughts, like living things, constantly urge us towards this fulfilment; hence the unabated exchange of embraces and whispers among human beings. A mind looks for another mind to relieve it of the burden of its thoughts, to have its own ideas contemplated by another. That is why women gather at the waterside steps, friend runs to friend, letters go to and fro; that is why there are meetings, arguments, writings, disputes—even scuffles and skirmishes. Human thoughts, in their search for fulfilment, impel human beings so strongly that no one can remain isolated. It is this urge that makes men and women around the world go on prating day and night aloud and in silence. We are wonder-struck when our mind's eye views all this prattle in various garbs and shapes, through appropriate and incongruous means, crowding and jostling through our world as speech and conversation, story and gossip, message and letter, image and picture, prose and verse, work and deed.

Thus throughout human society, the thoughts of one mind strive to find fulfilment in another, thereby so shaping our ideas that they are no longer exclusive to the original thinker. This often goes unnoticed. A little reflection would make us agree that when we say something to a friend, the statement moulds itself to some extent in accordance with the friend's mind. We cannot write to one friend exactly as we write to another. My idea adjusts itself somewhat to the particular mind of the particular friend in whom it secretly seeks fulfilment. In fact, what we say is shaped by the conjunction of speaker and listener.

In literature, for the same reason, the author tries to fit the work, even if unwittingly, to the nature of the person to whom it is offered. Dashu Ray's panchali† is not Dasharathi's sole possession; it is written in collaboration with the society that listens to it. It does not contain the thoughts of Dasharathi alone; the love, hate, piety, belief, and taste of a given circle at a given time find spontaneous expression within it.

Some authors wish to utter their thoughts to friends, some to a community, some to a society, and some to the eternal human spirit. The writings of those who succeed provide some glimpse or other of that friend, community, society, or universal humanity. Hence literature bears testimony not only of the writer but of those for whom it is written.

In the material world too, when the right thing holds court in the right place, it survives with the support of its environs. It is so with literature as well. Therefore, that which survives does not speak only of itself; it speaks of the world around it, because it survives more by the force of its surroundings than by its own strength.

Consider now that question of crystallisation—the first point I had made about literature. Let us look at one or two instances.

Early monsoon clouds, flights of herons, the fragrance of rain on the heated earth, the refreshing onset of Asharh—sombre with dark masses of clouds—over mountains and forests, rivers and waterfalls, towns and villages: down the ages, all these have left on the poet's mind shadows of ideas, ecstatic sensations of beauty, intimations of anguish. Whose mind is free of such impressions? The world touches our minds day and night, striking one chord or another on the soul's strings.

Once upon a time, these numerous chords of numerous days took form as beautiful crystals in Kalidasa's† mind, flocking one after another around a central thread and assuming clear shape. The images of many ideas of many ages had been soliciting for this auspicious moment. Now, seizing on the pretext of the pining Yaksha's message of love, they clustered in layer after layer of description, stanza after stanza of mandakranta† verse. On that day, each of them was justified by the next and redeemed by the whole.

We are all familiar with the mental image that the mention of a chaste wife evokes in the Hindu mind. Each of us must have seen one woman or another who impressed us in some measure with the virtuous power of chastity. That heavenly image of benediction, which we saw in glimpses amid trivial daily household chores, keeps floating through our minds like the play of light and shade.

As soon as Kalidasa began *Kumarasambhavam* in mid-narrative, how these floating ideas about chastity yielded themselves and assumed firm shape! The austere discipline of devoted wives, glimpsed amid the daily chores in every home, was endowed with enduring lustre in the image of the goddess's ascesis beneath the rocky Himalayas, in the shade of deodars washed by the waters of the Mandakini.

The kind of poem we call a lyric—that is, a poem which develops a single idea in small compass, such as Vidyapati's†

> It is Bhadra:† the rain pours down,
> My house is all forlorn—

that, too, takes shape by seizing on a sentiment lying unexpressed in one's mind for a long time. Many minds have been mutely haunted by the gloom of an empty house amidst the swelling rains of Bhadra. The instant the right word was uttered in the right metre, this old and universal feeling crystallised into form.

Vapours float in the air; but on touching the cool petals of a flower, they condense into dew. Vapours were adrift in the sky, invisible; the moment they hit the mountains, clouds gathered and the pouring rain made springs and rivers stream forth. So also in the lyric, a single idea condenses and glistens like a pearl, while in more expansive poems the massed cluster of ideas descends as waterfalls. But the basic point is that the mute, vapour-like ideas are touched by the poet's imagination in such a way that a various and beautiful form takes visible shape around it.

Like the season of the rains, there are moments in human history when the air is heavy with the vapour of ideas. Such was the air of Bengal after Chaitanya's† arrival. Its sky was then moist with the rasa of love.† All the poetic minds that had then sprung up in the land helped to condense that moisture and make it rain down in all directions, plentifully and powerfully, in fresh diction and new rhythms.

During the French Revolution, a wave of ideas propagating love of humanity had likewise filled the air. Striking against the hearts of various poets, it showed itself in numerous ways and forms, now in compassion and now in rebellious notes. The fact, then, is that the human mind constantly throws up many unexpressed ideas which roam and cloud over the vast mental sky of universal humanity—now as pain, now as reflection, now as utterance. The individual poet's imagination acts like a gathering point and unites a distinct cluster of these ideas around an imaginative thread, thereby articulating them clearly to the human sensibility. This process gives us joy. Why? It is because in every mind, the effort to view itself is perpetually at work. Hence, when the mind sees in an integrated entity a particular manifestation of itself, it is rewarded in its incessant effort and that gives it joy. Why only literature—it is so with philosophy and history as well. Philosophical questions and reflections lie unexpressed and dispersed in all human minds. When the philosopher's genius gives a group of them a certain unity, their features and principles become manifest; we view a specific manifestation of our own thoughts. History is reported as hearsay: as soon as the historian's genius draws these reports around a single thread, we can grasp the manifest form of the history that had so long eluded expression.

The critic's task is to consider which particular aspect of the human heart, concentrated in a particular poet's imagination, depicts through beauty a distinct and exquisite manifestation of the heart's infinite variety. It is not enough to say that Kalidasa's similes are fine and his language pleasurable, that the descriptions in the third canto of *Kumarasambhavam* are beautiful, or that pathos is plentiful in the fourth act of *Abhijnanashakuntalam.* A particular cast of the human heart is enshrined in the entire body of Kalidasa's verse. The critic has to decide which unexpressed feature of humanity's mental universe was brought to specific beauteous expression by the poetic imagination serving as a focal point for the forces of attraction and repulsion, acceptance and rejection. Once born into the world, Kalidasa saw, thought, suffered, imagined, and created; this life of thought, feeling and imagination has expressed for us, through words, one particular form from among the endless forms of humanness. What form is that? Had we all been exceptional poets, each of us would have imaged forth one's heart in a unique way, and that infinite variety would have expressed an infinite unity. But we lack such powers. Our speech is fractured; we do not express ourselves well: what we propagate as the truth may not be true to our natures, but the habitual parroting of common wisdom. I am unable to show clearly all that I might see, understand, and achieve in my lifetime. It is not as if poets can do this fully either. Their words are not uniformly lucid, true, or beautiful; their efforts do not always make good the intentions lying deep within their nature. But unknown to themselves, from a realm beyond their endeavours, and urged by a mysterious worldwide effort, an ideal form that 'we think we grasp but that escapes our grasp'[†] continues to unfold itself through every obstacle and uncertainty—sometimes only a little, sometimes in fuller measure. A thinker who can look deep and discern this total form in the poet's work is the true judge of literature.

The purport of what I am saying is that the creation of our ideas is governed not by whims but by inexorable laws, just as much as the creation of material things. The urge for expression that we observe in the atoms and molecules of the physical world is powerfully at work in our mental faculties. Hence the eyes with which we regard mountains, forests, rivers, deserts, and oceans ought to be the same as those with which we look at literature: literature, too, is neither yours nor mine but part of universal creation.

When we look at literature in this way, we cannot rest content with judgments of good and bad. We also feel an eagerness to trace a method in its development and discern a large causal nexus. I shall try to make myself clear by citing an instance.

I said in an essay entitled 'Rural Literature' that among the common people of a country, a few ideas initially take the form of verse fragments and wander about in clusters. Subsequently, a poet gathers those fragments around the thread of an extended poem and unites them into a mass. Many legends about Shiva and Parvati not found in any of the Puranas, and many stories about Rama and Sita absent from the original *Ramayana*, have for long circulated orally in village meeting-places, in broken metre and rustic idiom, on the lips of rural bards and Puranic storytellers. Then a court poet, invited to sing at a large distinguished gathering rather than in a rustic courtyard, appropriated those rural stories, made them exalted and presentable in polite metre and formal idiom. When the old is displayed as new and the fragmented as one, the whole country seems to derive pleasure from seeing its own heart more clearly and expansively. It is as if it then crosses a phase in its life's journey. Mukundaram's *Chandimangal*,[†] Ghanaram's *Dharmamangal*,[†] the songs of Manasa[†] by Ketakadas[†] and others, Bharatchandra's *Annadamangal*[†] belong to this category of verse; they are attempts to bind together the poetic fragments of rural Bengal into a larger literature. In this way, after merging its vital substance into a larger entity, rural literature withers away, like petals from a flower that has brought forth its fruit.

Panchatantra,[†] *Kathasaritsagara*,[†] the *Arabian Nights*, the Arthurian legends of England, and the Scandinavian *saga* literature were born in this way. In each of them, orally dispersed narratives seek to converge and crystallise into a larger entity.

This effort of scattered ideas to achieve unity has found marvellous expression in a few instances, such as Homer's poems in Greece and the *Ramayana* and the *Mahabharata* in India.

It is now almost universally believed that the *Iliad* and the *Odyssey* became single poems by the gradual and layered adhesion of diverse fragmentary lays. It is not surprising that at a period prior to the manuscript and the printed book, when poems were sung by roving minstrels, a poem should be fleshed out by various hands at various times. But the structures that gave these poems standing room as integral works were undoubtedly the handiwork of great poets, because these structures saved the new adhesions from straying beyond the confines of unity.

If we observe how the songs of Vidyapati of Mithila became Bengali padabali,[†] we shall realise how one thing turns into another by the law of its inherent nature. The padabali current in Bengal as Vidyapati's cannot really be called his. Most of the pieces contain hardly anything of the original poet's work. In course of time, their language, meaning, and even affective content altered so much through contact with Bengali singers and listeners that they became something altogether new. Only a few of Vidyapati's original lyrics as published by Grierson[†] can be traced in the Bengali padabali; it is impossible to match the rest with corresponding poems in Bengali. Yet in spite of the changes made at different times by different hands, the lyrics did not degenerate into incoherent nonsense, because a keynote ran through their midst and alertly absorbed every change. On the strength of this keynote, we call these lyrics Vidyapati's; again, on the strength of the radical changes, we can place them without compunction among the literature of Bengalis.

It will thus be seen that when orally transmitted song-fragments are colligated in a poem, and that poem is then sung for a long time among the populace, it is subject to further interventions from every side by various people at different times. Such a poem automatically draws its nourishment from all parts of the country, and thus gradually becomes the possession of the entire land. The history of the whole country's inner spirit, its philosophical wisdom, its religious feeling, and its code of work converge of themselves in the poem. This is made possible by the wonderful genius of the poet who has laid the poem's foundations. He has laid such a base in such a place, according to such a broad *plan*, that he can make the entire country toil for him for ages to come. We cannot claim that nothing ever gets crooked or awry from being tampered by so many hands over the years; but such distortions are overwhelmed by the grandeur of the basic design.

Our *Ramayana* and *Mahabharata*, especially the latter, are instances of this process.

A poem may be called a true epic when it is composed in this way by an entire race over the ages on the basis of an author's poetic ground plan.

I would compare it to rivers such as the Ganga and the Brahmaputra. At first, springs issue from secret mountain-caves and meet to form a river. Then, when it flows down its course, many tributaries from many lands join the river and merge into it their discrete identities.

But there are few rivers in the world as large as the Ganga of India, the Nile of Egypt, or the Yang-tse-kiang of China. Each of these rivers, like a mother, nurtures a vast country from one end to another. Each of them has nursed an ancient civilisation at her breast.

Similarly, there are only four epics in the literature known to us: the *Iliad*, the *Odyssey*, the *Ramayana*, and the *Mahabharata*. The artificial canons of rhetoric force the *Raghuvamsham*,† the works of Bharavi† and Magha,† Milton's *Paradise Lost*, Voltaire's *Henriade*† and so on into the ranks of epics. In recent times, the regime of the modern printing press has destroyed even the possibility of an epic's growth.

We have lost the ancient legends about Rama's life current among the people before the *Ramayana* was composed. But the rudiments of the *Ramayana* were no doubt present in them, scattered across the country.

The heroes who are acknowledged in our country as divine incarnations had certainly performed some exceptional deeds for the good of the world. Before the *Ramayana* was written, some such popular tradition about Ramachandra must have been in circulation. That he went into exile in the forest to honour his father's promise, and rescued his wife after destroying her abductor, prove his greatness; but the *Ramayana* contains only faint hints of the extraordinary good he had done for his people so as to win their hearts.

The Dravidians, who had occupied this country before the Aryan conquest after defeating its earliest inhabitants, were by no means uncivilised. They did not capitulate easily to the Aryans. They disrupted the Aryans' rituals and their farming, and disturbed the forest retreats set up in clearings by the clan leaders.

In some remote part of the Deccan, a Dravidian royal dynasty grew extremely powerful and founded a prosperous kingdom. Hordes sent by them would suddenly emerge from the forest and terrorise the Aryan settlements.

Through patient effort and strategy, aided by the monkeys—that is the primitive inhabitants of India—Ramachandra destroyed the Dravidians' power. It is for this reason that songs to his glory began to circulate among the Aryans. Just as Vikramaditya† won renown by rescuing the

Hindus from Shaka oppression, so the hero who curbed non-Aryan influence and ensured the Aryans' safety came to be loved and worshipped by the people.

At that time, there was rising and widespread anxiety about who would deliver them from this menace. Vishvamitra† had concluded that it would be Ramachandra, having observed all the favourable signs in him while he was still young. Under Vishvamitra's encouragement and guidance, Ramachandra was groomed from his boyhood to fight the enemy. He had early begun to devise his winning strategies by making friends with the forest-dwelling Guhaka.†

Cattle in those days was accounted wealth, and farming was sacred work. Janaka† had ploughed the land with his own hands. It was through the plough that the Aryans were then making India's soil, by degrees, their own. The plough was pushing the forest back and spreading agriculture far and wide. The rakshashas† were obstacles to that expansion.

That Janaka was one of the foremost among the great names of ancient Aryan civilisation is supported by many popular legends. He was an enterprising leader in the spread of agriculture in India. He even named his daughter Sita.† He had resolved that he would marry her to the champion who could prove his extraordinary strength by breaking the bow.† In those troubled times, he was waiting for such an exceptionally powerful man. It was a way of choosing the man who would be able to withstand a formidable enemy.

Vishvamitra brought Rama to Janaka's court, having trained him for the task of defeating the non-Aryans. There Ramachandra proved himself the fittest man for this calling by breaking the bow.

Later, he nobly left for the forest to honour his word, after entrusting the kingdom to his younger brother, Bharata. Taking the advice of sages such as Bharadvaja and Agastya, who were bent on spreading Aryan settlements in the difficult southern terrain, he disappeared into the dense unfamiliar forest, accompanied by Lakshmana.

There he killed one of two rival brothers, Bali and Sugriva,† and made an ally of the other. He brought the monkeys under his sway, and built up an army by teaching them the arts of warfare. With this troop, he devastated Lanka after shrewdly creating division in the enemy's ranks. The rakshasas were skilled architects. Yudhisthira's astonishing palace was constructed by the demon, Maya.† Till today, the Dravidian style of temple architecture is recognised as distinctive in India. It is not entirely unjustified that some scholars should consider them related to the ancient Egyptians.

At any rate, the familiar traditions about the golden city of Lanka must have had a basis. The rakshasas were not uncivilised. Rather, in the cultivation of art they were superior to the Aryans.

Ramachandra subdued his enemies, but did not steal their kingdom. Vibhishana,† having turned his ally, went on to rule Lanka. Rama won the lasting loyalty of the monkeys by entrusting to them the kingdom of Kishkindhya.† In this way, it was Ramachandra who brought the Aryans and non-Aryans together and established ties between them. Dravidians and Aryans thus gradually became part of the same society and founded the Hindu community. Peace was established in India as the social customs and religious rites of both races were merged within that community.

When this union of Aryans and non-Aryans was finally complete and the exchange of faith and knowledge accomplished, the old story of Ramachandra started to change in form and idea as it travelled by word of mouth. If a complete union of the Indians and the English is achieved some day, would there be reason to celebrate Clive's exploits? Or could there be any natural enthusiasm for making expressly memorable the deeds of Outram† and other warriors of the *Mutiny*?

The poet who strung together into an epic the biographical sagas current in the country played down the theme of the subjugation of non-Aryans, magnifying instead a total ideal of the noble soul. It is perhaps wrong to say that he magnified the ideal. With changes of time and place, Ramachandra's sacred memory was adapting its own sanctity to the demands of popular piety. The poet's genius concentrated and clarified this process in one place. The devotion of the common people was thus gratified.

Since then, however, the poem has not remained stationary at the spot where the first poet installed it.

The original poet of the *Ramayana* had made Rama the embodiment of every virtue of a family-centred Hindu society. As son, brother, husband, friend, protector of brahmanical religion, and finally king, the Rama of Valmiki had demonstrated the qualities worthy of popular reverence. He did kill Ravana, but only to rescue his wife; in course of time, he abandoned her, but only to satisfy his subjects. He conducted himself ideally for preserving social order by governing all his natural instincts in strict accordance with the shastras.† The *Ramayana* could become the epic of Hindu society because Rama's character exemplified the sacrifice, forgiveness, and self-mortification demanded at every step by our civilisation which values stability above all else.

In the original *Ramayana*, the life of Rama, though touched by the supernatural, was portrayed as a model for human beings. But the supernatural cannot be confined to one place: once let in, it keeps spreading. So it was that Rama came to acquire the status of a god. Thus a further change invaded the basic tone of the *Ramayana*. We may see its evidence in the *Ramayana* of Krittibas.†

The feats accomplished by Rama do not seem arduous if we call him a deity. Hence an account of these exploits is no longer enough to glorify his character. The trait that makes a god adorable to humans now becomes dominant in the poem.

That trait is love for the faithful. The Rama of Krittibas loves and cares for his devotees. He redeems everyone, the base and the sinful. He embraces the outcaste Guhaka† as a friend. He blesses the monkeys, beasts of the forest, with his love. He fulfils Hanumana's life by imbuing it with devotion. Vibhishana becomes his follower. Even Ravana is redeemed when killed as an enemy by his hands. This *Ramayana* presents nothing but the lila† of piety.

At one time,† there was such a wave among the people of India. That the learned do not have an exclusive right to God, that there is no need for cults and rituals to reach Him, that the lowliest outcaste can win Him through simple devotion—this truth had come like a sudden revelation and released the Indian populace from an intolerable sense of inferiority. The literature that appeared when this great joy was flooding the country was a literature of this new glory acquired by the people. Ordinary mortals such as Kalketu,† Dhanapati† and Chand Sadagar† were its heroes; literature began to propagate in different ways that God belongs to the lowliest in society, not just to the brahmans and the kshatriyas, or to the eminent, the wise, and the pious. This idea is captured in Krittibas's *Ramayana* too. That God befriends even the monkeys who know no shastra and observe no ritual; that He accepts even the humblest service of the squirrel† and redeems even the sinful rakshasa by vanquishing him in just retribution—this particular notion became dominant in Krittibas and led the stream of the *Ramayana* legend in India down a special course, as the Bhagirathi† branches out from the Ganga.

The stream of the Ramayana legend that we have followed has a very recent distributary in the *Meghnadbadh Kabya*.† Even while following ancient lore, the poem has assumed a contrary character to Valmiki† or Krittibas's work.

We often say that the literature we are producing after learning English is spurious, unworthy of being considered indigenous literature at all. If we count as authentic only that which has achieved a lasting characteristic and is incapable of further change, we are not likely to find any such thing in living nature. Idea meets idea in the human world, and from their union new variations are born. There is no limit to the number of such unions that have taken place in India, and the transformations our minds have undergone. Did not the Muslims, who occupied the throne in our country not too long ago, touch our minds? Was there no natural mingling of their *Semitic* spirit with the Hindu? Muslim elements have fused with our art and literature, dress and ornament, song and melody, work and religion. This meeting of minds cannot but take place. It would indeed be shameful for us if we proved the only exceptions to this rule.

A flow of ideas has reached us from Europe, and we are naturally feeling its impact. Such buffetings have roused our mind: to deny this would be an unjust slander on our sensibilities. In time, the outcome of this meeting of ideas will take clearer shape.

Since it is true that the impact of new ideas from Europe is stirring our hearts, our literature is bound to express this truth in one new form or another, despite our best efforts to preserve our purity. By no means can the old repeat itself; if it does, I would call such literature unnatural and false.

We notice an unprecedented change not only in the metre and technique of *Meghnadbadh Kabya*, but also in its innate idea and rasa. This change is not unselfconscious: it harbours a revolt. The poet has broken the shackles of the payar[†] couplet, and has likewise dared to defy our age-old inhibitions about Rama and Ravana. Ravana and Indrajit are greater in this poem than Rama and Lakshmana. The sacrifice, penury, and self-denial of the god-fearing nature, that always measures fastidiously the good and bad in all things, did not appeal to the modern poet. He found joy in the fearsome play of instinctual power. This power is surrounded by enormous wealth; its towers impede the passage of clouds; the world trembles under its chariots and charioteers, horses and elephants; it overwhelms the gods with its temerity and holds Vayu, Agni, and Indra[†] in its thrall; it balks at neither the shastras, nor the might of weapons, nor any other impediment to its desire. The sky-high treasures amassed for so long fall to pieces and turn to dust all around it; the sons, grandsons, and kinsmen, dearer to it than life, die one by one fighting the pauper Raghava;[†] their bereaved mothers curse through their tears—yet the epic ends with a sigh at the seaside cremation ground after the fall of this colossal sacrilegous pride, this unwavering might that refuses to admit defeat in the midst of a fearsome disaster. As though secretly despising a cautious and compliant strength, the muse departs after bestowing her tear-drenched garland upon the arrogant power that spurns all submission.

The might of Europe has appeared before us today on the summit of worldly glory, with diverse weapons and unmatched wealth; its lightning-studded thunder rolls continually over our bowed heads; meanwhile, in this modern age, a new-strung chord of the *Ramayana* narrative is inwardly attuning itself to the hymn praising such power—could this have been brought about by an individual's whim? The scene was being set for it all across the country; we are forced to recognise it at each step, even if the bruised vanity of the weak makes us say we will not; hence we are unable to resist its music even while rehearsing the song of the *Ramayana*.

I have tried to show through the example of the *Ramayana* that the production of ideas in literature is a process that rests and moves over a vast space. It appears to be unexpected; so for that matter do the frequent showers this Chaitra.† But they come from a far place in the west, borne on a sequence of cause and effect, chancing upon some help here and some hindrance there, and rain down on my patch. The stream of ideas flows in the same way: through innumerable big and small causes, it disperses and changes into so many forms, passing from parts into a whole and from the whole into a hundred fragments. The greater mind of collective humanity spreads its exquisite creations through the world by expressing itself in accordance with the mind's profound and unerring law. The forms and rasas of these creations are many, and their movements diverse.

When we view the writer as too close to us, the relationship between author and work appears preponderant; we then feel as if the Gangotri† creates the Ganga. Hence I have tried to draw your attention to the innate material process powerfully at work in the creation of ideas, citing poems that seem written by untraceable hands, as though continually self-created, yet whose thread remains unbroken.

TRANSLATED BY SWAPAN CHAKRAVORTY

The Sense of Beauty

This essay makes repeated and notable use of the word mangal. *It is clearly aligned with the 'good'* (bhalo) *which Rabindranath contrasts with the 'beautiful'. But the consistent use of* mangal *suggests a wider and more active goodness than the simply moral. (See note on* mangal, *p. xiii.) Hence the word has been translated, according to context, as 'beneficence / the beneficent', and sometimes 'benign(ity)', as well as 'godness / the good'.*

The title phrase, soundaryabodh, *has been rendered as 'the sense of beauty' in general psychological contexts and as 'the aesthetic sense' in the more specific context of art.*

In early youth, one must observe brahmacharya† and build up one's life through regime and restraint—if this ancient Indian precept is cited, many will think: 'This is too severe a sadhana.† Such discipline may make a tough person, you may become a great saint by breaking the cords of desire—but where is the place in it for rasa?† Where will literature, picture, and music have gone? If you wish for fully developed human beings, you cannot afford to neglect the cultivation of beauty.'

Indeed, we do need beauty. The purpose of sadhana cannot be self-destruction; rather, its goal is the development of the self. In fact, the student's practice of brahmacharya is not a striving after aridity. The farmer does not labour to turn his land into a desert. When he breaches the soil with the plough, crushes clods with the harrow, uproots the grass and shrubs with a weeding tool until the patch is bare, the novice might think that he is torturing the land. But that is the way to make the land fruitful. Likewise, rigorous tilling is needed initially if one wishes to be truly eligible to imbibe the rasas. The path leading to rasa is strewn with many distractions. One who wants to avoid the perils on the way and achieve fulfilment needs regime and restraint all the more. One must accept such desiccation for the sake of rasa.

Unfortunately, human purpose is often stifled by the pretext. One wishes to learn music, but ends up acquiring mere virtuosity; one wants to be rich, but becomes pitiable by amassing money; one desires the good of the country, but feels smug by simply passing *resolutions* in a *committee.*

Similarly, we often see that regime and restraint have entirely replaced their ultimate purpose. Those who consider the rigour itself a gain and an act of piety become altogether covetous of rigour. The greed for rigour becomes a seventh enemy of the human state in addition to the original six.†

This is a symptom of human inertia. Once people start accumulating, they do not want to stop. We hear of people in Britain who collect cancelled postage stamps from home and abroad like maniacs, sparing no pain or cost. Crazed by this obsession with accumulation, some wear themselves out collecting china; others, old shoes. The urge to plant a flag anyhow at the exact centre of the North Pole is a similar sort of thing. There is nothing there except tracts of snow; but that does not dissuade the mind: people are obsessed with calculating who came within how many miles of the centre of that polar desert. Mountaineers count their gain by the number of feet each is able to climb. To achieve this hollow gain, they are killing themselves and forcing unwilling porters to their deaths; yet they do not wish to stop.

The more the waste and the hardship, the greater seems the glory of useless accumulation and fruitless conquest. The lust for rigour too feels pleasure in proportion to the degree of hardship. One might start with sleeping on a hard bed; one then grows greedier and longs to sleep on a mattress on the ground, then on a single rug, and at last on the bare floor. Once the practice of austerity is reckoned a pleasure, there is no stopping till one destroys oneself. This is nothing but to turn self-denial into a fierce appetite, to strangle oneself in the effort to tear off the noose.

Thus, if one can turn regimen into an object of desire, one can doubtless squeeze away the sense of beauty from one's nature by piling on the weight of austerity. But if we can restrain the practice of restraint itself with an eye to achieving fullness of development, every ingredient of true humaneness will be enriched and none depleted.

The fact is that a foundation is naturally hard or else nothing can rest on it. Whatever forms a base or gives shape has to be firm. The human body, no matter how soft, would be a mere lump and lack clear shape without its framework of bones. Equally hard are the foundations of knowledge and of joy. If its base were not firm, knowledge would have been a fanciful dream; if its foundation were not strong, joy would have been just crazy intoxication.

Restraint is nothing but this hard foundation. It entails judgment, strength, and sacrifice; there is in it an unrelenting firmness. Like a god, it bestows boons with one hand and destroys with the other. This restraint is as resolute in building up as it is unyielding in destruction. It is necessary if one wants to enjoy beauty to the full; or else, if the instincts are unbridled, our plight with objects of enjoyment is like the child's who grabs food from his plate, but achieves the opposite of what he desires—very little of the food reaches his stomach, while the rest is spattered over his body or strewn on the floor. In the same way, we smear our bodies with the objects of our desire, but profit little from it.

The creation of beauty too is beyond the means of an intemperate imagination. No one lights an evening lamp by setting the whole house on fire. One has to have mastery over fire because it goes out of control at the slightest opportunity. The same applies to our appetites. If we let any of them flare up to the full, it burns beauty to cinders when it is required merely to set it aglow. In trying to pick a flower, it tears it to shreds and flings it in the dust.

It is true that when our hungry impulses lay out their feast, beauty usually has a welcome ready close by. A fruit does not merely satisfy our hunger: it is beautiful in taste, smell, and appearance. Had it not been so at all, we would still have eaten it to fill our bellies. But in spite of such an enormous compulsion, the fruit still delights us aesthetically as well. It is a gain that exceeds our need.

This surplus gain called beauty that we obtain from the world—which way does it lead our minds? We notice that beauty strives to ensure that the urge to satisfy hunger does not hold power like a sole god over us, to see that its stranglehold over our minds is somewhat eased. Hunger, like the fiery raging goddess,† commands, 'You must eat. That's the last word.' At once, the gracious goddess of beauty hides the glare of over-importunate need with her honeyed smile, preparing a joyous feast in the upper quarters and confining the belly's gnawing to the lower. There is something about inescapable need that demeans human dignity. But beauty, one gathers, is always ahead of need; hence it dispels such indignity. It is because beauty is always adding a higher note to the satisfaction of our appetites that those who were unrestrained barbarians once are today humanised—one who had recognised only the appeal of the senses now comes under love's sway. Today we cannot, even if we are famished, sit down like beasts or demons to eat just anyhow; we lose the urge to eat if we cannot observe a modicum of civility. Thus hunger is no longer our sole urge; it has been softened by decorum. We try to shame a child by saying, 'Shame on you, does one eat in that greedy way?' That kind of eating is ugly to the view. It is beauty that disciplines our appetites, establishes ties of joy with the world in place of those of mere necessity. In ties of need are our poverty and servitude; in ties of joy lies our freedom.

Thus we see that beauty ultimately draws human beings towards restraint. It offers them an elixir which, when drunk, increasingly enables them to quell the rudeness of appetite. One who revolts at the idea of rejecting unrestraint as evil, freely wishes to renounce it as ugly.

Just as beauty gradually draws us towards decorum and restraint, restraint deepens our enjoyment of beauty. We cannot extract the joyous essence from the heart of beauty unless we learn to be still in contemplation. It is the chaste wife steadfastly devoted to her husband, and not the wanton, who can realise the true beauty of love. Chastity is the serene restraint that enables one to reach love's innermost essence. What happens if we do not have the same chaste restraint in our love of beauty? It keeps hovering restlessly around the outer pale of beauty and mistakes inebriation for joy; it never obtains that which, if acquired, would have let it rest in peace, forsaking everything else. True beauty is perceived only by the absorbed votary, not by the lustful epicure. The glutton is never a good judge of food.

King Paushya told Utanka,† the sage's son: 'Go to the inner quarters: you will see the queen.' Utanka went inside, but failed to see her. A defiled person could not behold the chaste woman, and Utanka was then unclean.

The chaste beneficent goddess dwelling in the inner quarters of all the world's beauty and splendour is ever present before us, but we cannot see her if we are unclean. When we wallow in luxury or giddily chase sensory delights, the world's chaste goddess, clad in light, disappears from our sight.

I do not say this to preach moral principles: I speak on behalf of joy, what in English is called *art.* Our shastras too instruct us: practise self-control not for the sake of piety alone, but also for the sake of happiness: *Sukharthi samyato bhavet.*† That is, if you want your desire fulfilled, keep it in check; if you want to enjoy beauty, be calm by quelling the lust of your appetite and purifying yourself. If one does not know how to subdue one's appetite, one will mistake its gratification for that of the aesthetic sense; what is a thing of the mind, one will crush with one's hands and think one has possessed it. That is why I said the practice of brahmacharya is necessary for a proper arousal of the aesthetic sense.

Those not easily fooled will instantly grow suspicious and exclaim,

'Why, this is an invasion of pure poeticism!' They will say, 'We often see in this world that gifted and skilled creators of beauty were no models of temperance. Their biographies are not fit to read. We must set poeticism aside and consider this material truth.'

My point is, why do we trust reality so much? It is because of its perceivable presence. But in many cases, much of what we declare as the reality about human beings is inaccessible to our perception. We feel we have seen the whole because we see a small part; thus, in accounts of reality concerning human beings, what one calls white another might call black, though we might have been relieved if the latter had at least called it grey. Some call Napoleon a god, others a demon. Some say Akbar was a liberal and benevolent ruler; others claim that he was the root of every evil that plagued his Hindu subjects. Some argue that the caste system has preserved Hindu society; others blame it for our ruin. Yet both sides speak in the name of material truth.

In fact, in matters relating to human beings we see contrary things in one and the same instance. The contrasts expressed in the part visible to us must surely be resolved, in a mysterious way, in the part that is hidden. Thus it is not as if the real truth is floating atop the visible; rather, it is submerged in the invisible. That is why there are so many disputes and factions over it and rival parties swear by the same events in history.

When we see similar contrarieties in the world's gifted artists, we cannot abruptly say something perverse on the plea of material truth. To say that beauty is created out of weakness, restiveness, and unrestraint is to make a glaringly discrepant statement. Even if material truth were to bear witness in its favour, we would say, 'Surely all the witnesses have not been brought forward; the key witness must have slipped away.' If we see a bunch of bandits prosper, we cannot appeal to material truth to argue that robbery is the route to prosperity. One can say, without having to adduce proof, such prosperity as we see among robbers for the moment is chiefly owing to their unity, that is, their keeping of mutual faith. Again, when this prosperity wanes, we will not call their unity its cause; we will rather say that their wickedness towards others is the cause of their decline. If we see that the same man has frittered away in self-indulgence a fortune that he had earned in trade, we will not say that those who waste money are the ones who know how to make it; rather, we will say that the man was prudent in earning money, his restraint and acumen then were greater than in an ordinary man; but at the time of spending, his wasteful propensity got the better of his provident wisdom.

Artists, in so far as they are really talented, are ascetics: in that sphere, wilfulness will not work; there must be discipline and temperance of the mind. Few people are so entirely strong that they can put their moral sense to full use. One always deviates in some degree. That is because we are all progressing from deficiency to fullness; we have not reached the final resting point. But whatever lasting and significant thing we build up in life, we do with the help of our inward sense of rectitude, not our deviancy. So too, talented artists have displayed their character in their artistic creations; they have expressed deficiency of character in destroying their lives. They have suffered by letting their depraved impulses† draw them contrary to the beautiful ideal of rectitude in their minds. Restraint is needed to build, intemperance to destroy. One needs restraint to comprehend, intemperance to misconstrue.

An objection will be raised at this point: 'Aesthetic ability and intemperance of character can then coexist and ripen within the same person. So we see that the tiger and the cow can drink at the same watering-hole.'†

Truly, the tiger and the cow do not drink together. But when is it true? When the tiger is fully grown and the cow too is fully a cow. The two can play together in their infancy. Once they grow up, the tiger pounces on the cow, and the cow tries to run away.

In the same way, the truly mature state of the aesthetic sense can never survive alongside a restive appetite and an unruly mind. The two states are inimical to each other.

There is a reason, if you want to know why. Vishvamitra† quarrelled with the Creator and constructed another universe. It was a creation of his anger and pride. Hence that universe could not be reconciled to God's; instead, it insolently assaulted God's world. It thus remained an aberration and an anomaly that could not tune itself to the universe, and finally perished after inflicting and suffering much torment.

When one's appetite grows too insistent, it seems to create in the teeth of God's created world. It then becomes incompatible with its surroundings. Our belligerence and avarice produce such aberrations around us that the petty is magnified and the great shrinks into smallness; the ephemeral appears enduring and the abiding eludes our sight. What we covet, we magnify so falsely that it overshadows the world's great truths, obscuring the sun, the moon, and the stars. Our creation thereby enters into conflict with the Creator.

Imagine a flowing river. Each of its ripples may rear its crest separately, but they sing in unison all the way to the sea: not one of them impedes another. But if the water eddies at a point, it keeps madly circling the same spot, trying to drown everything by impeding progress. By obstructing the course and aim of the whole river, it can achieve neither stability nor progress.

When an appetite goes berserk, it too drags one away from the flow of the universe and makes one whirl around the same spot. Trapped within the confines of that vortex, one's mind wants to cast all it has into it and destroy everything belonging to others. Some people find a sort of beauty in that madness. As a matter of fact, it seems to me that European literature has taken greatest delight in this all-destroying round dance of whirling appetite, with no conclusion and no rest. We cannot call this the culmination of education: it is a perversion of human nature. What might appear delightful on a casual glance within narrow confines, strikes us as aesthetically anomalous when seen against the wider universe. The drunkard forgets the world at his tippling den and mistakes it for a celestial palace, but the sober onlooker perceives its hideousness by comparing it to the world around. One's appetite may acquire an unnatural lustre when it becomes importunate, but one does not take long to see its deformity once it is held up against the great world. One who does not know how to compare the great with the small, the whole with its individual members in this composed manner will mistake excitement for joy and distortion for beauty. That is why, to acquire the sense of beauty fully, one needs peace of mind: intemperance will never achieve that.

Let us see which way the perfection of the sense of beauty leads us.

It has been seen that a civilised race flings away what an uncivilised one adores as beautiful. The main reason for this is that the civilised mind is not limited to the space within which the barbarian's mind ranges. Outside and within, in space and in time, the very world of a civilised race is large and its components extremely diverse. Hence the magnitude and weight of things can never be the same in the world of the barbarian and the world of the civilised.

A man ignorant of art is pleased merely on seeing a quantity of bright colours and rounded shapes on a canvas. He does not see the picture in a wider context. There is no higher discrimination to bridle his senses, and he yields to whatever appeals at first sight. He is overwhelmed by the beard and livery of the porter at the palace gate and takes him for the most important person; he does not feel the need to cross the gates and enter the court. But a man who is less of a rustic is not so easily impressed. He knows that the porter's glory strikes the eye excessively of a sudden, because the porter has no glory beyond the visible. But the king's glory is not merely something one sees, it has to be perceived with the mind as well. That is why there is a strength, serenity and solemnity in the king's majesty.

The connoisseur, therefore, is not overwhelmed by the excess of colour in a picture. He looks for a harmony between major and minor, centre and periphery, foreground and background. The eye is beguiled by gaudy colours, but one needs the mind to discern the beauty of harmony. One must look deep for it; hence its pleasure is deeper.

That is why we find many artists ignoring small outer graces; their compositions seem to have a certain severity. Their dhrupad is shorn of the taans of khayal.† The vulgar want to avoid it because of its unadorned exterior, yet the deeper riches of its pristine sparseness afford greater pleasure to distinguished minds.

Thus we see that the eye is not enough: beauty cannot be seen in a broader light unless the mind's vision is added to it. One needs special training to acquire this mind's eye.

The mind, again, has many levels. What we see with reason alone acquires a farther dimension if we bring our affective dispositions to it; the addition of the moral sense makes us see farther; and if the spiritual eyes are opened, the field of our vision has no limits.

Hence the seeing that engages the greater part of our mind gives us greater pleasure. The human face attracts one more than the beauty of a flower, because the former has, besides grace of form, the glow of consciousness, the vivacity of the intellect, the comeliness of the heart: it takes hold of one's consciousness, intellect and heart, and is not easily exhausted.

Again, the most excellent of human beings, those who manifest the benevolent divine self on earth, draw our minds so far that we ourselves cannot measure the reach. That is why the loveliness of the prince who left his kingdom† to devise means of relieving human suffering continues to inspire endless poems and pictures.

Sceptics will say at this point, 'You started out with beauty, now you stray into ethics! Why mix up the two? The good is good; the beautiful, beautiful. The good draws our mind in one way; the beautiful, in another. They differ in the manner in which they attract us—that is why they are given different names. We are moved by the utility of the good, while we are not sure why the beautiful moves us.'

I wish to make a point here. We do not express the whole truth about the benign if we say it is called good because it benefits us. The truly benign serves our need and it is beautiful: that is, it has an unaccountable attraction that surpasses its use. Experts in ethics try to propagate the benign through moral counsel from the standpoint of its benefit to the world; poets reveal the benign to the world in its ineffably beauteous form.

In fact, the benign is beautiful not because it is of use. Rice serves our need, so do clothes, umbrellas, and shoes: yet rice and clothes, umbrellas and shoes do not infuse our minds with the thrill of beauty. But the news that Lakshmana has accompanied Rama to the forest strikes a chord in our minds, like music struck on the veena. It is something to preserve for ever, adorned in beautiful language and metre. I do not say so because society benefits if the younger brother serves the elder, but because there is beauty in it. Why? Because whatever is beneficent is in deepest unison with the whole world, in secret harmony with the mind of all humanity. When we see this absolute accord of the true and the beneficent, the beauty of truth no longer eludes our perception. Compassion is beautiful; so are forgiveness and love. They bear comparison with the hundred-petalled lotus and the full moon. Like the hundred-petalled lotus and the full moon, they are in unassailed harmony within themselves and with the world around them: they are favourably disposed to the world and the world is propitious to them. In our puranas, Lakshmi is the goddess of not only beauty and riches, but also beneficence. The image of beauty is the fullest manifestation of the good, and the image of the good the consummate self of beauty.

Let us consider the space in which the beautiful agrees with the good.

We have shown at the outset that beauty exceeds what is necessary. That is why we recognise it as wealth. That is also why it delivers us into the freedom of love from the indigence of merely serving our selfish needs.

In goodness, too, we discover that wealth. When we see a brave man abandon his self-interest or sacrifice his life for the sake of moral principle, we witness a marvel that is greater than our pain and pleasure, larger than our self-interest, nobler than our lives. By virtue of this wealth, goodness does not count loss as loss or stress as stress. It remains unhurt by any injury to self-interest. That is why goodness as much as beauty induces us to willing sacrifice. Beauty expresses God's plenty in all the world's functions; goodness does the same in human life. Goodness has made beauty more than something to be seen with the eye or understood with the intellect; it has rendered beauty, for humanity, as something deeper and more far-reaching: it has turned divine things into intensely human possessions. In fact, the good is the beauty innermost and closest to humankind:

that is why we often cannot readily recognise it as beautiful, although our hearts well up like monsoon rivers when we do. Then there is nothing that appears to us more lovely.

It is well if you can lay out the feast with leaves and flowers, strings of lamps, and plates of gold and silver; but the guest will find no savour in all that wealth and beauty if there is a lack of welcome and cordiality in the host—for in such cordiality lies the wealth and abundance of the heart. The sweet smiles, sweet words, and sweet manners of cordiality are of such beauty that they turn the plantain leaf† into something more precious than a golden platter. I cannot say that this is true of everyone. We find many people who will swallow insults to gain admittance to an ostentatious feast. Why? Because such a person does not realise the greater significance, the larger beauty of the feast. As a matter of fact, neither the food nor the decoration is the vital aspect of a feast. The strength of the selfish is for ever folded inward, like the petals of a bud. The moment you loosen its knots and turn it outwards, it exfoliates to the universe in utmost beauty, full of the sweetness of union. The person who cannot see the deeper benign beauty at the heart of the ceremony treats the abundance of food and drink and the opulent embellishments as greater matters. Intemperate appetite and excessive greed for food and drink, gifts and fees, hide from such a person the generous sweetness of the feast.

The shastras say, *Shaktasya bhushanam kshama*: Forgiveness is the ornament of the powerful.† But not everyone can appreciate the beauty of strength expressed in forgiveness. On the contrary, the dull and the vulgar revere power when it is a menace. Modesty is the woman's adornment. But who discerns this beauty of modesty rather than of clothes and ornaments? That person who does not take a straitened view of beauty. One must have a broad view from a height in order to see the generous beauty of that larger epiphany within which the ripples of more straitened expressions are calmed. For that, one needs training, seriousness, and peace of mind.

Our ancient poets never felt constrained in describing the beauty of a woman with child. European poets feel a certain inhibition and privation in this matter. Indeed there is not much to feast the eyes in the beauty of a pregnant woman. When the highest fulfilment of womanhood is imminent, the wait for it invests the female form with glory. What that form lacks by way of visual pleasure is more than compensated by the reverence it evokes in the mind. When the setting sun touches the airy cloud of early autumn, drifting idly without care or cause after the last showers are shed, the eye is dazzled by a burst of colour. But the dense cloud of Asharh,[†] weighed down, like a black milch cow, by imminent rain—the cloud in whose amassed moisture there is no restiveness of shifting colours, embraces our mind in a dense clasp that leaves no void anywhere. Its soothing darkness is spread with the liberal promise of cooling the heated earth, relieving the impoverished farmlands and restoring the lean rivers and lakes: it is silent with the sublime tenderness of a ripe beneficence. Kalidas could have employed the spring breeze for the pining Yaksha's[†] embassy of love. It is reputed to be skilled in that task: moreover, the south wind would not have had to sail upstream in order to head north. But the poet has preferred the new cloud of early Asharh. It cools the heat-oppressed earth—would it then merely babble the lover's message in the beloved's ear? Rather, as it went, it would infuse the rivers, mountains, and forests on its way with its various perfection. The kadamba tree would bloom, rose-apple groves would fill with fruit, herons would fly along, the brimming river would lap against the clumps of cane on its bank, and the monsoon sky would be made more replete by the glance of the country bride whose artless eyes are tender with love. The poet's heart, thirsting for beauty's rasa, is satisfied only by linking the lover's embassy at every step with the world's benign operations.

The poet of *Kumarasambhavam*[†] does not set the final union of Shiva and Parvati amidst the enchantment of floral darts showered at the sudden advent of an untimely spring. With the waters of peace,[†] he first quenches the destructive blaze that flared up at the heady encounter of man and woman: only then can he set the scene for union. The poet has shown the loveliest image of Gauri's love as illumined by the flame of ascesis. Spring's wealth of flowers pales before it, and the koel's chatter is stilled. In *Abhijnanashakuntalam*[†] too, the union of the royal couple becomes meaningful when the beloved becomes a mother, when the restiveness of desire has attained solemnity through the ascesis of suffering, and when forgiveness is joined to remorse. The first union spells disaster; the second, deliverance. In both poems, whenever the poet has shown the perfection of beauty in peace and beneficence, his brush is sparse in colour, his veena unfrenzied.

In fact, wherever beauty has achieved fulfilment, it has shed its volubility. There the flower has transformed its excess of colour and fragrance into the profounder sweetness of the fruit: in that fruition, beauty becomes one with beneficence.

One who has witnessed this union of beauty and beneficence can never confuse beauty with indulgence. The ingredients of one's life are then usually simple—not because one lacks a sense of beauty, but because one has it in abundance. Where was Ashoka's garden of pleasure? We see no trace of it in his palace. But the stupas[†] and pillars[†] erected by him stand at the foot of the bodhi tree in Bodh Gaya.[†] Their craftsmanship is of no ordinary kind. The holy spot where the divine Budha discovered the way to assuage human suffering—there it was, at that memorial-place of supreme beneficence, that the emperor Ashoka installed the beauty of art. He did not bring to his own indulgences the same kind of worshipful offering. In India, we find so many shrines and holy monuments of great artistic beauty on remote mountaintops and lonely seashores; but where are the remains of the pleasure palaces of the Hindu kings? Why did they leave the capital to install such beauty in forests and mountains? There is indeed a reason. By its own creations of beauty, humanity in such instances has actually expressed its enraptured devotion for that which is greater than itself. Beauty created by human beings salutes with raised arms a beauty superior to itself; it silently propagates with all its nobility that which is nobler than itself. Through that silent speech replete with art, human beings have said, 'Look, behold with open eyes Him who is beautiful and great.' They have never said, 'See, what a mighty epicure I am.' Or, 'Cast your eyes on the place I walked on when I lived, and see my glory also in the spot where, once dead, I have mingled with the earth.' I do not know if the ancient Hindu rulers decorated their houses of pleasure elaborately, but this much is certain that the Hindu race has not prized and preserved them: such houses have crumbled to dust with those whose glory they were built to proclaim. But where human power and piety have found blessedness by installing its creations of beauty at the left hand of God's benign image, those temples of union we have tried to preserve even in the remotest places. Beauty's perfect union is with beneficence, Lakshmi's with Vishnu.[†] This idea is latent in all civilisations. Surely the day will come when beauty shall not be constrained by personal interest, nor stabbed by envy, nor corroded through self-indulgence—when it will unfold in joy and purity amidst peace and benignity. We do not see beauty whole unless we see it free of our desire and greed. What we see with our untrained, unrestrained, partial vision excites rather than slakes our thirst: it does not nourish us with food, and moreover destroys wholesome appetite by plying us with drink.

It is out of this fear that moral preachers advise us to salute beauty from a distance. They forbid us to set foot on the path of profit lest we suffer loss. But the true precept is this: we must practise restraint to acquire a full claim on beauty. That, and not aridity, is the goal of brahmacharya.

Since we have broached the subject of sadhana, the question may be asked: what is the fruit of this self-culture? Where does it culminate? We can understand the purpose of our other faculties of work and knowledge, but why has the aesthetic sense found a place in our minds?

To answer the question, we must briefly examine once more where the path of the aesthetic sense leads us.

When the aesthetic consciousness takes the help of our senses alone, what we apprehend as the beautiful is very clear: it strikes our eyes at a glance. The conflict between the beautiful on one side and the ugly on the other is, at this stage, precisely defined before us. The difference between the two recedes once the intellect comes to assist the aesthetic sense. What then engages our minds may not seem worthy of notice as soon as we set our eyes on it. When we derive pleasure by seeing the deeper concord of the beginning with the end, the major with the minor, one part with another, we no longer accept servitude to the beauty that beguiles the eye. Once the ethical sense joins the aesthetic, our minds' jurisdiction extends further, and the conflict between the beautiful and the ugly is at an end. The chaste and good wife then appears to us as beautiful, not the woman who is merely good-looking. Where patience and courage, forgiveness and love shed light, there we feel no need for the display and dazzle of colour. In *Kumarasambhavam*, the disguised Shiva vilifies his own looks, virtues, age, and fortunes to Uma in her ascetic meditation.[†] She replies, '*Mamatra bhavaikarasam manahsthitam*: My mind is disposed towards him only in the rasa of the mental state.' Joy, that is to say, needs no other ingredient. The conceptual rasa makes the stern divorce between the beautiful and the ugly recede far away.

But there is a conflict within goodness as well. The ethical sense entails a clash of good and evil. But nothing can finally end in such conflict: there can only be one conclusion and no more. The river needs both its banks as long as it flows, but at the end of its journey there is only the shoreless sea. In the flow, there is conflict; in the end, the resolution of that conflict. One needs to rub two sticks of wood to light a fire, but the friction stops once the flame is lit. In like manner, one's aesthetic sense would cease to be fragmentary and restless if it once lit up fully, after scattering sparks from the friction of what is agreeable and disagreeable to the senses, of the benign and the malefic in one's life.

What follows then? Contradictions are resolved and everything turns beautiful: truth and beauty are then one and the same thing. Only then do we see that every genuine realisation of truth is in itself joy and the highest beauty.

Where does one find the savour of truth in this fleeting world? Where one's mind can engage itself. People pass down the street—they are shadows to one: one does not find joy in them because one only apprehends them dimly. But the truth of a friend is a profound truth and a refuge for the mind; the friend gives one happiness in proportion to that truth. The people of a land that to me is a mere name in geography give up their lives for their country. They can sacrifice their lives because they know their country as intensely true. The study that is a nightmare to the ignorant is to the learned a thing of supreme joy with which one happily spends one's life. Thus we see that we find joy wherever we apprehend truth. The lack of joy is nothing but the incomplete apprehesion of truth. A truth which offers us no joy is merely known, not possessed. My love and joy dwell in that truth which to me is exceedingly true.

Once we understand the matter in this way, the apprehension of truth and that of beauty become one.

Knowingly or unknowingly, all literature, music, and the fine arts are moving in this direction. Human beings have illuminated every truth and only the truth in their poetry, painting and art. The poet brings before our eyes what was earlier untrue to us because it had escaped our notice; he thereby extends the frontiers of our realm of truth and joy. Each day, literature reveals all that is small and neglected, clad in the glory of truth and stamped with the beauty of art. It makes a friend of one who was a mere acquaintance, and draws the mind to that which merely struck the eye.

The modern poet has said, '*Truth is beauty, beauty truth.*'† Our goddess Sarasvati, clad in white and seated on a lotus, embodies both *Truth* and *Beauty*. The Upanishad too talks of *anandarupamamritam yadvibhati* [the being that shines forth in joyous and immortal form]:† whatever is manifested in His aspect of joy and immortality. From the dust beneath our feet to the stars in the sky, all is *truth* and *beauty*, all is *anandarupamamritam* [joyous and immortal in form].

The aim of poetry is to see the joyous and immortal face of truth and express that joy. We can express truth in literature only when we receive it with the heart, not when we see it with the eye or grasp it with the intellect. Is literature, then, only a discovery made by the heart, not a creation of craftsmanship? Creativity does have a role in it. The heart with its own wealth inscribes the wonder and joy of its discovery in language or sound or colour: herein lies creative skill, and this is literature, music, painting.

Standing amidst the sandy expanse of the desert, human beings have inscribed it with the exclamation-mark of two pyramids as a sign of wonder. They have marked the shores of a deserted island by carving rock-caves of great artistry, as if to say, 'This has made my heart glad': the Elephanta† caves in Mumbai are that mark. Facing east, they saw the glory of the sun rising from the sea, on which they left the impress of their hands joined in prayer by hauling stones over hundred of miles: that impress is the temple at Konarka.† Humanity has left its stamp on whatever has helped it experience truth intensely, that is as joyous and immortal. That mark is sometimes a statue and sometimes a temple, now a place of pilgrimage, now a capital city. Literature too is a mark. Through language, the human heart tries to pave every waterfront it touches in the world and to turn it into a lasting place of pilgrimage. In this way, it makes every place along the world's shores fit for the pilgrim heart to land at and use. In water, land and sky, in autumn, spring and rain, in piety, work and history, it constantly inscribes its exquisite traces and thus invites each human heart to the beauteous image of truth. Across nations and down the ages, this mark and this invitation are continually extending their reach. We cannot even imagine how constricted our world would have remained if humanity had not left its heart's imprint everywhere through literature. That this world of the eye and the ear has, to a great extent, become today a world of the heart is largely because the literature of humanity has adorned it with the signs of the heart's discoveries.

There are other disciplines to tell us that truth is an equilibrium of the stasis and movement of a mass of matter, or that it is a chain of cause and effect. Literature tells us that truth is joy and the elixir of immortality. Literature is for ever elucidating the mantra of the Upanishad:

Raso vai sah. Rasam hyevayam labdhvanandibhavati.

He indeed is rasa; this rasa it is that makes humankind feel joy.†

TRANSLATED BY SWAPAN CHAKRAVORTY

Bengali National Literature

The word *sahitya* [literature] comes from *sahit* [together]. Hence, if we take into account its etymological sense, we find in the word *sahitya* the idea of a union. It is not simply a union of idea and idea, language and language, book and book: nothing except *sahitya* or literature can establish deeply intimate ties between one person and another, between past and present, between far and near. The people of a country deficient in literature have no vital bonds to join them: they remain isolated.

They have no living ties with their ancestors either. The ties of inert custom, passed on by tradition, are no ties: they are mere fetters. It is impossible to preserve a conscious mental kinship with one's forefathers without the continuity afforded by literature.

We have in our country ties of convention linking past and present; yet somewhere within us, a vital artery has been so ruptured that the vital juice of the mind cannot flow to our times in a continuous stream from the past. We have no thorough knowledge of how our ancestors thought, worked, and fashioned new conceptions; how their vital and mental powers, awake at the heart of all their shruti, smriti, puranas,† poetry, theology, politics, and social order, devised and regulated everything; how society grew and changed daily; how it expanded on every side and assimilated changes. How do we bridge the infinite chasm between the age of the *Mahabharata* and our own? When we are overcome with wonder by the architecture and sculpture at Bhubaneshwar and Konarka,† we wonder if these amazing feats of craftsmanship surfaced like stone bubbles at some accidental upheaval in the outside world. Where lies the link between those artists and us? Those who had created such sky-topping beauty with so much love, patience, and skill; and we who watch with callous, half-shut eyes the stones tumble down one by one from these world-beguiling monuments, and neither can nor will restore them to their proper places—what dire calamity divides us, so that the works of the past should appear enigmas to the present? Who was it that tore out several pages midway through our national chronicle, so that we cannot make sense of ourselves in the light of our past? We still have laws, but not the law-giver; there are no artists, but the land is thick with evidence of their artistic skill. We live among the ruins of a derelict capital; we smear mud and dung where the bricks fall off, ignorant of the mysterious art of building a city.

We are so cut off from our ancient forebears that we have lost even the ability to realise our distance from them. We think that the difference between ancient India and the present times is simply that between old and new. What was once bright is now tarnished, what was firm now slack; that is to say, if someone gave us a gold-wash to put a little gloss back into us, the India of yore would return incarnate. We imagine that the ancient Hindus, far from being flesh-and-blood people, were merely animated verses of the shastras,† that they treated the world as illusion and spent all day in prayer and meditation. That they fought battles, maintained kingdoms, practised the arts, cultivated poetry, and traded across the seas; that there was the encounter of good and evil among them, that there was judgment and rebellion, and variety of opinion—in short, that there was life: these are things we know but cannot deeply feel. The moment we try to image ancient India, the old brahman in the new almanac,† whose picture accompanies the last date of each month, springs to our minds.

One of the main reasons for this extreme distance is that the vital and intellectual stream of literature has not flown uninterruptedly from those days to the present. The literary works that we possess are detached and far-flung. The currents of thought, ideas, and life from the original Ganga† of those times have dried up, leaving only sporadic pools along its course. These are not nourished by some flowing primordial stream; how much in them is ancient water, and how much the rain-puddles left by recent popular convention, is hard to tell. We can no longer sail down the literary stream from the present to the past, riding the enormous, powerful, dynamic, and vital tide of Hinduism, which runs in many directions and builds up its banks. We now dig ponds at various spots along the dry stretch to suit our individual tastes and needs, and call them Hinduism. These confined, meagre, and isolated Hinduisms are our private possessions; one of them may be mine, another yours; but they are hardly the undivided, vast, and surging torrent that was the Hinduism of Kanva and Kanad, of Raghava and Kaurava, of Nanda and Upananda,† and of our common people.

The vital links between our past and present have been snapped because of this paucity of literature. A major reason for this paucity is the absence of national ties. In our country, Kanauj, Koshal, Kashi, and Kanchi† have all gone their own separate ways; nor did they desist from destroying one another occasionally by letting loose the horse of the ashvamedha sacrifice.† The Indraprastha† of the *Mahabharata*, the Kashmir of *Rajtarangini*,† the Magadha of the Nandas† and the Ujjayini of Vikramaditya† were not joined by a running strand of national history. Hence our national literature could not establish a firm foundation upon the collective heart of the nation. In disjunct regions and times, under the patronage of discerning monarchs, particular writers independently left their marks. Kalidasa† belongs only to Vikramaditya, Chandvardi to Prithviraj,† Chanakya to Chandragupta.† They did not belong to the entire India of their times; even within their respective regions, there are no links connecting them to earlier and later periods.

Only when literature builds its warm and secure nest in the collective heart of the nation can it perpetuate its kind and extend itself uninterruptedly and far. That is why I said at the beginning that *sahitatwa* or union is the main ingredient of sahitya; it unites the isolated, and installs itself wherever it finds union. An extensive literature can never be born where one person is separated from others, one time from other times, and one village from other villages. What is it that can unite a great many people in our country? Religion. Thus in our country we have only religious literature. For the same reason, ancient Bengali literature is a collection of Shakta† and Vaishnava† poetry. The glory of valour unified the Rajputs; hence their poets sung the praise of valour.

Even within this little land of Bengal, the winds of a common literature have begun to blow. It started with the preaching of religion. The first ones among us to learn English did so chiefly in the hope of preferment from our mercantile English rulers; their learning, geared to moneymaking, was of no use to the common people. No one had then thought of uniting the people through a common education: men of accomplishment were busy making their own separate ways in the world.

It was the Christian missionaries who first felt a lack of means to propagate their message to the people of Bengal; so they set about developing the language of the common people to impart education and disseminate knowledge.

But this was not a task that could be achieved entirely by foreigners. Raja Rammohan Ray,† the creator of modern Bengal, was in fact the first to lay the ground of Bengali prose.

Before him, our literature had been restricted to verse. But verse was not adequate for Rammohan Ray's purpose. The language of sensibility and beauty, the idiom of the connoisseur of the rasas, was not enough; the language of reason and statement, a language that could discourse on all matters to all people, was what he needed. Till then, there had existed only poetry for gatherings of contemplatives; there now appeared prose for the concourse of the people. Without such conjunction of prose and poetry, no literature can achieve fullness. The royal court of the empress Sarasvati[†] is unsuited for all her subjects unless it contains two halls,[†] the private and the public. Rammohan Ray came and, with his own hands, threw open the portals of Sarasvati's public court.

We speak prose from infancy, but we realise what a difficult thing it is only when we read our earliest prose writers. In verse, there is a pause for rest at the end of each line; after every couplet or quatrain, there is a regular break in thought. But in prose, one line has to be linked to the next: there is no way of leaving a gap. The subject, object, and verb within a sentence, as also the sentences themselves, must be so arranged as to bring out closely the intricate logical links between the beginning, middle, and end of an essay. Metre has its own inescapable drift. Once cast in its midst, the poem floats along as in a dance; but in prose, one has to find one's own way, walk on one's own feet, and keep one's balance. If this ambulatory art is not properly practised, one's steps are crooked, irregular, and unsteady. We have grown accustomed to the codified rule of prose, but this was not so even in the recent past.

In those days, not only was it difficult to write prose, people could not easily follow a prose essay because they were not used to it. We see that just as there was only water in the earliest phase of the earth, there was only the flowing and rippling rhythm of verse in the earliest phase of literature everywhere. I feel that in verse, the short lines, the regular pauses in thought, and the music of metre and rhyme imprint the words rapidly in the mind, so that listeners can quickly make sense of them. But to follow a substantial piece of prose, unregulated by metre, demands a special mental effort in threading together sentences and passages and following their course. That is why, when Rammohan Ray undertook to translate the *Vedantasutra*[†] into Bengali, he felt it necessary to explain in a Preface the principles for comprehending prose. I would like to quote the relevant passage:

> Till today, no shastra or poetry has been discussed in prose in this language. Many people in our country cannot readily grasp the sense of a piece of prose by connecting two or three sentences, since they are unused to the exercise. We feel this vividly when trying to understand the translation of a legal text.

He then proceeds to advise readers on what needs to be done in order to understand prose:

One should consider in particular the beginning and end of sentences. Whenever words such as *when, which, as,* are used, finish the sentence by joining these antecedents† with the corresponding words *then, that, so,* etc. Do not try to make sense of the sentence, thinking it closed, until you find the verb.

The puranas and history tell us that when a royal guest arrived unexpectedly in the forest retreats of the sages, they produced meat and wine by their yogic powers to entertain the king and his retainers. We can easily see that the sages had to employ the magic gifts of ascesis since there was no shop or market close by, and since myrobalan served on sal leaves does not make for a royal repast. Rammohan Ray faced a situation equally unready: there was neither prose nor the ability to understand it. What gift did Rammohan offer his readers in those primitive days, when one had to be taught to read prose by connecting the beginning to the end and the subject to the verb? He presented them with translations of abstruse texts such as the *Vedantasara,*† the *Brahmasutra,*† and the Upanishads. He did not think the common people unworthy and therefore thrust into their hands a ready store of myrobalan. He had a genuine respect for them. In our recent past, it was Rammohan Ray who first recognised the people as the true king. He told himself, 'I will entertain this ruler called the public in the appropriate manner; I have nothing in my forest fit for it, but I will produce a royal feast through arduous ascesis.'

For a supremely learned man like Rammohan Ray, it would have been easy to display scholarship to scholars and be renowned among erudite men. But he left the secluded heights of erudition for the plains of the populace, and proceeded to serve the rice of learning and the nectar of ideas in the concourse of all humanity.

In this way, a new age dawned in Bengal under the rule of a new Raja.† The first Bengali of a new Bengal anointed the common people as king, and set up a royal palace of literature on a deep, firm foundation on the extensive soil of Bengal. With new storeys raised on this foundation, the literary edifice will in time reach the skies, to provide a permanent home for the heart of all Bengal, both past and future—this no longer seems an impossible dream.

We thus see that the literature of Bengal was founded on a large and noble idea. When this work of construction began, the Bengali language had neither worth nor esteem; it brought fame or money to none; it was difficult even to express one's thoughts in it; and if expressed, it was almost impossible to spread such thoughts among the people. No king gave it shelter, no educated public encouraged it. Those who cultivated English ignored Bengali, and those who knew Bengali failed to see the importance of the new effort.

The founders of Bengali literature had before them only a distant future and a vast public—that indeed is the lasting basis of genuine literature. Neither self-interest nor fame, but 'endless time and the vast world'† are the only unwavering targets of real literature. It is their presence that makes literature join one human being to another, one age to another, with the bonds of life. The growth and diffusion of Bengali literature will not only unite the hearts of Bengalis with the most intimate ties: it is already becoming apparent that it will one day attract the other races of India to the hall where the feast of its knowledge is served to guests and the nectar of its ideas freely dispensed to all.

Those who have sought to advance Bengali literature have so far worked in isolation. All tasks are difficult when done alone, and this is particularly true of literary labours. That is because, as I have said already, one of the main ingredients of literature is union or contact. In a society where ideas are constantly gathering in people's minds and stirring them, where mental contact with each other allows many forms of mutual empathy, ideas from the friction of minds and literature from the friction of ideas are spontaneously engendered and dispersed in all directions. To direct one's solitary mind through the rugged desolate fields of duty—impelled only by firm resolve, deprived of the vital contact of other minds—to think in solitude, to try and attract the attention of the indifferent, to persevere in the attempt to make flowers of ideas bloom with the warmth of one's love alone, and to remain ever doubtful of the success of one's best lifelong efforts—is there a more unhappy predicament than this? It does not merely pain the toiler, the task itself remains unfulfilled as a result. The flowers of literature do not show their full colours amidst such privation; its fruits never fully ripen. The light and heat of literature cannot spread in full measure everywhere.

Scientists tell us that a major function of the earth's atmosphere is to diffract the sun's rays and disperse them in all directions as evenly as possible. If there were no air, even at noon we would have had sharp light in some places and the most dense darkness in others. There is need for such an aerosphere around our intellectual and mental realm as well. The winds of intellectual practice must blow through all society in such a way that the rays of thought and learning are diffracted in every direction.

When English education was introduced into Bengal, when that intellectual aerosphere was yet uncreated in our society, learning and ignorance existed side by side without any contact, like the white and black squares on a chessboard. Those who knew English were clearly marked off from those who did not; there was no communication, only conflict. The educated man could hold his uneducated brother in heartfelt contempt, but could find no easy way to share his learning with him.

But one is not fully entitled to anything one cannot give away. The rights of consumption and life that women and children enjoy are only partial rights. There was a time when those of us who learnt English well were very erudite, but their erudition was limited to themselves; they could not gift it to the people of the country. Consequently, their learning produced only conflict and turmoil. That partial erudition gave off plenty of heat but very little light.

The stagnant learning, so narrowly confined, became somewhat fanatical; besides, its greatest shortcoming was that it failed to distinguish the important aspects of the new education from the minor ones. Hence the earliest people to learn English[†] proved an unnecessary nuisance to those around them, resolving that wine, meat, and volubility were the chief ingredients of civilisation.

To sift rice from grit, one has to empty the sack and spread everything out. In the same way, unless the new education is spread among many, its grain remains hard to separate from its grit. When the new learning does not altogether yield good results at first but creates all kinds of unwarranted excess, it is not always wise to panic and attempt to staunch it. That which spreads on its own rectifies itself; the stagnant becomes polluted.

That is why when English education was confined within narrow limits, the refuse of English culture collected in that small space and contaminated everything. Now that the learning has spread everywhere, it has begun to take effect.

However, it is not as though English education has spread through the English language. Its real support is now Bengali literature. Bengalis had once helped establish English rule in India; in today's India, Bengali literature is the principal help in furthering the dominion of English ideas and knowledge. It was when English ideas found easy passage through Bengali literature, at home and outside, that we consciously began to seek freedom from a blind servility to English culture. English education is now inextricably fused with our society; we have thus acquired the right to judge freely what in it is good and what evil, what is major and what minor. Various minds are now examining it under various conditions. English education has vitalised the Bengali mind, and reliance on the Bengali mind has invigorated that education itself.

A mental aerosphere is created in this way around the realm of our knowledge. As long as our minds were inert, we did not feel the lack of this air around us; the more our intellectual life is energised, the keener is our desire for it.

All these days, like submerged divers, we had to draw air through a snorkel from the literary sky of England. We have not cast away the snorkel as yet. But with the slow infusion of life in us, air has begun to flow all around. There is now a rising wind of native literature in our native language.

Bengali literature could make few claims as long as the literary wind had not begun to blow, as long as there was no stir—as long as it existed in seclusion, clinging to a few isolated and lonely peaks of genius. At that time, some strong men alone had cradled it in their arms and nurtured it by their own prowess. Now it has built its dwelling in the heart of the common people and won unrestricted right of access everywhere in Bengal. It now enters the inner quarters like a familiar relation, and sits in learned assemblies like an honoured guest. Those who have received English education now consider it a privilege to express their ideas in Bengali; the most arrogant claimant to Western learning does not think it beneath his efforts to gain fame among Bengali readers.

When the current of English education first reached our society, it merely laid down a sandbank of Western learning. The grains of sand were devoid of mutual contact: one could neither build a permanent dwelling upon them, nor grow crops to sustain the life of the people. When the alluvial soil of Bengali literature was deposited over it, not only was a firm shore built up so that the scattered people of Bengal begin to draw into a unity, but the heart of Bengal found food and shelter for all time. At present, that living and life-fostering mother tongue is pleading for its rights in the society of its offspring.

The moment being right, a movement suited to the times has sprung up spontaneously. It is now being said that our schools should introduce more instruction in Bengali. Why is it necessary? It is necessary because without the Bengali language, one cannot hope to fulfil the desire and the need that education has instilled in our hearts. There would have been no problem if we were content to work for the sahib and serve as office clerks at the end of our training. But the ideal of duty that education has implanted in our minds is that of serving the people. We have to link ourselves to the people with the bonds of service, impart education to all, imbue everyone with the vital juice of thought, unite everyone with the ties of nationality.

Without recourse to our indigenous language and literature, this task will never be accomplished. What we have received from the hands of others, we must parcel out with our own hands when the moment comes for us to give it away.

Under the influence of English education, the desire is gathering strength in our minds to discharge our duty to the people, to save for them what we have gained, to prove before them what we have concluded, to distribute among them what we have enjoyed. It is our misfortune that the means to gratify that desire are still not easily available. We are learning of the ends from English schools, but not acquiring the means.

Some people say that there is no need to introduce Bengali in our schools, because until now, English-trained writers have always written in Bengali out of love—they did not have to make a special effort to learn Bengali.

But as I have already said, times have changed. Bengali literature no longer depends on talented writers alone; it is the property of the educated public. Nowadays, on one occasion or another, we see society demanding of educated persons that they should express their ideas in Bengali. But not everyone is equally gifted; it is not possible for everyone to discharge this responsibility across the hurdles posed by lack of training and practice. Moreover, because Bengali is a relatively immature language, one needs special training and skill to put it to use.

Bengal is now inviting all its educated children to its literature through Bengali newspapers, monthly magazines, meetings, conferences, and fraternities. Those who are unready or unable to respond are to some degree abashed. No one other than the exceptionally shameless now dares to boast of being ignorant of Bengali. If our schools still do not groom our students to suit our current ideals, do not make them fit to improve our society in every way, deny us the right to pass on our education to others even as they have bestowed it on us, deprive us of the power to serve that learning to our starving kin—then we must admit that such schools are seriously inadequate for our times and conditions.

Anglers often find that the hooked fish which seemed enormous when thrashing in the water does not look as big when pulled out of it; the inchoate idea which seems great and new to the writer is exhausted in a few words and loses the gloss of novelty when articulated; things that seem infinitely prodigious and vast in dreams pall and shrink when we wake up. In the same way, we cannot gauge the real extent of our gain from an alien education until we have hauled it onto our native shore. Much of our learning is thrashing about in the deep lake of the English language like hooked fish, while we are thrilled and exultant trying to guess its weight. If we could haul it to the shore of the Bengali language, our learning would perhaps seem slighter. It could nonetheless be consumed and, despite its small bulk, taste delicious, cooked by her own hands by the benign goddess of the household with pure mustard oil† and undiluted love.

It is said in the Bible† that unto everyone that hath shall be given. It is difficult for the destitute to accept a gift. Rainwater collects in pools and lakes; the parched desert has no place to store it. Where shall we receive and store the new learning? If it is sucked in at every instant by our dry self-interest, our momentary needs and pleasures, how will that education gradually acquire permanence and depth, bloom delightedly in Sarasvati's lotus† of beauty, make its banks soft and verdant, reflect the sky, steep many people for many years in purity and joy?

There is one other thing to be said for Bengali literature. Without an exchange of views, no education becomes a vital part of ourselves. No subject to be taught and learnt becomes truly fit for general human use unless it has rolled through many human minds. In a country long accustomed to cultivating the sciences, science is intertwined with everything—the inner and outer worlds, conventions and conduct, language and ideas. For such a country, science is not dry unfamiliar knowledge: it is organically fused in various forms with the human mind and human life. That is why in such a country, the love of science easily becomes genuine and the notion of science deeper. Passing through various minds, science there becomes a living thing. Similarly, in a country where the practice of literature is ancient and widespread, it is not the pastime of a select few. Literature is part of the air that society breathes; it is intermixed with human life, day and night, in many forms; hence love of literature is easy there, its appreciation natural.

There is not enough exchange of learning among the learned people in our country, and it was minimal before Bengali literature began to flourish. The reason is that without the all-round development of native literature, it is impossible to have many people cultivate a subject; deprived of such discussion, the learned remain cut off from their surroundings and imprisoned within themselves. Their tree of knowledge cannot draw enough vital sap from the human minds around it.

This deficiency is one of the reasons why we see such a profound, humourless gloom in our educated ranks. We seem to be unable to determine how to spend our time. We lounge and smoke silently near the door in the morning, go to office around midday, and play cards after returning home in the evening. There is no general current in our society, flowing everywhere and keeping us afloat, upon which all of us can be towed together. Enclosed in our own separate rooms, each of us sits, rises, lolls in bed, and dies when it is time or, more often, before it is time. The main reason for this is our isolation. Our education is imperfectly fused with our society, our ideal with our character, our idea with our action, our selves with our environs. We know the history of heroic deeds, but do not know what heroism is; we have read many discourses on aesthetics, but cannot create beauty around us; we feel many emotions, but cannot find people to share and enjoy them with. These pent-up emotions gradually become distorted and unnatural, and assume unreal forms. What is deeply authentic in other countries turns into hollow and ridiculous excess in ours.

If snow kept piling up on the peaks of the Himalayas, the mountains would have gained an enormous, grotesque and tottering height, *na devaya na dharmaya* [fit for neither the gods nor for piety].[†] But when that snow melts into waterfalls, the Himalayas shed some of their superfluous load and the invigorating streams water the parched, far-stretching plains and make them fertile. As long as English education remains confined, it is like that inert and lifeless pile of snow; when contact with native literature makes it thaw and flow, that learning becomes fruitful, the youth of Bengal can keep their heads, and our country's thirst may be quenched. Once the pent-up ideas spread among the many, they are cured of the distortions caused by excess. The English ideas that our people can truly assimilate—that is the ideas that are universal rather than peculiarly English—survive while the rest decay. An intellectual current is generated among us: the unity born of an ideal and a joy grows among the common people, knowledge is subjected to scrutiny, ideas are exchanged; what students learn at school they find rehearsed at home, and it is no longer necessary to shed the burden of learning outside the school door when they enter adult society. We are thus rid of the unnatural state in which there is an absolute divide between school and home, an absolute distance between student days and working life, a drastic difference between one's own training and that of one's kin. The unifying impetus provided by native literature allows each Bengali to achieve a unity within one's self. Our education can thus be whole and our lives fruitful.

But there are still those among us who feel no need to teach Bengali students more Bengali, and who even object to the suggestion. If asked directly whether they feel that we should all have the basic ability to disseminate our newly acquired knowledge and express our new-born ideas in the language of our native country, they answer, 'Yes.' But according to them, there is no need of special training to that end. They say that any Bengali boy should be able to learn and write Bengali if he so desires.

But why should there be such a desire? Everyone is aware that the subjects we come to love on acquaintance are those we might well have detested when they were unknown to us. To provide room for this love to grow is also a responsibility, and our sense of duty might readily make us follow the right path if it were even slightly more accessible to start with. Our dutiful impulse naturally refuses to be aroused if it sees an untrodden path ahead.

But we argue in vain. There is a group among us who have no love, taste or respect for the Bengali language; no matter which way you turn them, their compass needles will always swing back towards English. Many of them scorn English food and clothes as alien; they do not like the fleshly bodies of our tribe to come in contact with English dishes or English dress. But they do not deplore seeing the intellectual body of the whole race apparelled in a foreign language and nourished by the cuisine of foreign literature. Clothes do not fuse with the body in the same way as language does with the mind. Those who deny their own children the opportunity to learn their mother tongue; those who feel no shame in writing to their closest relations in English; those who in sport trample upon Bengali spelling and grammar 'like frenzied elephants in a lotus garden' but ask the ground to part[†] and swallow them if by mistake they get a dot or dash wrong in their English; those who remain unmoved when called *hastimurkha* [elephantine dunce] in Bengali, but faint if called *ignorant* in English—it is hard to convince such people that they are not the most delectable products of English education.

But we do not wish to blame the Bengali youth who despises his mother tongue and is proud of his English. This vehement bias towards English is only natural, because that language is the king's daughter and, on top of that, our second wife:[†] that she should be excessively favoured is hardly surprising. She is as rich as she is beautiful, and we hope for a little respect from our own princes on her account. Everyone knows that thanks to her, we are allowed the occasional place near the threshold of the aforesaid princes' palaces; at other times, our ears suffer molestation† —we try to laugh it away as a joke, although tears stream from our eyes.

And our hapless first wife, our poor Bengali language, toils in the kitchen; the work is not really humble—one doubts if there is anything more essential—but we are ashamed to claim her as our own. We hide her lest she should be seen in her shabby clothes by our rich new in-laws; when asked, we say we do not know her.

She comes of a poor home. Her father has no kingdom. She cannot procure us honour; she can only give us love. He who loves her does not move up in the world; he has no hope of remuneration, and no identity or influence to flaunt at the palace gates. But the orphan girl fully requites his love in secret. And one who has received that love knows that office, honour, and power are trivial beside it.

We see here something like what we are told in fairy tales.† The new lady of our household is the favoured queen, fruitless and barren. All this time she has been the queen consort, treated with care and respect, but no child of ours has been born in her womb. We have not been able to express any living thought through her. Even if she is not entirely infertile, her offspring are stillborn. A few poems were born to her initially, and then a number of essays; but newspapers were the bed on which they were born and the pile under which they were buried.

On the other hand, in the quarters of our neglected elder queen was born our native literature, the future hope and only lasting glory of our unfortunate land. We do not lavish affection on this child; we leave it naked in the corner of the courtyard and say disapprovingly, 'Look at him! No clothes or ornaments, but covered with dust.' Very well, I accept that. He has neither clothes nor ornaments, but he has life. He will keep growing. One day he will be a fully grown human being and make human beings of others; while even if we swaddled the favoured queen's still-born infants in rich clothes and jewels and dandled them in our arms, we would still fail to infuse life into them.

We trust no one will mind if the few of us gathered here at the call of the Bengali language, who have accepted the charge of bringing up this infant literature as best we can, feel proud to hold this naked, dust-clad child to our breast. Those who have a place at the court of the rulers are blessed; triumphant cheers greet those who sit in the assembly of the ruled: we express the joys, sorrows and anguish of our hearts in the tongue current in this neglected and enslaved country, we pay out of our own pockets to print them although no one wants to pay to read them—please allow us at least a little pride. That pride too is not for the present but for the future; not our own pride but the pride of the Bengal to come, possibly of the India to come. Where will we be then, and where will be the huge victory flags that fly today? But this literature, then decked with ornaments, will be enthroned in royal splendour in the country's heart. In those prosperous times, he will recall the names of his childhood friends—we do confess to this affectionate vanity.

We cannot now make the unreal boast that the young Bengali literature of today is fit for a place in company with the rich and mature literatures of the world. We concede that renowned writers and commendable books are still very few in Bengali. And yet we do not feel Bengali literature to be meagre. Is it only out of blind affection? Not really. The time has come when Bengali literature has consciously begun to feel its own future possibilities. Hence it cannot consider itself negligible, even if the tangible results are still insignificant. At the first arrival of spring, when new shoots in the forest and new leaves on the branches are yet to appear in plenty, when the spirit of the woods has not had the chance to fully display her boundless floral riches—even then she feels in her limbs and veins a secret infusion of life and, sensing her imminent glory, becomes joyous with the pride of nascent youth. Just so does Bengali literature today feel within herself a new vitality, the thrill of a large faith; she feels in her veins the joys and sorrows, hopes and desires rocking the heart of all Bengal; she knows that her place is secure in the inner quarters† of Bengali hearts; she no longer stands begging at the door of the mighty; her unassailable right to her own palace of glory is being enhanced and strengthened each day. For all Bengalis, in their dream and wake, joy and sorrow, prosperity and adversity, she is henceforth

Grihini sachivah sakhi mithah
Priyashishya lalite kalavidhau:
[Housewife, aide, friend and favoured pupil in the fine arts.]†

It is about a hundred years since the new Bengali literature was born. If this Bangiya Sahitya Parishad celebrates its centenary a hundred years from now, the fortunate speaker at that festival will stand here to sing the triumphs of Bengali literature. He will not tune his song like us to the soft, tentative notes of a solitary bird, startled at early dawn; nor will he have his eyes fixed only on the first stirrings of a faint and distant glory, bereft of proof, armed only with heartfelt hope and love, and driven only by the fervency of desire. In the garden of Bengal, then fully awake under a brighter sun, he shall lead a chorus of varied voices, and raise the joyous notes of his enthused times. No one shall then remember that only dark night reigned here once, and that when the pitiful song of our weak voices was over, we went to sleep, torn between the weariness and the peace, the hope and the despair of this present twilight.

TRANSLATED BY SWAPAN CHAKRAVORTY

The Historical Novel

Where is now that childhood of the human race when the natural and supra-natural, event and imagination grew up like brothers and sisters, eating the same food and playing together? No one had ever dreamt their house would be so divided today.

The *Ramayana* and the *Mahabharata* were once history. What is history today feels deeply ashamed to acknowledge kinship with them: they have lost caste by tying the knot with poetry. So hard is it for them to regain their standing that history wishes to pass them off as poetry. Says poetry: 'Dear History, you have a lot of falsehood and I have a lot of truth: come, let us live in amity as we used to do.' History replies: 'No, brother, it's better to divide up our property between us and go our own ways.' The surveyor named knowledge has set about that task of division. He is determined to draw a firm line between the realm of truth and the realm of the imagination.

The charge brought against the historical novel, that it deviates from history, goes to prove this rift in the family of letters.

The charge is not special to our country: Bankim Babu† and Nabin Babu† are not the only offenders. Even Scott, the ideal and original of all historical novelists, has not been spared.

The name of Freeman† is well known among modern English historians. He has expressed his ire at the distortion of history brought about by the novel. He has said that those who wish to find out about *the Age of the Crusades* in Europe should refrain from reading Scott's *Ivanhoe.*

No doubt we need to learn the authentic facts about the Age of the Crusades; but we also need to learn the abiding truth about perennial human history enshrined in Scott's *Ivanhoe.* So intent are we to learn it that students cannot resist the temptation to hoodwink Professor Freeman and secretly peruse *Ivanhoe*, at the risk of being misinformed about the Crusades.

The point at issue is this: could Scott not have written *Ivanhoe* in such a way as to preserve both the particular truth of history and the perennial truth of literature?

It is hard for us to say whether or not he could have done so. What we plainly see is that he did not.

This may have been unintentional. Scott did not know as much about the Crusades as Professor Freeman does. Historical investigation and the analysis of evidence had not advanced so far in Scott's day.

The critic will say: 'If he sat down to write at all, he should have informed himself thoroughly before he started.'

But when would this informing have reached an end? When shall we be able to say confidently that we have exhausted all the evidence about the Crusades? How can we tell that what we conclude today to be firm historical fact will not be dethroned tomorrow with the emergence of new documents? If somebody writes a historical novel based on history as current today, what shall we say if the new historians of tomorrow find fault with him?

The critic will rejoin: 'That's why I say, write as many novels as you like, but don't write historical novels.' True, no one has said such a thing in our country as yet, but there have been hints towards it in English literature recently. Sir Francis Palgrave[†] says that the historical novel is the enemy of history on the one hand and of fiction on the other. In other words, such a novelist impairs history in the interest of the story, and that impaired history then destroys the story itself. The poor story thus loses caste vis-à-vis both her own family and that she has married into.

Why then do historical poems and novels find a place in literature, in spite of such dangers? Let us try to articulate the reason as we know it in our hearts.

Our poetics defines poetry as utterance whose soul is rasa. I have not come across such a brief yet comprehensive definition anywhere else. Of course, it is impossible to explain what is meant by rasa. To a person endowed with the faculty of taste, it is superfluous; and the person who is not does not need to know such things.

Our poetics names nine principal rasas; but there are many indefinable mixed rasas which it has not attempted to name. Of these unspecified rasas, we may perhaps designate one the historical rasa. This rasa is the vital principle of the epic.

An individual's joys and sorrows are no small matter to his or her self: they overshadow the great events of the world. If the rise and buffets undergone by such an individual or a few such lives are suitably recounted in a novel, it intensifies the rasa; the force of that concentrated rasa then assails us from close quarters. For most of us, our joys and sorrows are confined within a small compass; the surging waves of our lives do not break beyond the circle of a few friends and relatives. We can experience as our own the dangers, comforts, pleasures, and pains of Nagendra, Surjyamukhi, and Kundanandini in *Bishabriksha*,[†] because they are centred on Nagendra's family circle. There is no difficulty in thinking of Nagendra as our near neighbour.

But a few people appear on this earth whose joys and sorrows are bound up with the great events of the world. The rise and fall of kingdoms, the far-ranging sequence of events surging and breaking through all time to the sound of the ocean's roar—the private loves and hates of such persons are attuned to that noble harmony. When their tales are sung, one string of the rudraveena[†] plays the main tune, while the other four fingers keep up a stern, diverse, far-ranging accompaniment on the strings of varying diameter behind it.

This progression of time along with a human career is not perceptible to one's daily gaze. Even if such an exceptional being, maker of a nation's history, stands before us, we cannot simultaneously view the person and that extended history from the brief fragmentary perspective of present time. Hence even if we have the opportunity, we cannot properly see such people implanted on the true soil of their greatness. To view them not only as individuals but as elements in the great process of time, one must stand back, place them against the past, and see them in unity with the wide arena of action where they played the principal part.

This distancing of ourselves from everyday joys and sorrows, this momentary realisation that while we are toiling at our jobs, crying and wailing, eating and drinking, great charioteers are driving the chariot of time down the world's highroads—this is what frees us from our petty confines. This it is to savour the rasa of history.

It is not as though such things cannot be conceived of purely by the imagination. But it is easier for a writer to win the reader's confidence if by some device or other he can link such matters, of their nature remote from us and beyond our experience, to some actual event. The poet's purpose is to generate rasa; towards this end, he does not hesitate to draw on historical ingredients, precisely to the extent that they will help his task.

The principal business of Shakespeare's *Antony and Cleopatra* is a familiar and tested truth of our daily lives. Many unknown, unrenowned yet worthy men have surrendered both this life and the next by being caught in the magic toils of womanly illusion. The world's path is strewn with the depressing debris of these minor exemplars of nobility and humanity.

The poet has enlarged this much-observed play of love between man and woman, full of poison nectar, into something immense by setting it in a wide historical arena. The thunder of civil upheaval roars from behind the upheaval of hearts; linked to the conflict of love by a common bond, Rome is led to war by being sundered from its own self. The lyre plays in Cleopatra's pleasure-chamber; from the distant ocean shore, the apocalyptic strains of Shiva's horn† resound to the same tune. This expansive effect of distancing and enlarging the subject has been achieved by mingling the rasa of history with the erotic (*adi*) and sorrowful (*karuna*) rasas.†

If the learned historian Mommsen† were to turn the fierce light of evidence upon Shakespeare's play, it would no doubt show up many *anachronisms*, many errors in the history. But the spell that Shakespeare has cast over the reader's mind, the historical rasa that he has proffered even through erroneous and distorted history, can never be impaired by the discovery of new historical facts.

This is why we had written in an earlier critical essay,†

> The novel generates a special rasa by commingling with history. The novelist prizes this rasa of history; he has no regard for its truth. If someone, not satisfied with this distinctive scent and savour of the past, sets about extracting a sustained history from a novel, he will be looking for whole spices in a curry. If someone can give the curry its flavour through whole spices alone, let him do so; but I cannot quarrel with someone else who wants to grind and mix them together. After all, they have the common purpose of imparting a taste to the curry; the spices are only a means to that end.

In other words, it is immaterial whether a writer leaves his history whole or chops it up into pieces. What matters is his success in infusing his work with the *rasa*, the sap and juice† of history.

Is there then no offence in depicting Rama as a villain and Ravana as a righteous man?† Indeed there is, but it is an offence against poetry, not against history. If the universally known truth is utterly inverted, it impairs the rasa: the readers feel they have been hit on the head. The poem overturns and sinks before a single such blast.

Even if a falsehood of history has won general belief down the ages, it may be wrong for poetry to lay hands on it in defence of history and the truth. Imagine that it is proved beyond doubt that the tribe of Yadu,† drunkards and dissolute all of them, were Greeks, and Krishna a free-ranging, forest-haunting, flute-playing Greek shepherd; that his complexion was as fair† as his elder brother Balaram's; that the exiled Arjuna had abducted the Ionian princess Subhadra† from some Greek kingdom in Asia Minor, and that Dwarka† was located on a peninsula in Greece; that from their state of exile, the Pandavas† managed to recover their kingdom with the aid of that talented military expert, the Grecian hero Krishna, and that his novel and outlandish tactics, politics and work-oriented doctrines set him up as a divine incarnation in wonderstruck India—even so, Vedavyasa's† *Mahabharata* would not be defunct, and no upstart poet would dare turn black into white.

These are general observations. Whether Nabin Babu or Bankim Babu have transgressed so far against traditional history in their poems or novels as to vitiate the poetic spirit, is a matter to discuss in specific criticisms of their work.

What then are we to do? Should we read history, or should we read *Ivanhoe*? The answer is very simple: read both. Read history for facts and *Ivanhoe* for pleasure. If we are so wary of misinformation as to deprive ourselves of the rasa of poetry, our natures will dry and wither.†

If we learn something wrong from poetry, we can correct ourselves by reference to history. The person who reads only poetry, with no opportunity to read history, is unfortunate. But the person who reads only history, with no leisure to read poetry, is perhaps more unfortunate still.

TRANSLATED BY SUKANTA CHAUDHURI

A Poet's Biography

The poet Tennyson's son has published his late father's life and letters in two massive volumes.†

We do not have detailed accounts of the lives of ancient poets. People in those days were not keen on biographies. Besides, the lives of people, big and small, were more private. Nor were letters, newspapers, meetings, conferences, literary debates so plentiful. Consequently, the opportunity to see the personal life of a genius mirrored from many angles was rare.

Travellers have ventured into inaccessible terrains to track the sources of rivers. One feels the same curiosity about the wellsprings of great poems. One would have hoped that the biography of a latter-day poet would meet that curiosity. The modern world seems to leave the poet with no place to hide: the railways have reached the peaks from which the poetic streams course down.

I finished the two huge volumes with that eager hope. But I could trace neither the poet, nor the cave from which his verse streamed forth. This may very well be the life of Tennyson, but it is certainly not the life of the poet. We do not get to know when he cast his net in the sea of the human heart and drew in such a rich catch of knowledge and ideas, or where he sat to rehearse the notes of the cosmic melody on his flute.

The poet did not compose his life as he did his poems. His life was no poem. Men of action shape their own lives. Just as a poet builds up his rhythm despite the constraints of the language, finds exceptional music for common thoughts and great meanings for small words, so do men of action fashion the rhythm of their lives despite the stubborn resistance of the world, and by some marvellous power ennoble the pettiness all around them. They exalt their lives with the humble ingredients close at hand, and they exalt the ingredients in the process. Their life's work is their poetry, and for that reason people cannot ignore their biographies.

But of what use will a poet's life be to the world? Where is the enduring stuff in it? To tie it to the poet's name and display it aloft is to embarrass the commonplace by enthroning it as great. Biography belongs to the great man; poetry, to the great poet.

A few rare individuals may express their genius in their lives as well as their verse; for them, poetry and work are both fruits of the same genius. To see their poetry undetached from their lives is to enlarge its meaning and deepen its ideas. Dante's poetry is fused with Dante's life; to read them together is to see them both heightened.

Tennyson's life was different. It was the life of a decent man, but in no way far-ranging, grand or copious in its impact. It is not of the same weight as his poetry. Rather the biography mirrors those aspects of his verse which are narrow and uncatholic, reeking a bit too strongly of the shops and factories of contemporary English culture. But it does not express his greatness, the way in which he was able to integrate human beings with one another, and creation with its creator, within an expansive harmony.

There is no biography of any poet of ancient India. That makes me for ever curious, but not sad. No one would consider the legend current about Valmiki to be history. But according to us, that legend is the true account of the poet. The biography that his readers have created out of his poetry is truer than his actual life. What was the blow that struck at the fount of poetry and made it well out of his heart? It was the stroke of compassion. The *Ramayana* is a spring of compassion's tears. At its core one hears the mournful cry of the heron which has lost its lover.[†] Ravana too tears the lovers apart[†] like the hunter: the war canto in the *Ramayana*[†] is the beating of the deranged lover's wings. The separation forced by Ravana is worse than that of death. The rift does not heal even after the reunion.

The conditions for bliss seemed so perfect! A father's affection, the subjects' love, a brother's devotion, and, at the centre of all this, the union of the new couple Rama and Sita. His investiture as crown prince came as a consummation and exaltation of such bliss. Precisely at this point, the fowler took aim: the arrow found its mark when Sita was abducted. From then on there was no end to the separation. Conjugal bliss was most rudely cut off at the point of its keenest onset.

The story of the coupling herons is a miniature allegory of the basic idea of the *Ramayana*. In sum, people have indubitably discovered the truth that the epic poet's clear, cascading anushtupa metre thawed and began to flow under the heat of compassion, that the conclusive and premature rupture of conjugal love had stirred his tender poetic soul.

Then there is the story of Ratnakar.† It deals with another idea, and comments on a different aspect of the poetic nature of the *Ramayana.* The story is directed at its portrayal of Rama. It says that the epic's mainstay is not an immeasurable pity at the sad separation of Rama and Sita; its root is in a devotion to the figure of Rama. Rama's virtue is such that it can make a poet out of a brigand—such is the strength of devotion. The legend seems a measure of the colossal stature of Rama in Indian eyes.

Both stories seem to say that the source of poetry is not to be found in everyday conversation, letters, socialising, chores and lessons. At its root is the welling up of some powerful emotion, like a sudden, preternatural revelation: it is beyond the control of the poet. The poetry written by the Kabikankan† too was divinely ordained in a dream, under the spell of the goddess.†

The familiar legend about Kalidasa† is similar in bent. He was unlettered and dull, the butt of his learned wife's ridicule. He was gifted with poetic effluence by the sudden intervention of providence. Valmiki was a cruel bandit, Kalidasa dull and insensitive to poetry: both stories have the same import. They are no more than attempts to express the compassionate purity of Valmiki's work and the pleasurable erudition, raised to a supra-natural plane, in Kalidasa's.

People gathered these stories not from the lives of the poets but from their poetry. The facts one could have pieced together from their lives would have had no deep and lasting connection with their verse. Valmiki's everyday conversations and activities could never be set alongside the *Ramayana,* because they were momentary, transient. Perennial and undivided nature, operating within him, brought the *Ramayana* into being: it was the expression of an ineffable and immeasurable power, not the stirrings of the moment like his other activities.

One could write a poetic biography of Tennyson. Its roots would not lie in his material life but in his poetic life. It could not be made authentic without the aid of the imagination. In such an account, the times of the Lady of Shalott and King Arthur would strangely merge with that of Queen Victoria; in it, Merlin's magic would be reconciled with the inventions of science. The modern age, like a cruel stepmother, had banished him as a child to the forests of the imagination. That long story is yet to be written of how he found Aladdin's lamp while living there alone in an old ruined fortress; how he met and won a princess; how he stepped out into the present-day world dressed as a prince and laden with antique treasures. If such an account were attempted, one person's effort would be unlike another's. Tennyson's life would take on new forms with different people at different times.

TRANSLATED BY SWAPAN CHAKRAVORTY

Vidyapati's Radhika

Just as motion and heat are two manifestations of the same energy, in the poetry of Vidyapati and in that of Chandidas† we have two expressions of the same power of love. In Vidyapati love is sportive, dancing, restless; in Chandidas it is intense, burning, luminous. That is why Vidyapati's songs are so full of rhythm, music, and colour; that is why they ripple so with a joyful luxuriating in beauty. It is the overflowing delight of the onset of youth: unmixed bliss, uninterrupted music. It is not that there is no sadness, but the sadness is clearly set apart from the joy. There is either sadness or joy, either union or separation, clearly categorised. We do not find, as in Chandidas, joy and sorrow, union and separation interwoven with each other. Thus in Vidyapati love has the freshness of youth, and in Chandidas the depth of mature years.

It is the way of youth to look upon joy and sorrow, good and evil as two completely separate entities: as if there were pure good and pure evil, entire joy and entire sorrow, ranged on two sides, facing each other as antagonists.

At that time of life, one's heart is filled with perfect ideals of all things. When we see one virtue, we imagine that we see them all; a single vice assumes in our eyes the shape of a devil with all the vices combined in him. A single glimpse of happiness makes every trace of sorrow vanish from our world, and as soon as sorrow appears, there remains not the least suggestion of joy. That is why music is always pitched on a high, rapturous note. That is why in Vidyapati it is always springtime. His Radha is coming into bloom little by little, brimming over with loveliness. She meets with Shyam, and the air around them turns vibrant with youthfulness: a little smile, a little deceit, a few sidelong glances—also a little eager anxiety, a little swaying between hope and despair, but not such as to really hurt.

In Chandidas we have

> My eyes are birds clamouring to drink the moonlight:
> Their gaze does not falter for an instant.†

In Vidyapati there is no such agitation, though there is some sense of being distracted. It is half revealing and half concealing oneself, as though partly unveiled by a sudden boisterous breeze. Vidyapati's Radha is a young plant, just coming into bud. She knows neither herself nor others well. From a distance she appears a laughing, yearning, playful girl; draw nearer, and she is trembling, alarmed, confused. She makes bold to touch the strange object of love very cautiously, with the tips of her champak-like fingers, and then turns to flee. She is just like a timid girl, drawn by her natural love of animals, now venturing to touch a strange deer and now running away, until at last she loses her fear.

It is the time of youth, and that too at its first onset. Everything then seems full of mystery. A heart just opening out suddenly becomes aware of its own sweet perfume. It has only just become conscious of itself. Bashful, timorous, joyful, hesitant, it cannot decide whether to conceal or to express itself:

> Now she'll bind up her bosom, now make it bare;
> Now cover her body, and now unveil it.†

Her fledgling desires now want to spread their wings and take to the air, but do not yet know how to go about it. Curious and inexperienced, they venture forth just a little, then withdraw and take shelter in the soft secluded nest of her hastily gathered-up sari-end.

Love at this stage carries more of indulgence than of agony. It has none of the unshakable firmness of deep feeling, only the distracted playfulness of newly awakened yearning. To read the verses of Vidyapati is to look on the surface of the sea stirred by a breeze: tossing waves, foaming surf, the shadows of clouds, sunbeams diffracted into a thousand fragments; waves now touching, now running away from each other; the sound of voices and laughter and clapping of hands. It is all dancing and singing, fleeting glimpses and commotion, colours and light.

In Vidyapati's songs we see how beauty breaks in a thousand rhythmic movements and gestures upon the waves of this young restless love. What we do not find in him is the profundity, the silence, the world-oblivious meditation that dwells in the depths of the sea.

Occasionally Radha and Krishna do see each other: sometimes while bathing in the Yamuna, sometimes when returning. But the meetings are unsatisfactory. Not only are they too brief, but they shatter into fragments the beauty reflected in the swaying, restive heart: there is not time enough to observe that beauty patiently with tranquil mind. All they can see is

Half the veil slips: half a smiling face,
    And half of an arch glance.
    It could not be seen clearly.†

Then there is much coming and going and talking, many artful ways to express oneself, many fears and anxieties—and then at last, in the sweet season of spring, the first union. Even that is not deep, intense, extravagant. It is full of fear and reassurance, fun, playful archness, affected hurt and cajolery. Then again, Radha going into a huddle with a companion, calling her to an intimate session in some nook or corner, and by all sorts of artful means, bringing the talk round to her sweet memories. It has all the infatuation, the variety, the sportive eagerness that goes with the newly awakened love of a girl in her first youth.

Chandidas is deep, passionate, yearning; Vidyapati is fresh and sweet.

In a new† Vrindavan,† new are the trees,
New the flowers, and new the southern breeze.
In the new spring, the bees are mad with joy;
And walking in their midst, the stripling Boy.
On Yamuna's bank, the newly bedecked grove,
    Enraptured by new love.
New blossoms on the mango tree now spring,
And maddened by their nectar, koels sing.
All the young maidens wander gardenward,
Distracted hearts by a new passion stirred.
Young is the Prince, and young his paramours:
New radiance now shines forth with all its fires.
And Vidyapati's heart, day after day,
In such new sports is ever held in play.

This would not be complete without adding another song to it:

Sweet is the season,† sweet the swarm of bees,
Drunk on the sweet honey of sweet flowers.
And in the midst of our sweet Vrindavan,
Sweetest of all, the King of sweet passion.
In the sweet company of girls, he plays
His sweet games with his sweet sportive ways.
Sweet is the music of his instrument,
While hands clap in a sweet accompaniment.
Sweet are the steps, the gestures of the dance,
As girls and youths in their sweet play advance.
Sweet, sweet the songs of love, that in his verse
Sweet Vidyapati to you does rehearse.

We might have stopped here, but it would have left things badly incomplete: the music would not have come to a proper close. That is why Vidyapati has added one last word. We can also call it a word without end. After all the joyful play, all the thrills of delight, this is the concluding word:

Ever since birth, your face have I descried;
 Yet the eye's unsatisfied.
Aeon after aeon, my heart on yours has lain;
 Yet the hearts will not join.†

In a moment, the new-born love becomes a million years old. It is time for a change of rhythm and ragá. The role of ever-new love has been played out. Now Chandidas arrives on the scene to begin a song of ever-familiar love.

TRANSLATED BY BHAWANI-PRASAD CHATTOPADHYAY,
VERSE TRANSLATED BY SUKANTA CHAUDHURI

The Nature of Krishna

The Bengali title of this essay (as of the work by Bankimchandra of which it is a critique) is Krishnacharitra. Charitra *is usually translated as 'character'—meaning either a person's mental and moral propensities, or a figure in a play or narrative. But there can be a deeper implication of 'nature' or 'kind of being'. Bankimchandra's work and Rabindranath's essay explore the nature of Krishna's being, whether divine or human, and the constituent elements of his personality. Hence 'nature' seems a fitter rendering than 'character' in this case, though 'character' and 'being' have been used at certain points where these words better suit the immediate context.*

When, on beginning to receive English-type education, we first embarked on political criticism, our social and religious principles too could not escape that pitiless examination. Every student started to feel doubt and dissatisfaction about our society and religion.

After criticism comes action. It is easy to decide what is good and what is bad in theoretical terms. It is far more difficult to determine one's practical duty accordingly. There is little we can do in the field of statecraft because we have no right of governance. That is why *political* criticism these days is so intense and virulent: there are no grounds for any doubts or inhibitions in the matter. But what we do about our social and religious duties is up to us. Hence if we fail to perform what we judge to be our duty in religious and social matters, we cannot blame anyone but ourselves.

One cannot blame oneself and do nothing about it; nor is it good for one to blame oneself without letting it dusturb one's peace. Hence we took to comforting ourselves by finding one excuse after another to defend our society and our religion, till things came to a point where we started declaring rather too stridently, with all the force at our command, that whatever we had was the best there could be and perfect in every respect.

I am not suggesting that such behaviour was hypocritical or false. In fact, society and religion have their roots so deep in national character that any attempt to interfere with them encounters enormous obstacles from many quarters, and new evils raise their heads in place of the old. Dismayed at such a situation, one seeks refuge in inaction. In this retreat into passivity it is not unlikely that one should exhibit a somewhat excessive arrogance. One wants to strike a heroic pose and declare to the world that one is in fact not the loser but the winner.

It was in such a perverse phase of Bengal society that Bankimchandra wrote his *Krishnacharitra* (*The Nature of Krishna*). When so many of us, big men and small, were adding their voices unthinkingly to the general cry, genius struck a different note. Bankimchandra's *Krishnacharitra* did not join the chorus. It did not uphold the popular ideas; it admonished the people.

If one considers the trends of that age and the postures and attitudes of the conformists around him, one perceives in *Krishnacharitra* the strength of a genius—powerful, emancipated.

This strength is a permanent gain for us. It is something the Bengali sorely needs. At times, this power has transgressed the boundaries of fairness and good manners; but it is still an unwavering support for us, faint-hearted weaklings that we are.

At a time when even men of education in our country forgot themselves and blindly championed the shastras,† Bankimchandra in *Krishnacharitra* boldly hoisted the flag of the unvanquished human intellect. He subjected the shastras to minute examination through historical analysis, and tested even time-honoured beliefs by reason, thereby restoring the despised intellectual faculty to its throne of glory.

In our view it is not Krishna who is the protagonist of *Krishnacharitra*: it is the sovereign intellect, the active faculties of the mind. In the first place, Bankim makes it clear that we will not offer homage in blind conformity to scripture or custom, but be judiciously guided by our highest ideals. He then goes on to show that everything in the shastras is not worthy of belief; rather, that everything worthy of belief is shastra. This principle constitutes the spiritual force of *Krishnacharitra*: this is what ennobles the work.

In this work the greatness and historicity of Krishna are subject to proof. In the first part of the book the author goes into history. The nature of Krishna is here critically considered for the first time from a truly historical point of view. No one had ventured into this field before, so Bankim had to take upon himself the tasks of both demolition and construction. Before we can find out what is history, we must, with great labour and discernment, determine what is not. In our view, in the present work Bankim has largely accomplished the work of demolition, but could not properly set his hand to the work of construction.

He has mainly depended upon the *Mahabharata*. He has proved beyond doubt that the great epic contains much that is apocryphal, but he has not pointed out which parts are genuine. He has himself asserted: 'The *Mahabharata* as we know it is not the original composition of Vedavyasa.† It is known as Vaishampayana's;† but it is doubtful whether what we have is truly Vaishampayana's work either. We have gone on to prove that almost three-fourths of it is apocryphal.'

Bankim has discovered three strata of composition in the *Mahabharata*. At the first level, the composition is elevated and of high poetic quality; the second is narrow in outlook, with its poetical parts somewhat warped; while the third is the work, over a very long period, of very many people who permitted themselves all kinds of freedom.

It is hardly necessary to point out to the reader that to distinguish different planes of composition by differences in poetic quality is purely a matter of conjecture. Tastes differ and men differ in their views of poetry. Then again, instances are not rare where works by the same poet vary greatly in poetic quality. Hence a historian should concern himself with differences in language rather than in poetic quality. To separate the work of different poets on a linguistic basis, and thus to determine the original text of the *Mahabharata*, is an arduous task.

Secondly, while the work of a good poet may contain good poetry, historical truth is unrelated to poetical power. Many stories about the battle of Kurukshetra† circulated orally in many parts of ancient India, on the lips of many people. It is possible that from these stories, some good poet may have gathered material suited to his poetic talent and shaped it into a good, well-constructed poem. It is also possible that many bad poets, and others who were no poets at all, may have added on to that poem the facts of history as known to them. In such a case, the inferior poetry may be more dependable as history than the superior. As we all know, if poetry is to be fully poetry, it cannot use everything in history without modification. Suppose that latter-day sticklers for historical accuracy were to take up one of Shakespeare's historical plays and, in order to make good its deficiencies as history, thoughtlessly insert passages of their own creation. We can easily imagine the bad poetry, the departures from the original, the conflicts with the characters as depicted by Shakespeare. In such an event, a literary critic might rescue Shakespeare's original play by applying the test of poetic quality. But I am not sure that a historical scholar would depend solely on Shakespeare's original text for the facts of history.

In any case, there is no denying that the *Mahabharata* contains the work of many men from many ages. What is yet to be ascertained, however, is how to tell them apart, and to determine their dates and relative accuracy.

All we can say is that Bankim Babu has found out an unquestionable mark of unhistoricity: namely the supernatural. In the first place, we cannot credit the supernatural sections. Secondly, we can be fairly certain that those parts of the history in which the supernatural makes its appearance are of much later date than the actual events.

The other characteristic of unhistoricity that Bankim Babu has hit upon is also worthy of notice. Those parts where a great historical figure is deified are without doubt later additions.

It follows, therefore, that where Bankim has purged Krishna of supernatural, non-human elements, no historian can cavil. But where he has rejected something that he regards as inconsistent with some other part of the *Mahabharata*, the reader might raise questions. This is because various legends gain currency around a great figure or a great historical event. A poet can cull and refine these legends to create his own poetry according to his own ideals. Some will see Krishna as a supremely religious-minded, god-like man; some will paint him as a cunning politician and intriguer. Both pictures might be incomplete; but though contradictory, each may contain a part of the truth. In fact, it is difficult to say which is historically more accurate.

Hence we do not think that Bankim's detailed exposition of every statement and opinion attributed to Krishna in the *Mahabharata*, and his construction of a historical character on that basis, is sufficiently based on fact. He himself says from time to time that not everything put into Krishna's mouth in the *Mahabharata* was actually uttered by him: it only shows what the poet thought of Krishna. But to accept the poet's ideal as entirely in conformity with the ideal enshrined in history, it is necessary to find supportive evidence outside the poet's work. Let us quote an instance. Bankim Babu says:

> Recalling the sufferings of her sons and daughter-in-law, Kunti† shed many tears before Krishna. What Krishna said to her in reply is of immeasurable value. Leave aside a fool, only someone who fully knows every province of human nature can appreciate how invaluable those words are. Shri Krishna says, 'The Pandavas† have conquered sleep, drowsiness, anger, joy, hunger, thirst, cold and heat, and

are enjoying the felicity deserved by the brave. They have renounced sensual pleasures, and are content with the pleasures appropriate to the brave. Such immensely mighty, immensely ardent heroes never find satisfaction in small things. The brave experience either great sorrow or supreme happiness. Those seeking to gratify their senses, on the other hand, are content with the middle state; but that is a source of misery. True happiness is to be found either in gaining a kingdom or in dwelling in the forest.'

These words of Krishna quoted by Bankim Babu out of the *Mahabharata* are full of the profoundest wisdom. But we do not believe that they help us a great deal in determining the character of the historical Krishna. Those words establish the *Mahabharata* poet's knowledge of human nature and the loftiness of his mind. These utterances of Krishna belong to the ninetieth chapter of the *Udyogparva*, the Canto of Preparation for Battle. Some forty chapters later, Kunti narrates the old story of Vidula's dialogue with Sanjay.† The spirited Vidula's words to inspire her son, unwilling to enter battle, with kshatriya† ideals is no different from the words of Krishna quoted above. Says Vidula:

Even now, take on yourself the burden of manly thought. Do not idly insult your illimitable soul by being content with small things. Little streams are filled with small amounts of water. It takes very little to fill the paws of a mouse. So also the faint-hearted, asking for little, are easily satisfied. It is better to burst into flames, if only for a little while, than to smoulder for ever. A man of true wisdom in this world scorns meagreness. To one whom it takes little to satisfy, that little is sure to do harm. Those who, knowing how transient are the gains of human endeavour, nevertheless engage in action, may or may not attain their goal; but those who, convinced of the uncertainty of gain, totally desist from action cannot ever achieve anything.

We see from this that the poet of the *Mahabharata* set a very high ideal of devotion to duty, and propagated that ideal in many passages with the help of examples. It would not even be inadmissible to suppose, from a close reading of the *Mahabharata*, that the poet has made an epic out of the legendary war of the Kauravas and the Pandavas in order to declare the erstwhile supremacy of the ethos of action in India. All the great heroes of the *Mahabharata*—Krishna, Arjuna,† Bhishma,† Bhima,† Karna,† Drona†—are, each one of them, a supreme example of the doer of great deeds, the *karmavira*. Even Gandhari† and Draupadi† are resplendent in their devotion to duty. That is why Gandhari proposes forsaking Duryodhana,† and Draupadi asserts, 'If it is a sin to kill one who should not be killed, it is equally a sin not to kill one who should be.'†

Thus, if what Bankim says is truly argued, it goes to prove that there was an unknown poet who held very high the ideal of nobility, and that the Krishna of his creation is an embodiment of that lofty ideal. It may be that Krishna is a historical character; but there is nothing to prove that the Krishna of the *Mahabharata* is in all respects a true representation of the historical Krishna. We also see that in the *Mahabharata* itself, different people have constructed different Krishnas, according to their respective ideals.

When one witness contradicts another, we have to call a fresh witness to find out the truth. Bankim Babu, however, argues that the part of Krishna's life described in the *Mahabharata* is not to be found in any of the other Puranas. This makes it impossible to arrive at the truth by comparing the evidence given by different witnesses.

According to Bankim Babu's argument, Vyasa's original *Mahabharata* is no longer extant. The *Mahabharata* that we possess travelled orally from Vyasa to Vaishampayana, from Vaishampayana to Ugrashraba's father,† from him to Ugrashraba, and finally from Ugrashraba to some unknown poet. Second, even in this version there occurred, in course of time, many interpolations by many hands. No reliable means has been found so far to distinguish these later additions beyond doubt. Thirdly, we have no means of ascertaining the authenticity of the *Mahabharata's* account by comparison with other ancient texts.

Bankim chiefly discusses the character of Krishna to investigate, quite incidentally, the historical authenticity of the *Mahabharata*. But it is only after identifying the historical parts of the entire *Mahabharata*, through proper evidence and judgment, that we can establish the historicity of Krishna's character to our satisfaction.

To take an example, Bankim doubts the factual basis of Draupadi's having five husbands.† We must therefore see whether we can expunge, from the whole of what he calls the original *Mahabharata*, those parts where Draupadi is shown as having five husbands; and also whether Draupadi's wifely attentions to five husbands are inextricably woven into those parts from which he has culled the evidence for the historicity of Krishna.

If Bankim is able, on adequate evidence, to cleanse his ideal *Mahabharata* of all that he considers unhistorical, we can accept the parts retained by him as a credible historical account. But he does not clearly indicate just how much of the *Mahabharata* might be historical. All he does is to trace the strand relating to Krishna's character. At one point he says:

I too do not believe that Drupad† got his daughter out of the ceremonial fire, or that the daughter had five husbands. It is, however, not impossible that Drupad had a daughter born to him; nor is there reason to doubt that she had a *svayamvara* marriage,† or that at the gathering where she chose her husband, Arjuna hit the target with his arrow. Whether she subsequently married five husbands or one, is a question we do not need to decide.

Indeed there is need, because Bankim regards the *Mahabharata* as history, and hence the character of Krishna, as presented in the *Mahabharata*, as historical. Draupadi's marrying five husbands is not a trifling matter; if such an important event is an invention, and if the invention finds a place in the text approved by Bankim, it certainly detracts from the credibility of the *Mahabharata* and hence diminishes the historical validity of Krishna's character as described there. When there is only one witness, we can trust any one piece of his evidence only if the rest of it is free from the taint of falsehood.

But to insist on such intensive preparation would probably have meant no *Krishnacharitra* for the Bengali reader at all. It is doubtful if a lifetime would suffice to analyse the *Mahabharata* by appropriate methods and extract its authentic parts. It is therefore a matter of good fortune, and no little wonder for us, that Bankim has commenced laying out a narrow path through the vast dense forest of the epic. All we wish to say is that his work is not conclusive. We cannot rest contented at the point where his genius has brought us. He has set before us an example of scepticism for us to follow: we must strive to extend the kingdom of truth. He has not handed us a pearl; he has shown by example that if we want pearls, we must dive into the ocean. Very likely we shall salute him and say, 'We have no use for pearls—we cannot go diving in the ocean.'

Bankim, citing Macaulay, Carlyle, Lamartine, Thucydides, and others, contends that the *Mahabharata* is poetised history. We hold that it is a historical poem. But we do not want to enter into a long argument on whether the ideal of Krishna is derived from history or from poetry, or from a mixture of the two. Indeed it is not as if history were gospel truth. It is well known that few people can accurately register and report even on something that happens before their eyes.

To take fragmentary reports and build up from them the being and the history of a whole man is a task even fewer can accomplish. As everybody knows, even close relatives can be mistaken about one another; friends too can misunderstand each other. It is even more difficult to really know an exceptional man. Undoubtedly, to build up the true picture of such a man from far off, out of ancient report, is largely an imaginative exercise. Mixing evidence with conjecture, one can depict the same man in so many ways that to accept any one of them as authentic must be a matter of individual disposition. It cannot be doubted that history is very largely a matter of the writer's conjecture and the reader's beliefs. In such a situation, it is not unlikely that a poet's conjecture will come closer to the real history than the historian's. The life of Strafford published by Mr Forster[†] is popularly believed to have been virtually written by the poet Browning; but the play *Strafford* that Browning wrote shortly after was later shown to be truer than the history he composed. Similarly, what the poet of the *Mahabharata* did was to take the stray accounts of the battle of Kurukshetra scattered in popular legend, flesh them out by his imagination, and make them into an integrated whole. There is no reason why it need be less true than the history written by a historian.

Truth extends far beyond information, or what in English is called *fact*. Reason and imagination draw truth out of a heap of facts. History often supplies masses of facts which are like dry firewood; it is the poet's genius that ignites truth into poetry. We think it virtually impossible, so late in the day, to set about determining the historical basis for the character Krishna in the *Mahabharata*; nor would it be germane to our purpose.

The renowned historian Mr Froude[†] has said that the real and natural greatness of a truly great man lies beyond the reach of prose; it can only be described by a poet's pen. Whatever may be the reason for this, it is true in practice. Poetry has this life-giving power; prose lacks it, and that is why the poet is the best historian.

We take Froude's observation to mean that a catalogue of a great man's deeds is mere fact; his greatness is the truth. To give the reader a sense of this greatness needs poetic genius more than historical research.

Judged in this light, every fact the poet conveys about the being of Krishna may not be accurate; every word put in his mouth, every act ascribed to him, may not be authentic to the last detail; but the impression of the glory of Krishna's character, stamped by the poet on the reader's mind, is a truth of the greatest value. If we had a history of the life of Krishna, it would have contained a thousand incidents which, though enacted by him, would in no way express his Krishna-hood, and hence have no permanent value. For that matter, because we cannot finally know everything, many of those incidents might have appeared to contradict Krishna's true nature. Every person, in many deeds, acts against his true nature. No doubt, in depicting the Krishna of the *Mahabharata*, many such unnecessary and adventitious facts have been shed, retaining only those that are true to his nature. Indeed, by making Krishna say things that he did not but that he alone might have said, do things that he did not but that he alone might have done, the poet has made his Krishna truer than the real Krishna. In other words, the poet has eliminated what was un-Krishna-like in the real Krishna; he has thus given full, rounded expression to the ideal that the real Krishna, by virtue of his qualities, had inspired in the poet, yet which could not everywhere find steady, unhindered, and articulate expression on account of ulterior factors. He has thereby liberated from factual history the veritable, timeless Krishna.

Thus, since it is Bankim's aim to implant in the Bengali reader a sense of Krishna's glory, he went about it the right way when he drew upon the poet's work. Unfortunately, the *Mahabharata* lies buried under the compositions of many men in many ages. It is not easy to extricate the original vision of the poet. Once all the dross is purged away, not Krishna alone but Bhishma, Karna, Arjuna, Draupadi, and the rest will all stand before our eyes in fuller and brighter form. Rescuing the original work of the original poet would mean an unsurpassed gain for mankind.

Bankim, however, follows his own ideals in trying to discover the original poet's ideal of Krishna. Before we can judge conclusively of his success, we have to draw out the original *Mahabharata* from the ocean of its eighteen cantos. For the present, we only wish to direct the reader's attention to one matter.

Bankim admits that the poet to whom he ascribes the first stratum of the *Mahabharata* did not believe that Krishna was God. He even takes this as a principal means of identifying the first stratum of composition.

But Bankim believed that Krishna was God. This profound divergence made it difficult for him to pick out the original poet's ideal of Krishna. The Krishna Bankim was searching for was the Krishna born of his own desire. He was searching fervently for an ideal being, rendered perfect by the full exercise of all the faculties of the mind. What his theory of religion had given him as an idea, he was undoubtedly most eager to find exemplified historically in flesh and blood. In this state of mind, it would have been difficult for any person to draw out the ideals of another poet in undistorted form.

Some may say in reply that even though Bankim believed Krishna to be God, he has repeatedly asserted that when God appears on earth in human incarnation, He is entirely human and does not perform miracles in order to manifest His divinity. Thus it was Krishna as man and not Krishna as God that Bankim set out to discover in the *Mahabharata*.

But the man he sought was without any imperfection; all the faculties of his mind were in perfect harmony. In other words, he was a *theory* in human shape. But the Krishna of the *Mahabharata* was probably not a deity, nor a refinement of the developed human faculties; he was simply Krishna.

The poet of the *Mahabharata* has not created a character who is only a theory or a moral principle in human form. This shows his high poetic powers. He has made even his great heroes perform unworthy acts, such as a lesser poet would not have dared ascribe to them. Lesser poets can construct, they cannot create; they build, from top to bottom, according to rules. They cannot allow any exceptions or contradictions. But when something is truly great, even its imperfections indicate its greatness. When nature makes a mountain, it does not feel compelled to give it a perfectly rounded shape. With all its broken lines, its slapdash appearance, it is still majestic in its towering presence. It carries its imperfections with such ease that they become a measure of its colossal completeness. In a small thing, however, a minor blemish can be fatal. You must make it perfect if you wish it to attract attention and regard.

The poet of the *Mahabharata* has created a class of heroes evincing an exalted harmony of being but not petty consistency. Many high-minded Bengali writers today, known and unknown, can very likely create a species of chaste women with names like Sarala, Bimala, Damini, or Jamini who, in the faultless purity of their morals, utterly consistent from start to finish, can beat Draupadi time and again. Yet in the forceful primal limitless amplitude of her spirit, the Draupadi of the *Mahabharata*, bravely bearing all her imperfections, will tower for all time above the little anthills of morality raised by these termites of modern times.[†] The shameful acts perpetrated by Karna towards the Pandavas in the *Sabhaparva* (Canto of the Royal Court) would not be emulated by any Dinesh, Ramesh, Ganesh, or Dhanesh of our plays and novels; they are only too ready to sacrifice themselves at any time and place. Nonetheless, the poet of the *Mahabharata* has effortlessly secured for Karna a place among the immortals; the latter worthies, with all the first-class tickets and moral travel money bestowed on them by the critics, can scarcely climb the first step of that ascent.

That is why I said, if it is true that the original author of the *Mahabharata* did not regard Krishna as a god, neither does it seem possible that he set him up as a fully formed moral exemplum. Bankim has determined that the first textual stratum of the *Mahabharata* is the work of a great poet; on that ground, he has purged the character of Krishna of all inconsistencies and deficiencies at many points. But we would hold that consistency is not a mark of poetic greatness. Nobody so far has plausibly found consistency in the character of Hamlet; yet no one has doubted that in the world of poetry, Hamlet is a character supremely true to nature.

Hence we gravely doubt whether, by casting out all that is bad from the character of Krishna in the *Mahabharata*, Bankimchandra has brought to light the ideal Krishna of the original creator of the work.

It can still be argued: what if it is not the ideal of the original poet? If Bankim's own ideal is a truly exalted one, that too will be a great gain for the Bengali reader.

We do not for a moment doubt that Bankim's ideal was lofty and that the *Krishnacharitra* is a priceless acquisition for Bengali literature.

But that is precisely why, while reading the book, we constantly regret that Bankim did not set about establishing his ideal in a manner appropriate to literature.

As Froude has justly remarked, history cannot capture the true greatness of a great man; poetry can. The quality of greatness must be instilled in the consciousness of the reader as an integrated, living thing. One might demonstrate it to the reader in piecemeal fashion, by argument and reasoning; but mere reasoning cannot send the perception of greatness coursing through one's entire being.

From the outset, Bankim has fought his way forward, sword in hand. Never for a moment has he found time to hold the total picture of his Krishna calmly before our eyes.

Nor can we blame him for this. Except among the devotees of Krishna, or perhaps even within their circle, the character of Krishna had been painted in such dark colours that it required immense efforts on his part to cleanse our minds of such prejudices. He had to take up an axe to clear the jungle at the site where he wished to set up the image of his god. What Bankim's *Krishnacharitra* teaches us is that the Krishna of our tradition and the real Krishna, worthy of belief, are two very different propositions.

What we find most irksome, however, is the gratuitous disputation that Bankim has introduced. When writing this book, Bankim had set a firm ideal before himself. A proper reverence for that ideal required that it should inform all his language and ideas. When Bankim engages in petty quarrels and narrow-minded carping, that disturbance impairs the timeless tranquillity of the ideal. Such disputes are more appropriate to the cut-and-thrust of weekly journals; they are unworthy of place in a memorable work of permanent value.

The author has showered copious vituperation on 'western ignoramuses'—that is, European scholars. In the first place, to do so is wrong in itself; in the second, it ill becomes a book of this nature. In the presence of a respected person, unwarranted rudeness towards any member of the company is not only uncivil to the person addressed, it is discourteous to the respected one. Bankim is trying to set up an ideal image of Krishna as the first among men, personifying both valour and mercy, often desisting from taking up arms without cause or indeed with cause, despite his power to do so. It is an affront to that ideal to display the frivolous commotion of petty bickering before its very seat.

Not to western scholars alone, but to the European nations in general, the author has often expressed a strong and undiscriminating hostility. Let me cite an instance or two.

When Shishupala† abused Krishna,

> that ideal being, supreme vehicle of mercy, supreme yogin,† did not make any reply. He had the power tc destroy Shishupala at once, as the reader learns later. Nor is Krishna known ever to have been abused in such harsh language. But he did not heed that abuse. He did not, like a European, grandly declare to Shishupala, 'Shishupala, forgiveness is a great virtue. I forgive you!' He silently forgave his enemy.

This unjust hit at Europeans while recounting the quality of mercy in Krishna is not only uncalled for; it harms Bankim's prime purpose. It prevents the reader's mind from being suitably prepared to appreciate Krishna's great power of forgiveness. A book like *Krishnacharitra* should not be meant for present-day Hindus alone; it should be addressed to all men of all times. The reader can easily imagine how a European's spirit would rebel when he reads this passage. It is specially hard to say how the author derives the notion that it is in the European character to eulogise the virtue of forgiveness while practising it. Our own shastras, on the other hand, have plenty of instances of somebody doing just that.

When Vishvamitra was forcibly taking away Vashishtha's miraculous cow Nandini,† and the ill-used Nandini came to Vashishtha and wailed piteously, Vashishtha said to her, 'O gentle Nanaini, I hear you calling again and again; but when King Vishwamitra is forcibly taking you away, what can I do? For I am a brahman, given to forgiveness.' When Nandini again called to him in pain, he said, 'A kshatriya is distinguished by his valour, a brahman by his forgiveness. Hence I am drawn to the virtue of forgiveness.'

To take another instance, Krishna observes, 'Those seeking to gratify their senses . . . are content with the middle state; but that is a source of misery. True happiness is to be found either in gaining a kingdom or in dwelling in the forest.'

Quoting this lofty sentiment, Bankim remarks: 'With ideas like this in Hindu mythological history, we waste our time reading novels written by memsahibs, or gathering at meetings where we chatter like birds.'

Such repeated outbursts of irascibility ill become a book like *Krishnacharitra.* The ideal character described in the book loses its lustre by the work's failure to sustain, in its language, mode, and style, a solemnity, beauty, and large-heartedness.

Bankim picks a quarrel on the slightest pretext with Europeans, with his readers, or with those whose misfortune it is to differ from his views. This belligerence is unbecoming in such a work. Moreover, he raises any number of irrelevant issues, thereby unnecessarily distracting the reader's attention. First, when he presents Krishna as the greatest of humans, the general question of whether divine incarnations are possible only raises an irrelevant issue in the reader's mind but does not properly solve it. To those who ask how God, who is bodiless, can take on material form, he replies that it is impossible that the All-Powerful should not be able to assume form. But why should he need to, if he is all-powerful anyway? some might ask. He could destroy Ravana[†] or Kumbhakarna,[†] Kangsa[†] or Shishupala by His mere wish. Bankim replies that it is not just to kill Ravana or Shishupala that God assumes form; His purpose is to set up an ideal of humanity for humans. If, in destroying the evildoer and preserving the good, He acts as God, there is nothing that humans can learn from Him. But if as a human He shows what humans can do, that can work to our lasting good. At this point, a third objection might be raised. If God is omnipotent and His aim is to establish an ideal of humanity for humans, could He not evolve a human being to manifest that ideal? Has He no recourse but for Himself to be born in human shape? Is His power limited in this way? Bankim neither raises this objection, nor does he refute it.

This contention, however, is not unconnected with the overall purpose of the book. At many places, Bankim has acknowledged that a human ideal is more effective than a divine one. We may not feel inspired to follow the example of an all-powerful Being. It is easier and more natural for us to hope and believe that what humans have done, we too can achieve. Hence, by trying to prove that Krishna is God, Bankim has detracted from his value as a human ideal: everything being easy for God, we find little to wonder at in the nature of Krishna.

By raising social controversies at many points, Bankimchandra has merely disturbed the tenor of his book without achieving anything. In the chapter entitled 'The Many Marriages of Krishna', after establishing that Krishna had no wife except Rukmini, Bankim ends with the contention that for a man to have many wives is not wrong in all circumstances. He says:

> It is generally wrong for a man to have more than one wife without good reason; but it is not so in all circumstances. If a man's wife suffers from leprosy, or is so sickly that she cannot render support in domestic life, I fail to see why it should be sinful for him to seek another wife. If someone's wife strays from virtue and brings shame and disgrace to his line, our small intelligence cannot fathom why he should not marry a second time without going to court in the matter. . . . If someone needs an heir and his wife is barren, I cannot understand why he should not take another wife. . . . Had Europe not been taught these very wrong ideas, Bonaparte would not have fallen into the damnable sin of abandoning Josephine, and Henry VIII would not have had to kill his wives on trifling pretexts. This is why these days, in the radiant light of civilisation, so many people in Europe are killing their wives or husbands. Our educated classes believe that whatever comes from Europe is superior, holy and immaculate, ensuring salvation down the generations. I for one believe that just as we can learn many things from England, there are many things England can learn from us. One of these latter is the philosophy of marriage.

As Krishna did not marry more than once, this debate about marriage is quite uncalled for. Besides, what conclusion does it reach? First, it is upheld that one whose wife is sickly or unchaste or barren can take a second wife. But it is not as if so many wife killings are taking place in enlightened Europe because husbands with sickly, unchaste, or barren wives cannot marry again. More often, such murders result from disaffection towards one's wife and love for some other woman. If such killings are to be prevented, love for another woman must be recognised as just ground for bigamy. In that case, to hold that 'It is generally wrong for a man to have more than one wife without good reason' is to say that if you wish to take a second wife, you must have a reason for it, it must not be done wantonly. Which amounts to granting that if your wife is weak and sickly, you may marry again; also that if you feel the desire to marry another woman, you are free to do so, since Henry VIII killed his wives on being thwarted in that wish. We are finally left saying: Do not commit bigamy if you have no motive for doing so.

The question now arises, can we allow the wife the same freedom on the same grounds that we are according the husband? Again, for lack of such a right, are many women in our society 'falling into damnable sin'?

Shortly after this, the author tries to argue that Krishna's abduction of Subhadra† was no wrongful act. In order to do so, Bankim takes a jab at a Parsi named Malabari†—the flower of whose fame has probably been consumed by worms within the leaves of certain recent journals—and thereby raises another social controversy, which too is not satisfactorily resolved. All that the author achieves is to pick a needless quarrel with a number of persons in harsh and intolerant language.

There would have been no occasion for all these arguments, and Bankim could have observed restraint all through his book, had he not regarded Krishna as God and harboured a *theory* about the entire perfection of every faculty of Krishna's mind. He could then have presented the reader, calmly, impartially, and free of distortion, with the ideal Krishna as depicted by the *Mahabharata* poet. He would not then have vented his anger in advance against any sceptical reader who might find the least fault with his *Krishnacharitra*. He thus banishes from his book the serenity that is the hallmark of great literature.

Off-stage directives can interfere with our enjoyment of the acting on stage: the beauty of the dramatic verse cannot fully imprint itself on the minds of the audience. So too in Bankim's presentation, the constant arguments and disputations prevent the true nature of Krishna from establishing itself integrally in the reader's mind. But Bankim may object that *Krishnacharitra* does not concern stage action; it belongs off-stage. 'I am,' he may say, 'the stage manager who, fighting against all odds, put the act together by collecting materials from many sources, and dressed up Krishna as the Supreme Man. Now let some poet come to raise the curtain and begin the play to everybody's delight. He will not have to shoulder any burden of labouring, thinking and judging.'

TRANSLATED BY BHAWANI-PRASAD CHATTOPADHYAY

The Meghadutam

From Ramagiri[†] to the Himalayas ran a long stretch of ancient India over which life used to flow to the slow, measured mandakranta metre of the *Meghadutam.* We are banished from that India, not just during the rains but for all time. Gone is Dasharna[†] with its groves hedged with ketaki plants where, before the onset of the rains, the birds among the roadside trees fed on household scraps and busily built their nests, while in the jaam copse on the outskirts of the village, the fruit ripened to a colour dark as the clouds. And the village elders of Avanti,[†] who used to tell the story of Udayana and Vasavadatta[†]—where are they? And Ujjayini[†] on the bank of the Shipra? Of course it also enjoyed great prosperity and enormous riches, but our memory is not burdened with a detailed account of that. All we have is the fleeting scent, that once wafted from the mansion windows, of the incense with which the women of the city perfumed their hair. We sense within us the deserted streets of the vast teeming city and its deep slumber through the dark night, when the pigeons were asleep on its rooftops. And we catch a glimpse, like a fleeting shadow, of the woman going to her lover with eager steps and trembling heart, through the dark lonely streets of that capital with its sleeping mansions and closed doors. How we wish we could throw just a ray of light at her feet, like the thin trace of gold on a touchstone!

And then, how charming are the names of the rivers, mountains, and cities of that segment of ancient India: Avanti, Vidisha,[†] Ujjayini, Vindhya,[†] Kailas,[†] Devagiri,[†] the Reva,[†] the Shipra,[†] the Vetravati.[†] There is a comeliness, a dignity, a purity about those names. It seems as if, since those days, the times have become more and more vulgar: our language, manners and outlook have withered and declined. Our naming of things these days follows the pattern. We feel that if we could only find our way back to Avanti or Vidisha, on the bank of the Reva, the Shipra or the Nirvindhya,[†] we would be freed of the vulgar cacophony that surrounds us today.

The yaksha's cloud thus sails over hills, rivers,[†] and cities, and with it go the sighs of the reader, afflicted by the sorrow of separation from his loved one. It was the India of the poet, where the loving-tender eyes of village wives had not yet learnt the artful play of eyebrows, and the town wives' long-lashed dark eyes, adept at beguiling play, sent out curious glances like swarms of bees.† We are banished from that India. We have only the poet's cloud to send there as a messenger.

I remember an English poet† saying that each man is an isolated island; we are separated by an immeasurable sea of salt tears. Viewing each other from a distance, we feel that once we were parts of a single continent; now, who knows by whose curse, the foaming sea of separation moans between us. From this narrow sea-girt present, when we look at the shores of that ancient land described in the poem and think of the women gathering flowers in the jasmine groves beside the Shipra, the old men who told tales of Udayana in the town squares of Avanti, and the sojourners away from home, who, looking at the first clouds of Asharh,† yearned for their wives—we feel that between them and us there ought to have been a bond. Our common humanity binds us intimately together, but remorseless time separates us. Thanks to the poet, that distant past has been transformed into the city of Alaka,† an everlasting visionary land of beauty. From this present world of ours, overcast by the grief of separation, we send out to it this cloud-messenger, our imagination.

Not only in the past or the present as a whole: in each man there is the bottomless sorrow of separation. She whom we pine for lives by the inaccessible shore of her own Manas Sarovar,† the lake of her solitary mind. We can only send our imagination there, never reach it in the flesh. Look where you are, and where am I! What lies between us? Nothing less than infinity. Who can cross it? That deathless, most beloved being at the heart of infinity—who can hope to meet her? All we have today, through words and gestures, hints and suggestions, errors and misapprehensions—in darkness and light, mind and body, among the swift currents of life and death—is a gentle breeze blowing from her. If I could only get a touch of that south breeze wafting from you, I would count myself fortunate. No one can hope for more in this world of separation.

Bhittva sadyah kisalayaputan devadarudrumanam
Ye tatkshirasrutisurabhayo dakshinena prabrittah.
Alingyante gunavati mayah te tusharadrivatah
Purvam sprishtam yadi kila bhavedangamebhistaveti.

[The breezes from the snowy peaks have just burst open the leaf-buds of deodar trees and, redolent of their oozing resin, blow southward. I embrace those breezes, fondly imagining they have lately touched your form, O perfect one!]†

Rabindranath Tagore: 'Woman going on tryst'.

By courtesy of Rabindra Bhavan, Shantiniketan.

It was this eternal separation that the Vaishnava poet was thinking of when he sang

In each other's arms, they think of parting and they weep.†

We stand, each one of us, alone on a lonely mountain peak, gazing northwards. Between us, the sky, the clouds, and the fair earth with its Reva, Shipra, Avanti, Ujjayini, its beauties, wealth and delights, stretch out like a painting. They arouse memories, but do not let us approach nearer. Desires are stirred but never satisfied. Two human beings, and so far apart!

But we are made to feel that once upon a time we together belonged to the same realm of the mind, from where we have been banished. That is why the Vaishnava poet says, 'Who took you out of my heart?'† How could this happen? Why did this denizen of my mind slip out into the world? You do not belong there. 'Lord, your Balaram's heart knows no peace,' sings Balaram Das. They were all one within the universal mind; now they have come out of it. So they cannot remain calm when they see each other. They are stricken by their separation; they are overcome with desire. We try to come together again in our hearts; but the vast world stands between us.

You on the lonely mountain top, sorrowful in separation—who has assured you that on a clear autumn night under a full moon, a night of such beauty as was never seen before, you will have everlasting union with her whom you embrace in your dreams, to whom you send messages though the cloud? You cannot distinguish between the sentient and the inanimate. Who knows, you may also have lost the distinction between reality and imagination.

TRANSLATED BY BHAWANI-PRASAD CHATTOPADHYAY

Kumarasambhavam *and* Shakuntala

In this essay and the next, Rabindranath follows a common Bengali practice by referring to Kalidasa's play Abhijnanashakuntalam *as* Shakuntala. *This simplified title, reflecting Rabindranath's own use, has been retained in translation, italicised to prevent confusion with Shakuntala the character.*

It is a common view that Kalidasa is purely a poet of the gratification afforded by beauty. That is why his character has been vilified in popular legend and report. These stories constitute the common man's critique of Kalidasa's poetry. They demonstrate that, whatever trust we place in the common man in other matters, we cannot blindly follow his blind lead in literary judgment.

The *Mahabharata* is swayed by an immense wave of activity; but there is a great calm unwavering renunciation at its heart. Action is not its own final prize in the *Mahabharata*. Through all its valour and heroism, anger and hatred, violence and counter-violence, strife and fulfilment, there sounds from the cremation-ground the renouncing, annihilating music† of the Great Departure.† It is the same in the *Ramayana*: consummate preparations are frustrated, fulfilment comes to hand yet eludes the grasp—everything ends in relinquishment. Yet it is through this loss, suffering and frustration that the nobility of action and manly assertion rises shining to the skies like the argent Mount Kailas.†

So also in Kalidasa, the renunciation of material satisfactions lies silently in the midst of the stirrings of beauty. Just as the *Mahabharata* can be called at once the poetry of action and of renunciation, Kalidasa can be called a poet of the enjoyment of beauty as well as the cessation of that enjoyment. His poetry does not come to rest in a luxuriance in beauty; he stops only after passing beyond it.

Where Kalidasa has stopped and where he has not must be discussed in distinction from present-day ideals. In assessing him, we cannot halt just anywhere on the road; we have to bear his destination in mind.

I firmly believe that a European poet would have ended the play of *Shakuntala* on a note of fruitless contrition at the point where Dushyanta receives the ring from the fisherman and realises his error. Shakuntala's union† with Dushyanta in the last act, on the latter's way back from heaven, was not necessary or inevitable by the rules of European dramatic practice. This is because the seed sown at the start of the play bears final fruit in their parting. Their subsequent reunion has had to be effected by external means, invoking a gracious destiny. There was no means to this union implicit in the events of the play, or in anything in the conduct of Dushyanta or Shakuntala.

Similarly, a poet today would have ended *Kumarasambhavam* with the thwarted Parvati's† sorrow and shame.† Through the grove of blood-red ashok flowers in an untimely spring, lit by the divine radiant anger of Shiva, slayer of the love-god, the daughter of the Himalayas would have come blushingly with bowed head, her unavailing flower ornaments about her, to stand upon the red lotus of the reader's pitiful grieving heart: the pain of unfulfilled love would have surrounded her for ever. In the judgment of present-day critics, this would have provided the poem with the brightest possible sunset: the subsequent wedding night† would have been lustreless by contrast.

Marriage is the prelude to everyday domestic life; it is part of the social order. Marriage points down a path with a single simple destination, where forceful appetite is as forcefully disallowed from carrying out its depredations. That is why poets today do not wish to magnify marriage in their work. The chief matter for poetry is now a love that, by its violent onrush, frees men and women from their thousand encircling bonds, that draws them out of the habitual path of social existence—a love that empowers men and women to think that they are sufficient in themselves, that they need fear nothing and lack nothing even if the whole world turns against them: a love that impels them, like planets thrown off course by some whirling motion, to detach themselves from everything around them and draw them more intensely into their own beings.

Kalidasa has not neglected to treat of the turbulent beauty of that unsought love: he has painted it in the bright hues of youthful grace. But he has not concluded his poem amidst this excessive brightness: its final purport lies in the serene outcome in muted colours towards which he has directed the work. As in the *Mahabharata*, all actions end in the Great

Departure, so too in *Kumarasambhavam*, all the impulsions of love end in beneficent union.

One cannot but compare *Kumarasambhavam* and *Shakuntala*. The subject of both works is at heart the same. In both, the union that Madana the love god tries to effect falls under divine malediction: unaccomplished, unconcluded, that union is struck dead by a divine hand on its exquisitely beautiful, variously embroidered marriage bed. The union forged subsequently, through stern suffering and a resolution born of unbearable separation, is different in nature: in garb of rare immaculacy, it casts aside all the trappings of external beauty, and instead draws grace from the holy light of beneficent virtue.

The union undertaken by the audacious Madana needed a great deal by way of appurtenance. With as much skill as elaboration, the poet has provided this sudden new causeless love with a fitting space between two forest retreats, outside the circle of society.

Shiva, clad in a tiger skin, was then meditating as an ascetic on a terrace of the Himalayas. The cool breeze,† bearing the scent of musk and the songs of kinnaras,† swayed the deodar trees watered by the Ganga. With the untimely arrival of spring,† the bride of the southern horizon† at once began to sigh there with hot breath, sending a murmur through the sprouting leaves of the fresh-flowering ashok trees. Pairing bees quaffed nectar together from the chalice of a single flower; the blackbuck rubbed his horns on the flanks of his doe, who closed her eyes at his touch.

The advent of spring in the forest hermitage—the sudden unfolding of Nature's true image amidst the enclosing walls of stern restraint, born of ascetic meditation! The vernal nature of spring does not appear so enchantingly in a pleasure garden.

The great sage Kanva's hermitage beside the river Malini is similar in nature. The leaves of the trees in that forest retreat have lost their colour from the smoke of ritual fires; the pathways to the lakes are traced over with water dripping from the bark dress of hermits back from bathing; the trusting deer listen to the sound of chariot wheels and the hum of bowstrings with fearless curiosity. But nature has not fled this place either: even here, Shakuntala's blooming youth breaks out unbeknownst from beneath her rough bark garment, straining at its tight bands. Even here the gesture of the mango tree, its leafy fingers shaken by the breeze, is not quite in consonance with the chants of the Sama Veda; and the malati creeper in her blossoming youth embraces the mango tree to declare her eagerness for union with the beloved.

All round, the endless array of untimely spring: in what enchanting guise does the daughter of the Himalayas appear in its midst! Adorned with ornaments of ashok and cassia flowers, robed in the colours of the young sun, a girdle of kesara flowers slipping down her waist time and again—Gauri,[†] her eyes restless with fear, waving the lotus she holds to drive off the insistent bees.

And set against her, Shiva, seated on a tiger skin upon a platform below deodar trees, in a knotted blackbuck hide with serpents coiled round his upgathered locks, contemplating his own being with eyes subdued in meditation, like a becalmed sea.

Madana busied himself in bringing about a union of this unmatched couple at this inappropriate place in an untimely spring.

It is the same in Kanva's ashram: on one side the hermit's foster daughter, clothed in bark; on the other the ruler of land and sea. Kalidasa has shown the power of the fish-pennanted god,[†] who can so confound place, time, and personalities in an instant.

But the poet has not stopped there. He has not paid his full measure of poetic tribute to this one power. He has indeed reported its sudden victory, but concluded the poem by effecting a full and final union through another unconquerable force. He has not only shown Madana as vanquished, although encouraged by the king of the gods[†] and aided by the enchanting power of spring; in his place, the poet has set up one with neither array nor resource, lean with meditation and pale with suffering.[†] The king of the gods had never given him a thought.

Kalidasa has acknowledged the power of the love that has no bonds or rules, that suddenly overwhelms men and women and sets its triumphal flag atop the ruined fortress of temperance; but he has not surrendered to it. He has shown that the blind amorous indulgence that intoxicates us with self-assertion is crossed by a master's curse,[†] thwarted by a holy man's,[†] and turned to ashes by divine wrath.[†] When the law of hospitality[†] became as nothing for Shakuntala, when Dushyanta was all-in-all, there was no longer any goodness in her love. Such violent love, that forgets everything except the loved one, antagonises the universal law and hence soon grows unbearable: it cannot sustain its own weight against the thrust of all things else.

Neither god nor man can strike at the permanence of a self-restraining love in harmony with the world, that does not overlook anyone around it—great or small, akin or alien; that places its near ones at the centre but spreads its benevolent sweetness across the universe. Even if its fixity is threatened, it is not impaired. But the love that enters the hermit's retreat to shatter his meditation, or the householder's yard to suddenly overthrow the laws of domestic life, might, like a typhoon, destroy others, but it carries its own destruction as well.

Bowed by the weight of her own high-piled youth, Uma† came like a swaying creeper† in leaf, fell at Shiva's feet, and made obeisance: a leaf dropped from her ear, and fresh cassia flowers from her hair. With a hand glowing like copper, she gave the ascetic her offering of a string of prayer-beads, made from the seeds, dried in the sun with her own hands, of the lotus growing in the Mandakini river. Their hands touched. The distracted yogin† opened his three eyes† wide at Uma's face and her lips. Uma's frame was overcome with excited delight, her eyes bashfully lowered, her face averted to one side.

But the god did not trust this glee, roused so suddenly by the sight of this exquisite beauty: he angrily rejected it. The shamed and mortified woman somehow made her way back home in the knowledge that the beauty of her graceful youth had been affronted.

Kanva's foster daughter† too had to go back humiliated one day with the full store of her youthful grace. Durvasha's curse is no more than a poetic allegory. The secret uncommitted union between Dushyanta and Shakuntala was doomed by an immemorial malediction. The effulgence of intoxication breaks out only for an instant; it is then assailed by the darkness of fatigue, dishonour, and oblivion. That is the law of all time. Age after age, in land after land, humiliated woman, *vyartham samarthya lalitam bapuratmanashcha*—'knowing the grace of her body to be in vain'—*shunya jagama bhavanabhimukhi kathanchit*, 'somehow makes her way back home with empty heart'.† The beauty of a graceful body is not a woman's ultimate beauty or her greatest glory.

That is why *nininda rupang hridayena Parvati*, Parvati dispraised beauty in her heart, yet *iyesha sa kartumavandhyarupatam*, wished that her own beauty might be fulfilled.† How can beauty be fulfilled? Through dress or ornaments? That test had failed.

Iyesha sa kartumavandhyarupatam
Samadhimasthaya tapobhiratmanah.

She desired to make her beauty unsterile through ascetic meditation.†

Now Gauri† no longer wrapped her body in robes coloured like the sunrise; she did not put mango leaves in her ears or fresh cassia flowers in her hair; she belted in her bark dress with a girdle of rough munja grass, sat down in the posture of meditation, and darkened the corners of her long eyes. Rejecting Madana, companion of spring, god of the five darts, she took hard suffering as her attendant in love.

Shakuntala too, burning up Madana's intoxicating torment in the fire of grief, garbed herself as a virtuous ascetic to await the coming of fulfilled love.

The three-eyed god who had instantly rejected Gauri when she came adorned with spring flowers now unquestioningly, with full heart, surrendered himself to the hermit woman, lean and pale as the crescent moon seen by day, her tawny mass of hair hanging down behind her. Disdaining youthfulness as fortified by grace and beauty, Parvati's unadorned mind-sustained form arose like a ray of clear light. Her desired one was not disturbed but fulfilled by that beauty. No shame, fear, hurt, or agitation remained in him; his soul gladly admitted bondage to that beauty, without feeling defeated thereby.

After so long,

> *Dharmenapi padam Sharve karite Parvatim prati*
> *Purvaparadhabhitasya kamasyochchhvasitam manah.*
>
> When dharma drew Mahadeva's mind towards Parvati, the love-god, so long fearful because of his earlier offence, now felt his mind swelling with hope.[†]

Where righteous virtue brings two hearts together, there is no conflict with Madana. It is when he wishes to revolt against virtue that a conflict occurs: there is no longer steadfastness in love or tranquillity in beauty. But in due place under the governance of virtue, Madana constitutes part of that fullness: he does not disturb its harmony. That is because virtue implies harmony: harmony protects beauty and beneficence and, making them one and the same, imparts a joyful completeness to both. Where beauty extends beyond the senses into the realm of ideas, the edict of external loveliness no longer prevails over it. It has no more need of ornament: the beauty created in the mind by love's holy spell cannot be judged by the laws of external beauty. Such laws cannot quite reconcile a meditative ascetic like Shiva with a young girl like Gauri. The disguised Shiva himself said as much[†] to her when she was seeking him through meditation. She replied, '*Mamatra bhavaikarasam manahsthitam*' (My mind is centred in him in a oneness of ideational spirit.)[†] This spirit, this rasa is the rasa of an idea, a state of mind: there is no questioning it. Here the mind has triumphed over external things to create, of itself, its own bliss. Shiva too had once spurned external beauty; but the beauty he now saw in the light of love, virtue, and beneficence vanquished him, although it was unadorned and lean with ascesis. This happened because his own mind assisted the victory: the authority of the mind was not impaired.

When dharma effected such a union of the male and the female ascetic, all heaven and earth appeared as aides and witnesses to their love. The call of that love reached to the constellation of the Seven Sages;† its festive spirit spread from one world to another. It no longer harboured any deep conspiracy, any advent of an untimely spring or Madana's secret archery. Its unfading beneficent loveliness became matter for joy to all the world: the entire universe brought this auspicious union to fruition by attending it as delighted guests.

The seventh canto shows this universal rejoicing. The wedding festivities constitute the essence of *Kumarasambhavam*.

Beauty finds its fullness in the midst of peace, not conflict. Kalidasa has brought the rasa flowing through his poem to a noble culmination, merging it with a fully accomplished peace pervading earth and heaven: he has not left it half way, *na yayau na tasthau* (neither here nor there).† He has indeed disturbed that peace once, midway through, but only to show up the serenity of the achieved beauty as deeper by contrast—to present its clear, steadfast, beneficent image more brightly against a distracted beauty in varying guises.

When Shiva saw Arundhati,† model of wifely devotion, among the Seven Sages, he realised what a wife's beauty consists in.

Taddarshanadabhut shambhorbhuyan dararthamadarah
Kriyanam khalu dharmyanam satpannyo mulakaranam.

Seeing her, Shambhu became eager to take a wife. A virtuous wife is the chief motivator of righteous works.†

The glorious comeliness of a married woman, as etched on the face of a devoted wife, is the steady beauty of beneficent works, unremittingly performed. In Shiva's imagination, that beauty was reflected from the serene image of Arundhati to touch the brow of Gauri in bridal array. The Daughter of the Mountain thereby evinced a grace beyond the loveliness that all the flowers of the untimely spring had bestowed upon her.

On her wedding-day, Gauri

Sa mangalasnanavishuddhagatri
Grihitapatyudgamaniyavastra
Nivrittaparjanyajalabhisheka
Praphullakasha vasudheva reje.

cleansed by the auspicious bath, she put on clothes appropriate for union with her lord, and appeared with a presence like the earth joyful with kash flowers at the end of the first monsoon rain.†

What peace, what comeliness, what fullness in this glowing beneficent vision! All effort, all array finds its end here. It evinces no design of Indra's court, no illusion woven by Madana, no assistance from an untimely spring: it is serene and perfect in its own unstained beneficence.

In our country, a woman's chief role is that of mother: the birth of a child is for us a holy and beneficent matter. That is why Manu† has said of women, *Prajanartham mahabhagah pujarha grihadiptayah*: 'They give birth to offspring, hence they are great of soul, objects of worship, and the shining light of the home.'† The entire poem of *Kumarasambhavam* is a fit prologue to the great event of Kartikeya's birth.† Madana brings about a union by secretly shooting his arrows to break down the barriers of restraint; that union is not worthy to engender a son, for its members desire each other, not the son. That is why the poet has shown Madana as reduced to ashes,† and made Gauri undergo ascetic meditation. That is why he has replaced the restlessness of appetite with a steadfast intensity, the illusory toils of beauty with the comely light of beneficence, and the rapturous springtime forest with a universe steeped in joy: then and then only could the birth of Kartikeya be set in process. It is to convey the nature of this birth that the poet has immolated Madana on the fire of divine wrath, making the widowed Rati break out in lament.

In *Shakuntala* too, the poet has shown the unavailing love of Dushyanta for his beloved in the first act, and then, in the last, his fulfilling union with the mother of Bharata.†

The first act is steeped in radiance and restlessness. It unfolds an exquisite scene, redolent of intoxicating beauty. A corner of the forest retreat becomes a haven for the sage's foster daughter in the ferment of her youth, her two high-spirited companions, the blooming nabamalika creepers, the scent-besotted honey bee—and, from behind a tree, the enthralled king. From this paradise of delight, Dushyanta's beloved is ignominiously exiled; but the holier forest hermitage† where the beneficent figure of Bharata's mother finds shelter presents a different scene. There no young hermit girls water the bases of trees, or sprinkle their sibling creepers with loving looks, or feed fawns with handfuls of wild rice as if they were their sons. There, a single boy† has acquired all the restlessness of the trees, creepers, leaves, and flowers; he fills the lap of the entire forest. Nobody observes whether the mango branch bears blossom or the nabamalika bursts into flower: the hermit matrons are preoccupied with affectionate concern for this unruly child.

In the first act, Dushyanta had been attracted and enthralled by Shakuntala's fresh youthful grace, seen from afar before he made her acquaintance. In the last act, Shakuntala's child has taken the place of all Shakuntala's own graces to infuse the deepest recesses of the king's heart.

At such a time

Vasane paridhusare vasana
Niyamakshamamukhi dhritaikavenih.

Shakuntala of cleansed mind, her love-separation assumed as a vow, entered in soiled, greyed clothes, her face parched from her rigorous rule of life, her hair bound in a single plait.†

Can such ascesis not be rewarded with a lasting boon? By prolonged adherence to vows, the torment of the first union has been consumed, and a moving, beneficent maternal image raised in its place, decked with the supreme ornament of a son: who can reject it?

In Shiva, Gauri saw no lack, no poverty. She viewed him with the eyes of the mind, which does not take count of wealth or looks or youth. Shakuntala's love too brought no charge against Dushyanta in their hour of union, even after so much ignominy; only her eyes flowed with tears. Where there is no love, there is no end to want and ugliness and impoverishment, only offences everywhere. Gauri's love saw her beloved ascetic as comely and divine in the light of its own beauty and riches; so too Shakuntala's love distanced all Dushyanta's misdoings by the power of its own beneficent vision. There is no such forgiveness in the infatuation of young lovers.

Along with Bharata, the son of her womb, Shakuntala was also nurturing patient forgiveness, like a daughter, to fullness in her heart during her later forest sojourn. The boy Bharata pointed to Dushyanta and asked, 'Mother, who is this calling me his son?' Shakuntala replied, 'My darling, ask your destiny.'† There was no resentment in the reply: it meant simply, 'You will obtain your answer if it pleases destiny.' So saying, she awaited the king's pleasure. And as soon as she understood that Dushyanta was not denying her, this forgiving, unpresuming woman laid her melted heart as a worshipful flower-offering at Dushyanta's feet, seeing no offence on anybody's part except that of her own fate. If we view another with the eyes of self-regard, we see him piecemeal, so that his offences are magnified; when we view him in entirety, with love and understanding, they disappear.

As the first verse of a shloka awaits completion through union with another verse, the first meeting of Dushyanta and Shakuntala craves to be completed in this second meeting. All the suffering that Shakuntala has undergone cannot be held in suspense: that would negate its purpose. If, at a solemn feast, only the fire is lit but no rice is cooked upon it, how will the guests fare? The last act of *Shakuntala* has been devised not in accord with the external conventions of dramatic art, but by a deeper rule.

We therefore see that the two poems, *Kumarasambhavam* and *Shakuntala*, have the same theme. In both, the poet shows how what is frustrated by deluded infatuation finds fulfilment in beneficent virtue. He shows how only that beauty is constant which is upheld by virtue, and how the serene, restrained, beneficent image of love is its best image; how true loveliness is realised through constraint, while a state of disorder quickly perverts beauty. The poet of ancient India has not granted love to be its own greatest glory, but declared beneficence to be the highest end of love. In his view, the love of man and woman cannot be lasting or beautiful if it is barren, if it remains constricted within itself—if it does not give birth to beneficence and spread itself across the world as a varied range of blessings among our children, guests, and fellow humans.

On one side, the beneficent ties of virtuous domesticity; on the other, casting off the ties of the unattached soul: both these are concepts distinctive to India. In this world, India is attached to many persons by many ties: none of them can be cast off. On the seat of meditation, India is entirely alone. In *Kumarasambhavam* and *Shakuntala*, Kalidasa has shown that there is no lack of consonance between these two spheres: they are linked by channels of movement and exchange. Just as the lion cub plays with the human child in his forest retreat, the ethos of the yogin and that of the householder commingle in his poetic hermitage. Madana had attempted to sever that bond; that is why the poet hurls a thunderbolt upon him, and re-establishes, on a basis of ascetic endeavour, the holy bond between the beneficent household and the desire-free hermitage. He has built a home on the foundations of a hermit's retreat; rescuing the relations of man and woman from the sudden attack of desire, he has set them on the yogin's immaculate seat, sanctified by meditation.

In Indian scriptural edict, the man–woman relationship is restrained and confined by stern enjoinments; in Kalidasa's poetry, it is fashioned from the ingredients of beauty. That beauty is radiant with the light of comeliness, modesty, and beneficence. In depth, it is intensely unicitous; in expanse, it harbours the world. It is fulfilled through renunciation, gratified through suffering, and constant by virtue of righteousness. In such beauty, the destructive force of man and woman's irresistible love curbs itself and achieves ultimate silence in the great ocean of beneficence. Hence it is nobler and more awesome than that other unbound, intractable love.

TRANSLATED BY SUKANTA CHAUDHURI

Shakuntala

For the use of Shakuntala *as a title, see the headnote to the previous essay.*

Many of the illustrative passages from Kalidasa were attractively rendered by Rabindranath in Bengali verse for this essay, sometimes simplifying or modifying the Sanskrit original. They have been represented here in English verse, following Rabindranath's imaginative re-creations of the Sanskrit. In a few cases the Sanskrit original has also been quoted elsewhere in the essay, and is rendered here by a closer equivalent in prose. The contrast between the two versions can be significant.

A comparison between Shakespeare's play *The Tempest* and Kalidasa's *Shakuntala* readily suggests itself. Their external resemblances and inner disparities are a matter for discussion.

The love between Miranda, nurtured in seclusion, and Prince Ferdinand resembles the love between the hermit's foster daughter† Shakuntala and Dushyanta. The locales are similar too: in one case a sea-girt island, in the other a forest retreat.†

We thus find a similarity in the basic narrative; but as soon as we start to read, we sense a total difference of poetic spirit.

Goethe,† that wise master in the line of European poets, has written a critique of *Shakuntala* in a single stanza: he has not dissected the work. His stanza is brief, like the flame of a tiny earthen lamp; but like the flame of such a lamp, it lights up the whole play to our view in an instant. He has put it in a word by saying that if someone wishes to see the flower of youth and the fruit of maturity, to see earth and heaven in one place, he can do so in *Shakuntala*.

Many readers take this remark lightly, judging it to be mere poetic effusion. They think it means simply that Goethe considers *Shakuntala* to be a highly delectable work. That is not so. Goethe's observation is not a hyperbolic expression of delight; it is the considered judgment of a connoisseur. There is something singular about it.

The poet has specifically said that *Shakuntala* contains a strain of deep fulfilment: the fulfilment leading from flower to fruit, from earth to heaven, from nature to dharma. In the *Meghadutam* there is the 'Early Cloud' and the 'Later Cloud':† having traversed the various beauties of the world on the cloud's earlier journey, we can arrive at the sole timeless beauty of the celestial city of Alaka in the later account. So too in *Shakuntala* there is an early union and a final union. The play spans the journey from the early union of the first act—earthly, various, full of changing beauties—to the final union in a celestial forest retreat, full of eternal joy. This is not merely to present a single theme or the growth of a particular character; it is to transport the entire poem from one world to another. It elevates love from the realm of natural beauty to the imperishable heaven of beneficent beauty. I have discussed this matter in another essay,† and do not wish to repeat it here.

Kalidasa has brought about this union of heaven and earth with great ease. He has made the flower grow into the fruit by natural process; he has mingled the borders of earth with the territory of heaven so skilfully that no one can discern any division between them. In presenting the fall of Shakuntala in the first act, the poet has not glossed over the earthly element in the least. Through the conduct of both Dushyanta and Shakuntala, he has clearly shown how far the power of desire is present in the scene. He has fully brought out the demeanour and restless play of intoxicated youth, the conflict between profound diffidence and fierce self-assertion.

This testifies to Shakuntala's simplicity. She had not been prepared for such a sudden burst of rapture at a moment so conducive: she had no ready strategy to restrain herself or hide her feelings. The doe that has never known the hunter is quickly shot. Shakuntala was not properly acquainted with the five-darted love-god: she had therefore left her heart unprotected. She distrusted neither Kandarpa† nor Dushyanta. In a forest where hunting is common, the hunter has to carefully conceal himself; similarly, in a society where the union of man and woman is easy and habitual, the love-god has to proceed with great caution, hiding himself from sight. But the girl of the forest retreat is as unguarded as its deer are unafraid.

Shakuntala's surrender is simply and directly rendered; but her deeper purity of character in spite of it, her natural inviolate chastity is as readily expressed. This too testifies to her simplicity. The artificial flower that adorns a room must be dusted every day, but one need not employ anybody to dust the flower of the forest. It is undraped and exposed to dust, yet how easily it protects its immaculate beauty! Shakuntala too had been touched by dust, but she did not even know it. Like the innocent forest doe, like the water from a spring, she is effortlessly pure even in contact with dirt.

Kalidasa has set free his ashram-nurtured† Shakuntala, in the fresh flower of her youth, to travel the road of undiffident human nature: to the end, he has never blocked her path. Yet he has depicted her as reticent of speech, sobered by suffering, regulated in her ways, an ideal image of chastity. She follows the bent of her nature unselfconsciously, like a tree, creeper, flower, or fruit; yet her inner womanly being is restrained, forbearing, single-mindedly contemplative, totally governed by the discipline of the good and beneficent. With singular skill, Kalidasa has placed his heroine at the estuary where playfulness and patience, nature and rule, river and ocean come to meet.

Shakuntala's father is a hermit, her mother a celestial courtesan. She was born by the breaking of a vow but brought up in a spiritual retreat. A forest hermitage is a place where nature and contemplation, beauty and restraint are united. It is not bound by the artificial dictates of society, but the stern law of dharma rules there. The ritual of the gandharva marriage† is of the same order. It displays the intractability of human nature, but also the social tie of marriage.

By being placed at the meeting point of constraint and freedom, the play *Shakuntala* has acquired a rare quality. Its joys and sorrows, unions and partings are all brought about through the encounter of these two elements. It is apparent on consideration why Goethe, in his critique, proclaimed the union of two disparates in *Shakuntala*.

This strain is not present in *The Tempest*. Why must it be? Shakuntala is beautiful, so is Miranda; but who would expect their noses or their eyes to be exactly similar? Their situations, experiences, and natures are totally different. Miranda has been reared in solitude from her childhood; Shakuntala did not experience the same solitude. Miranda has grown up in the company of her father alone, so that her nature has not been encouraged to develop naturally. Shakuntala has grown up among girls of her own age: they have developed naturally in one another's warm proximity through mutual imitation, exchange of ideas, laughter, jests, and talk. If Shakuntala had stayed continually beside the hermit Kanva, her growth would have been impeded: her simplicity would have been synonymous with ignorance, making of her a female Rishyashringa.†

In truth, Shakuntala's simplicity derives from her nature, while Miranda's is the outcome of external circumstance. This accords with the difference in their situations. Shakuntala's simplicity, unlike Miranda's, is not girt round by ignorance. Shakuntala's youth has just come to flower, and her high-spirited companions do not let her forget it: we see this in the very first act. She has also learnt to be bashful. But all this is external to her being. Her simplicity lies deeper; her chastity is more inward. The poet shows to the end how no external experience can touch her. Shakuntala's simplicity lies within. It is not as though she knows nothing of worldly things. The forest retreat was not really outside society; it observed domestic rule. Although inexperienced in external matters, Shakuntala is not ignorant; but in her heart, implicit trust sits enthroned. That trusting simplicity of nature lets her lapse for a moment, but redeems her forever; even under the blow of fiercest betrayal, it preserves her unwaveringly in patience, forgiveness, and beneficence. Miranda's simplicity is not tested by fire: it does not encounter any conflict with worldly wisdom. We see her only in the first stage of development; Shakuntala has been shown by the poet in all stages, from first to last.

In such a case, there is no point in critical comparisons. We too admit that. If we place these two poems side by side, their difference appears more clearly than their similarity. But even a discussion of that difference might help us to understand the two plays clearly. We have undertaken this essay in that hope.

We see Miranda in the midst of a wave-lashed, desolate, mountainous island; but she has no intimate relationship with nature on that island. If she were to be plucked from that maternal soil where she has lived since infancy, it would not cause any wrench to her being. Her state of being reflects only the lack of human company in such a place; we find no mental affinity with the ocean and mountains there. We see the lonely island only through the poet's descriptions or in course of events; we do not see it through Miranda's eyes. The island is only required for the plot; it is not essential to the character.

This cannot be said of Shakuntala: she is one with the forest retreat. If the hermitage were to be kept at a distance, not only would the dramatic action suffer; Shakuntala herself would remain incomplete. Shakuntala is not an isolated being like Miranda; she is linked in spirit to her surroundings. Her sweet nature expands and flowers among the forest shades and the blossoms on the madhavi creeper; it is deeply drawn to the unfeigned affection of birds and beasts. The external nature that Kalidasa describes in his play does not remain external: he displays it through Shakuntala's being. That is why I said that Shakuntala cannot be brought out of the fold of her poetic environment.

We know Miranda chiefly through her amour with Ferdinand. We also see her distressed pity in her anxiety for the shipwrecked mariners during the tempest. Shakuntala is much more comprehensively presented. Even if Dushyanta had not appeared on the scene, the sweetness of her being would have found many other expressions. Her heart's creeper binds everything, animate and inanimate, with graceful tendrils of love. When she waters the plants around her home, she anoints them also with sibling love. She takes the youthful, newly blossomed nabamalika flower into her tender heart through her soft gaze. When she leaves the forest retreat for her husband's home, every step is fraught with ties and with pangs of parting. Of all the literature of the world, only the fourth act of *Shakuntala* shows us how grievous and heart-rending the parting between a human being and a forest can be.

In this poem, as there is the union of nature with rule and principle, there is also the union of nature with humankind. I think no country other than India could have brought about this sense of implicit union between dissimilars.

In *The Tempest*, external nature takes on human shape in the figure of Ariel, but keeps away from any kinship with man. Ariel's relationship with humankind is that of unwilling servant. He wishes to be free; but bound and oppressed by human force, he is made to work like a slave. He has no love in his heart, no tears in his eyes. Nor has Miranda's womanly heart extended any affection towards him. When Prospero and Miranda leave the island, they exchange no tender farewell with Ariel. In *The Tempest*, oppression, rule, rigour; in *Shakuntala*, love, peace, and fellowship. In *The Tempest*, nature assumes the shape of man yet is not bound to him by the heart's ties; in *Shakuntala*, trees, birds, and beasts retain their own shapes yet unite with man in a pleasing relationship.

When, at the start of the play, we hear this moving call to the king who has raised his bow, *Bho bho rajan ashramamrigoyam na hantavyo na hantyavyah* (O King, do not kill, do not kill the ashram deer)† it strikes a principal chord of the play. The canopy of pity held out by the forbiddance protects the ashram girl Shakuntala as well as the ashram deer.

Turn your bow from the tender deer!
Who would set a flower on fire?
Here is the deer's life, O King,
And there your dart comes thundering.†

This also applies to Shakuntala. Towards her too, the king shoots a fearsome arrow of love. The king is indeed a hard veteran trafficker in love—how hard we know from other evidence—while the inexperience and simplicity of this young girl raised in an ashram is all too tender, all too moving. Alas, she needs pleas for protection as much as the deer. *Dvau api atra aranyakau.* [They are both forest-dwellers.]†

No sooner have the echoes of this pitiful call died away than we see the daughter of the hermitage, dressed in tree bark, watering the furrows with her companions: she is carrying out her daily task of love towards the trees, her brothers, and the creepers, her sisters. It is not just the bark she wears; her gestures and movements make her appear one among the plants. That is what makes Dushyanta say

Lips as red as tender leaves,
Like young branches her two arms,
Form infused with blooming youth
Like a flower that tempts the heart.

At the very start of the play, we encounter this full life—replete with beauty and peace, with the daily tasks of the ashramic order among secluded leaves and flowers, with hospitality, companionate affection and nurturing universal love. It is so integral, so joyful that we are in constant fear that it might shatter at a blow. We wish to block Dushyanta's path, our arms raised, and say, 'Do not, do not shoot your arrow! Do not shatter this full and perfect beauty!'

As Dushyanta and Shakuntala's love swiftly grows deep, a sudden outcry rises from behind the scenes at the end of the first act: 'O hermits, take guard to protect the creatures of your hermitage. King Dushyanta is about to approach on his hunt.'

Such is the tearful call of the whole terrain around the forest retreat—and Shakuntala is one of the creatures of the hermitage. But it could not protect her.

When Shakuntala is about to leave that forest retreat, Kanva calls out, 'O assembled trees of the hermitage,

She who never quenched her thirst
Had she not watered you first;
She who loved to dress, yet never
Your beloved leaves would sever;
She who would rejoice as soon
As your flowers had come to bloom—
With her lord she goes to dwell:
All of you, bid her farewell.'†

Such is her intimate kinship with all things, conscious and unconscious: such the tie of affection and beneficence.

Shakuntala said, 'O Priyamvada,† my heart is yearning to see my husband, but my feet will scarcely move to take me out of this ashram.' Priyamvada replied, 'Not only are you distressed at leaving the hermitage; the hermitage too is in the same state at your impending departure:

The grass drops from the deer's jaws,
    The peacocks dance no more,
And every creeper sheds its leaves
    As if the tears did flow.'†

Shakuntala said to Kanva, 'Father, when this deer's wife grazing beside the hut, heavy with child, has safely given birth, send somebody to me to give me the good news.'

'I shan't forget,' said Kanva.

Then Shakuntala felt a tug from behind her and said, 'Who is it that pulls me by my clothes?'

Kanva said, 'My daughter,

    He whose jaws, when chafed by kusha grass,
With oil of ingudi you would smear,
He whom you fed with fistfuls of green paddy—
    This is your son, that baby deer.'†

Shakuntala said to it, 'My darling, why are you still following the companion who is leaving you? When your mother died as soon as you were born, it was I who brought you up. Now I am going. Father will look after you. Go back.'

She took leave of all the plants, animals, and birds in this way, and left the forest retreat shedding tears.

Shakuntala had the same natural relationship with the forest retreat that the flower has with the creeper.

Like Anasuya or Priyamvada, or Kanva, or Dushyanta, the natural setting of the forest retreat is also a character in *Shakuntala*. Nowhere except in Sanskrit literature, I believe, has mute nature been given such a central and essential place in a drama. One can write an allegorical play by personifying Nature and putting words on her lips; but to keep nature natural, yet make it so living, so immediate, so pervasive, so intimate, to make it perform so many dramatic functions—we have not seen this anywhere else. Where external nature is regarded as something distant and alien, where humanity raises walls around itself to create divisions throughout the world, such creations of literature are impossible.

In *Uttararamacharitam*† too, there is this affectionate kinship between nature and humanity. Even in the royal palace, Sita's heart weeps for the forest. The river Tamasa and the bountiful goddess of the springtime forest were her favoured companions there; the peacock and elephant calf were her foster children; the trees and creepers her kinsfolk.

In *The Tempest*, man has not enlarged his being by extending himself into the universe beneficently in a tie of love; he has tried to dominate the universe by curtailing and tyrannising over the latter. In fact, the principal theme of *The Tempest* is the conflict and strife to dominate. There Prospero, ousted from rule over his own kingdom, establishes stern rule over nature by the power of magic. When a few creatures reach the shore of the island after somehow escaping death, they too engage in conspiracies, betrayals, and attempts at assassination, to dominate over what is virtually a desert island. By the end, their efforts have been stayed; but no one can say that they have finally ended. Demonic nature falls silent, like the persecuted Caliban, out of fear, oppression, and lack of opportunity; but its fangs and talons still bear venom. Everybody gains what is due, but that is only an external gain. It might be the goal of a mercenary community; it cannot be the final outcome of a poetic work.

The Tempest is in content as it is in name: a conflict between nature and humankind, between one human being and another—and, at the root of that conflict, the struggle for power. It is full of strife from beginning to end.

Intractable human nature raises such tempests. These propensities then need to be restrained, like savage beasts, by discipline, suppression, and persecution. But to ward off force with force in this way can only be a temporary measure for limited practical ends. Our spiritual nature cannot admit this to be our ultimate goal: it wishes that evil should be eradicated, extinguished from within by beauty, love, and beneficence. There may be a thousand obstacles to this end in practical life; yet it constitutes a deeper human purpose. Literature expresses a profound endeavour to achieve that purpose. It makes the good, beautiful; the superior, lovable; the virtuous deed, the heart's treasure. To keep us on the path of beneficence by weighing consequences and inspiring terror is an external-minded business; it might form the subject matter of penal law or religious ethics. But higher literature seeks to pursue the interior path of the spirit: it washes away stains with heartfelt tears, burns up sin with heartfelt despise, and ushers in virtue with simple joy.

Kalidasa too, in his play, has quenched the forest fire of indomitable impulse with the rain of tears from a penitent heart. But he has not discussed the malady at excessive length: he has merely hinted at it, and then drawn a veil. What in mundane life might have happened naturally, he has made to happen by Durvasa's curse;[†] or else it would have been so intensely cruel and distressing as to impair the balance and serenity of the whole play. The rasa that Kalidasa has aimed for in *Shakuntala* could not have survived such a grotesque disturbance. He has preserved sorrow and pain in full measure, veiling only the ugly and horrific.

Yet Kalidasa has left a little gap in that veil through which we might glimpse evil. Let us talk about that.

The fifth act shows Dushyanta's rejection of Shakuntala. At the start of the act, the poet has briefly drawn away the curtain from the spectacle of the king's amorous sports. From behind the scene, the royal paramour Hamsapadika sits and sings to herself in the music room:

O honey bee, so greedy for new honey,
　　You dwelt once in the lotus-grove—
But now, the mango blossom having kissed,
　　How could you have forgot that love?[†]

This tearful song of a grieving heart, rising from the women's quarters of the palace, pains us deeply—the more so because our hearts had earlier been won by Dushyanta's love sport with Shakuntala. In the immediately previous act, Shakuntala had set out for her husband's home—with a very tender sadness, a very sweet sanctity of spirit, fortified with the blessings of the old sage Kanva and the auspicious invocations breathed forth by the whole forest. The picture of love and home life we may have been drawing for her on hope's canvas is stained over at the very outset of the next act.

When the comic companion[†] asks, 'Did you understand the implications of this song?', the King smiles a little and says, *Sakritkritapranayoyam janah*:[†] 'A person only loves once and then gives over; hence I have come to deserve this rousing reprimand on account of Queen Vasumati.† Madhava, my friend, tell Hamsapadika from me that she has rebuked me very skilfully. . . . Go, tell her this with due gallantry.'

This glimpse of the king's fickle amours at the start of the fifth act is not without significance. The poet is informing us very skilfully that what happens as a result of Durvasa's curse had its germination in Dushyanta's nature. It is shown as fortuitous to suit the poetic fable; but it is in fact natural.

As we pass from the fourth act to the fifth, we enter a different atmosphere. We have dwelt all this while in a realm of the mind: its laws were different from the one we now enter. How can the music of that forest retreat match these other notes? We are fearful of the possible outcome, in such a place, of the events transacted so easily and attractively in the hermitage. So when we see, in the courtly practices commencing the fifth act, that hearts here are very hard, love full of wiles, and the path to union anything but easy, our beautiful forest dream seems about to shatter. The sage's disciple Sharngarava† remarks as he enters the palace, 'I feel I am entering a house encircled by fire.' Sharadvata† observes, 'As the man who has bathed feels when he sees one who has only oiled himself, or the pure person when he sees the unclean, or one who is awake when he sees the sleeping, or the unfettered man when he sees the bound, so feel I on seeing all these worldly men.' The young ascetics readily sense that they have stepped into a totally distinct world.

At the start of the fifth act, the poet thus prepares our minds by many hints and suggestions, so that we may not be too suddenly or severely hurt at the rejection of Shakuntala. Hamsapadika's simple sad song comes to serve as prologue to this canto of cruelty.

When after this, rejection lights upon Shakuntala's head like a thunderbolt, this child of the forest hermitage keeps gazing distressedly, overcome by amazement, fear, and pain, like a doe struck by an arrow from a trusted hand. Flames engulf the flowers of the forest retreat. The hermitage which had extended around Shakuntala, mantling her within and without, in shadow and in brilliance, visibly and invisibly, is stripped away forever by this blast: she stands nakedly exposed. Where now is Father Kanva, where Mother Gautami,† where Anasuya and Priyamvada, where that loving bond and tender link with all those plants, birds, and beasts—that pleasing peace, that pure life? We are aghast when we realise how much of Shakuntala has been annihilated by this moment's devastation. The music playing through the first four acts is stilled in an instant.

What profound silence, what desolation now surrounds Shakuntala! The same Shakuntala who, by virtue of her tender heart, made everyone her own in the world around her—how lonely she is now! She now subsists by filling and perfecting that vast vacancy with her one great, noble grief. That Kalidasa did not take her back to Kanva's hermitage tesifies to his exceptional poetic judgment. It would have been impossible for her to mingle as before with her once-familiar forest. When she set out from Kanva's hermitage, she had undergone only an external separation from the forest retreat; that separation is completed when she is thrust out of Dushyanta's palace. That old Shakuntala no longer exists: her relation with the universe has changed. It would now be a cruel and grotesque incongruity to re-establish her among her old relationships. This grieving woman now needs a solitude appropriate to her great ennobling grief.

Kalidasa has not directly presented the sorrow of the parted Shakuntala in her new companionless forest retreat. Rather, by staying silent on the matter, he has intensified in our hearts the silence and emptiness that surrounds Shakuntala. If he had restored her to Kanva's ashram and then been silent, the ashram itself would have spoken: the weeping of the plants, the lament of her companions, would have kept on resounding in our hearts. But in Maricha's[†] unfamiliar hermitage, everything for us is silent and still: there only appears, seated in meditation before the mind's eye, the controlled, gravely patient, immeasurable grief of a Shakuntala grievingly separated from the world. The poet stands by himself, his finger to his lips, before this meditatively absorbed grief: by that forbidding gesture, he silences all questions and keeps the whole world at a distance.

Dushyanta is now consumed by repentance. This repentance is in the nature of meditation. Had he not won Shakuntala through such repentance, there would have been no honour in winning her. Simply to receive in hand is not to receive: gaining something is not such a facile business. Dushyanta could not have completely obtained Shakuntala by wafting her away on a passing gale of youthful intoxication. The best way to gain something is through dedicated labour and meditation. What comes easily to hand is also easily lost: what is grasped by infatuation falls to the ground when the grip slackens. That is why the poet made Dushyanta and Shakuntala undertake long and arduous meditation, that they might truly and lastingly gain each other. If Dushyanta had drawn Shakuntala to him as soon as she set foot in the royal court, Shakuntala would simply have swelled Hamsapadika's band to lodge in a corner of the women's quarters. Many such lightly won paramours of promiscuous kings are living out their useless lives the darkness of neglect, sustained only by the memory of their momentary good fortune. *Sakritkritapranayoyam janah.* [A person only loves once.]

Shakuntala's good fortune was that Dushyanta should reject her with such cruel violence. It was the rebound of that cruelty upon himself that did not let Dushyanta remain unconcerned about Shakuntala any more. Unceasingly, in the heat of his great pain, she began to blend with his dissolving heart: his inner state was confounded with the exterior. The king had never had such an experience in his life: he had never found the means or the opportunity truly to love. He was deprived in this respect because he was a king. Because he could easily realise his wishes, the prize of dedicated labour eluded him. Now, by casting him in severe affliction, the Creator vests him with the right to true love: his philandering days are over.

In this way, Kalidasa immolates sin in its own fire, rising of itself within the heart: he does not merely cover it under ashes from the outside. The play ends after all that is evil and inauspicious has been burnt to nothing, and the reader's heart brought to peace through an assured, fulfilling close. The poison tree that sprouts from a seed suddenly landing from outside cannot be rooted up except deeply from within. Kalidasa leads the external union of Dushyanta and Shakuntala along a path excavated out of suffering, to its fulfilment in an inward union. That is why the poet Goethe has said that if someone wishes to see the flower of youth and the fruit of maturity, to see earth and heaven in one place, he can do so in *Shakuntala*.

In *The Tempest*, Prospero tests Ferdinand's love through physical hardship; but that is external. To carry logs is not an adequate trial. Kalidasa has shown us by what inward heat and stress coal turns to diamond. He has made blackness glow from within, imparted solidity to the fragile through pressure. In *Shakuntala*, we see the purpose of evil: how by divine dispensation, even wrongdoing is employed to beneficent purpose in this world. Kalidasa's play gives us a perfected instance of this process. Unless buffeted by evil, beneficence does not acquire its timeless strength and lustre.

At the start of the play, we see Shakuntala in a world of unstained beauty where she mingles in ready joy with her companions and with plants and animals. Evil enters unperceived into this paradise, and the paradisal beauty breaks apart and falls like a cankered flower. Then come shame, doubt, suffering, separation, repentance; and finally, in a higher, purer heaven, forgiveness, love, and peace. *Shakuntala* might be called a *Paradise Lost* and *Paradise Regained* in one.

The first paradise is exceedingly weak and vulnerable: beautiful, integral, yet ephemeral like a dewdrop on a lotus leaf. It is best to be free of the delicate grace of this narrow perfection: it cannot last for ever, nor can it afford us full satisfaction. Malefaction enters like a rogue elephant and breaks down the lotus-leaf fence around this territory: the entire spirit is thrown into upheaval. The easy-won heaven is thus easily despoilt; there remains the heaven of dedicated labour. Once that heaven is won through repentance and meditation, there need be no more fear. That heaven is eternal.

Human life is like this. A child's simple heaven is beautiful, integral, perfect, but puny. The full flowering of life requires all the turmoil and disquiet of middle age, the blows of every kind of wrongdoing and repentance. If one does not pass on from the tranquillity of childhood to the conflicts and upheavals of this world, one may hope in vain for the perfected peace of mature years. The repose that spreads across world upon world at evening can be achieved only if the tenderness of dawn is burnt up in the midday blaze. Sin and wrongdoing break what is fragile, and suffering and penitence build up what is everlasting. In *Shakuntala*, the poet has recounted the whole process from the loss of paradise to its recovery.

Universal nature is outwardly serene, but a tremendous force works continually within it. In *Shakuntala* we see an image of this state. No other drama exhibits such remarkable restraint. European poets seem to grow wild at the least chance of displaying the force of nature and impulse. They love to bring out, through hyperbolic utterance, how far our impulses can lead us. Examples aplenty can be found in plays like Shakespeare's *Romeo and Juliet.* Among all Shakespeare's dramatic works, there is no play as serenely profound, as restrainedly complete and perfect as *Shakuntala.* Such love dialogue as passes between Dushyanta and Shakuntala is very brief, and chiefly conveyed through hints and signs: Kalidasa never slackens the reins. Precisely where another poet would have looked for a chance to let the pen race, he quells it.

Having returned from the forest to his capital, Dushyanta makes no enquiry after Shakuntala. In such an event, much could have been said by way of lament and imprecation; but Kalidasa does not put one such word on Shakuntala's lips. We must imagine, as best we can, the hapless woman's state simply owing to her remissness in attending to Durvasa. With what moving gravity and restraint is Kanva's deep affection for Shakuntala brought out at their parting, and in how few words! Anasuya and Priyamvada's sorrow at the loss of their companion seems to attempt, every now and again, to break through some barrier with a word or two, but subsides at once into the heart. In the rejection scene there is fear, shame, resentment, pleading, upbraiding, lament—everything indeed, yet in such brief compass.

In times of joy, Shakuntala had surrendered herself simply and unquestioningly; now, in her days of grief and abject indignity, who would have thought she could maintain a dignified reserve with such amazing self-restraint? And how pervasive, how profound, is the silence that follows this rejection! Kanva is silent; so are Anasuya and Priyamvada; so is the forest and the banks of the river Malini; and Shakuntala is most silent of all. Has the opportunity to stir up the emotions been so wordlessly scorned in any other play?

To cover over Dushyanta's wrongdoing with Durvasa's curse also shows the poet's restraint: he has overcome the temptation to present the depradations of corrupt nature in open and uncontrolled form. The presiding goddess of his poetry forbids him to do so, saying

Na khalu na khalu vanah sannipatyoyamasmin
Mriduni mrigasharire pushparashavivagnih.

Do not, do not let the arrow fall on the tender body of this deer, like fire on a heap of flowers.†

When in the play Dushyanta enters, intoxicated with the opportunity to set up a great agitation, this sound rises from the poet's heart:

Murto vighnastapasa iva no bhinnasarangayutho
Dharmaranyam pravishati gajah syandanalokabhitah.

The elephant, terrified by the sight of the chariot, enters our sacred grove like an incarnate hindrance to our rites. The startled deer flee at the sight.†

The king-elephant has entered the holy forest like an incarnate threat to meditation. It seems the poem's serenity must now be broken—but just then, Kalidasa binds and restrains this visible danger to the holy forest and the poetic grove by postulating the curse. Thereby he prevents the brute from churning up the slime in which his lotuses grow.

Had he been a European poet, he would here have imitated material reality: he would have made events fall out exactly as in life. He would not have cloaked anything beneath a curse or any other supernatural business—as though poets owe allegiance only to earthly things and none at all to poetry. Kalidasa has not honoured material reality above poetry; he has not consigned anyone to the slavery of reproducing what happens on the streets. Rather, the poet must obey poetic discipline. He must reconcile each incident of the plot to the totality of the work. Leaving the inner form of truth unimpaired, Kalidasa has matched its outer image to the particular beauty of his poem. He has presented penitence and meditative labour in all their radiance, but somewhat screened evil from view. Had he not done so, it would have destroyed the peace, beauty, and restraint that engird the play from beginning to end. Materiality would have been duly imitated, but the presiding goddess of poetry would have suffered grave hurt. This could never have been possible from Kalidasa's tenderly skilful pen.

Thus the poet, without ever unduly disturbing the external beauty and composure of the work, has kept its inner force uniformly strong and active in the midst of silence. Even external nature, in the forest scenes, participates all through in the functions of the mind. Now it submits its own sweet sportiveness to the play of Shakuntala's youthful being; now it mingles its beneficent sighs and sounds with the general benediction; now, through its mute words of farewell, it adds pity and tenderness to the agony of departure and, by its exquisite spell, irradiates Shakuntala's nature continually with a holy chastity, a soothing grace. There is much stillness in *Shakuntala*; but stillest of all, yet most pervasive, is the way the forest retreat functions in the work. It is not an external function, like that performed by Ariel in *The Tempest* through the rigours of servitude; it is the operation of beauty, of love, of kinship—the deep secret workings of the mind.

In *The Tempest*, power; in *Shakuntala*, peace. In *The Tempest*, conquest through force; in *Shakuntala*, fulfilment through beneficent power. In *The Tempest*, interruption halfway through the process; in *Shakuntala*, cessation at its close. In *The Tempest*, Miranda is constituted of graceful simplicity, but that simplicity is based on ignorance and inexperience. Shakuntala's simplicity, having endured wrongdoing, suffering, experience, patience, and forgiveness, is mature, sober, and permanent. Following Goethe's critique, let me say again that in *Shakuntala*, the fresh beauty of the opening achieves fulfilment in the ultimate beneficent close, and thereby unites earth with heaven.

TRANSLATED BY SUKANTA CHAUDHURI

The Ramayana

Written as the foreword to Ramayani Katha *(Ramayana Themes) by Dineshchandra Sen.*

Before the *Ramayana* and the *Mahabharata* came to be classified with the great poetical works of the world, they used to be designated as history. Now, having adjudged them against the literary treasures of foreign lands, we call them *epics.* Our Bengali equivalent for the word *epic* is *mahakabya*, a great poetical work. Today we refer to the *Ramayana* and the *Mahabharata* as *mahakabyas.*

The name *mahakabya* is apt enough. It seems to contain its definition within it. If now we refuse to admit that it is a translation of a foreign word, there is no harm done.

If we acknowledge that the word is a translation, the work so called must render account if it does not accord in every point with the features of an *epic* as laid down by some foreign school of rhetoric. I do not think it right to accept such accountability.

We are ready to explain what we mean by *mahakabya*, but we cannot undertake to make it conform to the *epic* in every respect. How can we? Even *Paradise Lost* is generally called an *epic.* If that be the case, the *Ramayana* and the *Mahabharata* are not *epics*; they cannot possibly be put in the same class.

Poetry can be classified into two broad groups. Some poems are the utterances of an individual poet, some of a larger community. We do not mean that the work of the individual poet is inaccessible to anybody else: that would make it a lunatic's babble. What we mean is that such a poet has the power to sound, through his own joys and sorrows, his imagination and experiences, the eternal emotions of universal man and the innermost truths of human life.

There we have one class of poets. So also there is another, through whose poetry a whole nation, an entire age gives voice to its soul and its experience, thus making their poetry a timeless treasure for mankind.

It is the latter group that may be called epic poets (*mahakabi*). The muse of a whole nation descends upon them; what they create does not seem to be the work of an individual. It appears to have been born like an immense tree from the womb of the nation's soil, and now to give shelter to the nation itself. Kalidasa's *Abhijnanashakuntalam* and *Kumarasambhavam* bear the marks of Kalidasa's particular skill. The *Ramayana* and the *Mahabharata*, like the Ganga and the Himalayas, seem to belong to India: Vyasa and Valmiki[†] merely provide the occasions for their coming into being.

As a matter of fact, there never was anybody called Vyasa or Valmiki. Those names were merely invented to serve a purpose. Two works of such stupendous dimensions, poems reaching across the whole of India, have absentmindedly let go of the names of their poets: so completely have the poets grown obscured by their own work.

Just as we have our *Ramayana* and *Mahabharata*, ancient Greece and Rome had their *Iliad* and *Aeneid*. They sprang from the lotus of the heart of all Greece, and within that lotus they dwelt. Homer and Virgil gave voice to their ages and lands: what they uttered sprang from the deepest beings of their respective countries, and have gone on flooding them with their tide.

No poetical work of the present day possesses that kind of expansiveness. For all its sublimity of style, prosodic grandeur, and depth of aesthetic emotion, *Paradise Lost* is not a common possession of the land; it is a treasure of the library.

Hence, if we must put this handful of ancient poems in a separate category, what name can we give them except epic (*mahakabya*)? They were built on a gigantic scale, like ancient gods and giants. They are now an extinct breed.

The ancient Aryan civilisation branched into two streams. One flourished in Europe, the other in India. The European stream has two epics, and the Indian two, to preserve their lore and their songs.

As foreigners, we cannot say whether Greece and Rome were able to express their entire beings in their two epics; but from the *Ramayana* and the *Mahabharata*, without a doubt, India has withheld nothing of herself. That is why century after century, their stream flowing across the country shows no sign of abating. They are still read daily in every village, in every home. They are as highly valued in the royal palace as in the grocer's shop. Blessed indeed are the two poets whose names are lost in the vast wastes of time, but whose words still bring strength and peace in a thousand streams to millions of homes, carrying the rich alluvial soil from countless centuries to keep the soul of India fertile as ever.

Hence it will not do to call the *Ramayana* and the *Mahabharata* just epic poems. They are also history: not the history of actual events, for such a history is limited to a particular period of time, but the history of the timeless life of India. Other histories change as time passes; this history has known no change. Within these two vast poetic edifices is enthroned the history of all that India strove for, worshipped, and purposed.

The criticism of the *Ramayana* and the *Mahabharata* must therefore be different from the criticism of other poetry. It is not enough to debate whether Rama's character is noble or base, and whether you like Lakshmana† or not. We must consider calmly, in a spirit of reverence, how the whole of India has received them over thousands of years. However great a critic I may be, it would be shameful presumption on my part not to bow my head before the judgment of a great and ancient land over all time.

What we must humbly ponder in the present case is what India has to say through the *Ramayana,* what ideal India has enshrined in that work. It is commonly believed that an *epic* is a poem in which the heroic rasa† dominates. This is because the *epic* naturally excels in the heroic rasa in a land and age where the glory of the heroic spirit is of primary value. There is enough of warfare in the *Ramayana* too, and Rama is no mean soldier; but the dominant rasa of the *Ramayana* is not the heroic rasa. The *Ramayana* does not proclaim the glory of physical prowess, nor are the battles its principal object of interest.

Neither is it merely concerned with the divine sport whereby a god is incarnated as man. It is for scholars to prove that to Valmiki, Rama was not God incarnate but a mere man. This introduction has nothing to do with scholarship. I can only observe briefly that if the poet had presented a god and not a human protagonist in the *Ramayana,* it would have detracted from its value and thereby harmed its poetry. It is because he is a man that Rama is sublime.

When in the first section of the Adikanda† Valmiki, seeking a fit hero for his poem, cites a number of qualities and asks Narada,†

> *Samagra rupini Lakshmih kamekam sangshrita naram?*
>
> Who is that single individual in whom the goddess Lakshmi† has fully manifested herself?

Narada says in reply:

> *Deveshvapi na pashyami kashchidebhirgunairyutam*
> *Shruyatam tu gunairebhiryo yukto narachandramah.*

> I do not find a person of so many virtues even among the gods. But hear the tale of a human moon, who combines all the virtues in himself.

It is of that human moon that the *Ramayana* tells, not of a god. In the *Ramayana* a god has not cut himself down to the size of a man; a man has become god by virtue of his many qualities.

It was to set up that ultimate ideal of humanity that the poet of India composed his epic. And ever since that day, Indian readers have been reading, with the greatest avidity, that account of ideal human life and conduct.

What distinguishes the *Ramayana* most of all is that it is a tale of domestic matters on an immense scale. The bond of piety, the relation of love and respect between father and son, brother and brother, husband and wife—the *Ramayana* has so ennobled them as to make them readily appropriate for epic. Conquest of territories, destruction of enemies, violent conflicts between powerful antagonists—these are the things that usually move and excite us in an epic. But the greatness of the *Ramayana* does not depend on the war between Rama and Ravana. That war too is an occasion to glorify the conjugal love between Rama and Sita. The *Ramayana* demonstrates the utmost reach of a son's obedience to his father, one brother's self-sacrifice for another, the mutual devotion between husband and wife, the duty of a king towards his subjects. No epic of any other country has taken up such domestic concerns of an individual as its subject matter.

This tells us not only about the poet but about India. It shows how much the home and the domestic virtues mean in this country. That the domestic stage of life† was accorded a very high status in India, is clearly shown in this work. Domestic life was not just for comfort and convenience; it underpinned the whole of society and made human beings truly human. Domestic and family life were the true foundation of Aryan society in India, and it is of that domestic sanctuary that the *Ramayana* sings. It invests the ideal of domestic piety with a special glory by subjecting it to the incongruous milieu of forest exile. The nefarious designs of Kaikeyi and Manthara† had struck a cruel blow to break up the royal house of Ayodhya; yet the *Ramayana* proclaims the invincible strength of the domestic virtues. Not brute force, nor desire for conquest, nor national glory: upon a foundation of noble valour, the *Ramayana* has set up the ideal of domestic piety, vessel of the rasa of serenity† anointed with the tears of compassion.

A sceptical reader might object that in such a case, the depiction of character becomes exaggerated. We cannot decide summarily where the bounds of decorum lie, or what limits of imagination poetry cannot transgress without falling into excess. To the foreign critic who has observed that in the *Ramayana*, character portrayal has crossed the bounds of nature, my reply is that the same thing may appear natural to one man and supernatural to another, according to their dispositions. India has not seen supernatural excesses in the *Ramayana*.

If one grossly exceeds the received ideals of a particular place and time, the people there will not accept it. There is a limit to the range of sound waves our ears can capture; a tune pitched above that limit is inaudible to us. The same goes for the invention of characters and ideas in poetry.

If that is so, a thousand years have gone to prove that for India, nothing in the *Ramayana* crosses the limit in the least degree. The young and the old, men and women, the high and the low in India have been not only edified but also entertained by the narrative of the *Ramayana*. They have not only venerated it but taken it to their hearts. To them it is not only religious scripture; it is poetry.

Rama could never have been both god and man to us, the *Ramayana* could not have drawn at the same time our reverence and our love, if the poetry of this great work had, in Indian eyes, belonged to some faraway land of the imagination instead of coming down to the confines of home and family. If some foreign critics, applying their own critical standards, describe such a work as supernatural in character, it only brings out more clearly a feature that sets India apart from their country. In the *Ramayana*, India has had what it desires.

That is the way I, for one, look at the *Ramayana* and also the *Mahabharata*. The heart of India has, for a thousand years, beat with the rhythms of its simple anushtupa metre.

When my friend Dineshchandra Sen asked me to write a foreword to his reading of the *Ramayana*, I could not refuse, despite my ill health and lack of time. By rendering the poet's words in the language of the devotee, he has given ultimate expression to his own devotion. This interpretation, informed by the spirit of worship, is in my opinion the truest criticism. It is thus that the feeling of devotion is transmitted from heart to heart. Or if there are such feelings already in the reader, they are stirred up anew. What goes by the name of criticism nowadays is estimating the price something may fetch in the market place, for literature is now merchandise. Afraid of being cheated, everybody is anxious to seek the help of an astute valuer. No doubt such assessments have their uses. But I would still maintain that true criticism is an act of worship. The true critic is a worshipping priest, who merely gives expression to his own mingled wonder and adoration or that of the public at large.

Dineshchandra the devotee has begun his worship in the temple courtyard, and has invited me all on a sudden to assist in his devotions. That is what, standing in an inconspicuous corner, I do. I would not presume to overwhelm his worship with too much noise. All I want to say is that readers should not look upon Valmiki's story of Rama as one man's poem, but as something that belongs to the whole of India. Then, knowing the *Ramayana*, they will know India, and knowing India they will know the *Ramayana*. They should bear in mind that what India wanted to hear was not the history of some glorious event of the past, but the ideal life story of a total, fully realised human being. That is the story she has been hearing till this day with undiminished delight. She has never said it was overdone, never said it was just poetical invention. To an Indian, one's nearest relations are not so real as Rama, Lakshmana, and Sita.

India has a life-felt desire for the full and perfect. She has not despised it or disbelieved it as transgressing the bounds of reality. She has accepted it as implicitly true and rejoiced in it. It is this craving for the full and perfect that the poet of the *Ramayana* has stimulated and satisfied, thereby putting India's worshipful heart for ever in his debt.

Nations that attach more value to fragmentary truths, that never tire of pursuing material reality, to whom poetry is nothing but a mirror of nature, have accomplished much in this world. They have covered themselves with glory in many ways. Humankind is greatly indebted to them. On the other hand, there are those who have said, *Bhumaiva sukham bhumatveva vijijnasitavyah.* [True happiness lies only in the whole; this totality is what we should seek to know.] They have devoted themselves to realising the harmony among all fragments, the peace that all discords attain in the whole. Our debt to them too can never be repaid. If we forget their teachings and let them sink into oblivion, then human civilisation—trapped among the crowds in dusty, sooty factories, the stagnant air polluted by their own breath—will day by day sicken, shrivel up, and die. The *Ramayana* bears the deathless imprint of these seekers thirsting for unimpaired immortality. If we can retain our simple respect and heartfelt devotion towards the brotherly love, regard for truth, chastity, and loyalty depicted in the *Ramayana*, the clean breeze from the mighty ocean will find entry through the windows in our factory shed.

TRANSLATED BY BHAWANI-PRASAD CHATTOPADHYAY

Literature (1924)

The Upanishads speak of three distinct selves within the absolute—*satyam, jnanam,* and *anantam* [being, knowledge, and the infinite]. Based on these three selves of the eternal, there must surely be three aspects to the human soul as well. One of these is 'We are;' another, 'We know.' There is a third aspect which is the subject of my discussion today. It is 'We express.' There are these three facets of a human being—to put it in English, *I am, I know, I express*—and these together constitute an integral truth. Truth in these three aspects is constantly urging us to do and devise things. We must survive, hence we need food, clothes, shelter, health. These involve the various activities of gathering, preserving, and making. 'I am'—this aspect of truth makes us undertake these various things. Then there is the spur of 'I know' which is no less insistent. The provisions for the acquisition of knowledge are enormous: these are continually expanding and are of immense importance to human beings. Along with these there is the third aspect of the truth about us: 'I express.' 'I am' is contained in the selfhood of the absolute as truth; 'I know,' in its selfhood as knowledge; and 'I express,' in its selfhood as the infinite.

Just as the defence of the truth 'I am' is a form of human self-preservation, so is the defence of the truth 'I know,' because the human self is also self-as-knowledge. Hence it is not enough for us to know how to nourish ourselves and with what food. Our self-as-knowledge obliges us to sit up nights to determine what the web of traces visible on Mars might be. The investigations might seriously upset our workaday lives. The sciences are best understood when seen as accordant with the nature of the human self-as-knowledge; it is not enough to regard them solely in terms of the human self-as-being.

'I am, I must survive'—when this idea remains within narrow limits, only self-preservation and reproduction preoccupy our egos. But in as much as one says, 'I survive only in the survival of others,' by so much does one testify to the presence of the infinite in one's own life; and by so much does the distance between 'I am' and 'others are' dissolve for one. The nobility achieved through this sense of union with others is the wealth of the soul; that union inspires people to express themselves in many different ways. Where a person is alone there is no self-expression: it becomes impossible to keep the sense of the infinite in existence—the sense that 'I exist in the existence of others'—hidden in the obscurity of petty day-to-day private life. We are drawn to service and sacrifice by the demands of that greater life; we express its passion and joy in literature, architecture, sculpture, painting, and music.

I have said that we need knowledge even for mere selfish survival. But that knowledge has no lustre. When the inspiration to learning comes from the infinite, one sees so much enterprise devoted to education, so many schools, universities, studies, experiments, discoveries, inventions. Knowledge then takes on a pan-human and timeless character, and thereby declares the human soul's right of universal access. The varied provisions for the exercise of this right enlarge themselves in science and philosophy; the pure strain of its joy, however, is expressed in various compositions of literature and the arts.

We can thus see that while human beings are like beasts in their strong desire for survival and indefatigable curiosity for useful knowledge, they have something which beasts lack, something which constantly takes them beyond the bounds of the merely creatural. It is here that one must seek the true nature of expression.

Expression has to do with wealth. Where human beings are poor there is no expression; there they consume what they can gather. What I on my own cannot exhaust by consuming is what I use for expressing myself. Iron is devoid of expression until it is heated enough to glow. Light is the wealth of heat. The carnival of human expression draws on feelings which are not consumed by their particular occasions, which cannot contain their own abundance within themselves, and which are naturally luminous. When is money rich in that kind of wealth? When it outgrows my own private needs, when it is no longer hidden in my pocket, when its lustre is not totally blotted out by the blackness of my ego. It is then that the infinite appears within it, and manifests itself in so many forms. The nature of that manifestation is such that all of us can say, 'This is mine.' When money admits the claims of the infinite, it is freed from the tainted bond of consumability which ties it to one particular person. The world is tormented by the barbarity of money which is exclusively enjoyed and deprived of the grace of the infinite. No burden is heavier than that of poverty. When money becomes the vehicle of impoverishment, it grinds so many people to dust under its wheels. That poverty the world calls power: it sheds no light, but it can burn—it belongs only to its possessor: one can feel it, but accept it one cannot. Expression is another name for this universal acceptance.

Nature is busy cleansing the unholy blood-begrimed imprint of power with its green ambrosial salve. From the inner chambers of creation, the flowers stream forth laden with beauty and, with their shame, pave over power's sullied trail. They tell us, 'We are small, we are tender, but we are the ones who belong to all time, because everyone has accepted us. And that raised fist of hideous terror, that castle rearing up to the skies as one stone is piled on another—that indeed is nothing, since none other than itself accepts its power. Even the lovely shadow in the madhavi bower is more real.'

Consider the Taj Mahal. It is what it is because in Shah Jahan's heart love, and the joy born of the pain of separation, had touched the infinite. To whichever chamber he might have consigned his throne, his Taj Mahal he released from the confines of his own self. For the Taj, none is an alien and none its own: it is now the seat of the infinite. When Shah Jahan's power expressed itself in plunder, no matter how immense the booty, his bags were never quite full: the loot sank into the dark pit of appetite and was lost. But when the sense of fullness was born in his heart, he could not confine that divine injunction within his treasury or his vast empire. There was no option but to dedicate it to all people and all time. This is expression. In all our sacred rituals the mantra† of acceptance is *Om*,† that is 'Yes'. The Taj Mahal is that perpetually uttered *Om*, a visible embodiment of the world's mantra of acceptance. Shah Jahan's throne had no use for the mantra: however awesome it might once have been, it turned into a 'no' and sank without trace. In the same way, droves of big names, renowned incarnations of 'no', are proudly marching to their extinction even today. We are deafened by the roar of their cannons and the jangle of their prisoners' fetters. Yet they are but illusions, pilgrims carrying the oblation of their own deaths to the ocean of fatal night.† But what about one of the tearful songs of Shah Jahan's daughter, the princess Jahanara?† We have accepted it and said, *Om*.

But can we give just because we wish to? If we simply utter *Tubhyamaham sampradade* [I give (the bride) to you],† does the groom appear with outstreched hands? Eternity and the universe say, '*Yadetat hridayam mama* [as is this heart of mine]:† your gift must match with that. I may take only what is given by the infinite in you.' He has taken the gift of the *Meghadutam*:† it is not the exclusive property of Ujjayini,† the troops and sentinels of Vikramaditya† could not keep it locked in the inner quarters among the Hamsapadikas.† Let pedants dispute whether it was written half a millenium before or after the birth of Christ. It bears the stamp of all time. Let them argue whether it was written by the banks of the Shipra or the Ganga. Its mandakranta metre echoes the music of all rivers flowing east and west. On the other hand, there are panchalis† in which sparks fly from the friction of alliteration. They have captivated audiences of thousands; but no matter how enthused we might feel at their pure indigenous spirit, their time and place are clearly marked out. Rejected by the wider world and by abiding time, they needs must surrender their futile pride of lineage, like unwed daughters of pedigreed† brahmans, to a plantain tree and die childless.

Where the Upanishads describe the true form of the absolute as infinite, what do they have to say about its expression? They say, *anandarupamamritam yadvibhati* [the being that shines forth in joyous and immortal form].† This is the main thing. If the world were a prison, all its soldiers goading us with the staff of royal state would have failed to move us an inch. We would have squatted and gone on strike, refusing food and drink. But it seems clear to me that it is not just the goad that we feel all the time.

My heart, I know, has been enthralled again and again. Was there any need for that? The workers who slave to death in a jute mill at Titagarh† get their wages, but no one is bothered about their hearts. And the mills work none the worse for that. The owners who make a profit of 400 per cent would not dream of spending a paisa to delight their minds. But as I look around the world, I see no end to the efforts to enchant our hearts. We see, then, that this is poetry, not the formulas of Bopadeva's† *Mugdhabodha*. Put another way, the grammar trails behind like a waiting woman, and the goddess of the rasas leads the way. In that expression, then, do we feel the staff-bearer's rigour† or the poet's joy?

This sunrise and sunset, this wave of beauty flooding everything between sky and earth—I see no sign of a doughty watchman's livery in all this. There is, of course, a drive in appetite, but that is clearly something stamped 'no'. 'Yes' marks the fruit which satisfies that appetite, which the tongue with eager enjoyment greets as its own. So which shall we put in front and which behind? The grammar or the poetry? The kitchen or the invitation to the feast? Where is the intention of the host best expressed—

in the road down which I trudge, umbrella and invitation in hand, or at the place laid out for me? *Srishti* [to generate] is cognate with *sarjan* [to be generous, to relinquish]. Since He has given Himself so totally, meted Himself out among all things, He has soothed our souls so that our hearts can say, 'Ah, peace at last!'

The evening sky is brimming with the light of the waxing moon. We can remain oblivious of that amazing fact when we are busy bickering at committee meetings. But what do I say when I encounter that sight, returning home along the Maidan† at ten in the night, when that instance of expression finds its way through the mind's portals, piercing the dense mass of worries? I say, *anandarupamamritam yadvibhati* [the being that shines forth in joyous and immortal form]. What substance constitutes the being which expresses itself as joy? Can it be power?

The expression of power is latent in the kitchen; but is it power that finds expression in a banquet? The Mughal emperor wanted to express power. Does one call that gigantic show of material power 'expression'? Where is its embodiment? The various modern avatars of Aurangzeb† have made massive preparations for expressing power in a trail of blood. But He who is *abih* [the self-revealed], who expresses Himself as joy, has already begun to erase that trail. The refuse of those preparations is surely feeling the touch of His radiant broom, because His joy is expression, and His expression is joy.

If He had put his power to the fore, obscuring this expression, nothing could have been more humiliating for me than to submit to Him. When I was sailing to Japan,† the ship met with a fierce storm. I was sitting on the deck. A small puff of wind would have been enough to drown me; but the frenzied dance of the squall on the dark waters was designed to stir the mad heart lurking inside me. That spectacular turbulence enabled the mad to meet the mad and trade pleasantries. Let's say I would have died—would that have been more momentous than this encounter? Among the waves' foamy fury, the maestro of the rudraveena† treated His disciple to presto runs of a few swirling phrases. I was then able to say, 'You are my own.'

The word *amrita*† has two meanings—that which is deathless, and the ultimate rasa or source of joy. Joy assuming a form—that indeed is *rasa*. If *amrita*, too, is just that *rasa*, then one is being tautological. Therefore, I should say that here *amrita* means the deathless: that is, wherever joy has taken on form, its expression has transcended death. Everyone holds up time as the great bogey. Few care for that which lives under time's rule and yet does not cooperate† with it.

Now about ourselves. Poetry which is strung in metre, the form which is composed by the *rupadaksha*,[†] master of form, will conquer death only if it is also the expression of joy. This word *rupadaksha* is a new acquisition of mine. It was found in an ancient *inscription*, and is an excellent synonym for the artist.

The poem or the picture is not exhausted when it ends. We come away from listening to the *Meghadutam* or from looking at a picture, but we do not carry home a sense of exhaustion. When the song touches the final beat, having circled the measure, we shake our heads with spontaneous pleasure. The notes run out at the *sama*, the climax of the music; yet why do we feel joy? Because the form of joy is not exhausted when it ends. But when we run out of money, we do not shake our heads and exclaim in pleasure.

The song comes to a stop—yet why is it not a termination like darkness or emptiness? The reason is that there is a truth in the song which is also present in the soul of the entire universe. Thus its being survives on the strength of *Om*; there is no abyss lying in wait for it. It does not matter whether I actually hear the song, whether it is directly enjoyed by someone. So many priceless treasures have been lost with the poems and the pictures which held them; but that is an external, accidental fact. The important thing is that they had expressed the wealth of joy, not the poverty of necessity. If you want to witness that poverty, step inside the jute mill where the blood of poor peasants is being churned into profits several times over. The shrine in the shade of the banyan by the Ganga, which has now disappeared to make room for the mill belching black smoke from its giant maw, is less unreal than that factory. That is because the world of joy has no place for the latter.

In spring, buds fall off the trees in heaps: that is no cause for dismay, since there is no loss. The gifts of spring carry the mantra of the deathless, so that beauty's worshipful offerings are replenished again and again. Those seismic buffaloes from the early days of creation, that gored the earth into convulsions and tossed hot slime up into the air, have never come back. Those flaming hooded she-serpents that raised their heads, piercing the roof of the underworld, lunging at the earth's overcast skies, have long been tamed by some flute. But the tender kisses of the fresh green grass still charm the blue-eyed firmament again and again. They return each day. At my door the spring has pampered a few thornbushes into blossom. They are prickly nightshades. There is a fleck of gold in the centre of their flower's soft purple breast. It seems as if its contemplation of the sun as it gazes up at the sky has turned to a sweet trace in its bosom.

Who in the world knows of this flower? And does it not wither and drop? Yet that is no loss. It is more fearless than the world's doughtiest strongmen. It dwells in the joy within its soul: it is deathless. Even when it is not visible, it still lives.

In the court of eternity, the hammer of death puts the deathless to the test on time's anvil. That surely is what the tidings of Christ's death signify in the Gospels. Was it not the stroke of death that made the immortal flame in Christ shine forth? But one thing must be kept in mind: the deathless is not manifested because you or I give it the nod of recognition. Our vision may not reach to it: the measure of our memory is not the measure of its immortality. If it comes clutching to its breast the epiphany of fullness, it is able to show us eternity in an instant. It does not have to depend on my notions.

Maybe all this is part of philosophy. An amateur like me ought not to venture on a philosophical discourse at a university.† But I do not speak to you from the professor's rostrum. Moment by moment, I have gleaned the answers to my queries from the experience of joy out in the world and within my heart. Those answers are all that I have been recalling here. In our country the supreme being has been defined as *sacchidananda* [one who combines in His self being, consciousness, and joy]. *Ananda* or joy is the last of the three terms, and there is no utterance beyond it. Since the truth about expression inheres in joy, it is pointless asking whether art does us any good.†

TRANSLATED BY SWAPAN CHAKRAVORTY

Creation

A section of this essay, towards the middle, notably exploits the dual implications of the term rup(a), *'form' and 'beauty'. (See the note on this term on p. xii.) As the first meaning appears to be predominant, the rendering 'form' has been adopted. But there is a complementary sense of 'beauty', especially in the passage about 'gluttons for form'. At one point, it seemed most appropriate to render* rup *and its opposite* arup *as 'visible' and 'invisible'.*

As I was preparing to set out for this lecture meeting, the strains of the shehnai reached my ears from the lane outside. There was a wedding in a neighbouring house. The plaintive notes of the Khamaj raga were draping the city skies like the long loose end of a sari.

Why do we have flutes playing on a festive day? Their music covers over the broken ends and squalid refuse of everyday living—as if the chariot of foulness had never rolled down the iron road of official purpose, as if all the trafficking and spending were nothing at all. The music drew a veil over all that.

'Drew a veil' is not quite the right phrase. One should have said 'lifted the veil',† the veil drawn by the cacophony of tram cars, hucksters and criers. Lifting this veil, the music wafted away the bride and the groom to the sanctum of the timeless, the world of aesthetic joy.

The world of commerce and petty concerns cares little for brides and grooms. No one knows their names or gives up seats for them. In the timeless world of aesthetic joy, however, they are king and queen. We need to release them from all surrounding distractions, big and small, and crown them on brocaded thrones. On all other days they play mean roles: hence on all other days, they are as insubstantial as shadows. On this day they are revealed in their true forms. Their worth is now inestimable: strings of lamps, trays of flowers greet them, and the infinite arrives to bless them with Vedic invocations.

That this couple, these two human beings, are true, and no less true than a king or emperor—this true identity the whole world conspires to hide. The flute has taken on the task of revealing that abiding truth. Imagine a girl in the forest retreat of ancient times. Like thousands of other girls of the day, she too lived behind a mist of obscurity. A king was smitten by her, and one day he abandoned her. Who ever bothered to keep track of countless such events? The king therefore said of himself, *Sakritkritapranayoyam janah* [A person only loves once]:† 'I love each woman only once, for a brief while, and then let her go.' No one has time to notice and remember the daily leavings of the king's passing amours. One's daily chores never end, the buying and selling goes on and on, the crowd never leaves the market place. One can never trace there the steps of the Hamsapadikas† of this world, the throng just pushes them aside and surges forward. What was it, then, that lifted a simple forest girl out of a crowded world of trivialities and made her stand out, shining in the light of truth? That too was a poet's flute. In our neighbourhood alley today, the mournful notes of Khamaj drip rain like an elixir from heaven to revive the truth that is daily stifled by the trams' rattle and the hagglers' din.

Don't we know how radically human worth changes when we are released from the constrictions of fact and let into the boundlessness of truth? When Krishna† appears as the cowherd of Vraja,† do we honour him because he is the prince of Mathura?† Is his herdsman's staff any poorer than his mace† and his war-quoit?† Is his flute shamed by his panchajanya?† Truth is not ashamed to throw away the jewelled necklace and put on a garland of wild flowers. What can reveal the truth behind that herdsman's guise? The poet's flute.

What stupendous pains does an emperor take to parade his might! And yet how soon does he melt away beyond the horizon, like the cloud after a storm, carrying with him the mammoth load of that effort. But in the celestial city of literature, in the lasting hall of the arts, the unfragmented truth in which a wayside mendicant dwells suffers no decay. In the fictional universe, no fool ever asks how much money Romeo and Juliet had in the bank, how learned they were in the six schools of philosophy,† whether they feared gods and priests and said their prayers three times a day. They are true: that is their sole claim to glory, and that is what literature demonstrates. No one would be able to save them if there were the slightest deflection from that truth, even if the hero and heroine produced clever scientific interpretations of the ten avatars† of Vishnu or drew breathtakingly patriotic sentiments from the verses of the *Bhagavadgita*.

Why just men and women? Even inanimate things are enriched by the treasure of truth once we transport them on the chariot of poetry beyond the confines of fact. My plot of land in Calcutta may sell for five or ten thousand rupees a cottah,† but that price is never recognised in the kingdom of truth. Market value is there reduced to shreds, and draws the laughter of contempt. This release from the fetters of fact into the world of abiding joy is no small freedom. Human beings composed songs and painted pictures to remind themselves of this freedom. They preserved their true treasures from the marketplace and placed them lovingly in the lasting store of beauty. They expressed the wealth of their penniless state through the penniless flute, telling themselves time and again, 'Your true manifestation is in that world of joy.'

How can I explain to you what literature is, or painting? Can any analysis plumb their depths? One recognises their primordial source the moment one's mind casts itself upon their stream. Today, as the strains of the flute swept my mind along, I realised that there was nothing to explain; all things seem clear when the mind plunges into them. The blue sky had beckoned to us each day and said, 'Every one of you is welcome to the house of joy.' The soulful poet, moved by the spring breeze to think of his faraway love, had said the same thing. The sunbeam knocked at dawn. What was its message? It said, 'You are invited.' In the wistful noontide, the forest shade, thick with the murmur of honey bees, came as another messenger, knocked and said, 'You are invited.' The herald reappeared in the evening cloud lit by the setting sun and said, 'You are invited.' This messenger comes decked in so many costumes, so many garlands, so many crowns of glory! And for whom? For me. I am no king or sage; I have no rare gift. I am true, and so the message shines for me in the blue of the sky, in the green of the earth, in the burning letters of the stars. Don't I have to answer this invitation? And if I do not answer in the language of that house of joy, will it find acceptance? So the human respondent echoes back its reply in the same sweet tones, 'Your welcome has struck a chord in my heart. It reverberates in form, in idea, in deed. O beauty eternal, I accept your call. I shall send you a reply just as beautiful. As you have put the undying lamp of the stars in your messenger's hands, so must I light a lamp which does not go out, string a garland which never withers. I am human. If indeed I have immortal power within me, I shall answer your invitation with the wealth of its power.' That we have dared to say this is the highest human glory.

Today, as the flute was bringing to light the true form—that is, the joyful form—of the new couple next door, I asked myself what magic helped it to accomplish its task. Our philosopher tells us that the world rocks on the waves of uncertainty, that all we see around us is unreal. Our moralist says, 'The sandal paste you see on their brow is a hoax, it merely hides the skull beneath. Look behind that honeyed smile, and you will find a bare set of teeth.' The flute does not argue in reply. It only says, to the notes of the Khamaj raga, 'The skull and the teeth, no matter how long they last, are unreal. But the fragrant mark of joy inscribed on the forehead, the smile touched by a fugitive blush which, like a shadow or a dream, eludes your grasp: these indeed are the truth—truth that is moving, dulcet, and deep.' Making that truth shine above the world's busy traffic, the flute tells us, 'The day you see truth face to face is the day of real festival.'

Very well. But how does the flute establish this truth without an argument? I was discussing this yesterday.† The flute has lit the flame of the indivisible. It has filled the sky with its music, creating a beauty of form that has no purpose except to reveal with finality the One and the whole in rhythm and melody. Those touched by the magic wand of that One have shown to the world the deep indestructible truth for ever living and awake within them. The bride and the groom have said, 'We are not commonplace, we belong to all time. They see us falsely who look at us only across the barrier of death. We belong to the deathless world: hence we cannot let ourselves be known except through song.' The bride and the groom are no longer flotsam on the world's tide. They now display the fullness of the One within themselves like a sweetly set poem, like a song, like a picture. The mystery of this expression is the mystery of creation and of truth.

No matter how complete and enchanting a form it takes in a particular raga, music cannot, from the outside and in common-sense terms, be described as infinite. Form has limits. But when form shows up only the limits, it does not show the truth. Truth is expressed when the finiteness of form, like a lamp, lights up the flame of the infinite.

I felt this today, listening to the strains of the shehnai. After a cycle or two, I could tell that the player was a novice and the melody trite. The same tune was being played over and over again, and the notes were harsh, like the shadowless midday sun beating down on treeless soil. All the stress was on the sharpness of the sound, and all effort towards magnifying its extent. That is to say, the limits of music were flaunting themselves, so that one could not but take notice of them. The convolutions of those limits were impeding their own fulfilment. Limits express truth by their self-effacing restraint. Restrained simplicity is thus a crucial element in all art. Restraint is the gesture of the finite towards the infinite. When the parts exceed the whole, the result is intemperance, or the insurrection of the many aginst the One. As the many outside multiply, the One inside is eclipsed. Jesus said, 'It is easier for a camel to go through the eye of a needle, than for a person to enter the kingdom of God carrying an excess of wealth.'[†] This means that too much wealth constitutes an intemperance in external things. Material excess deprives human beings of the sense of the soul's wholeness and unity. Most of their ideas and efforts are broken and scattered outwards through multiple acquisitions. The expression in the self of the One that is whole, true, and infinite is destroyed when the rich dissipate it among the many and the various. They play a trite tune on life's flute, with doubled and quadrupled tempos, laboured twists and shrill, intolerable vanity. This may impress the dull-eared; but those seeking the full revelation of truth in the restraint of form try to escape the clutches of the bandits of excess in this wilderness of forms. There form calls out to you, 'Look at me.' Why should I? I have come into the world to see the formless enthroned in form. Just as science discovers non-matter behind material nature and says, 'This is truth', so art, in the world of forms, discovers a rasa beyond form and declares, 'That is my truth.' Once I see that truth, mere form can no longer tempt me, and I can scorn the laboured feats of the virtuoso.

The hunger in a glutton's mind outlasts the hunger in his belly. Women delightedly pile sweets on his plate; then one day they are called in to soothe his gastric pains. Literary gluttons seek too much material delight to satisfy their greed for form: there is no release for them. For truth frees us from form when it appears in form: those who pay for books by their bulk eventually let their minds be buried under them.

The problem in expressing the pleasurable truth[†] through the fine arts is that the invisible has to be shown in the visible; form has to be seen enveloped by the formless. One has to accept the precept of the *Isha Upanisad* to look upon fleeting appearances[†] as covered by the full and perfect, and follow the edict *Ma gridhah*: Do not covet. That is the mystery of creation, be it the creation of the world or artistic creation. One has to admit form and yet dismiss it; grasp form, yet obscure it. Desist from the lust for form.

Consider this amazing body of ours with so many amazing machines—to digest food, to transport blood, to breathe with, to think with.

The creator seems immensely embarrassed by these, and has taken great care to cover them well. That we chew our food with our teeth is not a fact we are keen to publicise. The face is the arena for the play of our emotions. It expresses something which is beyond flesh and blood, beyond form and sense. That is its primary identity. Muscles are essential, and they have plenty of work. But we are enchanted only when the play of their movements expresses the body's music. The creator says to those who have taken anatomy lessons at the medical college, 'Spare me your praises.' For creation is not justified by its ingenuity. The creator says, 'That I am a skilled engineer in devising the universal machine is a piece of information you can do without.' What should we know then? 'Know me in my form as joy.' The structural history of the earth is written in cipher on the great rock carvings of the geological strata. The maker has hidden that secret under layer upon layer of soil. But the surface, the dwelling-place of joy and life, is the scene of his unending play lit up by the sun and the moon. Until the cover was in place, there was fearsome tumult: what blows of the hammer, what churning of giant wheels, what furnaces, what sighs of steam! And when all that was over, the maker shut up his workshop, washed everything in a green, blue, and golden flood, and, in his joy, ascended the throne of form with a wreath of stars on his head and his feet on a footstool of flowers.

Here I am reminded of something else. The civilisation that is flaunting its muscles and shaking the world with its bluster, that is turning the factory chimneys into comets' flagstaffs to blacken the shining sky—don't you see how the creator is shamed by its shamelessness? It beats its brazen drums, and its ranks swell here and abroad. In every port and every military base from New York to Tokyo its wild, arrogant trumpets are mocking the benediction of the conch. The insolence of naked might wants to ravish the honour of the eternal realm of joy with its foul, soiled fists. This today is the greatest pity and the biggest insult visited upon the human world.

The highest human distinction is that of creator. Civilisation at present makes of us drudges, tinkers, and usurers; it demeans the creator by whetting our greed. Human beings construct for profit; they create at the bidding of the spirit. When the claims of profit become too insistent, the spirit falls silent. The rich efface the waymarks to the heavenly house, and ensure that all roads lead to the marketplace.

Where does the final truth about human beings lie? It lies in the human bonds which cross the barriers of extrinsic fact and lead us into the deepest ties of the spirit: the ties of beauty, well-being, and love. That is the realm of human creativity. There each person realises his own boundless glory; there the whole race strives with austere discipline for each of its members. The ascetic's contemplation, the hero's sacrifice, the sage's wisdom are dedicated to each one of us. Where one person fattens on ten others, where one grows powerful by robbing thousands of their freedom and many starve to overfeed one epicure—there the humanity that manifests itself as truth and peace cannot express itself in beautiful creations.

The greedy are for ever shameless. Those afflicted by the vanity of power had boasted of their mismatch with the universal order even in the unfallen past. But in those days, there were people to raise their voices against such insolence and pride. Humankind did not flinch from cautioning the covetous and the powerful, 'The tidings of the beautiful have reached the earth, stop your discordant meddling. The goddess of joyful abundance† is enthroned on a hundred-petalled lotus, don't trample on it like a mad elephant.' That was the message of the poet's verse and the artist's picture. On this wedding day, the flute is saying, 'O bride and groom, let the truth of your being be expressed in you above all other things. A lakh or two in the bank does not make you true. The truth I proclaim belongs to the rhythm of creation, not to the sums you can write in a cheque book. That truth is in the undying mutual tie joining one person to another, not in costly bric-a-brac to display at home. That is the truth of the whole, the indivisible One.'

I had decided that I would say a few things today about literary craft, prosody, and style. The flute changed all that, Lord Indra† sent word through the beautiful, 'That all things can be explained, or all ends achieved through austere endeavour, is common wisdom. But do you, as a poet, uphold this as the article of your faith? The fruits obtained by ceasing to analyse and shattering the ascetic's trance are the only whole, integral ones. They can't be pieced together, they grow and mature from within.' The shastras† tell us that Indra sends the delectable to blast the fruits of rigorous discipline. I do not believe in such envy and treachery on the god's part. Rather, Indra sends the delectable to show the full, indivisible form of the state of attainment. He tells us, 'This is not something you build up through strife. It does not form gradually, layer on layer. If you round off the song according to the right and true tune, it won't do just to plug and pound away day and night. Take the fourth and fifth notes of the octave as your steady ground notes, and realise the integrity of the melody in your heart. Only then will the unity of the whole song be made true.' Menaka and Urvashi† are those base notes, the integral image of perfection. They remind the ascetic of the nature of the fruit he seeks. Heaven-seeker, is it really heaven you seek? Is that why you mortify yourself? But heaven was not built by the labour of masons. Heaven is creation. Consider the fleeting shadow of Urvashi's smile; you will get a hint of heaven's unforced music. Salvation-seeker, do you seek release? Shaking off the coils of mortal existence one by one is no release. Freedom is not an unfettered void; it is creation. Look at the parijat† in Menaka's hair, you will glimpse an image of freedom's perfection. God's arrested joy finds release in that flower: formless joy achieves fulfilment by being expressed in form.

When the Budha was mortifying himself under the bodhi tree, his tormented heart whispered to him, 'I have failed. I have found nothing.' When did he discover in the outside world the full image of what he had achieved within? When Sujata† brought him food. It was not just food for the body. It was an offering of devotion, love, service, and beauty: the elixir of the deathless state found such effortless embodiment in that sweetened milk and rice. Was not Sujata sent by Indra? Did she not carry a message from heaven, 'Austerities bring no release, love does.' Is not the truth of the maternal heart, latent in Sujata's devout food offering, echoed in the Budha's precept, 'To range in the realm of the absolute is to regard the whole world with the immeasurable love a mother feels for her only son'? That is to say, freedom is to be sought not in nothingness, but in plenitude—a plenitude that does not destroy but create.

When did Jesus see the simple manifestation of the human soul's love that rejoices in total surrender to the infinite soul, wanting nothing beyond it? It was Indra who sent him that vision from the realm of his own creation. Martha and Mary† had both come to serve him. Martha was dutiful, preoccupied with the rigours of service. Mary did not express the fullness of her self-submission through such busy, various chores. Instead she poured out all her costly ointment of spikenard upon Christ's feet. Everyone said, 'This is sinful extravagance.' 'Let her alone,' said Christ. Is not creation itself an extravagance? Does music profit anyone? Do paintings supply the lack of food and clothing? In matters of aesthetic creation human beings receive the wealth of plenitude by offering up the plenitude within themselves. That wealth is not expressed only in literature and art; its sportive self-surrender finds arenas for expression in many other creations of human society. That creativity cannot be priced by its practical uses, but in the unfolding of the total form of the human spirit. It is without cause, and it is self-sufficient. When Jesus saw the form of Mary's simple and supreme self-surrender, he saw his own inner plenitude mirrored in the world outside, and she stood before him, with exquisite sweetness, like a creation of his own soul. In the same way, the human artist desires to witness his own fullness in his creation—not in austerities nor in acquisitions. It is heaven he has to generate out of his soul's joy—not the millionaire's treasury, nor the victor's monument. Let him not be tempted by greed, nor vanquished by pride. For the human maker is not a gatherer or builder; he is a creator.

TRANSLATED BY SWAPAN CHAKRAVORTY

The Poet's Defence

What to us is *jivalila,* the play of living creation, is known across the western seas as the struggle of life.

There is little harm in that. If I call something navigation and you call it oarsmanship, or if I call a poem the *Ramayana* and you call it *The Battle of Rama and Ravana,* we need not take the matter to court.

The problem is, we are much too embarrassed with the word *lila*[†] nowadays. Life as mere play! What would the race of swaggerers, busy shaking up the three worlds with their bluster and brawling, say if they heard such a word?

I must confess that I feel no shame on this count. My English mentor might shoot the surest dart at this point and say, 'My dear fellow, you are *Oriental* after all.' But that won't kill me.

The word *lila,* play, tells the whole story; call it 'struggle', and you chop off head and tail. Where does the struggle start and where does it lead? What madness have we unleashed on a sudden, crazed by the holy narcotic offered to us by our drugged deity![†] Why, may I ask you, this pointless struggle?

— For life.
— What's the point of being alive?
— You are dead else.
— So what if I die?
— You don't want to die.
— Why don't I?
— You don't because you don't, that's why.

If you were to sum up this reply in a word, you have got to call it *lila,* play. Within all life there is an inexplicable desire to live. That desire is the last word. We struggle, we accept hardship, all because of that desire. Beyond all infliction there is a joy—there is no way of going past that, nor is there a need. A game of chess is a game from start to finish, although it involves making moves and anxiously deliberating. Without that hardship there would be no point in the game. On the other hand, if there were no joy in the game nothing would be more cruelly meaningless than that ordeal. Given the situation, if I called the game of chess 'play' and you called it 'the battle of chesspieces', I would not say you had expressed more of the matter than I had.

— But why say such things? Won't people slack off utterly as soon as they learn that life or the world is play?

— If work or idleness depended on hearing the word, then one would need to silence the Creator first of all. There is little glory in taking it out on a mere poet.

— Why, what does the Creator say?

— Whatever else He might say, He suppresses as far as possible that bit about the fight. Our science tells us that all through creation there is a battle of molecules and atoms. But when we turn our eyes to that scene of battle, we see that combat blossoming in flowers, burning in stars, flowing in rivers, floating in clouds. When we see it all together, in the realm of the multiform, melody harmonises with melody, line meets line, colour weds colour. Abstracted from that totality, science sees the factions, the friction, the feuds. That abstracted truth may be the truth of science, but it is not the truth of the poet, nor of the supreme lord of poets.

— Never mind other poets, speak for yourself.

— Fair enough. Your complaint is that words such as *khela* [play], *chhuti* [holiday], *ananda* [joy] appear repeatedly in my verse. If that is so, one is to understand that I am possessed by some truth. I have no way of eluding its grip. So from now on I will go on saying the same thing a thousand times, as shamelessly as the Creator Himself. If I had to make up things to say, I would be embarrassed if I failed to think up something new every time. But truth knows neither shame nor fear nor worry. It expresses itself, it has no other choice than to express itself: it is therefore reckless.

— That sounds like conceit.

— If it is no sin to criticise in the name of truth, then it should be no sin to be conceited in its name either. So in this we are quits.

— Don't let's get distracted. The point in question was—

— It was that to see the battle of strength in the world as the primary reality is to see it in abstracted form, like hearing the convolutions of the notes but not the song. To see joy is to see the whole. That is the highest wisdom of our culture. The ultimate truth of the Upanishads is *Anandaddhyeba khalvimani bhutani jayante, anandena jatani jeevanti, anandam samprayantyabhisamvishanti*: everything is born of joy,† everything lives in it, everything moves towards it.

— If that is the highest truth in the Upanishads, does the sage mean that there is no sin, no affliction, no strife in the world? Those are the things we wish to stress: how else can we rouse human beings to awareness?

— The Upanishads say in reply, *Ko hyevanyat kah pranyat yadesha akasha anando na syat*: who would have exerted body or life—that is, who would have brooked the slightest suffering or strife—if the skies were not filled with joy?† In other words, it is only because joy is the final truth that the world can endure pain and strife. Not just that, pain is the measure of joy. We know love to be true in proportion to the suffering it is able to bear. Thus suffering undoubtedly exists, but it exists because of the joy beyond it— or else there would be nothing, not even hatred and violence. When you acknowledge pain, you exclude joy; but by admitting joy, you do not rule out pain. Thus when you say that creation is that which survives the strife, you make a disjunct statement—what in English is called an *abstraction*. Everything is born of and lives in joy—that is the whole truth.

— All right, we accept what you say, but this is mere theorising. Of what use is it in the workaday world?

— The poet is not obliged to answer that question, nor indeed is the scientist. But the way things are now, even a creature of no practical use, such as the poet, can hardly escape the world's audit. Indian poetics has always conceived of rasa as causeless and ineffable; hence dealers in rasa in this country did not have to pay taxes at the mart of utility. But it is rumoured that some renowned wise heads in the West are unwilling to accept rasa as the essence of poetry: they wish to check and weigh the sediment under that distillate† before fixing the price of poetry. Therefore, people in our country too might condemn the appeal to ineffability as dated and *Oriental*. The censure would not be unbearable, but it is prudent to try and please practical people as far as possible. Although I am just a poet, I would still like to start from the beginning to explain the little I can judge of the matter.

The manifestations of being, consciousness, and joy† in the world may be analysed in the laboratory of human knowledge, but they do not exist in isolation from each other. The substance wood is not the tree, nor is the tree's ability to absorb moisture and take on life equivalent to the tree itself. Matter and energy gathered into an integral whole finds undivided expression in that which we call a tree: it is at one and the same time replete with matter, energy, and beauty. It is for this reason that the tree is a source of pleasure to us. And it is thus that trees are among the riches of the earth. There is no division of leisure and work, of work and play in the tree. So the heart finds rest among trees; it sees in them the true form of leisure. That form is not opposed to work. In fact, it is the fulfilled form assumed by work. This comprehensive manifestation of work takes the form of joy, of beauty. It is certainly work, but it is also *lila*, play, for in it work and rest exist together.

This wholeness gets broken and dispersed once the stream of creation reaches humans. The main reason for this is that a human being has an independent will; it does not always keep time with the play of the world. We have yet to get the measure of creation's rhythm: every now and then, we are out of time. That is why we split our own creations into small fragments and try to fix their beat within a manageable compass. But this destroys the pleasure of the whole symphony; nor do the small fragments sustain any rhythm. In everything we do, it is thus the discord and friction which declare themselves above all.

An instance of this process is the education of children. There is no harsher pain for the human child. A bird learns to fly, it learns to sing by hearing the song of its parents—that is part of its play of life: it is not a mortal combat between learning on one side and life and mind on the other. Such learning is entirely holiday lesson, it is work in the guise of play. Think of what our teachers and schools used to be. It was as if being born a human infant was such an offence that the guilty had to be sentenced for twenty years. I shall not argue the point, only declare on the strength of my poetic intuition that this is terribly wrong, because in the Creator's kingdom, Vishvakarma's[†] retinue is filling the world with the song

> As is our play so is our work—don't you know, friend?[†]

Once in the past the moralists had laid down, *Lalane vahabo doshastarane vahabo gunah* [Mildness fosters vice; rigour, virtue].[†] Sparing the rod, everyone knew, spoiled the child. But today it appears that the strains of the world's joy are at last reaching our classrooms—the rod is slowly losing out to the reed.

Let me cite another instance. On my voyage back from England, I was being dogged by two missionaries. Their carping against my country was infecting even the sea air. At the same time they furnished a long list of the selfless favours they were relentlessly bestowing upon my nation. It was not a fake list, and they had their sums right. They do in fact benefit us, but they could not do us a more cruel injustice. We would much rather they let loose Gurkha troops in our quarters. To me, where the principle of duty is limited to duties alone—that is where duty is an *abstraction*—it is a crime to practise it on living creatures. That is why our ancient books say, *Shraddhaya deyam* [Give with respect]:† for it is only when respect and love go with the gift that the giving is graceful and total.

But our habits have turned so graceless that we can brazenly claim that duty need not be a pleasure: in fact, it is better if it is not. Fight, fight, fight! We need to boast that we scorn joy—such is our machismo! We are ashamed to anoint ourselves with sandal-paste, so we jump about flaunting a blister-pack of mustard. It is the blister-pack I am ashamed of.

The trouble with human beings is that most of them are unable to express themselves. Yet it is in the full expression of oneself that there lies true joy. Whatever the difficulty of the task, the expert is happy as long as it lies within his expertise. The mother, no matter what her ordeal, is happy to be a mother: because, as I have said earlier, real joy is easily able to assimilate all pain, as Shiva drank poison† to save the gods. That is why Carlyle, viewing genius from the opposite end, described it as the 'transcendent capacity of taking trouble'.†

But it is not for self-expression that we do most things. Want or fear compels one to express one's master, or some powerful party, or some routine way of doing things. The work of the vast majority of people is someone else's work. They are forced to turn themselves into someone or something other than themselves. The Chinese woman's shoe does not match her feet: her feet match her shoes. The feet, therefore, must suffer pain and be misshapen. The great advantage of this kind of deformity, however, is that it is easy for everyone to be uniformly ugly. God has not made all humans alike; but if the moral theorist wants to make us uniform, it cannot be otherwise than by strife, deprivation, and disfigurement.

All men and women have to slave for the king, for the society, for the family, for the boss. They have been somehow forced into this strange situation. That is why we want to suppress the word 'play'. We stick out our chests and claim that the highest human glory is to fall flat on our face while running with saddle on back and bits between our teeth. This is the vaunt of a race of slaves proud of its slavery. The mantra of slavery is dinned constantly into our ears lest our soul become aware of its glory even for a moment. No, we were not born to die like hackneys in harness. Let us live like kings, and die like kings.

Our most profound prayer is *Abirabirma edhi*: O self-revealed One, may you express yourself in all your glory in me.† You are the whole, you are joy. Your form is the form of joy. That joyous form is not the firewood from the tree but the tree itself. In it, being and doing are one.

One might retort that this joyful form achieves its integrity and wholeness only after going through division and dispersal in human beings. As long as that does not happen, we have to chant day and night the mantra of struggle, we have to stumble and die with the bit between our teeth. In school and office and lawcourt and market, the hecatomb of human victims will continue. And it is best to play the drums very loud in the ears of the sacrificial animals, so that their minds are muddled by the din. It is better to tell them that this sacrificial block is the true deity, this stroke of the cleaver the true blessing, the executioner the true deliverer.

So be it. Let the sacrificial drums rumble on in offices and lawcourts; let them keep time with the jangling of prisoners' chains. Let all fall dead in the dust of the road from exhaustion, with perspiring bodies and parched tongues, the bit between their teeth. But the poet's veena will keep on playing, *Anandaddhyeba khalvimani bhutani jayante* [Everything is born of joy]. The poet's verse will endlessly repeat the mantra: 'Truth is beauty, beauty truth.'† Even if whole offices and lawcourts and colleges come rushing out bludgeons in hand, this melody will sound above all the commotion: it will sound in unison with the sea, the forest, and the lucent veena of the skies: *Anandam samprayantyabhisamvishanti*: everything that is, moves towards complete joy—not towards a slow, choking death, face down, in the wayside dust.

TRANSLATED BY SWAPAN CHAKRAVORTY

Modern Poetry

English passages quoted by Rabindranath in the original have been printed in italics. Where he offers a Bengali rendering, the original English has been placed in the text in Roman lettering, and substantive variations in the Bengali indicated in the notes. In E. A. Robinson' s poem 'Richard Cory', the original reading has been placed in the text except for Rabindranath's citing of the protagonist's name as 'Cody'.

I have been asked to write on *modern* poets in English. The task is not an easy one, for who is going to look up the almanac and fix the limits of the *modern*? Modernity is more about ideas than about periods.

A river flowing straight may take a sudden turn. Literature too does not always follow a straight course. When it changes course, one must call it a turn towards the *modern.* In Bengali, we might say *adhunik.* Such modernity is not about periods, but about temperament.

The English poetry I was introduced to in childhood was then deemed modern. It had changed course since Burns, and a number of great poets followed in that line—Wordsworth, Coleridge, Shelley, and Keats, for instance.

Rules of behaviour current in society at large are known as conventions. In certain countries, these conventions totally stifle the distinctness and variety of individual preference. They make puppets of people, whose conduct becomes flawlessly regular; a society favours these routine, time-honoured ways. Literature too is at times possessed by conventions, and people ascribe holy virtue to writings inscribed with the ritual marks of an impeccable convention. The period that followed Burns saw the individual will make its way into English poetry, breaching the barriers of convention. *Kumudakahlarasevita sarovar* [the lake bedecked with red and white lotuses]† is a lake glimpsed through a special aperture in the official blinkers produced at the workshop of sanctified wisdom.† When an intrepid writer takes off those blinkers, sweeps away the clichés, and looks at the lake with unconstrained vision, he clears the way whereby the lake may look different with changing gazes and fancies. Sanctified wisdom says 'Fie!'

When we started reading English poetry, this iconoclastic, personal temper was already accepted in literature. The uproar raised by the *Edinburgh Review* had died down. Our good old days marked the end of one particular era of modernity.

The mark of modernity in poetry then was the free rein given to the individual temperament. Wordsworth expressed in his own manner the joyous being he sensed in all nature. Shelley was a Platonic idealist, and moreover a rebel against all species of crude political and religious restraints. Keats's poetry was concerned with the contemplation and creation of the beauty of form. Poetry in that age was turning away from the outer world towards the inner.

The poet's deepest feelings seek to establish their permanence by assuming the beauteous form words give them. Love adorns itself so that beauty might demonstrate its inner joy to the world outside. There was an age when people made time to adorn in many ways the world with which they felt an affinity. These outer embellishments expressed the love in their hearts. Where there is love, there cannot be neglect. People in those days, revelling in the exercise of their taste, shaped the things of daily use into various attractive forms. An inner impulse taught their fingers creative skill. In every country and village, pots and pans, decorations to the home and adornments of the body joined the human heart to its material environs through colour and form. So many rituals were devised to give daily life its relish—so many new melodies, so many new crafts in wood, metal, clay, stone, silk, wool, cotton. A wife in those days was to her husband *priyashishyalalite kalavidhau* [a favoured pupil in the fine arts].[†] Setting up home needed artistic skill more than money in the bank. A garland was not to be strung just anyhow; young girls could embroider patterns and images on the trains of silk wraps; dance was crucial to their training; there were moreover the veena and the flute, there was song. Human ties had the beauty of spiritual kinship.

The English poets we encountered in our early youth saw the outside world in relation to their own spirits: their world became a personal one. Their private fancies, views, and tastes rendered that world not only human, not only a world of the mind, but specifically of a single poet's mind. Wordsworth's world was peculiarly Wordsworthian, Shelley's was Shelleyan, Byron's Byronic. The magic of their styles made the worlds the reader's as well. What pleased us in the world of each particular poet was the unique flavour of its hospitality. A flower invites bees by its distinct colour and fragrance: that is what makes the invitation delectable. So also with the invitations of these poets. In an age when one's private links with the outside world are predominant, that personal welcome needs specially to be kept alive. In such an age, people seem to compete to make their distinct identities shine forth even in matters of clothes, adornment, and personal grace.

We can see, then, that in the earlier nineteenth century, English poetry veered away from the conventions of the preceding age and turned towards individual self-expression. That, for those times, was modernity.

That modernity has now been dubbed mid-Victorian antiquity, and confined to the chaise longue in an adjoining chamber. Today's modernity comes cut and dried, with short dress and cropped hair. Not that it never powders its cheeks or paints its lips, but it does so openly, with an insolent lack of inhibition. It wants to say that we no longer have any use for infatuation. The creator has strewn our way with bewitchments; their diversity strikes different chords through different forms. But science has plumbed their depths and declared that there is no bewitchment at bottom, there are only carbon, nitrogen, *physiology*, and *psychology*. Old-fashioned poets that we are, we had thought these to be minor matters and fascination to be primary. We must admit that we tried to emulate the creator and sought to weave a web of illusion, cast a magic spell of metre and phrase, words and gestures. At times we played hide and seek among hints and suggestions; we could not shed that drape of modesty which adorns truth rather than hide it. In the tinctured light filtering through that thin mist, we beheld the beauty of dawn and dusk, soft and subdued like a new bride. Modernity is busy publicly disrobing the world, a Duhshasan pulling at Draupadi's clothes[†] in the open court. We are not used to such a sight. Do we demur just because of our old ways? Is there no truth behind our compunction? Is beauty not impoverished if we cast aside the veil that reveals rather than obscures the beauty of creation?

The modern age, however, has neither patience nor time. Livelihood is now more important than life. Hustled by machines, people rush through their business and race through their pleasure. The human species that once took its time shaping the world after its heart now farms out the job to a factory which hastily cobbles up a serviceable thing made to the measure of necessity and official standards. The feast has been called off, although we are yet to eat. There is no urge to see if things tune well with our minds, for our minds are lost among the throng pulling at the chariot ropes of livelihood's giant juggernaut.† There one hears no music save the chorus, 'Pull hard, heave-ho!' The mind has to dwell with the world of crowds more than with that of ties and affection; its ways are those of the workaholic. Swept on by the rush, it feels no urge to step aside from the unadorned and ugly.

Which road, then, shall poetry take and towards what destination? The days when one could choose, reject, and arrange as one pleased are over. Science does not choose, it accepts all that exists because it exists. It does not put things to the test of personal preference, nor does it adorn them impelled by a personal love. The chief pleasure of the scientific mind is in inquiry, not in kinship of the spirit. What I desire is not important; what the thing is in itself regardless of me, is what matters. If you leave 'me' out, no provisions need be made for bewitchment.

Embellishments are the first casualty of the spending cuts in the poetic economy of this scientific age. Fastidious attention to metre, phrase, and diction will soon be a thing of the past. This is not happening naturally; these strident denials have become the vogue to cure us of past addictions. The boundary wall has been crudely topped with broken glass so that fastidiousness, compelled by old habit, should not climb the wall and force an entry. A poet writes, '*I am the greatest laugher of all*, greater than the sun and the oak, than the frog and Apollo.'† '*Than the frog and Apollo*'—this is the broken glass, put there lest someone thinks that the poet is presenting some sweet contrivance. If the poet had written 'the sea' instead of 'the frog', our times would have resented it as routine poeticism. It may well have been so, but that frog is a far more mannered poeticism in an inverted way. It did not flow naturally from the pen; it jolts you by stamping on your toes. Such is the fashion of the times.

Yet it is a fact that the days are gone when the frog was not adjudged a creature fit to drink the same water as upper-caste verse. In the hall of truth, it is Apollo's equal, if not his superior. I too do not wish to scorn the frog. In fact, given the right occasion, the laughter of the poet's beloved could be compared to the frog's croaking laugh despite the beloved's protests. But even in the loftiest of scientific egalitarianisms, the frog's laugh is not of a kind with the sun's, the oak's, or Apollo's. Here it has been forcibly dragged in to break the spell.

Once the veil of enchantment is lifted, things must appear just as they are. What was coloured by enchantment in the nineteenth century has now faded; the mere trace of that sweetness fails to satisfy us—we demand something substantial. *Ghranena ardhabhojanam* [The food's aroma satisfies half our hunger][†] is a statement that is three-fourths exaggeration. Let me translate the exceedingly forthright language in which a modern woman poet has addressed a beautiful lady of yesteryear. If I try to sweeten the translation it would not be appropriate, nor would the effort succeed.

You are beautiful[†] and faded
Like an old opera tune[†]
Played upon a harpsichord;[†]
Or like the sun-flooded silks
Of an eighteenth-century boudoir.[†]
In your eyes
Smoulder the fallen roses of out-lived minutes,[†]
And the perfume of your soul
Is vague and suffusing
With the pungence of sealed spice-jars.
Your half-tones delight me,
And I grow mad[†] with gazing
At your blent colours.

My vigour is a new-minted penny,
Which I cast at your feet.
Gather it up from the dust,
That its sparkle may amuse you.

This modern coin is low on value but high on strength, and it is very distinct—its ring is of the most recent timbre. The sweetness of the past had a heady effect, but this has audacity. There is nothing fuzzy about it.

The subject matter of today's verse does not wish to seduce with loveliness. What, then, is the source of its strength? It is in its confident selfhood, what in English is called *character*. It says, *Ayamaham bhoh*[†] [I am here]: look at me. That woman poet—her name is Amy Lowell—has written a poem about a shop selling red slippers.[†] The situation is like this: the sleet blows in the evening wind outside, while inside the shop, rows of red slippers are seen strung behind the polished glass:

like stalactites of blood, flooding the eyes of passers-by with dripping color, jamming the crimson reflections against the windows of cabs and tramcars, screaming their claret and salmon into the teeth of the sleet, plopping their little round maroon lights upon the tops of umbrellas. The row of white, sparkling shop fronts is gashed and bleeding, it bleeds red slippers.

All this about those slippers.

This is what one might call *impersonal.* Neither as buyer nor as seller does one have reason to be particularly fond of that string of slippers. But the poem makes you stand and look; the moment its character takes form, the whole picture loses its triviality. The scrounger of meanings will ask, 'What does it mean, sir? Why this fuss about slippers, never mind if they are red ones?' One must say in reply, 'Try looking.' But there is no answer to the question, 'What's the use of looking?'

Ezra Pound has a poem about aesthetics.† A girl walks down a street. A small boy in patched clothes is excited by the sight. Unable to restrain himself, he cries out, 'Look! How beautiful!' Three years later, the poet sees the boy again. That year, there had been a great catch of sardines. The elders were busy packing them into wooden boxes for the market in Brescia. The boy leapt about, snatching at the fish. The older men snapped at him, 'Sit still!' Then the boy stroked the arranged fish and delightedly murmured the same phrase, 'How beautiful!' The poet says, 'Hearing this *I was mildly abashed.*'

Look at the beautiful girl, and at the sardines too: and don't be abashed to use the same words, 'How beautiful!' Such vision is impersonal—a mere sighting: the shop selling red slippers cannot fall outside its range.

In the nineteenth century, poetry had the selfhood of the subject; in the twentieth, it has that of the object. Hence the emphasis is now on the reality of poetic content, not on rhetorical embellishments: for the latter express individual preference, while genuine realism draws its strength from the expression of the content.

Before its appearance in literature, modernity of this kind had taken hold of the visual arts. It made a nuisance of itself in all kinds of ways in order to deny that the visual arts were part of the fine arts. It claimed that the task of art was not to delight the mind but to convince it; its characteristic trait was not loveliness but authenticity. It did not recognise the enchantment of appearance; it recognised only *character*, that is the self-declaration of a total entity. Such a visage wishes to say nothing about itself except to insist forcefully, 'I am worth taking note of.' The power of its noteworthiness comes neither from its demeanour nor from copying nature, but from the creative truth peculiar to its own self. This truth is neither religious, nor pragmatic, nor conceptual; it derives from its createdness. That is, we have to recognise it simply because it has come into being—just as we recognise both the peacock and the vulture, or cannot deny the pig any more than the deer.

Some are beautiful, some ugly; some are useful, some useless—but when it comes to creation, it is impossible to reject anyone on any pretext. So also with literature and the visual arts. If a form has been created, it owes no one an explanation; if it has not come to be, if its being is feeble, if it has only the elegance of an idea, it is to be discarded.

That is why the current literature which has accepted the creed of the modern is indiscriminate in its ways: it scorns to preserve its purity by assiduously scoring up the traditional marks of superior caste. Eliot's poetry is modern in this sense; the poetry of Bridges is not. Eliot writes:

The winter evening[†] settles down.
With smell of steaks in passageways.
Six o'clock.
The burnt-out ends of smoky days.[†]
And now a gusty shower[†] wraps
The grimy scraps
Of withered leaves about your feet
And newspapers[†] from vacant lots;
The showers beat
On broken blinds[†] and chimney-pots,
And at the corner of the street
A lonely cab-horse steams and stamps.

There follows the description of a muddy morning smelling of stale beer. Addressing a girl on that morning, the poet says:

You tossed a blanket from the bed,
You lay upon your back, and waited;
You dozed,[†] and watched the night revealing
The thousand sordid images[†]
Of which your soul[†] was constituted . . .

Then we hear about the man:

His soul stretched tight across the skies
That fade behind a city block,
Or trampled by insistent feet
At four and five and six o'clock;
And short square fingers stuffing pipes,
And evening newspapers, and eyes
Assured of certain certainties,
The conscience of a blackened street
Impatient to assume the world.

Between this tawdry evening and tawdry morning filled with smoke, mud, various stale smells, and tattered rubbish, a picture of a contrasting nature arises in the poet's mind. He says:

I am moved by fancies that are curled
Around these images, and cling:
The notion of some infinitely gentle
Infinitely suffering thing.

It is at this point that the parity of the frog and Apollo breaks down. Here the croaking of the frog in the well torments Apollo's laughter. It is clear that the poet is not dispassionate in the scientific manner. His disgust at the tawdriness of this world is expressed through the description of its tawdriness. Hence the harshness of the poem's conclusion:

Wipe your hand across your mouth, and laugh;
The worlds revolve like ancient women
Gathering fuel† in vacant lots.

The poet's distaste for this fuel-gathering, decrepit world is obvious. He differs from earlier times in having no desire to lull the mind with a fictitious world of coloured dreams. The poet is making his verse plod on through the mire without sparing a thought for its laundered clothes. It is not that he loves the mud, but he feels the need to know and recognise with open eyes the mud of this clayey world. If Apollo's laugh breaks out somewhere amidst all this, well and good; if not, he need not ignore the frog's high, leaping laughter. That too is something: one can regard it for a while in the world's context, there is something to be said for it as well. The frog would be out of place in the decorous parlour of language, but the greater part of the world lies outside that parlour.

We wake up in the morning, and start with a perception of our self, a fresh stirring of our consciousness. One could call this phase romantic. The newly awakened consciousness ventures out to test itself. In universal creation and in its own compositions the mind seeks to lend form to its thoughts and desires. What it wishes in its heart, it fashions outside itself by many spells. Then the light grows harsher, experience hardens, the world's turbulence tears away many a web of illusion. In the stark light, under a bare sky, one begins to confront a more blatant reality. This newly perceived reality is greeted in different ways by different poets. Some mistrust it and feel rebellious; some despise it so much as to be frankly and shamelessly rude. Others sense a profound mystery at the heart of this shape that looms all too clear in the harsh light: they do not feel that there is no secret, or that everything is fully contained in what is perceived. The experience of the last war in Europe was so harsh and brutal that the terrible crisis destroyed age-old decorum and modesty at a stroke; the stable social order in which people had rested securely, with implicit faith, was rent apart in an instant. The haven of gracious codes and beneficent policies lay in ruins; thus people began to take aggressive delight in scorning as weakness and self-deluding artifice all that had been so long deemed decorous. Wholesale carping is taken today for fidelity to truth.

However, if there is a theory of modernity, and if we describe it as a theory of the impersonal, it must be said that this arrogant mistrust and vilification of the world is also a perversion of personal feelings caused by a sudden upheaval. This too is infatuation; it lacks the profundity of a simple acceptance of the real with a quiet, dispassionate heart. Many take this aggressiveness and iconoclastic bluster for modernity; I do not. I refuse to say that influenza is the modern disposition of the body just because it attacks thousands of people nowadays. *Eha vahya* [That is something external].[†] Behind the influenza lies the body's fundamental nature.

If you ask me what pure modernity is, I will say that it is to see the world with dispassionate absorption, free of personal attachment. This seeing is bright and pure; there is genuine joy in such undeluded vision. Modern poetry will regard the world with its holistic gaze in the same dispassionate spirit that modern science brings to its analysis of reality: that alone is lastingly modern.

But it is pointless calling it modern. This joy of simple vision, free of attachment, does not belong to any particular period. It belongs to anyone who knows how to move in this unveiled world. It is more than a thousand years[†] since the Chinese poet Li Po wrote his verses. He was modern; his eyes had freshly viewed the world. He writes just four lines in plain language:

Why do I live among these green hills?
The question makes me laugh, I don't answer. My mind is still.
I live under another sky and on another earth—
In a world that belongs to no man.
The peach tree blossoms, the stream flows by.

Here is another picture:

Blue water . . . spotless moon,
The white herons fly in the moonlight.
Listen, the girls had come to gather water-chestnuts,
They are returning home in the night, singing.

Yet another one:

I lie naked in the green forest in spring,
So languorous that the fan of white feathers feels heavy.
I have left my hat perched on yonder hilltop,
My bare head feels the breeze
Blowing through the pines.

A wife says:

My hair was cut short, it didn't cover my brow.
I was playing near the front gate, picking flowers.
You arrived, my love, on your bamboo horse,
Scattering green plums.
In the alleys of Chungkan, we lived close by.
We were young, our hearts full of joy.
When I married you, I had just turned fourteen.
I was shy, too scared to laugh,
I hid in dark corners, head lowered,
Never looking round even if you called a thousand times.
At fifteen my scowl disappeared,
I laughed. . . .
When I was sixteen, you left for a far country—
Through the mountain pass at Chutang,
Over swirling rivers and piled rocks.
You had been gone five months, I could bear it no more.
I saw you pass down the road
By our gate, where the green moss, too deep to clear away,
Grew to hide your footsteps.
At length, the early autumn wind piled dead leaves on them.
It's eight months now, yellow butterflies
Skim the grass in our west garden.
My heart aches, I fear lest my beauty fade.
My love, when you return home crossing three districts,
Don't forget to send me word ahead.
I'll take the long road to Changfengsha to meet you.
The distance won't scare me at all.

The note of *sentiment* in the poem is not in the least shrill; but neither do we discern in it a frown of sarcasm and doubt. The subject is traditional, but does not lack vitality. If one had mocked it by an obliqueness of *style,* that would have been modern, because the moderns scorn to allow in verse what everybody else finds readily acceptable. A modern poet would probably have ended the poem by describing how the husband departed wiping his tears and casting backward glances, whereupon the wife promptly went off to fry dried-shrimp fritters. For whom? The answer would have consisted of a line and a half of dots. The outmoded reader would ask, 'What is this?' The modish poet would reply, 'This is what usually happens.' 'But it does turn out otherwise too.' 'Yes, but that would be too genteel. A bit of stench cures it of its overnice air, makes it modern.' In earlier times, there was a dandyism in poetry allied to courtesy. Modern poetry too has its dandyism—of a sort that revels in putrid flesh.

Beside this Chinese poem, the modernity of the poets in English does not strike us as natural. Theirs is a besmirched modernity, jostling the readers' mind with its elbow. The world that they view and show is crumbling, dustblown, and choked with *rubbish.* Their minds today are morbid, discontented, unsettled. In such a state, it is impossible for them to disengage their minds totally from the world-as-object. The goddess's broken image, with its timber and straw stuffing in full view, convulses them with laughter: they claim that the real thing is showing at last. Sharp talk, which stabs at the clay and the wood and the straw, is in their view the only firm means of asserting unalloyed truth.

In this context, I am reminded of a poem by Eliot.† Its subject is this: an old lady of a rich house has died. The shutters are drawn, the undertakers are busy making the appropriate arrangements. Meanwhile, the butler of the house sits upon the *dinner table*, with the second housemaid on his lap.

The incident is no doubt credible and natural. But the question will arise in the old-fashioned reader's mind, 'Is that enough?' Why should one be impelled to write such a poem, and why should one bother to read it? If a poet's work tells us about a beautiful woman's smile, I might say that is news worth sharing. But if the poem goes on to describe how the *dentist* walks in, plies his instruments and finds she has caries, one must say that this too is certainly news, but not of the kind to cry out to all and sundry. Should I find someone particularly eager to spread this news, I would suspect that the person's sensibility is caried as well. If it is argued that earlier poets were selective in their subject matter while ultra-modern poets are not, I must disagree: the latter are no less selective. Choosing fresh flowers is selectiveness, so is choosing flowers that are withered and worm-eaten. The only difference is that the moderns are always worried that people might accuse them of being finicky. The members of the aghori sect† assiduously choose an offensive diet and use unclean objects, lest it should be proved that they are partial to good things. The result is that their preference for things not good becomes a settled habit. If the aghori discipline is introduced into poetry, what place will there be for those who have a natural taste for clean things? The flowers and leaves of some plants are routinely infested by pests, while those of others are spared. Does one have to stress the former, and flaunt this as a rigorous commitment to reality?

A poet describes a respectable gentleman thus:

Whenever Richard Cody† went down town,
We people on the pavement looked at him:
He was a gentleman† from sole to crown,
Clean favored, and imperially slim.†

And he was always quietly arrayed,†
And he was always human when he talked;
But still he fluttered pulses when he said,
'Good morning,' and he glittered when he walked.

And he was rich—yes, richer than a king,†
And admirably schooled in every grace;
In fine, we thought that he was everything
To make us wish that we were in his place.†

So on we worked, and waited for the light,
And went without the meat, and cursed the bread;†
And Richard Cody, one calm summer night,†
Went home and put a bullet through his head.[1]

The poem is free of the snide sarcasm and cynical laughter of modernity; rather, it has a hint of compassion. But there is in it a moral message, and it is a modern moral. It says that whatever appears to be beautiful or wholesome may be mortally sick at heart. Someone we take to be rich may actually, behind that façade, be starving. Old-fashioned ascetics speak in the same vein. They remind the living that they will one day be carried on a bamboo litter to the cremation ground. In Europe, monks have preached how the decaying corpse feeds worms in the grave. Books of moral instruction have tried to jolt us into the awareness that the human body, which seems so beautiful, is really a gruesome assemblage of bone, flesh, fluids and blood. The best recourse for ascetic discipline

[1] I am having to translate from memory since the original is not at hand, and there may be some errors.

is to provoke repeatedly a contempt for that which is immediately real to our apprehension. But the poet is not a disciple of the ascetic; he is there to speak on behalf of love. Is the modern age so withered that even the poet is touched by the winds from the cremation ground? Does it please him now to declare that what seems noble must be rotten, that what we adore as beautiful is untouchable at the core?

Wizened minds lack the strength of the purely natural. Having grown soiled and morbid, such a mind tries to shake off its stupor by taking a contrary course. Like a fetid, fermenting substance, it needs the perverse to make itself pungent. Laughter can course through its wrinkles only if it sheds shame and disgust.

By deferring to reality, the mid-Victorian years had wished to feel it as worthy of esteem. The present age takes the demeaning and disrobing of reality as the theme of its efforts.

If excessive respect for the world-as-object is *sentimentalism*, an unbidden hostility to it can be called by the same name. A mind that has grown perverse, whatever be the cause, finds it hard to achieve clarity of vision. Hence, if you deride the mid-Victorian age as the file leader of over-genteelity, one could use a contrasting epithet to mock the Edwardian era. The present situation is unnatural; hence it will not endure. Be it in *science* or in *art*, a dispassionate mind is the best recourse. Europe has achieved it in *science*, but not in literature.

TRANSLATED BY SWAPAN CHAKRAVORTY

The Philosophy of Literature

In this essay, Rabindranath repeatedly uses the term byaktipurush *(Sanskrit* vyaktipurusha)*. It seems basically to mean the personalised, humanised expression of a universal, ultimately divine or divinely inspired being or force. This can find expression in an individual character or personality, but suggests the manifestation of a greater entity. No single word or phrase can adequately render the term. We have translated it according to context as 'individual self', 'particular self', 'personal(ised) self' or simply 'self'. Sometimes 'being' has been used instead of 'self'.*

Rabindranath here also exploits the full range of meaning of the word ras(a). *It sometimes reflects the technical use of the term in Sanskrit poetics (see p. xi above); the word* rasa *has been retained in such contexts. But such uses shade off into more general senses, rendered variously according to context by '(aesthetic) joy', 'savour' and 'pleasure'.*

I am and everything else is—in my existence are the two united. If I do not apprehend what is outside of me, I do not feel myself either. The stronger the sense of the world outside, the more robust is the sense of one's own inner being.

I am—this truth for me is of utmost value. Whatever enhances this apprehension therefore gives me pleasure. I cannot be indifferent to any external thing: whatever excites my eagerness—that is, whatever keeps my consciousness awake, even if it is as trivial a thing as flying a kite or spinning a top—makes me happy, since that eagerness spurs me on to a keener apprehension of my own being.

I am one; outside of me, there are the many. The many make my consciousness various; I am able to know myself through diverse things in diverse ways. It is through this diversity that my self-awareness remains constantly alert. We feel depressed when the world outside is monotonous.

According to the shastras, the One said, 'I shall be many.'† The One wished to realise its unity in the various. This we call creation. The one that is within me also wishes to find its own self in the many: the wealth of such self-realisation is in its multiplicity. Continually coursing through one's consciousness is the stream of the multifold—visual forms, aesthetic delights, the surge of various events: the feeling that 'I am' achieves clearer definition under their impact. Joy stems from the clarity of such self-revelation; obscurity, on the contrary, breeds weariness.

To the solitary prisoner, even if he suffers no other torture, the sense of his own self grows dim: he seems to come close to a state of non-being. 'I am' and 'The non-I is'—these two ceaseless streams are creating me by continually merging within my being: to stunt or distort this process of self-creation by impeding the union of the inner and the outer is to cause joylessness.

One might argue at this point that the union of the I and the non-I also gives rise to pain. That may be so. But one must remember that pain is the opposite of pleasure, not of joy. In fact, pain is included in joy. This might sound self-contradictory, but is true nevertheless. Anyway, let us leave this issue for the moment; we might take it up later.

Our learning is of two kinds: through knowledge and through apprehension, *anubhav.*† The etymological meaning of the word *anubhav* (feeling, apprehending) includes the sense of becoming in accordance with something else. It is not just receiving information from outside; it is a maturing within one's own self. To apprehend is to experience one's own self in some particular colour, form, or savour perceived through one's link with external matter. The Upanishad therefore says that a son is dear to us not because of our desire for a son, but because of our desire for ourselves.† The father realises his own self in his son: that realisation is the source of his happiness.

This joy of realisation born of the union of subject and object is the goal of what we call literature and the fine arts. The truer the sense of oneness of the outer world with the inner self achieved by the depth of experience, the more extended is the limit of life's joy, that is the limit of one's own being. The practical demands of everyday life confine our self-extension to small segments, chain our mind to the narrow limits of material concerns—the world of necessity hems us in with its strict vigilance; the inertia bred of this daily rehearsal of confinement makes us forget that the purely practical person is too little of a person—a human being pared down by necessity.

The claims of necessity are powerful, and they are innumerble, because our essential requirements hardly keep within their measure. Even after our wants are met, insatiable desire begs for more; acquisitions accumulate, and we seek after them without rest. Every sphere of life has been filled with the cry 'I want.' But on the margins of that marketplace, humankind looks for a vacant space where the mind says 'I do not want'—that is I do not want that which serves my desire for accumulation. Hence, in spite of the pressures of necessity, we see people amassing the ingredients of the useless—so great to them is the worth of inutility. Human glory and wealth lie where we have been able to transcend necessity.

Needless to say, pure literature is useless; the pleasure it provides is gratuitous. In that spacious recess exempt from obligations, humankind comes to know material objects within the human state of being, by touching them to life with imagination's golden wand. In that apprehension, that is in that particular realisation of the self, he finds joy. I do not know of any other purpose of literature except to provide such joy.

People say that the joy literature affords is that of beauty. The point is worth considering. I will not attempt the impossible task of explaining the mystery of beauty through analysis. Beyond the range of our direct apprehension, we observe that beauty is in command of certain bare *facts.* These are neither beautiful nor unbeautiful. The rose has petals and a stem of a particular shape and size, with green leaves around them. But there is a principle of unity that includes all these and yet transcends them: we call it beauty. This unity invokes the deepest unity within me—my distinctive self. Unbeautiful objects have expression as well, which too no doubt has a certian wholeness and unity. But their material factuality is the most important thing about them; the unity is secondary. The shape and dimensions of the rose, its grace, the harmonious proportions of its parts specifically point to the unity pervading its entirety. That is why, to us, the rose is not a mere fact: it is beautiful.

Why only the rose—any object that transcends its own factuality is as true to me as I am to myself. I too am an object which encompasses many facts but is indivisibly one.

The mathematician no doubt immerses himself in the profound beauty and formal unity latent in higher mathematics. The fact of its harmony does not belong to knowledge alone. It is a matter of intense apprehension: it provides pure joy, because the lofty peak of knowledge where it manifests itself is exempt from every kind of necessity—there, knowledge is free. We may naturally ask why this has not become a subject for poetry. It is because this experience is limited to a very few; it lives away from the gaze of the common people. The language through which one can engage with it is technical; such a language has not developed into a vital element touched by the heartfelt response of the multitude. The language that fails to enter the heart through unmediated emotions can create neither poetic pleasure nor poetic form. And yet the machine and the factory are finding their way into modern poetry. The machine may surpass the fact of its use and express itself in our imagination in its aspect as immense power: it may manifest itself, transcending its particular constituents, by the strength of its inherent tectonic coordination. The eyes of the imagination may discern an inner self deep within its components. That inner self is the partner of our own particular selves. The man who senses an intimacy with the machine through feeling rather than mechanical knowledge finds his own self in it, the way a captain lovingly senses his own self in the heart of his steamship. But the theories of natural selection or the survival of the fittest are not of this kind. It is not as if one cannot derive disinterested pleasure from knowing these theories. But it does not afford the joy of becoming, only the pleasure of acquisition. That is to say, such knowledge is distinct from the knower; it belongs not to the inner chambers of his private being, but to his storehouse.

Our rhetorical text tells us, *Vakyam rasatmakam kavyam* (Poetry is speech imbued with rasa or aesthetic pleasure).[†] Beauty affords aesthetic pleasure by its rasa; but we cannot say that all pleasurable rasas evince beauty. Aesthetic pleasure agrees with all other forms of pleasure in that it is something we feel or apprehend. Outside of feeling, rasa has no significance. Rasa, by its very nature, appropriates fact and transcends it by an inexpressible process. The stuff of rasa is a feeling of oneness that surpasses materiality and merges into one's consciousness without delay. Its expression is one and the same with my expression of myself.

The human race has set about mitigating the exclusive dominance of the clutter of material things. It is clearing a space for its feelings. Let me cite a simple instance. A man carries water in a vessel: carrying water is part of his daily necessity. Hence his head and waist have to bear the oppression of matter. If the rule of necessity were to be absolute, then the vessel would remain something alien. But human beings have made the vessel into a beautiful object. Beauty is irrelevant to the task of carrying water. But this artistic beauty clears a space around the starkness of necessity. The vessel which we had accepted under compulsion becomes a thing of our own. We have seen this effort at work ever since the beginnings of human history. Human beings confer the value of the useless on useful things, they turn material objects into something beyond materiality with the help of art. The creation of literature and art belongs to that cataclysmic sphere where there is neither burden nor compulsion, where the ingredients are illusory and their ideal form is true, where the human soul has appropriated the entire world into itself.

On the other hand, if you want an instance of abject surrender under duress to matter, look at the can of paraffin dignified into a vessel, the transporting of water by slinging two jerrycans from a shoulder-pole. It shows our utter defeat in the face of need. The man who built a beautiful vessel did not give in to thirst quickly; he took a fair bit of time to accommodate the claims of his own personality.

The world of matter is a ball stuffed with dust and mud and rocks and iron. The atmosphere has cleared a wide space around it. Its self-expressive function begins from this point. The breath of life flows from here: this life is ineffable. The brush of the artist painting that life draws light, colour, and warmth from here, filling the canvas of the earth with mobile pictures, time and time again. Here we see the world's aspect of lila or play, of creativity; here its distinctive self is expressed—a self which cannot be analysed or explained; here we find the earth's own utterance, its verity, its savour, its greenness, its billowing energy. Human beings too want an aerosphere of their own beyond the call of essential duties, a space where they are at leisure, where the ultimate purpose is to express oneself in one's creations engendered by the play of the unnecessary—a creativity that is neither learning nor acquiring, but simply becoming. I have said that *anubhav* means becoming. When the sense of becoming swells under the impact of a being outside of us, the play of creativity overfloods our minds. Our emotions have their use in the conduct of our material lives. We defend ourselves, kill enemies, raise offspring: our emotions provide these activities with impetus and make them desirable. Within these limits, there is no difference between humans and animals. The difference arises when human beings disengage their emotions from the burden of work and attach them to the imagination, when pleasure in feeling something becomes for them the sole object of a selfless enjoyment; when inspired to express their feelings, they forget the imperatives of material profit. These same men do not just wield weapons to wage war—they play martial music and dance the war-dance. Even when their violence is dedicated to a destructive traffic, they transport that sensation of ferocity beyond practical use and give it unnecessary form. This might well hinder the fulfilment of their purpose.

Humanity looks for symbols of its own feeling not only in human creations, but also in universal creation. Human love ranges among the flowery woods; human devotion sets out on pilgrimage to the confluence of river and sea, to mountain peaks. Humankind finds the sportive partner of its particular self neither in material objects nor in theory, but in play where the sky is blue and the tender shoots of grass are green. Where there is beauty in flowers, sweetness in fruits, compassion for living creatures, and self-surrender to the absolute, we feel in our hearts the eternal bond of kinship between the world and our individual selves. This we call reality—the reality in which my own intimate self comes true.

Where we are eager to express that self and perceive the infinite within it, we become extravagant, whether of money or of energy. When we wish to acquire money, we are anxious to account for every quarter-paisa; but when we wish to express the sense of wealth, we do not hesitate even to bankrupt ourselves, because the expression of wealth then also becomes the expression of one's distinctive self. In fact, no one in the world has wealth enough to adequately express the statement, 'I am wealthy.' When we have to protect our lives from an enemy, we must be extremely cautious about every movement and posture; but when we want to express our courage, we risk even death, for such expression expresses our distinctive self. In our everyday affairs, we spend judiciously; but this concern for the limits of our purse vanishes when we express our joy during a festival—because when we are strongly aware of our individual beings, we disregard worldly facts. One's behaviour with other people is usually measured. But one loses all measure when it comes to the person one loves, that is the person with whom my personal self shares the deepest bond. Of that person one can easily say

Ever since birth, your face have I descried;
    Yet the eye's unsatisfied.
Aeon after aeon, my heart on yours has lain;
    Yet the hearts will not join.†

As far as facts are concerned, there cannot be wilder exaggeration; but through the feeling of the individual self, the eternal can be concentrated within the confines of the momentary. 'Her body's breeze dissolves the stone'†—this statement is counterfactual in the material world; but in the world of the individual self, a statement pitched lower in the interest of fact misses the full reach of truth.

It is the same with universal creation. There, the facts of matter or cosmological forces cannot waver in the least. But beauty surpasses these factual limits: its account has no norm or measure.

The mass of vapour floating in the upper atmosphere constitutes an ordinary fact, but the exquisite play of colours into which it breaks at sunrise and sunset is extraordinary. It is not just *dhumajyotihsalilamarutam sannipatah* (born of the union of smoke, light, water, and air):† it seems an unbidden overstatement of nature's. It seems to transfigure a particular, finite, material fact into something infinite and inexpressible. In the same way, language surpasses the limits of lexical meaning under the impact of powerful feeling.

That is why when language utters 'Ten moons fall weeping upon his toenails,'† we cannot dismiss it as nonsense. That is why the facts of everyday life are abashed at being placed on the pedestal of art, because authenticity of artistic expression involves overstatement—it is a burden too heavy for mere facts. No matter how hard we strive for accuracy, there is always something in the choice of words, the style of speech, the implications of the rhythm which exceeds the accurate and constitutes a surplus. In a world of facts, this surplus is the individual self. Here lies the difference between courtesy and workaday conduct: some calculated purpose drives the latter, while courtesy has an excess which expresses the grace of the individual self.

The civilisations of ancient Greece and Rome are lost in antiquity. When they were living, they had many material obligations. Their needs were opaque, obdurate, and burdensome. Strong anxieties, fierce endeavours engirded them. Today there is no trace of all this: only those things have survived that were imponderous, immaterial, uncommitted—things which all nations have greeted with the extravagance of courtesy, just as we satisfy our feeling of reverence by prefixing five honorific 'Shris' to an emperor's name. The people had placed them at the summit of excess, not on the plain below, teeming with everyday transactions. Only that aspect of the distinctive human self which can bear the scrutiny of the timeless, has been accorded a welcome whose imperishable form and priceless value still endure, in verbal utterances and lines carved on stone.

That which is merely local and temporary, no matter how highly prized by the present, has never received the spontaneous welcome of excess from the genius of the land. That welcome has been accorded to the choric song heard from a boat floating into the full-moon night:

> Boatman, pick up your oar.
> I can row no more.†

It has also been accorded to the nightingale's song, listening to which the poet said to his beloved:

> Listen Eugenia,
> How thick the burst comes crowding through the leaves.
> Again—thou hearest?
> Eternal passion !
> Eternal pain![†]

I have said already that in every kind of rasa, that is, in every form of affective experience, we know ourselves in a special way, and that this knowing produces a special joy. One might object that it is a contradiction in terms to say that the knowing which causes pain also gives us joy. We think we should repudiate all causes of suffering or fear because they harm us, hurt our souls, and go against our interests. The urge to protect life and self-interest is very strong: we cannot bear it to be inhibited. Hence the experience of suffering, even though it stimulates one's sense of the individual self, is usually displeasing. It has been observed that people in whom the fear of injury or death is not strong enough willingly invite danger, make the most arduous journeys, plunge into impossible tasks. What is it that tempts them? Not the acquisition of some rare treasure, but the realisation of one's own self with intense feeling in an encounter with dread and peril. Many children are seen to be cruel: they find keen pleasure in torturing insects and beasts. Such pleasure is no longer possible when our sense of the right grows stronger and acts as an inhibition. Whenever instinct or habit enfeebles this sense, the pleasure in cruelty is seen to grow exceedingly keen: history provides many such instances, which are by no means rare among a certain class of prison staff as well. Slanderers find pleasure in the same unwarranted viciousness; it is not as if people slander when provoked by some particular harm done to them. In ritual seance among the ascetic votaries of calumny, the slanderer enjoys the impersonal malice of besmirching some unknown person who has done the defamer no harm. It is a cruel and ugly business, but it has a sharp relish. A person to whom we are indifferent affords us no pleasure, but the target of our slander strongly excites our feeling. Hence it is easy to see why, for a certain kind of person, someone else's pain is matter for luxurious pastime—why it is possible to dance a wild, bloody dance while sacrificing a huge and powerful animal like the buffalo. The experience of pain causes an upheaval in one's consciousness. Even when its acridity brings tears to our eyes, we enjoy its savour. Its sensation is stronger than that of easy comfort. This it is from which tragedy draws its value. Rama's banishment at Kaikeyi's instigation, Manthara's exultation, the death of Dasharatha† —there is nothing good in all this. It must be admitted that these events are not of the kind that in plain terms we may call beautiful. Yet so many poems, plays, pictures, songs, and ballads centred on them have come down the ages; they attract crowds and give pleasure to so many. Here lies the powerful self-apprehension of the particular being through dynamic experience. Stagnant water is dumb, and the still air without self-knowledge; in the same way, the continual rehearsing of dead, everyday habit does not stir the consciousness, but enfeebles one's sense of being. Hence in pain and peril, rebellion and revolution, human beings wish to realise themselves with an intensity of emotion, shaking off the torpor of the unmanifested.

I had said this once in one of my poems. I had said that the 'I' within me is lulled to sleep by indolence, languor, and easeful indulgence. I find that true self intimately only when, by a ruthless stroke, I can rouse it from its inertness; in that discovery lies joy.

Alas, for long I nurtured her
With every care
Upon her bed.
Lest she feel pain, or sorrows prove,
Night and day with lavish love
A nuptial bed I fashioned for her,
Flower-layered;
Behind closed doors I kept her there
In secret room,
With every care. . . .

Her happy bed tired her at length—
Her idle trance,
Luxuriance.
No longer did she wake when touched,
Her flower garlands weighed too much,
Sleep and wake were one to her,
Night one with day.
A numb inert aversion pierced
Her inwardly,
Luxuriantly. . . .

Hence have I thought to play today
A novel game
In the night-time.
Clutching fast the death-swing's ropes,
The two of us shall nestle close,
The storm will come and give a push
With laughter high:
We two shall play the swinging game
At midnight-time,
My soul and I.†

The shastras say, *Tam vedyam purusham veda yatha ma vo mrityuh parivyathah*: 'Know that knowable being so that death may not cause you pain.'† Know that being—that is that *personality*—who may be known through *vedana*,† that is the feelings of the heart. When my individual self apprehends the infinite being through unmediated feeling, knows Him by means of the heart, intellect and mind,† it confidently realises its own self in Him. To what effect? The pain of death—that is of emptiness—disappears, since the sense of that knowable being is a sense of fullness: it is opposed to the sense of void.

This truth pertaining to spiritual exercise may be brought to bear on the literary field. The sense of emptiness afflicts us in our lives; a dim sense of our own being makes for a diminished world in which our feelings are unresponsive, and no message clearly asserting 'I am' keeps our self-awareness awake. When Shakuntala's mind was listless from the emptiness of separation, there was the call at her doorstep, *Ayamaham bhoh*: 'Look, here I am.'† That call did not reach her ears, so her innermost self could not reply 'Yes, I too am here.' That was the cause of grief. 'I am'—if this message rings out clear in the world, my soul is bound to answer, 'I am.' Where does this message sound the strongest notes? In a truth that is replete with rasa, joy. We feel the being within us most intimately when we behold its joyous form outside us. Hence the wandering baul sings

Where shall I find the one
Who dwells within my heart?†

I desire the supreme Person in order to realise the person dwelling in my heart most intimately: we desire *tam vedyam purusham* [that supreme knowable being]—only then is emptiness powerless to hurt.

There are various skills, various efforts to provide one with food and relieve the wants of everyday life; there is literature and art to fill the void in one, to keep the person dwelling in one's heart awake in various ways, through diverse forms of aesthetic delight. How great their place in human history, how enormous their quantity! If some catastrophic earthquake wrecks civilisation and wipes them all out, what immense emptiness will spread like a black desert through human history! The farm, the office, and the factory are fields of human cultivation. Literature is the field of human culture: here humankind refines itself, fashions that self fully, becomes that self. It is therefore said in the *Aitareya Brahmana, Atmasamskritirvava shilpani* [Art is the reformation of one's own self].†

The boy Madhab has written in big letters on the classroom wall about another boy: 'Rakhal is a monkey.' He is obviously very angry with Rakhal. He does not notice any other boy as much as he notices the object of his anger. The proportions of the letters make clear how big Rakhal now looms as a fact of existence. In keeping with his meagre powers, Madhab has carried his feeling of anger beyond himself, and created out of it a shape in black letters on the wall which stridently declares that Madhab is angry and wants the whole world to know it. We may call that a midget incarnation† of the lyric.

The unformed and crippled poet in Madhab could not progress beyond the comparison between Rakhal and a monkey. Vedavyasa† had said the same thing about Shakuni† in the *Mahabharata*; but his language was of a different order, and no whitewash can ever erase those coal-black letters. The antiquarian may prove from assorted evidence that there was never any person called Shakuni. One's reason might agree, but one's unmediated feeling would bear testimony that he certainly exists. Indeed, Bhanru Datta† too is a monkey. The Kabikankan† has proclaimed it in black letters. But we derive pleasure from the feeling of scorn these monkeys arouse in us.

We find a kind of literary analysis in our country which cites various irrelevant reasons to devalue this immediate perceptibility of literature. Some expert in human character might say that such unqualified villainy as Shakuni's is not normal, or that Iago's motiveless malice should have been coupled with some noble virtue. He might add that since Kaikeyi or Lady Macbeth or Hirimba† or Shurpanakha† are women, belonging to 'the race of mothers', it is irreverent to besmirch their characters so thickly with envy and malevolence. Literature has this to say for itself: we need only to be convinced that the character rises to the level of a creation, that it is immediately present to us: all other considerations are invalid. Seized by a whim, the Creator devised the giraffe. His critics might say that its neck resembles neither a cow's nor a deer's, still less a tiger's or a bear's; its sloping hindquarters are not normal in quadruped society, therefore . . . and so on. The sole answer to all these objections is that the beast is a clear and perceptible presence in the order of animal creation. It says, 'I am'; it is unsustainable to say 'It should not have been.' Open manifestation is the highest vindication of what we call creation. Literary creation resembles the divine in this: in it, the camel has come to be because it has come to be; the ostrich too calls for no other justification.

From childhood, human beings have felt this joy—the joy of unmediated reality. This reality does not mean that which always takes place or that which conforms to reason. Whatever touches the consciousness unmistakably by assuming a form is real. When that reality comes to life in rhythm, words, style, and gesture, it becomes a work of art composed in language. It may not have any practical significance: it expresses something that can *tease us out of thought as doth eternity.*†

It's dark upon the other shore:
Jham, jham, the raindrops pour.
On this bank the chilli bush is hung with chillis red.
O my worthy brother, my heart begins to ache.†

The subject of the rhyme is trivial. But the swing of the rhythm has turned it into a tangible object, despite the grammatical error it contains.†

Come and see the cuckoo dance
On the pomegranate branch.
Tak-duma-dum go the drums.†

The child is delighted on hearing this. It is something mobile and well-defined, like a rhythmically structured insect: it exists, it flies—this is enough to cause amusement.

That is why human beings demand from infancy, 'Tell us a story.' Such a story is called *rupkatha*, a fairy tale. It is *rupkatha* indeed: it may not convey any historical fact or necessary information; it may not even make out a case for its own probability. It sets up a form or *rup* before the mind's eye, excites interest in it, and thereby fills a void: it is real. Let us begin the story:

A portly tiger once there was
Streaked in black from pate to paws.
He stalked a footboy to the hall
And spied a mirror on the wall.

The footboy vanished like a shot;
The tiger gazed on, quite distraught.
At last he roars in dudgeon high,
'Who did this to me and why?'
Aunt was busy husking grain:
The tiger pads up, stiff and vain.
His whiskers rear to their full scope:
'Quick,' he snaps, 'some glycerine soap!'†

The little girl listens wide-eyed and open-mouthed. I tell her, 'Enough for today.' She grows restless: 'No, tell me: what happened next?' She knows very well that the tiger fancies the soap less than it does its users. Yet this absurd story is entirely real to her, while the tiger of zoological accounts does not matter in the least. She is happy because her whole mind and soul has intensely felt that crazy mirror-gazing tiger. Such is the play of the mind: it creates out of nothing, and finds joy therein.

I have already said that manifesting the beautiful is not the only purpose of creative literature. There is a stage of aesthetic experience where beauty is easily apprehended. A flower is beautiful; a butterfly is beautiful; a peacock is beautiful. This beauty is single-storeyed: it lacks the mystique of inner and outer quarters; it is easily accessible and requires no effort. But when this edifice of life is enhanced by the largesse of the mind and the commingling of characters, its chambers multiply; the appreciation of beauty is then no longer easy. Take the human face. One risks error if one pronounces an instant verdict on the evidence of one's eyes. One might quite possibly call something delightful that is unbeautiful by a simple judgment. In fact, such delight may be deeper than that aroused by customary beauty. The mind is instantly excited on hearing a thumri in the tappa mode,† but a chautal composition in the Tori raga† inspires the consciousness to delve deep. *Lalitalabangalataparishilana*† may sound sweet, but *Vasantapushpabharanam bahanti*† gives delight. The one appeals to the ear, the other to the mind; one has a soft grace but no character, but character is of primary importance in the other—and can be recognised only by a cultivated mind.

What we call beautiful is limited in range; the scope of the delightful extends very far. It does not need to be exceptional in order to beguile us; it is distinguished even when it is trivial. If language represents exactly what we are used to seeing, we call it information. But when literature transforms that object of everyday experience into something special and presents it before us, it comes as something unprecedented: it is then uniquely and autonomously itself. Many people are driven by parental love to forget their wider obligations; Dhritarashtra† of the *Mahabharata* fits this banal description. The subtle touches of the poet's pen, however, make this blind king, deprived of the right of rule, appear to us as totally singular. There are many who share his basic trait, but there is only one Dhritarashtra in the world; his singularity is neither in his particular conduct nor in any partial account, but in his totality. No puny critic's analytic pen can fathom the easy deftness of genius that has so completely fashioned this unparalleled and distinct character, manifested by the poet's magic mantra of creation.

Most objects in the world appear to our observation as belonging to general categories. Thousands of people walk down the street: although each of them is a particular person, to me they are all just men and women, obscured and indistinct beneath the casing of a large generality. To my own self, I am certain and distinct; when someone else arrives with his or her own distinctness, we place that person in the same category as ourselves, and are happy.

One thing must be made clear. My washerman is certainly an indubitable truth to me; so is the beast of burden† that follows him around. The link of necessity brings him close to me because he washes my clothes, but he remains beyond the full affective ambit of my personal self.

I have said elsewhere that when utility is paramount in our relationship with an object, it becomes part of a general category; we cannot perceive its distinctiveness. The sajina† flower has entered poetry so late because we have known of it under the general category of food. The flower of the chalta† has not yet reached the portals of verse. The flower of the star-apple is not less worthy than that of the rain-tree, but when we set our eyes on the former, we see it as the phase preceding the fruit we eat: it does not manifest itself as its own culminating state. If it overtly declared its distinctiveness, it would have by now found recognition in poetry. A little thought will make us see why the beauty of the hen or the rooster is yet to be acknowledged in Bengali literature. Our consciousness does not see these things as their own selves; it sees them connected with or wrapped in something else.

I might recount an experience at this point, even thought it may be redundant for those who have read my poems.† I was living in the country, where I had a servant whose looks or intelligence were hardly worthy of notice. He would go home at night, return the next morning and go about his chores with a dusting-cloth on his shoulder. His major virtue was that he did not talk too much. I registered the fact of his presence on the day he did not turn up. That morning, I found the water had not been drawn for my bath, the rooms had not been swept. He showed up around ten in the morning. I asked in a rather brusque voice, 'Where were you all this time?' He said, 'My daughter died last night.' And he promptly picked up the dusting-cloth and went quietly to work. My heart stopped for a moment. The veil of necessity that had covered the servant was lifted, revealing a father. My self discovered its likeness with his: he became a perceptible presence, something distinctive.

Beauty carries a divine *passport* and is granted easy entry everywhere. But what am I to call this man, this Momin Mian? I cannot call him beautiful. There are countless fathers of daughters in the world—this banal fact is neither beautiful nor unbeautiful. But that day, at the touch of the rasa of compassion,[†] that rustic man was united with the self that dwells in my heart: beyond the bounds of need, on the plane of the imagination, Momin Mian became real for me.

The second daughter of a millionaire is getting married. Even the oldest inhabitants of the neighbourhood cannot recall having seen such a display. Its reports have made waves overspilling the columns of the newspapers. No matter how important the event is made to seem by the rumble of the rumour-mill, even this extravagance cannot raise the event above the trite factuality of a report entitled 'A Daughter's Wedding'. The commotion of the moment cannot make it memorable. But if a poet rescues this commonplace event from the ephemerality of its local and temporary self-proclamation, turning it into the stuff of literature resplendent in word and rhythm, it pierces the fog of thousands of everyday nuptials and appears as the unique wedding of a unique daughter—like Uma's[†] in *Kumarasambhavam* or Indumati's[†] in *Raghuvamsham.*

Sancho Panza is the mere servant of Don Quixote. Translate him among the world's fleeting clusters of fact and he will never catch anyone's eye: who will care to pick him out from the general category of countless servants? But Don Quixote's servant is now known for ever to people of all times, offering everyone the joy of his singular and immediate presence. If you put together the biographies of all the viceroys of India to date, they would pale into insignificance beside this servant. The debate on arms control raised by hordes of clever and eminent politicians is a formidable fact among facts; but if one can clearly express the pain that dogs the life of a single maimed soldier, people in all ages will give it more importance than serious political deliberations. We know this for sure, that at the time when *Abhijnanashakuntalam* was written, there were many political and economic problems whose urgency was a source of immense anxiety. There is no trace of them today; only the play about Shakuntala remains.

Human society is like the Milky Way in the sky. Much of it is strewn with the sprawling nebulae of detached concepts or *abstractions*: we call them society, state, *nation*, commerce, and much else. Their amorphous mists occlude the apprehensible reality of the individual human being. The burning ember of pain searing thousands of individual hearts is buried in ashes and hidden from reality: it loses substance under the single substantive, 'war'. If you uncover all the sins and horrors covered up by the word *nation*, humankind will have no place to hide its shame. The thing called 'society' has fashioned a prodigious range of folly and enslavement which, although conspicuous, escapes our sight: because 'society' is an abstract concept, it deadens the feeling for human reality in our minds. Rammohan Ray† and Vidyasagar† had to fight against this insentience. The terrible things perpetrated behind the phantasmal screen of the word 'religion' are enough to exhaust every infernal torment described in every sacred text. In school, there is an abstract concept called a *class*; here the individual student is hidden behind the generality of the group. That is why we remain indifferent when the living substance called their minds is wrung dry by rote learning like a flower pressed between the pages of a book. An abstraction known as governmental bureaucracy exists beyond the individual human's perception of truth; hence there is nothing to stop the monstrous heartlessness that goes under the name of an apathetic state administration.

Literature has illuminated the distinctive capacity for feeling amidst these vast nebulae of insentience in the human consciousness. These creations are finite in form, but infinite as expressions of the individual self. This self is the innermost integrating principle of human beings, and their ultimate mystery. It radiates from the centre of the human consciousness and spreads to the edges of the world; it is in the body but exceeds it; it is in the mind but transcends it; it occupies the present and floods the shores of past and future. As truth, this individual self continually surpasses the limits within which it appears as the manifested—it will not be held back. Hence it is anxious to express its own being in a form that is joyous and immortal. In the creation of such forms, the individual is at one with the world. Through these creations, the individual self answers the message of the absolute being, who, amidst the darkness of a mass of facts, constantly lights up before our eyes His own epiphany, in the boundless mystery of truth and the indescribable miracle of beauty.

TRANSLATED BY SWAPAN CHAKRAVORTY

VERSE TRANSLATIONS: 'ALAS, FOR LONG . . .' BY ANANDA LAL AND SUKANTA CHAUDHURI; 'EVER SINCE BIRTH . . .', 'IT'S DARK . . .' AND 'COME AND SEE . . .' BY SUKANTA CHAUDHURI; ALL OTHER VERSE BY SWAPAN CHAKRAVORTY

Presidential Address

At the Bengali Literary Convention of North India, 3 March 1923

Literary pursuits can take several paths. One of these involves organisational work. Chairing and livening up meetings and conferences, editing literary works, running newspapers—these are part of organisational activity. Those who follow this trail know how to run smoothly the affairs of the literary estate. Next is the road which involves knowledge, such as the study and discussion of history, antiquity, and philosophy. This kind of work can also stir up literary audiences, draw applause, and bring fame.

I have strayed from both these paths since childhood. The only road left is that which involves aesthetic pleasure. It is now no secret that having embarked on this path I have continued, whether ably or not, to cultivate imaginative literature. Years ago, I had on my own started on a love tryst with the rasas on this lonely road, seduced by the far-off strains of a flute.[†] But all who have walked this road towards a tryst will know that it is made difficult by abuse and insults from those near at hand.

In spite of the obstacles close to home, I had to start out, because I had heard the melody that leads one far beyond the domestic pale and the writ of the useful. That is why for so many years now I have been listening to both the flute and the abuses. The road I had taken did not lead to the market or the cargo jetty. I therefore feel rather lost in the kingdom of rules. The farers on the imaginative road have to flout rules at every step, and that bad habit is now in my bones. If you drag me into the domain of rules, I may fail to do things in a tidy way.

Why then did I agree to preside over this conference? The first reason is that the person who asked me[†] is someone I hold in high esteem; I cannot turn down an invitation coming from him.

The second reason is that since the invitation was coming from Bengalis living outside Bengal, the ties of blood made it impossible to resist.

The answer my heart made then, at the moment when the call reached me, is what I shall put before you in some detail in my address today.

All nature is thrilled to greet the south wind on this festive spring day, and the earth has sprouted stalks for new leaves. To this literary festival too the season has sent out a call. It is not the first time we are hearing it.

For a long while now, a quickening wind has been surging across the heart of Bengal. In no time, the literary buds that had so far remained shut burst open, breaking all barriers. And barriers there were in plenty. Students newly drunk on the heady delights of English literature had then scoffed at the Bengali language. At the same time, classical scholars, proud of the riches of Sanskrit literature, spared no effort to scorn their mother tongue. But just as a long-ignored beggar girl, despite all privation, comes suddenly one day to claim her place in the world of beauty through the abundant glory of her youth burgeoning from within, so did the spurned Bengali language, swept by a sudden onrush of feeling, overflow the banks of long indigence and achieve majesty. Your invitation brought back to the sanctum of my memory the image of that youthfulness of spirit triumphing over material poverty.

Human identity is complete only when one can truly express oneself. Expression, however, cannot take place within the private self. It is to be found in a true relationship between oneself and others. Unity involves not just the one, but a relationship of the one with the many. The reach and truth of that unity defines the genuine identity of a particular individual or group. We fulfil ourselves when we achieve that unity deeply and expansively.

Bengal as geographically defined gives us no sense of any deep unity: for Bengal is not just a tract of soil, it is also an idea. It does not simply have a physical existence in the world, it exists in a truer sense in our consciousnesses. Do not forget that Bengal is home to birds and beasts too. And yet, since the royal Bengal tiger's sense of union with Bengalis is not exactly steeped in the milk of kinship, it finds nothing more delectable than ingesting them. No real human identity is ever derived from one's birth within a certain landmass.

Human beings have also tried to define their identity in terms of national unity. Those who have been able, through the system and laws of a self-governed state, to evolve a polity whereby they can maintain the distinction between other states and their own, and who can codify and extend their collective interests through governance and cooperation within their territory—only they are to be regarded as a *nation*. It does not matter how much they may differ in other respects. One cannot call Bengalis a *nation*, since they are not yet in control of their political destiny. On the other hand, the inhabitants of a particular country can declare their identity through social and religious cohesion—by declaring, for instance, 'We are Hindus' or 'We are Muslims'. Needless to say, Bengal is divided on this count as well. As regards identity based on caste, there is in Bengal no end to divisions in this respect. Again, scientists have tried to determine racial identities, as fostered by scientism, by measuring fine distinctions of height, colour, length of the nose, circumference of the skull, and so on. One would soon feel lost if one were to ponder, on the basis of expert opinion, to which racial line we Bengalis belonged.

Birth for us is a kind of expression. The coming to fullness of this expression is the fullness of life. The better I fulfil the demands of my physical nature by overcoming disease, affliction, infirmity, and hunger, the more I express my creatural individuality. The vehicle of this expression is the natural world.

But we do not express our beings only in the natural world through our links with land and sea, light and ether. We are born into the world of human consciousness too. That expression in terms of the spirit fulfils itself through the fullness of the individual mind, as effected by its link with that world of common human consciouness. The vehicle of that expression of the spirit is language. Without language, the bond between human minds would have been very tenuous.

Hence a Bengali is not just someone born in Bengal; one is a Bengali only when one has been granted access to the realm of human consciouness by means of the Bengali language. Language is the medium of kinship; it is a more intimate possession than our creatural natures. The pride Bengalis take these days in their mother tongue is deeply gratifying, because the language has enabled them to know one another and to give others an authentic account of themselves.

There are two sides to human self-expression. On the one hand there is one's apprehension of oneself; on the other, the urge to express oneself to others. A self which remains hidden is of little consequence. One who is only dimly evident to oneself cannot claim the notice of others. In obscurity, one stays insignificant. One's greatness comes to light when one is able to express oneself.

To achieve such identity successfully, one needs a language that is strong and vigorous. If the language is unclear, mean, or stiff, humankind cannot express itself fully in the universe of the mind. At one time, the

Bengali language was rustic in nature. It was difficult to express deep emotions or abstract ideas in it. Hence the world then saw Bengalis as rustics. Those who studied Sanskrit and encountered universal ideas through its texts could therefore show no respect towards a mind totally confined within the Bengali language. They found little to cherish in its rude verse narratives and couplets. What does such neglect breed? The neglected start believing they deserve neglect, that they are by nature dull. But that cannot be the truth in any deep sense: such self-oblivion follows from the absence of self-expression. When one finds a fit occasion for self-expression, one no longer remains hidden from oneself. The lamp remains blind to its own flame until it is fitted with an oil chamber. Therefore, since the prime medium of human self-expression is language, the biggest task is to recover one's true identity by redeeming one's language from its impoverished state, and then to reveal that full countenance to the world. I remember that in our childhood Bankimchandra,[†] that savant of ideas, one day read a magic invocation in Bengal at which the dark moon turned over and a bright lunar phase began. It is not just that we were thrilled with the riches revealed to us. Suddenly we saw stretching before us a vista of inexhaustible hope. What might come next, what else we might acquire, what surprises the future might bring—such anticipations filled our minds.

This sense that there is no end to good fortune, these approaching footfalls of the infinite pulsating in our heart's beat, are what give creative work its momentum. This is true of every sphere of life. In politics, the aspirations of Bengalis and Indians were once strictly confined. The Congress thus felt that we could grow only upon the scraps the English doled out to us. The day our hopes broke free of this confinement, we felt that the power within ourselves was enough to invoke and receive the country's resources. Such boundless hope achieves miracles; nothing big is accomplished when one's hopes are fettered. Where did Bengalis get a glimpse of this boundlessness? Only where they could create their own world and dwell in it. The worst misery is when human beings cannot roam free in their own worlds, when they have to eat others' food and shelter in others' homes. We have, therefore, the saying *Svadharme nidhanam shreyah paradharmo bhayavahah* [It is better to die in one's own faith, and dangerous to adopt that of others].[†] My faith is the basis of my creative strength: I must create my own dwelling and reside in it. The creative output of every race takes its own divergent form in accord with its particular nature. It acquires the right of movement within the worlds it fashions in different pursuits such as politics, society, literature, and the arts. Bengalis as a race have found the Bengali language the only sphere in which they can express their joyous being. At one point of time, the great power generated by that language seemed to find almost excessive expression in different forms of writing, somewhat like a seed whose overwhelming vitality cracks its rind open and shoots forth a sprout. If that vital force had been feeble, its literature could not have stood its ground: the flood of ideas from abroad would have swept it out of existence.

We have witnessed such extinction elsewhere. In many other areas of India the study of English is very strong. In those places Indians write to one another, even to close relations, in English. So pitiful is the situation that father and son exchange not just ideas but the most trivial information in an alien language. They mouth *Vande mataram*[†] in their eagerness for political rights, but in the same breath insult the mother tongue, the highest privilege a mother can bequeath, without a hint of regret.

I cannot say that there are no signs of this self-abasement in Bengal. But Bengalis now have a sense of shame in this matter. At the moment, it is mostly Bengali letters that crowd the roads to post offices in Bengal.

In fact, no one who has acquired any respect for the mother tongue can ever sink to writing in English to one's kin and countrymen.

There was a time in Bengal when people were eager to write English verse. Writings and speeches in English were then considered proud achievements. The tide has now turned. There are some who lament that the Tamils speak better English than the Bengalis. May we flaunt this slander as a victor's crown.

Today this Bengali Literary Convention outside Bengal is suddenly eager to declare itself. The reason for this eagerness is that Bengalis, with their hearts and lives, have built up a living literature. When Bengal is just a claim to a stretch of land, it cannot transcend the borders in a map. There it is a territory fashioned by providence, not the land Bengalis can really claim as their own. But when a Bengali's soul inhabits a country of the mind in the world of language, that space is not restricted by any geographical boundaries; it is created by fellow Bengalis. Today Bengalis can see that country traversing rivers, plains and mountains, and stretching into the distance; and so their joy is extending beyond the physical limits of Bengal. They can now assert their soul's privilege beyond a broken fragment of space and time.

History tells us that there was once no end to the hostility between England and Scotland. How was that conflict resolved? Not just by putting a Scottish prince on the English throne. The fact is that since the time of Chaucer and his contemporary poets, the English language and its literature so enriched by them impressed and attracted Scotland. The English language won the heart of Scotland by the power of its own wealth. In this way two hostile races were brought together on the common ground of language: fellow travellers now on the same road of thought and learning, they acknowledged ties of kinship, and their surface differences melted away. That Bengalis want to cling to their language far away from home, that they resist submission to the language of their present environs, is because the power of the Bengali language, enriched by its literature, has won their hearts too. That is why, however far they might go, the pride in their language remains a deep bond tying them to Bengalis back in Bengal. They are pained by the thought of severing this bond; they are glad when they feel it.

I have even heard it said in my childhood that the care that Bengalis are taking to cultivate their mother tongue is an impediment to national unity—because if you strengthen a language, it becomes harder to loosen its firm bonds. If Bengali literature had not achieved excellence in that age, we might by now have relinquished our attachment to it and accepted any other commonplace language without regret. But the stuff of language is a living thing. You cannot mould or mill it to order. You can put it to best use only if you accept its laws. If you fly in their face, you render it sterile. Once, in the days of Frederick the Great, Germany eyed the French language with lust, but to no avail. For the French language will not answer the needs of your soul once you uproot it from the nature of French life. I can use a lion's hide to make a rug or drape the wall, but I cannot swap my skin for his.

We must accept that we are born as much in the lap of the mother tongue as in that of our mothers: both mothers are for us vital and indispensable.

Besides being of use to ourselves, the mother tongue can be meaningful in a larger sense. Only when my language is the proper vehicle for my own ideas can I establish an easy and just relationship with ideas in another language. Although I dodged school as a child, the school has reclaimed me in my mature years. I have thus gained some experience by teaching children. Among the different kinds of students who joined my school, there have been a few English-trained Bengali students. I have found that it is harder to teach English to these children. On what do I base my English lessons for a Bengali child who has no Bengali? The meeting of the beggar and the alms-giver is not a meeting of hearts. If that happens in the learning of a language—that is, if we have an empty beggar's bowl on one side and a fistful of alms on the other—the receiver has to start from scratch. But no good comes out of a vocation founded on begging. It is simpler to master a foreign tongue by paying from your own language for everything you get.

Therefore, it is only when each country achieves maturity in the use of its own language that it can forge authentic links with those of others. This synergy of languages offers the literature of every race the chance to shine forth with heightened lustre. The river that flows past my village can be used to conduct trade with foreign lands as well as to ferry people across from the village, because that coursing river has dynamic links with many others.

There was a time in Europe when Latin was the only common medium for the pursuit of knowledge. As long as this was the case, the unity of Europe was external and shallow. The greatness Europe has achieved today through the union of various streams of learning is unparalleled in the history of any other continent. This active and continuous convergence of knowledge from different countries was made possible only by the interaction of the various European languages; it would never have happened through any single language. There is no end to the political inequality in Europe at present, but its equality in learning still holds strong. This synergy of all learning has lit up and overwhelmed the whole world. Each country has brought its own flame to the great festival of lights in that continent. Wherever there is true union there is true strength. The real strength of Europe today is in its intellectual collectivism.

We ought to keep this fact in mind in our country as well. In India the medium for exchanging ideas is now the English language. The claims of another language as the instrument of national unity have also been advanced. But genuine integration does not lie that way: we may perhaps achieve uniformity, but unity we never shall. The reason is that this uniformity will be shallow and artificial—it is like tying us with ropes in an effort to keep us together. When hearts meet, true union is possible only if freedom and distinctness are preserved. But if people are forced into togetherness by some external bond, the outcome is a deep hatred: it is the unity of a chain gang,[†] unity through mere regimentation.

Russia tried to co-opt the small countries it conquered to the privilege of the Russian language by destroying their native tongues; the Belgians would be relieved if they could make the Flemish forget their own language. But the right of language is stronger than territorial rights, and bullying in this respect is of no avail. The Belgians could not stand the distinctiveness of the Flemish and tried forcing them into a political unity. That unity is superficial and can therefore have no lasting basis. The attempt at inducing unity in the name of imperial integration is a great nuisance. The big slave-trading nations of Europe have at present forced their conquered peoples under one yoke and lashed the chariot of *imperialism* into motion. The horses pulling it have no relationships in common, but that is immaterial to the charioteer. He is intent on moving ahead: strapping on the harness with all his might, he keeps tugging and flogging the horses, for else he must come to a halt. Those who desire such seeming equality will steamroll over every difference of language to ensure a level road for their imperial chariot. However, one cannot tear five different flowers to shreds, roll them into a lump, and call it a hundred-petalled lotus. The unity among the varied leaves and flowers in the forest is the unity of spring. They bud together when the south wind blows in early springtime. Behind their variety lies a single pathway for transporting the message of spring: there they meet and become one. The tough men of politics are fond of saying that they must accomplish their purpose by tying up people with thick ropes, flogging and maiming them—that the ropes are essential for unity. They do not desire the supremely free Shiva who dwells in the heart of the indivisible One.[†] They worship the counterfeit One obtained by stuffing the many into one sack. But those who have found the indivisible One in their hearts do not seek Him outside. Oneness in the outer world is destruction, it is uniformity; oneness of the heart is creation, it is unity. Uniformity leads to the disintegration of death; unity, to the concert of the living.[†]

We have here with us today many friends from regions neighbouring Bengal. If they have gathered here without any reservations about the honour of the invitation, that itself will have accomplished much. Let no inordinate pride of Bengali identity disturb this rite of union. It was Daksha's[†] pride in his lineage that made him provoke Shiva.

Bengalis living here have created some space for their language in a part of the country where Hindi is spoken. This has increased the responsibility of their organisation. We need to know what they have gained and observed, what they have achieved with the help of their friends here in northern India, at Varanasi. We who live far away are not familiar with all this; we view the people of northern India with the help of the atlas and the gazetteer. It will be a blessing when Bengalis can clear the path of friendship by using the Bengali language to extend our knowledge of them. A crucial step in the pursuit of love is the pursuit of knowledge.

Differences are magnified when people know little of one another. When there is no acquaintance of the spirit, surface differences hit the eye and induce contempt at every stage. Let the flow of genuine contact with northern India be carried today by the Bengali language towards Bengal. The writers here can collect the finest treasures of recent and ancient north Indian literature, worthy of everyone's esteem, and send them to distant Bengal. In this way, language can be the vehicle for bringing Bengal closer to northern India.

I do not know Hindi, but a friend at our ashram has acquainted me with some remarkable gems from the Hindi literature of the past. I have heard from him songs composed by ancient Hindi poets which still sound modern. It goes to show that poetry which is true is for ever modern. I realised that a language which has produced such a golden harvest can never lose its natural fertility, even if its fields have lain untilled for some time. They shall see happier seasons and rejoice in new harvest festivals. That is how a friend helped me develop a bond of esteem with the language and literature of these parts. Let that bond with these north-western parts be an object of our pursuit and care. *Ma vidvishavahai* [Let us never decry each other].[†]

The coming of spring today has thrilled the leaves in the forest. The last dry leaves have fallen off. Those who are busy turning the sapless leaves of their ledger-books on such a day have missed the rhythm of the countrywide festival of spring: they are lagging behind. However valuable the present *political* enthusiasm in the country, 'It is superficial'.[†] More momentous than a tally of its gains and losses is the message of that deep spiritual impetus which has enabled the Bengali language and its literature to grow so freely. Since the natural processes that preserve our health work invisibly, some impatient persons would place much greater value in the *joint stock company* of the pharmacy: they are even willing to risk their healths for its sake. People pray to be crowned with honour and fame, and there may even be a need for these things; but the crown does not make their heads any taller. The intimation of true glory is inside the head, not in the headgear; it is in the creative chamber of life, not in the workshop behind the store. Spring has brought the bounty of the lord of life to the garden of Bengal's heart. This is the inside news, not the news printed in the papers: poets have the job of announcing it to the world. I am here today to carry out that task of the poet. I come to tell you, Rama's foot has touched the cursed stone that was Ahalya.† We have already seen this happening in Bengali literature: that is our strongest reason for hope. Let that hope and that thrill spread today in the hearts of Bengalis living far from Bengal. It was not so long ago that it all began: Bengali literature has become powerful in word, rhythm, and song within sixty years at the most. That power is not yet exhausted. Let hope and faith rise in our minds. Let us make this power live for ever. Whenever human potency has expresed itself in language and literature; men and women have conquered mortality and won honour and love in the concourse of all humankind.

A few days ago Dr Otto, a professor at Marburg University, wrote to me that they wished to send a teacher to Shantiniketan to study Bengali literature. When he returned after finishing his course, a chair in Bengali would be instituted at that university. No foreigner would have thought of this ten years back.

Today the fount of Bengal's utterance has been unsealed. We have to serve those who have come to us, tracking the stream. We will certainly be able to accomplish the task if we have hope and courage. We all look forward eagerly to that future. If Bengal achieves special glory through such diligence, will it not redound to the whole of India? The flowers may blossom on one branch, but do they not belong to the entire tree? If the bees come swarming to a tree laden with flowers, the whole forest welcomes them in. There is no harm if today's guests stream through the courtyard of Bengal. Indians will have to recognise that all these travellers are meeting on Indian ground. Let Bengali literature usher in these seekers of honey with the utmost respect

TRANSLATED BY SWAPAN CHAKRAVORTY

The Poet Yeats

In this translation, a passage from a critic cited by Rabindranath in the original English has been printed in italics. An earlier unidentified passage, which he cites in Bengali translation, has been retranslated into English from his version.

The poet Yeats is not lost in a crowd. He stands out as somebody special. Just as he stands taller than almost anyone around him, so also, if you look at him, you get the feeling that he has an abundance of every gift: as if the Creator's powers gained particular intensity at one spot and thrust him up forcefully like a spring from the surrounding plains. That is why, in body and mind, he gives such an impression of profusion.

When I read the poets of modern England, many of them seem to me poets not of the great world around us but of the world of letters. Poetry has been written here in England for a long time, and a great deal of poetic language, metaphors, and figures of speech have piled up in course of time. Matters have now come to a pass where to be poetical, we need not go to the original springs of poetry. Poets have become somewhat like the ustads of Indian classical music. They feel no need to sing from the heart, but merely derive songs from other songs. When words are not born of pain but of words, the craft of words becomes more and more complex and adroit. Emotion, no longer deeply and prominently the substance of the heart, ceases to be simple: it does not believe in itself, and hence drives itself to excesses. Because it is not naturally fresh, it has to run after the bizarre in order to prove its novelty.

A comparison between Wordsworth and Swinburne will make my point clear. Swinburne is foremost in talent among those who are poets, not of the universal, but of the poetic. His extraordinary skill in the choreography of words intoxicates him with delight. With the many-coloured threads of sounds and echoes, he weaves vivid patterns in crudely vivid colours. They are amazing creations, but lack a broad base on earth.

The music of Wordsworth's poetry was struck out by a direct encounter between the world and the human heart. That is what makes it so simple: simple but not, therefore, easy. The readers did not easily accept it. When the poet writes directly from his feelings, his writing unfolds fully, spontaneously, like a fruit or flower. It does not explain itself, nor does it do any kind of violence to itself in order to be attractive or charming. It shows itself to be what it is. The reader accepts it and enjoys it because he wants to.

There are some persons born to let nothing stand between their feelings and the objects that evoke those feelings. They can express with unshakable confidence, in the true language of the heart, the beauty and joy of human life and of the world. Such people can boldly cut across all the artificiality of the poetry of their time.

Burns was born in such an age of artificiality in English literature. He felt with all his heart, and expressed what he felt. Thus it seemed as if, breaking the barriers of contemporary conventions, the unfettered heart of Scotland appeared—who knows from where—and confidently took its place at the centre of the poetic world.

If Yeats has won particular appreciation in English poetry today, it is for the same reason. His poetry, instead of echoing the poetry of his time, manifests the feelings of his own heart. We must undersand clearly what is meant by 'his own heart'. A diamond manifests itself by manifesting the light of the heavens. So also with the human heart. It cannot manifest itself within its own self alone: there it is dark. But when it reflects something greater than itself, it manifests itself in that greater light and also makes that light manifest. In the poetry of Yeats, the heart of Ireland has found utterance.

This too needs a little explanation. The same sun's rays fall on different clouds, but the clouds take on different colours according to their nature and position. But though different, these colours do not clash with each other. Their very variety enables them to unite within a single harmony. Dyed cotton wool could not have done so, however much it might have tried to mimic clouds.

Likewise, whether it is Ireland or Scotland or any other country, the light of the universe takes on a particular colour as it shines in the hearts of that particular people. Thus the sky of the universal human heart is made beautiful with a variety of colours.

The poet does not simply express the lustre of emotions and feelings; he touches them to a special beauty with the colours of his nation's heart.

I would not suggest that everybody can do this, but blessed are they who can. The songs of the Vaishnava† poets are universal poetry in the form of Bengali poetry. They give the world what is the world's, adding however an aesthetic quality of their own, filling the vessel of their particular form.

One who has to fight the battle of life must put on armour, must wear all the protective covering that the world has to offer; else one will be buffeted from all quarters. But if the aim is to express oneself fully, one's most fitting garb is the absence of covering. That was what I felt when I met Yeats. Here was a man who had accepted the world with his heart's senses wide open. He did not see what was around him as people usually do, through conditioning, habit, and emulation.

Whenever someone perceives the world with such immediacy and reports what is seen, we find it somehow accords with age-old human experience; it is not incongruous. Those who have seen with the eyes of innocence have seen like this. The Vedic poets too saw life and sentience in earth and water. River, cloud, dawn, fire, storm appeared before them not as scientific facts but as purposive beings. The experience of joy and sorrow operating in human life seemed to extend its play through earth and sky in many exquisite disguises. As it is in one's consciousness, so in all nature. The sensation of laughter and tears, the sportive play of asking, receiving, and losing, are to be found on a gigantic scale amid the light and darkness of the theatre of infinite space, no less than in the small compass of our hearts. The arena is so vast that we cannot see the whole of it. We see the water or the earth, but cannot see the cosmic sport within it all. But when humanity is not blinkered by education and habits, when one sees with all one's heart, mind and life, one feels such a sensation of emotional empathy playing among all things that one can express it only through tales and allegories. Humankind once saw itself on a grand scale in the affairs of the universe: it somehow sensed that there was nothing within it that was not there in the whole world, and whatever there was in it was also there in the universe on a vastly enlarged scale. Human beings then saw everything with the eyes of the poet—that is to say the eyes of the heart and of life, not the eyeballs, optic nerves, and brain cells. Such a truth does not lie in factual accuracy; it inheres in ideas and feelings. Similarly, its language is the language of music, the language of beauty and form. This is the oldest language in human literature; even today, when a poet apprehends the world through his own feelings, his language comes close to this ancient language of humankind. Hence even though the ancient legends are of no use in the age of science, for the poet's purposes alone they never go out of date. Humanity's new awareness of the universe has travelled down that path of legend and left its own imprint there. He whose heart has been awakened by such fresh sensations naturally turns his steps to that ancient path.

Yeats has let his poetry follow that age-old track of Irish legend. It was entirely natural for him to have done so, which is why such a course has brought him great fame. He touches the world with his life, not with his eyes or with his knowledge. That is why he does not see the world as mere matter; in its mountains and plains, he senses the sportive manifestation of a being that we can approach only through contemplation. If we try to express it by the customary methods of modern literature, we destroy its life and spirit; for the thing called modernity is not really something new, it is old and worn out: constant use has calloused it, so that it does not always respond to stimulus. It is like a fire hidden under ashes. The fire is older than the ashes, yet it is young; the ashes are modern, but they embody grey old age. Hence it is everywhere seen that poetry seeks to bypass the language of the day.

As we all know, for some time past there has been a surge of patriotic passion in Ireland. If it grew agonisingly powerful at one point, it was because the spirit of Ireland was being crushed in every way under British rule. For a long time, the agony sought to express itself in *political* uprisings. At length there came another kind of endeavour: Ireland woke up to the distinctiveness of its own soul and set about expressing it.

This puts us in mind of our own country. Here too for a long time, our effort to achieve *political* rights gathered strength among the educated. Those who led the endeavour were seen to have little touch with the language and literature, manners and customs of the country. They had hardly any contact with the common people of the land. All their efforts to improve the state of the nation related to the English government and the English language. They never considered that to undertake the business of the country, they needed to have the people of the country with them.

But we were lucky, at least in Bengal, in that we had begun to apprehend our own soul through literature. Bankimchandra's[†] chief glory lies in bringing about an era in Bengali literature when the Bengali could, with pride and delight, speak his own mind in his own language. Until then we had been schoolboys writing exercises in English, checking them against the English grammar and English dictionary: we looked down upon our own language and literature. With the appearance of *Bangadarshan*,[†] we suddenly discovered a new power in ourselves. We came to feel that we too could have a literature of our own which could truly satisfy the hunger of our minds. Thus it began; but it did not stop there. Up till then, we had been saying with our eyes shut that we had nothing. Now a search began to find out what we had. Even in *Bangadarshan*, those who had earlier enthroned Comte[†] and Mill[†] presently began a concerted endeavour to place the ethos of the country in the royal seat.

That endeavour is now proceeding along many channels. It lies with the King to grant our plea that there should be more Indian counsellors at his court; but it lies within our own powers to fulfil the desire that our mind should be free to attain their goal by their own path. Any one of us who, by his own efforts, can make his own powers fruitful in any direction will have promoted the nation's realisation of its own strength. The joy of that realisation is our only resource on the path to progress.

When one first becomes aware of one's powers, it greatly inflates the ego, thereby impeding the realisation of the truth. It tends to create delusions about oneself rather than to promote self-knowledge. It insults what is genuine by putting the spurious on a par with it. It forgets that only a clear knowledge of what I lack can tell me clearly what I have. We can gain strength only through such knowledge. Vanity blurs the limits of our self-knowledge, driving us to weakness and failure. Pride in oneself is founded on truth: it cannot be born of vanity. The more vanity is repulsed by the fortress walls of truth, the more we know ourselves.

As in our country, so too in Ireland, there has for some time been an endeavour to give the inner powers a distinct character. It is only natural that the first expressions of this endeavour should produce a great deal of froth. Overreaching itself, it often becomes grotesque and ridiculous. That something of the sort happened in Ireland we can gather from the book *Hail and Farewell* by the famous Irish writer George Moore.[†]

Be that as it may, in its efforts to express its distinctive spirit, Ireland turned to its own language, legends, and mythical tales, thus providing one or two persons of extraordinary powers with the scope to exercise their genius. The poet Yeats is one of them. He has won victory for the message of Ireland in world literature.

When Yeats took up the banner of Ireland in the field of literature, literary activities there had for some time lacked vitality. *Political* uprisings had given place to devious *political* moves; craftiness had elbowed out ideological force and assumed dominance.

A certain critic of Yeats writes:[†]

At such a time once again appeared the harbinger of war. But this time there were no thunderclaps of a cataclysmic social revolution accompanying the lightning-flashes of unbridled emotional upsurge. The all-conquering human soul that has attained self-knowledge, whose unseen fingers touch the mystery of each vast act of creation and destruction in the world of man—the great peace of that self-fulfilled human soul filled the firmanent. Manifesting in himself the fuller emancipation of the human soul, Yeats once again, with a deeper and subtler power, aroused the spirit of revolution. This time it was not the clamour of the world outside: the poet spoke of what lay in the heart of man: the message of Ireland and of all men. He thought deeply and rejected the poetic conventions of fifty years ago. But the way of writing he finally brought to perfection was an improved version of the practices of older poets. His poetry has taken heed of the minutest beauties of nature. It has mastered the innermost music of pleasurable sound. The thoughts he wove together in the incomparable lyrics of his earliest period were his heritage from his ancient Druid forebears. They enter into the mystery of the manifest universe and bring to light the profound unity between nature, man, and the gods.

The critic writes:

It was with the publication of The Wanderings of Oisin*—in 1889, if I remember aright—that Yeats sprang into the front rank of contemporary poets, and threatened to add to the august company of the immortals. In the qualities by which he succeeded—an exquisitely delicate music, intensity of imaginative conviction, intimacy with natural and (dare I say?) supernatural manifestations—he was typically Celtic.*

These words 'imaginative conviction' are very true of Yeats. Imagination for him is not a mere plaything. He could adopt in his life the truth of what he saw by the light of his imagination. That is to say, imagination to him is not merely the poet's stock-in-trade, it is an element of life itself. It enables him to derive nourishment for his soul from the entire universe. I have felt this every time I have had a private talk with him. I have not yet had full opportunity to learn by reading his poetry that he is a poet; but simply by entering his presence, I have realised that he animates his environment by the touch of a heart illumined by his imagination.

TRANSLATED BY BHAWANI-PRASAD CHATTOPADHYAY

The True Nature of Literature

I have been asked to say a few words on what poetry is all about.

I have examined the nature of literature on a few former occasions. I drew on what my heart had felt, not on external experience or on rational analysis. Poetry is an inner urge—I asked myself what that urge was. It is not easy to state simply the answer I found. The stock formulations that have accrued among experts push themselves to the fore whenever the subject is raised; it is necessary to hold them off if my own felt opinion is to find way.

To start with, the word 'beauty' creates trouble. As soon as some professor rules that the purpose of poetry is to make sense of our sense of the beautiful, unthinking habit prompts us to say, 'Indeed that is so.' The search for proof turns out to be baffling; we sit down to ponder the meaning of beauty. The groom's guardian, who makes a prospective bride stand, walk, talk, and untie her hair,† judges by a norm that would meet with hurdles at every step if applied to the evaluation of poetry. We can see that Falstaff hardly bears comparison with Kandarpa, the god of love, but the latter's omission would be no loss to the gallery of literary portraits, while Falstaff's certainly would. Sita is an exalted character in the *Ramayana*, but the valiant Hanuman is granted a stature no less colossal than his tail. Faced with such contradictions, one recalls the poet's utterance, '*Truth is beauty*'.† We savour the rasa of beauty in truth only when we apprehend truth intimately in our hearts—not through knowledge, but through recognition. That is what we call the real. The rash Bhima is more real than Yudhisthira, the paragon of every virtue; the irascible Lakshmana, who cannot brook injustice and is ready to seek unlawful redress, is more real than Rama, who accepts the ruling of the shastras and remains docile. Nilmani, our swarthy middle-aged servant invariably gets every word and chore wrong and, when scolded, smiles shyly and says, 'I made a mistake.' It does not matter what he would look like if he turned up draped in Benarasi silk like a bridegroom, but he is far more authentic than many renowned men whom I hesitate to name in such a context. That is to say, he would be far more enjoyable as the hero or the second lead in a poem than many eloquent champions of the people. The most familiar is not always the most real; but that person is real for me whom I may not know well, but whom I cannot help acknowledging as a positive presence. It is hard to analyse what precise virtue makes this so. One may call such persons *organic*; our taste or inclination might resist them, but nothing else hinders their assimilation. Some foods are bitter, some sweet, some pungent; we may not welcome them equally in practice, but they are all equal in that they are organic, useful for building up the body cells. From the body's point of view, they belong to the ranks of the positive and the acknowledged, not the negative.

There is this circle of positives around us in the world—a ring of such real things. One's being has gained in diversity and reach by intertwining itself with them all. They include not just people but dogs, cats and horses, parrots and cockatoos, the pond covered with water-hyacinth and ringed by ashshaora shrubs, the coral tree by the crumbling wall round the derelict garden of Gosainpara,[†] the smell of the haystack next to the cowshed, the lane winding through one's neighbourhood to the market place, the blows of the hammer from the blacksmith's shop, the ancient tumbledown brick-stack now sprouting a peepal tree, the elderly men under the hog-plum tree at their roadside rounds of cards and dice, and who knows what else—things that find no mention in history, nor leave any trace even at the corner of a map. They have been joined by the host of real things from the literary realms of various languages and from all parts of the world. When I get to know some of them across the barrier of language, I say, 'Ah, this is wonderful'—that is, they agree with my mind and soul. Among them are kings and paupers, handsome men and beautiful women, the blind and the lame, the hunchback and the ugly. Moreover, there are the fantastic and the freakish, untouched by the Creator's hands, whose existence defies zoology and physiology, and who are at odds with current ways and conventions. Then, again, there are those that arrive on the scene with a pretence at historicity. Some appear in Mughal turbans, some in Jodhpuri salwars; but their historical claims are three-fourths counterfeit. If you demand their credentials, they shamelessly reply, 'We don't *care* for proof—take us if you like us.' Besides, there is the reality of emotions—pain and pleasure, parting and union, shame and fear, courage and cowardice. These constitute the literary aerosphere: here we have sun and rain, light and darkness, the bafflement of mists, the brushwork of mirages. These things gathered by human beings from the external world but made their own, other creations born from within and assimilated with the human soul—they form the circle of reality for humankind and compose an intimate human universe within the larger cosmos. It contains all kinds—the beautiful and the ugly, the good and the bad, the rational and the irrational, the melodious and the jarring. I am delighted when they bring with them some intrinsic evidence that compels me to accept them. Let science and history call them false; the innermost feeling of the human heart finds them true. The apprehension of this truth gives us joy, and joy is its ultimate value. How then can we say that the purpose of poetry is to articulate the perception of beauty?

Besides the apprehension of its object's reality, there is another aspect to poetry: its craftsmanship. We need to prove what is accessible to reason; we wish to express what is joyous. The provable is easily proved; the joyous is hard to express. To express the feeling 'I am happy', you need music, you need gestures. You have to adorn the statement as a mother adorns her child or the lover his beloved, as gardens embellish the house or garlands the bridal chamber. Verbal artistry involves rhythm, melody, the ordering and selection of utterance. It will not do if the vehicle of joy is trite: my craftsmanship must express the fact that what I feel most intensely is undeserving of neglect.

At times, the craftsmanship overrides what is crafted and privileges its own autonomy, because craftsmanship too is inspired by the creative urge. Graceful and ornate language projects a distinct form that exceeds meaning: its distinctness lies in a lyricism dominated by sound. Pure music is autonomous in its own sphere—it has no need to share its power with language. The rasa of music that is expressed in rhythm and through the indirect workings of sounds and verbal structures is, however, answerable to meaning. But the intoxication of rhythm and cosmetic sound effects become in some poets an excessive addiction. It makes language turbid and cloying; made weak by unmanliness, such poetry becomes as unworthy of esteem as an uxorious husband.

Truth is beauty: that is the last word. The *truth* of poetry is the *truth* of beauty in form, not of fact. If the poetic form is not utterly apprehensible in the form of *truth*, it will be condemned in the royal court of poetry even when acquitted in the law court of fact. At the carnival of bewitchments, if its ornaments jingle[†] too loudly—that is, if it acts like beauty's glib lackey—its unreality is proclaimed all the more. At the risk of sounding rude, it must be said that those who applaud such verse are yet to outgrow their mental nonage.

I feel it necessary to say one last thing. It seems to be the case that for many people today, the definition of the real is 'all that is'. But in fact the real is a product of human selection, conscious or unconscious. Science indiscriminately values all that is. From that all-pervasive world of all that is, the things that gather round us bearing our own stamp constitute for us the real. The countless other things peddled at different markets at different prices are to us mere shadows, devoid of the worth of the real.

There is our local liquor shop: by admitting it to poetry in metrical or unmetrical lines, one may draw cheap applause from certain quarters. The inhabitants of those quarters say, poets have raved for long about the tippling at Indra's† court, but have failed to convey in metre the faintest whiff of the liquor shop, though they might have frequented the latter. I can judge the matter without bias, because, as far as direct acquaintance goes, Indra's bibulous court is to me no nearer than the local grog-shop. I have only this to say, that the magic touch of the pen and the alchemy of the imagination can make the drinking-bout as real as the quaffing of ambrosia. But that poetic effect must first be achieved. Times are such, however, that if the drunkards' binge at the pothouse is broached in broken metre, the appraiser will recognise the signs of modernity and declare, 'Yes, here is a true poet,' or, 'This is what you call *realism*.' I would say it is not. Too much tawdry poetising is now current in the name of *realism*. *Art* is not so cheap. It is indeed possible to write a poem on the list of soiled clothes sent to the washerman; one could bring in the rasas of sex, pathos, and revulsion† by the sackful, expressed in a realistic idiom. The couple that bicker and scuffle day and night have their clothes beaten together on the same waterside steps and then despatched, now spotless, on the same donkey's back: such a theme may well befit the quatrains of the new school. But its *realism* does not lie in the choice of theme: it must be brought out through the magic of the writing. Much selection should be at work here as well, or else it will end up as the most trivial rubbish. Instead of babbling on any longer on the subject, I request the editor to prove that *realistic* poetry is indeed poetry—but because it is poetry, not because it is *realistic*.

If the theme just mentioned does not please you, let me suggest another one: the autobiography of a husking pedal,† trodden by many feet for many years. You may accord it a higher place than the ancient story in which the touch of a beautiful woman's feet makes the ashok tree flower,† especially if the feet in your story belong to women handpicked for their ugliness. And if you wish to write on the withered date-palm, you might say how its youthful sap once induced in different lives different forms of intoxication—laughter among them, and tears and terror. Its addicts did not include the royal and the rich, nor even the distracted young man studying for his M.A. and sporting a wrist-watch, a pair of spectacles, and hair brushed back by the repeated effort of his fingers.†

As I say this, I am reminded of another subject. An unstoppered bottle of hair-oil, with its label scraped off and a bit of oil left at the bottom, set out in search of its lost world. For company, it had a toothless comb and a thin sliver of used-up soap. We might call the poem, 'A Modern Fairy Tale'. Its broken metre would bear the sigh that the quest had failed. These three relics of that bankrupt past may use the occasion to roundly mock the Creator and His laws. They could say, 'Disguised as a modish mirage, that clown used to play the dandy on the stage of abiding time. Peer behind the screen now, and you'll recognise him no more. In this world of shows, if you were to call anything true, its symbol would be us three, goods beyond the pale of price tags—this bottle of oil dregs, this toothless comb, this worn-out sliver of soap. We are the *real*; we feed modernity with its raw material from the basket of sweepings. The natey plant is lopped off as soon as our tale is over.'†

Time's cowshed has its doors open: the cow does not yield any milk, but chews up the plant. That is why that lopped plant of human hope, faith, and love sells today at such a premium in the markets of poesy. The cow, moreover, has to be scrawny, its bones showing, its horns broken, its back full of sores pecked at by crows, its tail loose-knotted and twisted out of shape by the carter. If the author carelessly allows it to be healthy and handsome, it will be branded with the stigma of mid-Victorianism, and driven through the fields of modern literature to its death at the critic's slaughterhouse.

TRANSLATED BY SWAPAN CHAKRAVORTY

The Prose Poem

There are certain things whose elements are of too subtle a substance: they tend not to manifest themselves readily. One can trade blows in debating tangible issues. But if a subject falls within the realm of the ineffable, how does one explain whether it is agreeable or not? One needs a natural capacity and wide experience to like or dislike such a thing. Mastering the sciences demands austere discipline. But taste is something that lies beyond the reach of discipline: there is no set route to it either through the intellect or through knowledge acquired by much hearing, *na medhaya na bahuna shrutena.*[†] All I can do is follow my personal taste and simply say, 'I like this.'

Individual nature, habits of thought, social ambience, and training converge on taste. If these are cultivated, catholic, and capable of subtle perception, one's taste may be taken as a lamp lighting up literature's way. But in order to recognise that this happy conjunction has achieved true fruition, the party judging must have a true ideal of the cultivation of taste. Hence there is always an uncertain element in judgments of taste. We have had proof of this in literary matters down the ages. One who has not made a sufficient study of science or philosophy will say quite humbly, 'I am not entitled to an opinion.' In the court of literary and artistic creativity, the din of warring opinions eventually makes one feel like saying in despair, *Bhinnaruchirhi lokah* [People differ in taste].[†] Where austere discipline is dispensed with, insolence finds liberty, and differences of taste may even lead to blows. Vararuchi's lament[†] hence comes to mind: *Arasikeshu rasasya nivedanam shirasi ma likha ma likha ma likha* [Do not, do not, do not, [O Brahma] destine me to serve rasa to those without a taste for it]. For the poet, the question of fit and unfit audiences one is a simple one. The distinction is between those who like what the poet has written and those who do not. That is why poets have always been at odds with their appraisers. Even Kalidasa undoubtedly had to suffer for this; we hear there are signs of ham-fisted meddling in the *Meghadutam.* Readers find it easy to move around at least in the outer precincts of poems that stick to conventional language and metre. But there are times when a poet deviates from the trodden path in search of a particular rasa. This disturbs the readers' comfort for at least some time, and they punish the poet by refusing to accept the innovation. Until the new path is defined by constant use, a hostility builds up between the travellers and the pathfinder. During this period of unrest, the poet dares his opponents; he says, 'My view is more authentic than yours.' Readers go on protesting that the consumer's claim is stronger than the producer's. But history does not bear them out. It is always seen that the way by which to welcome the new is made smooth by neglecting the new.

Of late, I have started writing some of my poems in prose. It is not fair to expect that these will at once be lauded by the public. But nor can I accept that this lack of instant acclaim is proof of their failure. In this dispute, the poet is obliged to respect his faith in himself. For a long time now, I have devoted myself to the creation of rasa. Perhaps I have pleased many; I may have failed to please many others. Nevertheless, I will say one or two things on the strength of my long experience in this matter; you are under no oath to accept them fully.

The point of contention is whether poetry can hold its own in the semblance of prose. The prose poem has departed from the form in which poetry has been hitherto viewed, and the pleasure that is associated with that view. Not only is it different in outward appearance, it has unsettled the idea of a poem's true nature. The point at issue, then, is whether the nature of poetry depends exclusively on its metrical array. Some think it does; I think it does not. Poetry can express itself with ease when freed from ornamental trappings. Let me cite an example of this from my own experience. You are aware that I have written a poem about the story of Jabala's son, Satyakam.[†] When I read this story in the *Chhandogya Upanishad* in simple prose, I did not have the least difficulty in accepting it as genuine poetry. Mere narrative that it is, the critic may well glance at its outward form and refuse to admit it to the ranks of poetry, since it is not written in the anushtubha or the trishtubha or the mandakranta metre.[†] I would say that it is the best sort of poetry precisely because of that, and not for any other accidental reason. If this story of Satyakam had been composed in metre, it would have lost much of its weight.

In the seventeenth century, a group of unnamed writers[†] translated the Hebrew and Greek scriptures into English. One has to admit that the Songs of Solomon and the Psalms of David are genuine poetry. Their poetic flavour and features appear with unmistakable clarity through the amazing power of the translators' language. It would have been disastrous if the free movement of prose rhythm in these songs had been arrested by the fetters of prosodic convention.

The lofty cadence we come across in the *Yajur Veda*† we do not call verse: we call it mantra.† We all know that the purpose of mantra is to carry the meaning of words deep into the mind with the help of sound. There it is sonorous as well as meaningful. I am certain that many have felt the effectiveness of this prose mantra, because even when its sounds cease, the mantra resonates in our minds.

Once, in an unguarded moment, I had translated my *Gitanjali* into English prose. At the time, distinguished English poets accepted my translation as part of their own literature. The English *Gitanjali* became the occasion for such praise that I felt embarrassed, thinking it to be excessive. I was a foreigner, there was no rhyme or metre in my poetry. Nonetheless, when they could extract the poetic sap from it in full measure, the fact could not but be acknowledged. I decided that translating my poems into English prose was no loss; on the contrary, a verse translation might have been condemned and held unworthy of esteem.

I remember telling Satyendra† once, 'You are the king of metre—let me see you make poetry stream forth by breaching its dykes with the force of the unmetrical.' There are few poets in Bengali who have introduced such diverse metrical forms as Satyendra. He did not take up my suggestion—perhaps habit made him desist. I tried my hand at such verse myself in *Lipika*,† though I did not make it look like verse with the usual line divisions. After *Lipika*, I did not write a prose poem for a long time. Perhaps I did not dare.

The language of poetry has a certain gravity and restraint: we call it rhythm. Prose is not so fastidious: it walks with a swagger. That is why the affairs of everyday life, such as politics, can be expressed in uncluttered prose. But one can render prose artistic by infusing it with poetry. Such poetic momentum expresses something that surpasses the everyday use of prose. Since it is prose, it rules out the intoxication of excessive sweetness and elegance. A restrained manner, combining the tough with the tender, grows naturally within it. A dancer's steps display trained skill and ornament. On the other hand, the walk of a graceful young woman has a poised, natural regularity. There is an untutored rhythm in her easy and graceful gait, a rhythm that is in her blood and body. The gait of the prose poem is somewhat like that—not irregular or chaotic, but a measured movement.

Just today I read someone in the journal *Mohammadi*[†] saying that he had already sampled the flavour of Rabi Thakur's prose poems in his plain prose. As an instance, the author says that things steeped in poetic rasa have found their way into *Shesher Kabita.*[†] If that is so, does poetry become an outcaste when it comes out of purdah? Have we not, I ask, read poetry which conveys a prosaic content—for instance in Browning? Again, have we not read prose which shows traces of the poetic imagination? I do not recognise a kinship taboo segregating prose and verse, like a woman from her husband's elder brother. To my eyes, they are like brother and sister: hence I do not object to an easy traffic whereby prose is touched by the essence of verse and verse by the seriousness of prose.

There is no point in arguing about differences of taste. I can only say this: I have written many prose poems whose content I could not have expressed in any other form. They have an easy everyday air; they lack frills, perhaps, but not beauty: hence I think they belong to the ranks of genuine poetry. One might ask, 'What is a prose poem?' I would answer, 'I do not know what or how. I know that its poetic essence is such as cannot be demonstrated by argument. That which gives me the taste of the ineffable, I will not refuse to accept as poetry, regardless of whether it comes in the shape of prose or of verse.'

TRANSLATED BY SWAPAN CHAKRAVORTY

Introduction to the Bengali Language (PART)

Section 3

The human being has a particular ability, in that he fashions images—be it on canvas, in stone, in clay or in metal. That is, he takes pleasure in making an object in the image of another one. Another ability of his lies in creating symbols, in the joy of play or for convenience at work. There is no hard and fast rule that a symbol should be in the image of anything in particular. It is unnecessary for the Viceroy to exactly imitate the appearance of the King by donning a mask. He occupies the position of the King on the throne of India and operates from there: he is the symbol or the representative of the King. A symbol is just something to be accepted by convention. While playing at schoolmaster in my childhood, I assumed for myself that the iron railings of the balcony were my pupils. It was not necessary to get hold of real-life boys in order to feel for oneself the cruel gratification of a teacher's disciplining. A piece of paper has no similarity in appearance with ten rupees, but everyone has collectively agreed that it is worth ten rupees, that it is a token for ten rupees. Transactions among people within the group have been made easy by this means.

In language, people deal in symbols. In order to discuss a tiger, it is neither easy nor safe to present the tiger physically. It is undesirable, for a variety of reasons, to try to demonstrate in real life the information that tigers eat people. People have adopted the word *tiger* as the representative symbol for the animal tiger. There may be a lot to be known about the nature of the tiger, all of which can be utilised and stored using the symbols of language. There is this vast world of symbols that has continued to be articulated alongside mankind's knowledge and sentiments. People have drawn innumerable truths from water, land and air, and been able to transmit these to far-off lands and ages, by means of this network of symbols. The power of creating symbols, which has made it easier for mankind to construct languages, is the greatest of all nature's gifts to humankind.

It is not merely that particular symbols, fashioned out of speech-sounds, are serving as names of particular objects: the task of the symbol is far more subtle. Language has to proceed in step with the mind. The trajectory of that mind is, after all, not merely confined to the visible. Our biggest dealings are with things that cannot be seen or touched but only thought of. Let me give a very simple example.

I wish to say 'three white cows'. That word *three* is not a simple one, and I cannot say that the word *white* is very 'white'† or straightforward either. There are a lot of things in the world that come in threes, such as three people, three-storeyed houses, three seers† of milk, etc.; but that there should be no material things and only a number three is impossible. If I proceed to think about it, perhaps I think of a digit signifying 'three' and call it *three*; but the digit is, after all, not the same as three. Hidden inside that figure of three and the word *three* are infinitely many sets of objects that are three in number. They do not even need to be named. Taking advantage of this capacity of language, people have coined a large number of words to denote numbers. In order to remind someone that three sets of three cows each add up to nine cows, we need not drag him to the cowshed. Leaving out cows and everything else, people formulated a clever rule of language: they said, 'Three threes are nine.' This was a snare of a sort. Not only cows, but anything that came in three sets of three began to get caught in it. Any being that lacks language is powerless to keep a grasp on this simple notion.

I remember an incident in this connection. To prove my ignorance of the multiplication tables to a little schoolgirl, I had jokingly said to her, 'Three fives are twenty-five.'

She opened her eyes very wide and said, 'Don't you know that three fives are fifteen?' I said, 'Tell me how I'm supposed to know: are all sets of three of the same size? If you multiply three elephants and three geckos five times each, do they both make fifteen?' She deeply deplored my stand, and said: 'The number three stands for three units: why bring elephants and geckos into it?' I, for my part, was struck with wonder at this. A unit that is neither thin nor thick, neither heavy nor light—a unit without attributes, that exists only by clinging to language—has become so clear to her that she does not hesitate to discard whole elephants and geckos. Such is the power of language.

The word *white* is wayward in the same way. It is an adjective and thus meaningless without a noun. If it is separated from white objects, no place can be found for it in the world, save the word in the particular language. So much for quality and quantity: now for the objects.

I remember once, when I was young, a teacher of mine had said, 'If we discard all the qualities of this table, we'll be left with a zero.' I could not accept this at all. I think I had the notion that the qualities of a table were external to it, sticking on like the varnish; one must call a porter to get rid of the table, but it would be easy to wash or wipe off its qualities. I had wondered at this point, open-mouthed, for a long time. Yet human language has transacted weighty deals with that which lacks all quality. Let me give an example.

There is an official word in our language, *padartha* [substance]. Needless to say, there is nothing specific called 'substance' in the world; there are water, earth, rock, iron. Why then do people tie down such indeterminate ideas in language? They do so because there is urgent need for it.

It is a basic premise of science that any substance occupies some space. That single word makes it possible to dispense with millions of words. We are oblivious of the value of this creation because we are accustomed to it. But it is an enormous feat of mankind to have captured such inconceivable entities in language.

Science and philosophy are filled with such formal labour-saving words. Literature does not lack them either. For instance, we use the word *hriday* [heart] with complete ease. We cannot explain as easily as we can utter it, that so-and-so has, or does not have, a heart. It is impossible to spell out fully what one has in having *manushyatwa* [humanity]. In this instance, it is possible to employ a symbol other than a vocal–auditory one. A formless substance called *manushyatwa* can even be expressed through some image. But an image takes up space, it has weight, it has to be carried physically. Besides, it cannot be endowed with variety. Verbal symbols remain fused with our minds and do not resist extension of meaning as our experience extends.

It is useful to know that these labour-saving words with formal meanings are called *abstract* words in English. A new word for this is needed in Bengali. Perhaps the word *nirbastuk* [non-substantial] will serve. The word *nirbastuk* may be worth using in order to express and convey the pure notion after all attributes have been abstracted from an object. The human mind has been able to travel by means of these *abstract* words to distances that its five senses cannot traverse, and where none of its vehicles can reach.

Section 4

Just as human beings convey items of knowledge by means of language, they also have to convey information about joys and sorrows, likes and dislikes, blame and praise. Much of these feelings can be communicated through expressions and gestures, non-verbal noises, glances, smiles, and tears. These constitute the mute language bestowed on man by Nature: the expression of man's feelings in this language is immediate. But feelings of joy, sorrow, and love can reach great subtleties, great heights: they cannot then be captured through mere signalling or description, but can only be implied as exactly as possible by the skilled use of language. Humankind's awareness of its emotions has developed to such an extent simply because language has been able to take it into the depths of its own feelings. In cultured persons, the rough edge of the sensibility wears away, and subtler, more delicate perceptions readily find place in their feelings. The stubborn heart is an uncultured heart. Those in whom crudeness of taste and feeling are ingrained by nature are, of course, beyond redemption. This holds true also of the capacity for knowledge. The pursuit of knowledge cannot much improve the intelligence of those whose natural denseness is impenetrable.

The language of intellection has found its fulfilment in science and philosophy. The highest expression of the heart's impulses occurs in poetry. There is a great deal of difference between these two kinds of language. The language of knowledge must be as clear as possible; the right word must bear its exact meaning, unobscured by an excess of frills and decorations. But if the language of feeling is to some extent inexplicit, if it does not express things with directness, if it has appropriate figures of speech, it is in fact more effective. The language of knowledge requires clarity of meaning; the language of feeling needs indirection, perhaps with a bending of meaning.

To convey a feeling of attraction, the poet said, 'Her body's breeze dissolves the stone';† he said, 'The liquid grace of [his] young form spreads over the earth.'† To take these words literally would be madness. Had these words occurred in a scientific work, one would have understood that a scientist had discovered a certain bodily vapour whose chemical effect would not let a stone remain solid but instead made it vanish in gaseous form. Or again, that a certain kind of ray had been found in some person's body which had been named *labani* [grace], which gradually diffuses itself across the ground because of the earth's pull. If one entirely trusts the meanings of words, there is no alternative to this kind of explanation. But we are not talking here about natural events; we are talking about what seems to be. Words have been created to denote what-is-exact; hence, in order to express what-it-is-like, their meanings have to be extended and bent a little. The language of what-it-is-like has not been codified in the dictionary; the poet has therefore to skilfully make do with ordinary language. This is what is called the poetic faculty. Indeed, the main reason why the poetic faculty has been held in such worth is that words cannot express all ideas by means of their plain meanings alone. The poet therefore eschews the exact denotation of the word *labanya*† [grace], and says something he has made up, as though *labanya* is a mountain spring that flows from the body onto the ground. There is an anxiety of expression here, following a complete annihilation of the meaning of the word; while saying something, it is simultaneously being said: 'I cannot say it.' Different poets try to seize the opportunity and exploit this ineffability to all kinds of hyperbolic ends. What can one call it but an opportunity?—it is the poet's good fortune to have the opportunity of expressing what cannot be expressed. It is by this opportunity that one may compare *labanya* to the fragrance of flowers, and another to the soundless playing of a veena—thus extending the inconsistencies even further. The poet's use of the term *labani* for *labanya* is also a poetic excess. By imparting the look of the unfamiliar to a familiar word, the denotative boundaries of the language are extended indefinitely.

In order to express what has no limits in emotion, the fences around delimited language have to be demolished. To poetic creation falls the task of such breaking of fences. This is why a mother calls her child things that are actually other than what they denote. She calls him *chand* [moon]; she calls him *manik* [jewel]; she calls him *sona* [gold]. Language is on the one hand the vehicle of clear statements, and on the other hand of unclear statements as well. In one direction, science has been proceeding along the stairway of language towards the uttermost bounds of language, and has arrived at formulaic symbols transcending language; in another direction, poetry too has reached the far end of ideation, step by step along the stairs of language, and finally begun to construct signals of thought, transgressing its own limited meanings.

Section 5

Besides conveying information and awakening in the consciousness the utterances of the heart, language has another major task. This is to give shape to what is imagined. In one sense this is the most dispensable of tasks; but in another, this is what gives people the greatest pleasure. However pervasive the business of living may be in animate creation, its embellishments are not on too small a scale either. From flora to fauna, the department of decoration, in all its colours and lines, is a vast one. In the religious creeds prevalent in the West, animals have been given a lowly place. It is my belief that precisely for this reason, the scientific mind of Europe has continued to judge beauty among living creatures by purely utilitarian ideals. In Europe, they do not readily acknowledge that through the decorations and embellishments gifted them by nature, the consciousness of living creatures might extend beyond their biological needs. But there is no reason why we must believe that beauty has come to human beings alone as the bearer of pleasure above and beyond the necessary, while the sense of pleasure among animals is confined to the business of survival.

At any rate, people have come to accept beauty as having no particular *raison d'être.* Hunger and thirst exert a pull on people through sheer necessity; beauty, too, attracts people, but it does not have the drive of necessity. We involve beauty with our artefacts of need merely to elevate our minds above the intense burden of need. Set within the territory of biological discipline, beauty has a mansion where man is free; hence it is there that man feels pure joy.

Man constructs out of need, but creates out of joy. In work involving language, therefore, man has made two divisions: one for his practical compulsions, the other for his pleasures and fancies. The surprising fact is that nowhere else in the world of language is so much human wealth so carefully preserved as in this area of pleasure. It is here that man has experienced a creator's glory, and been granted the seat accorded to divinity.

Creation denotes the kind of composition whose principal goal is expression. People give expression to their intellects in learned disciplines, to their abilities through achievements, and to their own selves through creation. When one finds something in the world that illuminates its own being markedly in one's consciousness by its beauty and its affective power, something that one cannot but acknowledge, something from which one expects no other benefit, one accords the greatest value to its self-expression through one's joy. Mankind's greatest creation in language is literature. When I accept as the ultimate what has found expression in such creation, for me it becomes as real as that banyan tree. If it bears no resemblance to the commonplace, and yet we acknowledge it with firm conviction and say, 'You are here,' then it, too, finds a place in literature as something real, as mountains and rivers have been admitted as real entities in the natural world. There is much in the *Mahabharata* that is real for me. There may not be any historical or even natural evidence of its reality, and I do not demand such evidence either: it is enough for me that I have felt it to be real. When one sets out to tour some new place, one clearly perceives even its ordinary scenes, simply because one's consciousness has not been dulled by everyday life there; the reality of what one sees is made bright by this clear perception, and so it gives one pleasure. Likewise, we call great the literature that makes its own created beauty and affective power unquestionable to discerning sensibilities. Perhaps even the writer himself cannot exactly define this skill of turning a verbal entity into something real to the human mind.

There is much in the natural world that escapes one's eye by its insignificance. But there is also much that is particularly beautiful, that is sublime, that is associated with the memory of some special state of being. Among a myriad other things, therefore, it specially draws our attention as something real. In the world of literature created by man, a sifting of that reality goes on. In literature, what the human mind chooses to welcome from the totality is continually being created as the truth: much is destroyed, while much remains. This literature constitutes the realm of man's joy, his real world. I call it real in the sense that what is true herein is not true merely because it exists—it is not a scientific truth: what is true in literature is true only because the human mind has accepted it as true.

Man knows, and imparts his knowledge; man feels, and evokes feeling in others. The human mind roams in the world of imagination, it creates imaginary forms; the more language assists in this task, the more it comes to acquire power.

What is spontaneously expressed in literature is our own nature. Man's inner identity is reflected there of its own accord. Why this happens might be discussed a little further.

A truth that does not depend on our liking or disliking it, that has no value apart from its existence, is a scientific truth. But whatever bears the signature of our perceptions of joy and sorrow, and is vivid to the eye of the imagination, is real. Which of these will deeply stir one's perception, and appear to one in a determinate shape, depends on one's education, one's nature, and one's special circumstances. Which one we accept as real is what truly reveals us. The world of this reality is wide for some, limited for others. Some have a certain alert liveliness of vision, whereby many things of the world, both great and small, register on their minds with ease. The Creator has equipped their eyes with telescopic and microscopic powers of feeling and perception. For yet others, from internal reasons or external circumstances, a particular confined area of their world tends to be illuminated. Hence people are properly revealed by the nature and extent of their perceptions of reality. If he is a poet, his poetry captures his mind and the world that his mind perceives. Everyone knows that the light of vision in British poets has changed after the War.[†] That violent impact has deflected the chariot of their minds from its predestined route: it is now moving in a new direction.

An example from our old literature may merit discussion in this context. At the very beginning of the *Mangalkabya*,[†] we find the poet leaving his homeland. There is no order in the kingdom; the rulers are tyrants. Mukundaram's[†] experience of state power in his own life led him to feel the irrationality of injustice with the greatest intensity; when, unfed in a foreign domain, he bathed and went to sleep, the goddess[†] commanded him in a dream to compose a poem in her praise. That poem of praise was a celebration of ruthless, unprincipled, malicious conspiracy. The poet stated in his verse that Shiva, revered as being merciful, is actually passive, and his devotees are vanquished at every step. The reason for the devotee's ignominy is that he has bowed in terror to the power of wrongdoing, and has thereby made his adored deity an object of disdain. He has accepted the power of good[†] as being simply the lack of power.

The *Manasamangal*[†] says the same thing. The deity is merciless, caring nothing for righteousness, capable of all manner of misdeeds through the pride inculcated by worship. A coward can achieve salvation only by abasing himself before the merciless deity and denying virtue and righteousness. For the poet, this was the intensely real law of the world.

Take, on the other hand, the character of Prahlad[†] in our Puranic literature. The creators of this character have not accepted man's submission to oppression as the only reality. Such indignity is common in the world, but they have not judged human reality merely by counting the instances. For them, what ought to be true of human nature has become the only perceived reality: what always happens is but a shadow compared to it. From this literature, one gets an idea of how heroic steadfastness of mind was valued by the era that composed it.

Take another poet, Shelley. In his poetry, man is held captive by the cruel god.† But the outcome is not defeat. Even under unbearable oppression, man has not been overpowered by the forces of injustice. For this poet, the invincibility of the tyrant's power to oppress does not emerge as the biggest truth: a more real truth for him is the unvanquished heroism of the oppressed.

It is necessary to comprehend a little better why I call the world of literature the world of the real. It is often debated why sad or unpleasant elements in the natural world, things we wish to eschew, should be welcomed into literature as a matter of course—so much so that a play that ends in parting is valued more highly than one that ends in union.

Whatever impresses our minds deeply influences us strongly in real terms. We cannot remain at all indifferent under the blows of grief. While this is undeniable, the question arises as to why we admit grief as enjoyable in literature, given that it is unpleasing. The simple reply to this is: suffering is not unpleasing, as literature itself testifies. We find our very own selves most especially in that which we experience most acutely. The pleasure lies in that finding. It is death for us to find nothing worth experiencing anywhere around us. Or else if there are only things in which one finds little or no interest, it tires the mind, because it cannot bring to consciousness one's experience of self. Sorrowful experiences arouse us most intensely; but in the real world, sorrow is mixed with loss and hurt, therefore our material beings recoil from the prospect of sorrow. In literature, we can savour the feeling in pure and simple form precisely because there is no real-life damage or loss. Children get a thrill from the sensation of fear aroused by ghost stories because their minds can experience the feeling without paying its price of suffering. Ghosts become intimately real to them from the impact of imaginary fear, and the feel of this reality is thrilling because of the addition of fear. The brave court the prospect of danger precisely because the fearsome holds pleasure. They go off to climb the summit of Everest for no reason. Because they have no fear in their hearts, they feel an intense pleasure at the possibility of occasions for fear. I have fear in my heart, therefore I do not go climbing remote mountains; but I enjoy sitting at home and reading the accounts of travellers to remote regions, because they give me the taste of danger without the actual risk. Travel accounts that do not contain sufficiently grave dangers do not appeal to me as much. In effect, intense feeling is necessarily pleasurable, since we come to know ourselves intensely through such feeling. Literature is the world of our self-discovery through a variety of means, yet it is a world where we bear no responsibility.

Thousands of currents of man's self-identification flow through literature. Some are muddy, others clear; some thin, others brimful. Some signal the time of people's death, while others indicate a reawakening.

One realises upon reflection that man creates literature out of two ingredients. One is what has caught his eye or left a special impression on his mind. It may be funny, it may be strange, or it may be trivial in terms of worldly utility. Its value lies in that one has conceived of it as a distinct image or event. That is to say, it has captured one's sensibility in a special way, salvaged it from one's feeble consciousness. It may evoke contempt or anger, but it is distinctive—as in the case of Manthara† or Bhanru Datta.† We avoid such characters in real life; but when we see their images in literature, we laugh or grow excited, and we exclaim, 'This is what they are like!' We find pleasure in affirming such a character or an event. Not all the myriad substances and countless events that pass through our lives and minds become objects of our experience in any significant way. But when an experience arouses and agitates our faculties—by its nature or by some special circumstance—its ingredients gather in the storehouses of our minds, and give fuller shape to our personalities in varied ways. Human literature is full of countless such possible, potential experiences of mankind. In Java,† I recently watched the dramatisation of the battle between Hanuman and Indrajit† in a remarkable dance form. For the Javanese these two mythological characters have become objects of such intimate experience that their beings and exploits have become much more intensely real than many real-life acquaintances and real events around them. The joy of this authentic experience finds expression in their dance and music.

Another task of literature is to give shape to what one desires deeply. It does so in such a way that the object of one's desire becomes immediately perceptible to our minds. The real world is imperfect: good and evil are entwined in it, and so our wishes are not truly satisfied there. In literature, man has been continually building up that world where our yearnings are fulfilled. He has been compensating for his discontent by giving form to what ought to have happened by his desired ideal, but never did. That creation, in turn, influences the making of his real world and his character. Through age after age, man has revered the literature that has shaped his greatest desires, and thereby secretly expanded the limits of his mind from within.

Alongside this, it should be remembered that literature presents the varying excellence of man's moral ideals at various historical points of time. Sometimes, for many reasons, man's good sense grows jaded; his reliance on the faith that gives him the strength to conquer himself becomes shaky; his taste is perverted by the drive of tainted urges; the chains of the chained beast are loosened; the poisonous influence of the infected personality becomes dangerous, and the contagion of the disease spreads through the air far and wide. Yet the touch of death often brings out in him evidence of a remarkable artistry. The pearl in an oyster is the outcome of its disease. In cold countries, when the wind of death blows through the autumn forests, their colourfulness finds picturesque expression in the foliage: that is the beginning of their destruction. Likewise, when the character of a people is enfeebled by the clutch of a self-destructive enemy within, an attractiveness can sometimes become evident in its literature and its art. Connoisseurs who pride themselves on noting this are enemies of mankind—because if literature and art keep diverging from humanity as a whole, they end up by distorting the ideals of their own artistic excellence as well.

Man cannot be a connoisseur of pleasure alone, and strut about and flaunt himself for that reason. He must live in fullness and perfection, he must arm himself with dispassionate heroism to fight evil of every kind. Let us not build a flower garden on the graves of our own people.

TRANSLATED BY TISTA BAGCHI

About Language

When there no bridge across the Padma, there was a broad-gauge railway line on this side and a metre-gauge one on the other. This interruption between the railroads was then bearable for us because there was a gap in between. This gap has now been bridged; but when one is still forced to change trains in the middle of the night, baggage and all, because of parsimony in the laying of new tracks, I cannot but blame the presiding deity of the railways.

So much for the passage of people and freight; but the passage of ideas is through language. For some time now in Bengal, routes of two different gauges have been current in the language. One of them is the way of the spoken tongue; the other of the literary language. One or two bravehearts have begun to say that it would be easier for everyone if the two routes were to be of the same gauge. However, a large number of people object to this. Indeed, they are so agitated by this that their utterances in defence of the refined sadhu language[†] scarcely contribute to refinement and honest speech in Bengali.

My name has been cited in this connection even though I have not entered the debate. Over ninety per cent of the people of my province—excluding me—have pretty much decided for themselves what my views are in this matter, and have not hesitated to speak their minds plainly about it. I had hoped to voice my own opinion in a cooler climate, when the heat generated around this issue had abated a little. I now realise, however, that there is no hope of this happening within my lifetime. I shall, therefore, waste no more time.

I have engaged myself in literary creation ever since childhood. I believe that is why I had no clear opinion regarding the nature of language. At the age at which I started to write, I did not have the courage or the intelligence to doubt that a book had to be written in the language of books. It had therefore become ingrained in my mind that the way of literary language was this metre-gauge track, not the broad-gauge track of colloquial Bengali.[†]

One does not feel like unsettling something that has become a matter of habit, because habit can be stronger than natural disposition. A bullock pulling a cart walks along the dirt-track of habitude all by itself, and no harm is done even if the cart-driver drops off to sleep. But a greater reason than this is that habit is linked to a kind of arrogance. We are chagrined to hear that what we have been doing for ages could possibly be done otherwise. This arrogance is in fact the main reason behind clashes over differences of opinion. I remember, when I had said a long time ago that the education of Bengalis should be conducted in the Bengali language, numerous educated Bengalis had not only disagreed with me, they had even been angry. However, this kind of disagreement does not come within the purview of the penal code. The real point is this: it is owing to arrogance that people who have grown up learning English flare up at the suggestion of growing up learning Bengali.

I confess that I once detected this trait in my own character. As I have said earlier, I developed my literary skill by writing books in the same language as I read in books; I did not find the time to form any kind of opinion on the subject. Evidently, though, the intelligence of the editor of *Sabuj Patra*† has not yet become ensnared in the toils of habit; he has therefore managed to remain disengaged and form an opinion on literary Bengali.

Long ago, when this opinion of his had reached my ears, I had not liked it at all. I had even become angry. Old practice flies out at new opinion, calling it arrogance; it takes time to realise that the arrogance of old practice is in fact more pronounced. Thus once upon a time I, too, mouthed the arguments heard today against the elevation of colloquial Bengali to the level of books.

In one area, my mind is relatively free of prejudice. I have never conformed to existing norms and rules in the composition of poetry. I knew that poetry was subject to the bond of language and metre, but it was the bond of ankle-bells, not of shackles. This is why I have never been afraid to ignore external strictures on poetry.

I first used colloquial Bengali and its rhythms in *Kshanika.*† It was then that I first understood with clarity the power, force, and beauty of this language. I saw that this language was not merely a vehicle for rustic sentiments in the manner of a village pony; its speed and carrying power far exceeded those of the artificial language of books.

Needless to say, I did not write *Kshanika* after constructing any well-defined opinion; nor can I claim that I am guided by any firm opinion even after writing it. My language has not entirely given up its claims on either the throne or the cowherd's life, either Mathura† or Vrindavan.† It is for others to judge, at a later date, which way it has been drawn by habit and which way by inclination.

It needs to be stated here that I have always used the colloquial language in written correspondence. There is evidence of this in my *Europe Jatrir Patra,*† written when I was seventeen. Apart from this I always use colloquial Bengali in public speeches, evidence of which will be found in the book *Shantiniketan.*†

In any case, my views on the matter are as follows. The beginnings of Bengali prose literature were at the behest of foreigners, and its initiator and protagonist was the Sanskrit pundit, whose relationship with the Bengali language was like the traditional remoteness between a man and his younger brother's wife.† They had never looked this language in the face. In their presence, this vibrant language remained stricken by silence behind its veil, and so they did not acknowledge its existence. They used the hammer of Sanskrit grammar to fashion with their own hands a strange substance that had rules but no movement. They banished Sita and built a golden Sita-image† at the command of the master of the sacrificial rites.

If Bengali prose literature had arisen out of natural forces, its language would not have been so highly wrought. It would then have been unformed in the initial stages, and gradually grown set according to mature rules. Natural, colloquial Bengali, as it developed, would then have drawn on the treasure house of Sanskrit as and when necessary, to make good what it lacked.

But Bengali prose literature proceeded in exactly the opposite direction. One finds it to have been, initially, the Sanskrit language, with only some little bits of Bengali mixed in as alloy to make it pass under the latter name. This was a kind of fraud. The ploy worked easily on the foreigner.

If Bengali prose had been used merely for the purpose of teaching Bengali to the English, the ruse of that fake Bengali would not have been detected even today. But the more this prose has come to be used by Bengalis, the more its shape has changed. Which way is this change tending? Towards natural, colloquial Bengali. Up until today Bengali prose has been fighting to reveal its true form and nature, sundering the bonds of the Sanskrit language.

To begin a business with little capital and then gradually increase it through profit—this is the normal method of business. But the business of Bengali prose began with no capital, rather with an enormous debt. It is now striving to work off that debt and free itself.

There are reasons for so many obstacles to the reconciliation of our written with our colloquial language. The prose in which Bengalis converse has progressed in step with the mental evolution of Bengalis. Colloquial Bengali prose is commensurate with the subjects and the ideas that the Bengali has normally talked about. The depth and width of a river bed are determined by the amount of flowing water. This is why even Bhagirath† did not dig a long and deep bed before he brought the Ganga down.

It is not entirely true that the Bengali has hitherto spent all his life in thinking about farming and housekeeping. But the ones who thought about larger matters were so long confined to a particular community. They belonged to the group of Brahman scholars. The mainstay of both their education and their profession was the Sanskrit text. This was why intellection or expression of views in the Bengali language did not come to them very naturally. Therefore the prose of those times failed to rise to the height of a language for high thought.

Even in relatively modern times, this conflict between language and thought has persisted in our country. Those who have received their education in English find it easy to think in English, especially since the ideas and subjects that they first received from English are extremely difficult to incorporate in the Bengali language. It follows that our English education and our Bengali language have been living separately, in the outer and inner quarters of our homes.

At such a juncture, the ones who tried to unite education and language found it impossible to make do with current spoken Bengali prose. If it were merely a deficiency of vocabulary, there would be no major problem; but the greatest difficulty was that colloquial Bengali does not have the capacity to coin new words. The reason is that the inventory and use of nominal derivational suffixes (*taddhita pratyaya*)† is extremely limited in Bengali. The word *prarthana* [prayer, asking] is a Sanskrit word whose true Bengali synonym is *chaoa*. If one ventures to implement the senses of *prarthita* [prayed for, desired], *prarthaniya* [to be prayed for, desirable] in unadulterated Bengali, one stumbles into darkness. No one to this day has had the temerity to suggest adopting *chayita*† [desired] or *chaoniya*† [desirable] in Bengali. Michael† has, in a number of places, converted Sanskrit nouns into new verb-forms by creating Bengali inflected verbs from them. So far, however, they have remained in Bengali as intrusions, instead of being recognised as treasures.

If Sanskrit nominal derivational suffixes (*taddhita pratyaya*) are adopted along with Sanskrit words, a good proportion of Sanskrit grammar necessarily comes in as well. In order to cope with conflicting pulls from trying to sail in two boats at once, one has thus to engage in the strong-man feats of a literary circus. Thenceforth there is no end to the debate as to how far the independent rights of Bengali *per se* extend and how far it is governed by Sanskrit. When the Sanskrit grammarian is entrusted with the survey records, the foundation post of Sanskrit grammar gets planted right in the centre of the ancestral homestead of Bengali. When the task falls to the other camp, they let all pandemonium break loose in the terrain of Sanskrit grammar within Bengali.

The problem, though, is that the general populace is more likely to stumble than to advance with every step in a language where one cannot proceed even one step without a wrestler's skills. Where the path itself is difficult of access, either a person does not feel motivated to walk, or else he has to follow both the path and a non-path according to convenience. In a land where port duties drive one bankrupt, the grammarian Bopadeva[†] himself would surely have winked at docking the goods where there is no port. But the little sliver of bamboo is spryer than the bamboo pole: it grew hard to trade in Bengali literature, using the Bengali language, at the port where Bopadeva's disciples sit guarding the pier.

The Japanese are in exactly the same predicament. The rule of the Chinese language over the Japanese language is extremely strong. The principal reason is that colloquial Japanese is like colloquial Bengali: it does not have the power to cater to new needs. The more ancient Chinese language has this power. Japanese has to move with the Chinese language on its shoulders. Count Okuma[†] was lamenting to me that Japanese literature has been suffering enormously beneath this weight-lifter's burden. It is not hard to see that in a language where the very expression of thought is a wrestling feat, thought itself must remain stunted. Crops are meagre where the soil is hard. Exceptional strength cannot be put to good use where strength can only be spent frugally. If the opinion of the pundits stands firm—that it is temerity to wield the pen in Bengali unless one is a monumental Sanskrit scholar—then those who have courage and love for the mother tongue must march in revolt, with the victory flag of colloquial Bengali on their shoulders.

Even before this, books like *Alaler Gharer Dulal*† had blown the conch-shell of revolt, but the time then was not yet ripe. Why should we declare that it is now so? There are reasons. Let me try to state them.

In the days when, in our land, we were trading with the currency of the English language in whatever we gained through that language, no correspondence had been achieved between the language of the land and the education prevalent in the land. From the time of Rammohan Ray† to this day, new sentiments and new ideas have constantly circulated in our language. In this way, our language has come to be the language of thought. It would have been calamitous twenty-five years ago to use the words that we safely use nowadays in everyday conversation in our homes. A Sara Bridge† has been built across our linguistic divide. We now use new and old Sanskrit words even in our spoken language; on the other hand, even words that were considered outcastes in elite language are now current in the language of books. Hence, despite the blow to our accustomed comfort and our ego, we cannot dismiss out of hand the proposal to lay railroads of equal gauge for both the language of books and the language of speech.

The real point is: we shall need to draw on Sanskrit to the extent that it is a help to Bengali, and discard the part of it that is a burden. If one needs must recognise Bengali as the offspring of Sanskrit, one must also recognise that it is now over sixteen, hence domination will not work now—it is time for friendship. But as long as the language of Bengali books does not accept the ways of the spoken language, the true boundary between Bengali and Sanskrit will not be established. Until then, the robber hordes of the Sanskrit grammarians will hold our writers in terror. The day we begin to write in the style of colloquial Bengali, the influence of Sanskrit grammar will naturally, out of regard for stylistic consistency, hesitate to cross the fence of Bengali and carry out its depradations.

I have already stated that a fenced-off plant sends out branches towards the light wherever it finds little chinks and gaps in the fence; in a similar manner, the literary language of Bengali had started peeping out through the fence of Sanskrit towards the everyday language. It had to endure no small amount of public criticism because of this. That was why Bankimchandra had to put up with a fair amount of abuse during his rise. Hence I feel that in our land, this gust of abuse is like the southern breeze of spring. It moves and shakes and agitates the foliage to exasperation. But this chastisement is merely the first drumbeat of the Chant of the Flowers.†

The aspect of literary Bengali that is the subject of special debate is the form of the verb. In the opinion of many, the purity of the language is sullied when one writes *habe*† [will be/happen] rather than *haibe*, *hachchhe*† [is happening] instead of *haitechhe*. When the Chinese had not yet cut off their pigtails, they used to regard the shortness of a pigtail as denoting shortness in social stature. Now that they have all cut off their pigtails they are heaving sighs of relief and saying 'Good riddance.' Once it was customary to write *hayen*† ['is', honorific] in the printed book, but now no one is bothered when one writes *han*. The long *a* vowel of *haiba*† [will become/happen'] *kariba*† [will do] is now gone, the *k* of *haibek*† [will become/happen], *karibek*† [will do] has been dropped, and where is the *ha* of *karaha*† [do!], *chalaha*† [go!]? Nowadays, if one writes *nay* [is not] in place of *nahe*, no one so much as notices. Just as we write *keha* [someone, anyone] now, people used to write *teha* for *tini* ['s/he', honorific]. Once the word *amardiger* [our] was considered the pure form; now our hands do not waver when we write *amader*. We write *seo* [even s/he] where we wrote *seha* earlier, and yet for fear of the pundit we cannot write *keo* or *keu* for *keha* [anyone]. We do not hesitate to write the future-tense form *kariha*† as *kariyo*, but dare not proceed even a little further.

But although we proceed so cautiously for fear of the pundit, the pundits did not pay us the slightest heed when they gave shape to the Bengali of books. When they introduced the words *jaiyachhi* [I/we have gone] and *jaila* [he/she/it/they went] in books of Bengali prose, they did not stop to think even for a moment that these verb-forms were not Bengali at all. The verb stem *ja-* (*ya-*) [go] occurs only in the present tense in Bengali: for instance, in *jai* [I/we go], *jao* [you go], *jay* [he/she/it/they go/es]. In addition, it occurs also in the verb-forms that are derived from an original form *jaite*: *jachchhi*, *jachcchila*, etc. But *jela*,† *jeyechhi*,† *jeyechhilum*† are not acceptable even in the homes of the pundits. In these cases, we say *gela* [he/she/it/they went], *giyechhi* [I/we have gone], *giyechhilum* [I/we had gone]. Then again, the pundits have imposed on Bengali the strange indeclinable word *ebang* [and, also], and now it is impossible to shake it off. Yet the use of this word does not seem to bear any similarity to Sanskrit usage either. Rather, the word *ar* [and], which is a descendant of the Sanskrit word *apara* [other], and which the general populace are in the habit of using, is in conformity with proper usage. There is an indeclinable word *o* in Bengali which is the Bengali form of the Sanskrit word *api* [also]. This is not the counterpart of the English word *and*, but of the word *too*. We say *Ami-o jaba tumi-o jabe*† [Both you and I will go]—but we never say *ami o tumi jaba* [You and I will go]. As in Sanskrit, we use *dvandva* (double-head) compounds instead of using conjunctive words. We say *bichhana balish mashari sange niyo* [Take with you the bedding, pillows, [and] mosquito-net].† If an item of a different category has to be mentioned, we say *bichhana balish mashari ar baiyer baksata sange niyo* [Take with you the bedding, pillows, mosquito-net, and the box of books]. Nowhere does *ebang* or *o* find a place in this. But the pundits have not recognised the laws of Bengali even in its own sphere. The reason why I am bringing up these examples is this: if the esteemed pundit can lean on Sanskrit rules and thus afford to ignore the rules of Bengali—why, then, do *we* hesitate to deviate where required from the rules of Sanskrit and to rely on the rules of Bengali? What do we have to be ashamed of in *manosadh* [heart's desire]? Why do we apologise as soon as we say *sabdhani* [cautious, vigilant]? And when we say *ashcharya hailam* [I/we am/are surprised], why should the esteemed pundit *ashcharyanvita hayen* (be taken by surprise)?

I have been saying that when there is a discrepancy between the language of writing and the language of speech, it is only natural that there should be a constant attempt to bridge the gap. This attempt was made for a long time during the very beginnings of English prose literature. Today, a certain harmony has been reached between the speech and the writing: the two have thus achieved a species of equality. In our language, their disharmony is acute: nature itself was therefore secretly preparing to bridge the chasm between the two. At such a time the law-makers suddenly appeared on the scene. They said the language of writing did not have orders to advance beyond the point it has reached today.

The editor of *Sabuj Patra* says the language of the books is pining, poor thing, to exchange wedding garlands with the spoken tongue. Her guardians are opposed to this. The editor, however, will play matchmaker to break the stern rule of caste purity and perform an auspicious wedding—because it is traditionally said that *Shubhasya shighram* [Good things should be accomplished without delay].†

The people who are opposed to this argue as follows: The spoken language of Bengal takes different shapes in different districts. Is the rebel faction trying, then, to create a state of anarchy? The answer is: Writing in the spoken tongue does not necessarily mean that one can write books in one's regional dialect in any way one pleases. Even wilfulness must have reason. It will not occur naturally to a person from Birbhum† to write books in his regional dialect out of animosity towards Calcutta. It might occur to some lunatic, but not to fifteen out of sixteen people. Rain falls everywhere, but a pool of rainwater forms in a particular spot according to the slope of the land. The same is true of language. Natural factors have generated a language in the Calcutta region which is the language of all of Bengal. Calcutta has a substandard speech form of its own, in which verb-forms such as *genu*† [I/we went], *karnu*† [I/we did], etc. are used, and corruptions such as *bheyer be*† [brother's wedding], *cheler dam*† [the price of rice] etc., are prevalent. This speech-form is not the cosmopolitan Bengali in question here. Supposing you say: Who will properly determine such a language? The answer is: If the authors using this language have the requisite talent, they will extract this common language of Bengal through their own natural abilities. Dante has determined, through his genius, which regional dialect of Italy will be the common language of all regions of Italy for all time. A similar process has been spontaneously at work for some time to establish which dialect of Bengal will be the universal language of Bengal. It is said that there has been a steady influx of regional dialect into Bengali prose from the time of Bankim until today; but which regional dialect is it? It is not of the Dhaka region, nor of any particular region of western Bengal. It is a language churned from several different regions in the capital of Bengal—just as the common language of all educated English people has gained world currency, overriding all the regional dialects of England.

True, this form of Bengali has not spread so completely, but it will know no bounds once it has found acceptance in literature. Is this not needed for unity of spirit among all the people of the land? Is a uniform book language the only bond of unity? Is it also not true that the language of books can never achieve full power if it remains divorced from our language of everyday use? When the impending threat of the partition of Bengal† made us shudder, a principle reason for our fear was that this was not merely a division of political geography: we feared a rift in the spirit of east and west Bengal along the lines of a linguistic divide. There being a single capital for all of Bengal, a common language for the whole of Bengal had been growing up there of its own. This is not an artificial language made to order: it has acquired life through the conflicts of existence, and is evolving according to the rules of that same life. Various foodstuffs enter our digestive system to produce blood. It cannot be belittled as the blood of the digestive system; it is the blood of the entire body. A capital is by nature the digestive system of the land. Different sentiments, statements, and powers are digested here, and the entire land derives life and unity by this means. If we say, out of chagrin and envy, that each region should bear its own autonomous digestive system, our arms and legs, back and chest may rebel against the Creator and say that they each want a separate digestive system of their own. However much we may rage and argue, we must defer to reality; this is why the pattern according to which cultured, Sanskritic Bengali is gradually taking the shape of natural, demotic Bengali is not the pattern of Dhaka or Birbhum. This is because Bengalis of many different regions have been gathering in Calcutta over a long time to learn, to earn, to spend, to make merry, and to work. The single language that has evolved through their coming together is slowly spreading across all the regions of Bengal. In this way, as in other countries, one particular version of the language has become the speech of all cultured households throughout Bengal. This is an auspicious sign. Of course, the natural entry to this language is through the language of southern Bengal. Not to acknowledge this with humility would be a failure of judgment. If the capital of the entire land had been located in Dhaka, our common language would by now certainly have grown out of the popular dialect of Dhaka. If the people of south-western Bengal had curled their lips at this, they would have abandoned their sulks of their own accord—they would not have required much persuasion.

This single language of Bengal, which is no longer a myth, yet which we still know imperfectly because we do not use it in literature—when powerful litterateurs express themselves in this language, then alone will it fully manifest itself. That will not only improve the language, it will benefit the land.

There is an argument against this proposal that needs some consideration. The language that we are using in Bengali literature today has developed a definite structure. Most people need this structure; otherwise literature lacks a restraining force. Moreover, people who are lacking in ability are also lacking in self-control. Hence the norms and usages of the colloquial language being proposed for literature have not yet become fixed: there is a real danger of unconstrained anarchy. In fact, writing in this current language is at present much harder than writing in the language of the books. The creations of the Lord are varied: decorum does not come naturally to everyone. Hence, if at least the rules of conventional decorum are not firmly in place, society becomes extremely unpleasant. If, under the edict of the editor of *Sabuj Patra*, every writer in Bengal began creating literature in the colloquial language, I can put it down in writing that the editor would be the first to shield his ears from the din and leave the land. Fortunately, there is no immediate danger of this calamity. Just as the people who usher in the new are soldiers of the Creator, the people who draw weapons against the new are also the Creator's armymen. The new must first fight the established law to seize its own kingdom; but until its own laws are firmly in place, who is to control the anarchy of the interim?

We must admit that the language we use in literature gradually acquires a distinctiveness. This is chiefly because, in literature, we have to think things through exhaustively and express them fully; we have to feel deeply and express movingly. That is to say, the domain of literature is a domain of permanence. The language has to be selected, arranged, and sounded out keeping this in view. That is precisely why the language of literature is naturally more comprehensive and distinctive than the spoken tongue.

What I have to say is this: the farther literature, in the arrogance of its singularity, diverges from the course of everyday language through which our life-stream flows, the more contrived it becomes. If the closeness of literature to the eternally flowing stream of life is to be maintained, it has to be general on the one hand and exclusive on the other. When the exclusiveness of literature exceeds its general appeal, its extravagance erodes its power. The literatures of all lands face this danger. In all lands, literature reaches a state of sterile artificiality at times owing to an extravagant exclusiveness. At such times it has to abandon its pedigree and look to its survival. What can sustain such survival? The language of the common people, where the life of the universe keeps revealing itself moment by moment. The literary language of the English was initially an elite hotchpotch of Latin, the scholar's language, and French, the royal tongue; but it grew assured only when it cast off its pedigree and came to dwell in the common man's home. Even afterwards, it has leaned towards artificiality several times, and has had to expiate for its sins before it could rise to the commoner's rank. We see this journey to a tryst down the common road even in contemporary English literature. Modern writers such as Bernard Shaw, Wells, Bennett, Chesterton, Belloc, and others are writing in a language that moves with a lighter step.

The editor of *Sabuj Patra* has begun a determined effort to draw down our literature, from its refuge in the fortress of linguistic exclusiveness, to the language of human habitations. His view is that true literature is popular in form and distinctive in nature. I acknowledge this point. But there is a saying in Hindustani, *Pahela samalna mushkil hai* [Beginnings are hard to control]. Even the Creator himself first made monkeys when he set out to make human beings. The ways of those original creations are still continually visible in human communities.

TRANSLATED BY TISTA BAGCHI

The Bengali of Maktabs† *and Madrasas*†

I read the article 'The Bengali of Maktabs and Madrasas' in the Vaishakh number of *Prabasi.*† I have not read the original books† reviewed in the article, and assume that the author of the article has written on the basis of sufficient evidence. Every day, we find instances of how horrifying people can become in communal conflict, but in this instance one saw that it was not impossible to be ridiculous either. This too might have been cause for concern, but luckily a farce of this sort mocks itself to extinction.

Every language has a vital framework of its own. Authors can lead it in new directions only by respecting the laws of that vital framework. One cannot assume that its anatomical parts can be changed simply by patching them up in whatever way one can. Let us suppose that the province of Bengal is Mag† country and that the Mag kings cannot tolerate the facial features of Bengali Hindus and Muslims: they see those as an affront to themselves. The only possible solution that might present itself to their imperial judgment is the annihilation of all races except the Mag. Even the inveterate Mag would not think it feasible to impose a Mag cast with needle, thread, and glue on the Bengali's nose, mouth, and eyes while letting him remain a Bengali.

There is no civilised language that has not absorbed some foreign vocabulary through many kinds of interaction with a variety of peoples. From prolonged contact with the Muslims, the Bengali language too has borrowed numerous Persian words, and a certain number of Arabic words. Indeed, there is enough natural evidence in the language that Bengali is considered by both Bengali Hindus and Bengali Muslims to be their own. No one, however devout a Hindu, feels embarrassed to utter strings of original and naturalised Islamic vocabulary in everyday usage, even in times of great animosity. Not only this: if Sanskritic counterparts of all those words were to be used in their stead, people would laugh at it as affected pedantry. It is easier to come to the market and change a *hajar*-rupee note than a *sahasra*-rupee† one. Half of the word *saman-jari*, 'proclamation of summons', is English (*summons*), half of it Persian (*zaari*)—but not even a title-holding Sanskrit pundit would venture to say *ahvan prachar*, even in elite prose. This is because, unless they are of especially contrary disposition, people are less afraid of taking a beating than of inviting ridicule. It is easy enough to utter the sentence 'I'm in a bad (*kharap*) mood (*mejaj*),' but if one wants to avoid foreign influence by saying, 'The disposition (*gatik*) of my mind (*man*) is disturbed (*bikal*),' or 'depressed (*bimarsha*),' or 'fatigue-stricken (*abasad-grasta*),' one's kith and kin will surely have doubts about one's normalcy. If one sees a purist pandit thrashing a boy to teach him the rules of spelling, one usually says, 'Oh, don't beat the poor fellow (*bechara*).' If one says, 'Don't beat the succourless one (*nirupay*),' or 'the forsaken one (*nihsahay*),' even the revered pundit would naturally feel amusement rather than pity. If I call a dope addict (*nesha-khor*) a consumer of intoxicants (*madak-sebi*), he may be suddenly roused from his addictive fog, or even believe that a high honour has been conferred on him. If a rogue (*badmayes*) is called a mischief-prone person (*durbritta*), he will not feel so hurt. These words have acquired such force because they have become linked in a natural way with the life of the Bengali language.

If the assiduous Muslim regards virtue to lie merely in Persianising and Arabicising the children's Bengali readers, why indeed does he not sanctify the language of English school readers by sprinkling them with Persian or Arabic? Let me provide an example of my own. The subject of Keats's poem 'Hyperion' is taken from Greek mythology; if, despite that, it is not to be eschewed by the Muslim student, let us see how its beauty is enhanced when Persian is mixed in with it:

> Deep in the *saya-i-ghamagin* of a vale,
> Far sunken from the *nafas-i-hayat afza-i*-morn,
> Far from the *atshin* noon and eve's one star,
> Sat *bamoo-i-safid* Saturn *Khamush* as a *Sang*.[1†]

[1] I do not want to aggrandise myself by creating the mistaken impression that I have any expertise in the Persian language. Before I am exposed, I confess that I have taken someone else's help. In order to author the kind of textbook for use in maktabs exemplified by the sample in *Prabasi*, many Muslim writers will need assistance from others. I have a Muslim friend with whom I occasionally discuss points about Persian. The Persian he knows is not the mongrelised Persian current in India—he has acquired and refined his knowledge of Persian from the people outside India for whom Persian is the mother tongue. However, even he is not aware of the use of the word *tambu* for 'sun'.

I know that no Maulvi Sahab† will attempt this sort of Islamisation of English literary style in a state of sanity. Even if he does, those for whom English is the mother tongue will frown from their lofty thrones at this mockery of their language. In conversing among ourselves, we make comical admixtures of English expressions with our own language all the time; but there is no fear of such farcical practice becoming current in the language of literature. I know that such a blow will not be dealt to the English language even in the most orthodox maktabs of Bengal, and not merely to escape the wrath of Englishmen. The teacher knows that if tampering with the English of prescribed school reading is encouraged, the students' learning of English will suffer, and they will not be able to use the language effectively. In such a situation, it would be better even to teach Keats's 'Hyperion' in a complete Persian translation; but it would not be at all admissible to mongrelise its English, even in the interest of one's own community. For this very same reason, one must teach Bengali in its unadulterated form to one's students in their own interest. The Maulvi Sahab may, however, say: 'The Bengali we speak at home is intermixed with Persian and Arabic; that is what we will promote as the Bengali meant for Muslim boys.' Everyone knows that the English spoken at home by the people termed *Anglo-Indians* in present-day English is not *undefiled,* ideal English. If they say, out of bias towards their own community, that they will be belittled if textbooks are not produced in the said *Anglo-Indian* language, such a statement cannot be received seriously, without a laugh. On the contrary, it will be imperative to convince them that they will be belittled if this variety of English is promoted in school for their children. If even the jibe that the Hindu Bengali's *surya* is the true sun and the Muslim Bengali's sun is merely *tambu,*† does not embarrass us; if even after ages of coexistence, neighbourly animosity extends beyond the breaking of heads here on earth and reaches for the skies to dispute linguistic rights over the sun and the moon, shall we say that our *national* destiny is humour-loving, or that it is merely quarrelsome? The earthly agents of that planet of destiny are probably laughing up their sleeves; we too try to laugh, but the laughter chokes in our throats. Communal conflict has taken many different forms in different countries of the world; but the grotesque shape that it has taken in Bengal makes it hard for us to hold our heads high.

TRANSLATED BY TISTA BAGCHI

Notes

Silent Poet, Untaught Poet
(*Nirab Kabi o Ashikshita Kabi*)

The condensed version of an essay published in the magazine *Bharati*, Bhadra 1287 (Aug.–Sept. 1880) under the title *Bangali Kabi Nay* (The Bengali Is Not a Poet); included in its present form in *Samalochana* (Criticism), Rabindranath's first collection of critical essays, published on 14 Chaitra 1294 (26 March 1888). It was later included in the collection of his writings brought out by the Hitabadi published in 1904, and then in vol. 2 of the *Achalita Sangraha* (Uncirculated Works) of the Visva-Bharati edition of his Collected Works.

The essay was prompted by the charge against contemporary poets that they lacked the spontaneity and naturalness of the poets of the pre-British period. Rabindranath never accepted the idea of the 'silent poet', which means no more than a sensitive reader. The matter recurs in a letter of July 1893 to his niece Indira Debi Choudhurani *(Chhinnapatra* no. 107), where Rabindranath rejects it as a confusing category. Again, in the essay *Sahityer Samagri* (The Materials of Literature) included in the 1907 collection *Sahitya* (Literature), he observes that 'to call him a poet who looks at the sky and remains speechless like it, is like calling an unignited log fire'.

Their eyes meet . . . wedding rites: a reference to the *shubhadrishti*, the item of the Bengali Hindu wedding ceremony where the bride and groom first formally look at each other. *Shubhadrishti* literally means 'auspicious sighting'; hence Rabindranath's pun in the next sentence on *ashubhadrishti*, 'inauspicious sighting'.

Ram Babu, Shyam Babu: common Bengali names, used here of fictitious poetasters.

forest-human . . . humanoid: The Bengali words for an ape and a monkey are, respectively, *banmanush* (forest-human) and *banar*, whose possible root meaning is 'like a man'.

Bhajahari: an old-fashioned, potentially comic name, used here of a fictitious person.

children: Rabindranath uses the word *balak*, which commonly means a boy but can be applied to children of either sex. As the present remarks obviously apply to all children, the word has been translated as 'child'. Cf. the headnote to 'Children's Rhymes'.

Marlowe's well-known poem: 'The Passionate Shepherd to His Love'. Rabindranath inserts here his Bengali translation of a seven-stanza version of the poem whose authenticity is doubted by scholars because of the very inconsistencies noted by Rabindranath.

Kabikankan: literally 'bracelet (i.e. jewel) of poets', a title given to the poet Mukunda (once commonly called Mukundaram) Chakrabarti (*fl.* mid-sixteenth century).

Kamaley Kamini: literally, 'the woman on the lotus'. Refers to an incident described in Mukunda Chakrabarti's *Chandimangal* or *Chandikamangal*, among the most important of the cycle of medieval Bengali poems about the goddess Chandi, an aspect of Durga. In the poem, the merchant Dhanapati sees Chandi in the middle of the ocean, seated on a lotus, swallowing and regurgitating an elephant.

(Footnote 2) *Durga kissing Ganesh*: Ganesh, the elephant-headed god, is Durga's son.

yoginis: 64 goddesses said to accompany Durga.

Jaya: another name for Durga.

the rasa of wonder: The phrase used by Rabindranath is *bismay rasa*, which is not one of the nine traditional rasas of Sanskrit aesthetics. He may be thinking of the *adbhuta rasa*, the sense of wonder aroused by the marvellous.

Copleston: Reginald Copleston, sometime Bishop of Calcutta in the nineteenth century, makes this observation in his *Aeschylus* (William Blackwood and Sons, Edinburgh & London, 1870), ch.1, p. 9.

'De Profundis'

The poem '*De Profundis*' (literally 'Out of the deep', the opening words of the Latin version of Psalm 130 and of the poem), was begun by Tennyson in 1852 on the birth of his son Hallam, but not completed till 1880.

This essay was published in *Bharati*, Ashwin 1288 (Sept.–Oct. 1881), and later included in *Samalochana* (see headnote to 'Silent Poet, Untaught Poet'). It is the only one of his early critical writings which Rabindranath chose to reprint again: it was included, deleting the first few paragraphs, in the 1907 volume *Adhunik Sahitya* (Modern Literature). It is interesting not only as evidence of Rabindranath's deep interest in contemporary English literature, but also for its defence of Tennyson's poem against the British response of the time, which was mechanically endorsed by most Bengali readers. Rabindranath, on the contrary, defends Tennyson against what he sees as the failure of European taste to appreciate 'great ideas beyond matter'. His reading assumes the dichotomy of matter and spirit that provided Indian nationalists with a paradigm for the vaunted spiritual superiority of Indian civilisation.

'*Come, let us be men*': This translates the way the words are rendered in the Bengali paraphrase: an obvious deviation from the English 'Let us make man', which Rabindranath himself quotes immediately above.

'*Who art not Matter*': another deviation—from the actual reading 'who wrought / Not matter', quoted by Rabindranath immediately above. With this change, Rabindranath quotes the words in English at this point.

On Changes in the State of Poetry
(*Kabyer Abastha Paribartan*)

Published in *Bharati*, Shravana 1288 (July–Aug. 1881), and included in *Samalochana*, the Hitabadi collection, and the *Achalita Sangraha* (see headnote to 'Silent Poet, Untaught Poet').

Here the young Rabindranath examines the prediction made by some Western thinkers of the gradual extinction of poetry with the advance of civilisation and the impact of industry and technology. By finding a correlation between social demands and the development of genre, he expresses optimism about the emergence of new forms of poetry.

Vedavyasa of this epic: i.e. its collective author. Vedavyasa is the putative poet of the *Mahabharata*.

Abhijnanashakuntalam: 'Shakuntala's Memento', the famous play by Kalidasa.

Uttararamacharitam: 'The Later Life of Rama', a Sanskrit play by Bhavabhuti (seventh–eighth century).

As Tennyson said: in 'Locksley Hall', line 142.

one demon of mystery: an allusion to the demon Raktavija ('Seed of Blood'). A new demon would spring from each drop of his blood that was shed onto the earth.

Lord Shiva: According to the Markandeya Purana, it was Shiva who gave Raktavija the above miraculous attribute.

Puranas: eighteen ancient texts of Hindu mythology; more generally, all Hindu mythological texts.

Baul Songs (*Bauler Gan*)

Published in *Bharati*, Vaishakh 1290 (Apr.–May 1883), as a review of the anthology of songs *Sangit Sangraha: Bauler Gatha* (see first note here). The present text replaces the last part of that essay with a passage adapted from a review of Part 2 of the anthology, published in *Bharati*, Ashwin 1291 (Sept.–Oct. 1884). This is the composite text offered in *Samalochana* (see headnote to 'Silent Poet, Untaught Poet') and in the Visva-Bharati edition of Rabindranath's Works (*Achalita Sangraha*, vol. 2).

The Bauls are members of a non-conformist and eclectic religious sect of Bengal, marked by a spirit of liberation. They are socially and culturally peripheral, although their songs have now become a prominent ingredient of Bengali folk culture. Contrary to popular belief, however, they have their own dogmas and elaborate, esoteric religious practices. Rabindranath was attracted to the Bauls by their religious liberalism and heretical attitude towards institutional religion. Their moving lyrics, and the simple music to which they are set, deepened the bond. Rabindranath himself collected some of the songs, translated them into English and wrote about their philosophical significance, besides composing many original songs on Baul models. In his English prose work *The Religion of Man* (1930), he entitles a chapter 'The Man of the Heart', translating the recurrent Baul phrase *maner manush*.

This article was one of the first attempts to introduce the Bauls to educated Bengalis. It has deep links with the essays in the volume *Loksahitya* (Folk Literature). But as these very connexions indicate, the term 'Baul song' is taken somewhat loosely, as in the book of which this is a review. It is made to cover a range of folk songs, not all of them derived from the Bauls. It was only later that Rabindranath acquired a deeper and truer understanding of the Baul ethos, through an intimate absorption of the songs of the great Baul singer and philosopher Lalan Fakir (1772–1888).

Sangit Sangraha: *Bauler Gatha*: a collection of Baul and other folk songs, published in two parts *c.* late 1289 and 1291 (1883 and 1884) respectively. These volumes have proved unobtainable, so that some of the rare songs cited in this essay cannot be identified.

Durgeshnandini (1865): the first Bengali novel by Bankimchandra Chattopadhyay or Chatterjee (1838–94), the pioneering novelist in the language.

Bishabriksha (serialised 1872, book form 1873), *Chandrashekhar* (serialised 1873–74, book form 1875): two later novels by Bankimchandra.

Jagai and Madhai, etc.: an anonymous song found in many collections of the period. Not a true Baul song, but belonging to the more general class of 'Harisankirtan'.

Jagai and Madhai were two ruffians who would attack and persecute Chaitanya (1486–1533), the scholar-saint of medieval Bengal. On one occasion, they broke his pitcher and attacked him with the shards. But finally, he converted them with his love.

Chaitanya was a leading exponent of the Vaishnava bhakti movement, a major source of inspiration for the Bauls. As the excerpts in this essay show, Chaitanya and his doctrines constantly recur in their songs.

Hari: roughly, 'the Lord'—used in Bengali of many major male gods of the Hindu pantheon.

Gour: another name of Chaitanya.

Chaitanyadeva: 'Lord Chaitanya'.

Bird of the mind, etc.: a song in the Baul mode composed by Trailokyanath Sanyal.

Brahmo songs: *Brahmasangeet,* the religious songs of the Brahmo Samaj or community of reformed Hindus, to which Rabindranath himself belonged.

Vrindavan: the haunt of Lord Krishna as a cowherd and lover, and setting for his *lila* or divine love-sport.

Nitai: Nityananda, Chaitanya's principal disciple and companion

Shyam: Krishna.

Govardhan: a hill near Vrindavan, which Krishna is said to have once held up with his hand.

LITERATURE (*Sahitya*): 1889

Written in a manuscript family album or memory-book (*Paribarik Smritilipi Pustak*) now in the Rabindra Bhavan, Shantiniketan. The album was maintained by the Tagore family during 1888–90 for comments and observations by its members and friends on various subjects. This piece was entered on 17 Ashwin 1296 (2 October 1889), and first published in *Rabindrabiksha,* vol.1, Shravan 1383 (July-Aug. 1976).

creation, construction: The contrast between the two is a recurrent theme in Rabindranath's writings. He uses these English words to express it, in an English lecture entitled 'Construction versus Creation' delivered at Ahmedabad in 1920. See S.K. Das (ed.), *The English Writings of Rabindranath Tagore* (New Delhi, 1996), vol. 3, pp. 401 ff.

A FIRST ACQUAINTANCE (*Parichay*)

This and the next six pieces are from the work *Panchabhut* (The Five Elements), published on 30 Vaishakh 1304 (12 May 1897). The items included in this collection had appeared in *Sadhana,* a journal edited by Rabindranath himself, between 1892 and 1895. The present essay inaugurated the series in the Magh 1299 (Jan.–Feb. 1893) number.

Panchabhut is a curious and happy blend of diary and dialogue. The interlocutors are five characters, two women and three men, named after the five basic elements constituting the universe in Hindu tradition: earth (*kshiti*), water (*ap,* here Srotaswini), heat or radiance (*teja(s),* here Dipti), air (*marut,* here Samir), and space (*vyoma,* here Byom). The narrator too is male, appropriately named Bhutanath (Lord of the *bhutas* or elements; but also an appellation of Shiva in his wandering disorderly aspect, consorting with *bhutas* in the sense of 'spectres' or 'ghosts').

Rabindranath's biographer Prabhatkumar Mukhopadhyay has traced the origin of this work to the family album cited in the headnote to 'Literature' (1889). Prabhatkumar suggests that some of the pieces in *Panchabhut* appeared in embryonic form in this private literary record.

Srotaswini: a feminine adjective derived from Sanskrit, literally 'she who flows swiftly'.

Dipti: a feminine noun derived from Sanskrit, literally 'radiance'; often used as a proper name.

Samir: a masculine noun derived from Sanskrit, literally 'breeze'; often used as a proper name.

feeling and apprehension: The word *bedana* (Sanskrit *vedana*) basically signifies 'feeling, apprehension, empathy', but in Bengali has chiefly come to mean 'pain'. Rabindranath often uses the word (as in several essays in this volume) in the original, basic sense. However, the sense of 'pain' is also rele-vant here in the light of the next sentence.

PROSE AND VERSE (*Gadya o Padya*)

First published in *Sadhana*, Phalgun 1299 (Feb.–Mar. 1893).

Bhavabhuti: a Sanskrit dramatist of the seventh–eighth century.

Four-Faced One: Brahma the god of creation: one of the three deities (Brahma, Vishnu, Shiva) held to preside over the cycles of creation, preservation, and destruction respectively. He is said to possess four faces as well as four hands. The verse cited, disdaining the *arasika* or insensitive undiscerning reader, is ascribed to Vararuchi in the *Subhashitaratnabhandar*. Vararuchi was a renowned poet and scholar, one of the legendary 'nine gems' at the court of King Vikramaditya.

rasa: As *rasa* literally means a juice or liquor, there is a punning reference to the actual serving of a drink.

quota allotted to criticism: a humorous allusion to the reservation of places in public bodies for members of select groups or communities. Already by this time, the practice was being widely discussed and sometimes implemented. During Lord Lansdowne's Governor-Generalship (1888–94), eight members of the regional legislative councils were elected from various bodies and institutions.

inner quarters, outer rooms: the traditional division of the Indian household, women being confined to the inner quarters while male visitors were admitted to the outer rooms only.

an upstart Nawab: *hathat-nabab* [suddenly made Nawab], a Bengali phrase for an upstart. Rabindranath's elder brother Jyotirindranath translated Molière's play *Le Bourgeois gentilhomme* under this title.

Vishvakarma: a god of the Hindu pantheon, the divine architect and craftsman.

The Significance of a Poem
(*Kabyer Tatparya*)

First published in *Sadhana*, Agrahayan 1301 (Nov.–Dec. 1894).

Kacha and Devyani: The legend is recounted in the text itself a little later. In the battle between the gods and the demons, Shukracharya was reviving the demons by his art of *sanjivani* or revival of the dead. Kacha the son of Vrihaspati (see below) was sent to him to learn the art so that he could revive the slain gods.

The reference is clearly to Rabindranath's own poem *Biday-Abhishap* (Farewell Curse), first published as *Kach o Devyani* in *Sadhana*, Magh 1300 (Jan.–Feb. 1894).

Madhusudan the Pride-Destroyer: a traditional appellation of Vishnu, said to humble the proud, as being *Madhusudan* or the slayer of Madhu the demon and his brother Kaitav.

Vrihaspati: the priest of the gods.

twelve hands. . . thirteen hands: applying a proverbial Bengali expression, 'a twelve-hands-long cucumber with a thirteen-hands seed'.

Ever since birth, etc.: from a poem once attributed to Vidyapati but by modern scholars to Kabiballabh. See 'Vidyapati's Radhika'.

Mathura: where Krishna went to become king, abandoning Vrindavan and his beloved Radha.

Lakshmi: the goddess of wealth and beauty.

Sarasvati: the goddess of learning and the arts, hence of 'feeling and idea' (*bhab*).

shastras: the Hindu scriptures.

the disrobing of Draupadi: an episode in the *Mahabharata*, where an attempt is made to publicly strip the captive Draupadi, wife of the five Pandava brothers, at the court of their opponents the Kauravas. Draupadi prays to Krishna; by his boon, her robes are endlessly replaced, saving her from humiliation.

Sabha Parva: The section of the *Mahabharata* containing the above episode.

connoisseurs: The Bengali carries a pun on *rasagna*, 'one who knows or can appreciate the rasas'; but the literal meaning of *rasa* is 'juice', as of a fruit.

Lucidity (*Pranjalata*)

First published in *Sadhana*, Chaitra 1301 (Mar.–Apr. 1895).

the Treta age: the second of the four ages or *yugas* into which the world is divided in the Hindu mythological calendar. The events of the *Ramayana* (in which Hanuman the monkey-hero, a devotee of Rama, takes part) occurred during the Treta Yuga.

Khana: a legendary woman of ancient times, credited with traditional sayings about the weather, the seasons etc.

panchali: a type of traditional lay or ballad on mythological or other themes.

Krishnanagar: a town in Bengal, headquarters of Nadia district; renowned for its clay toys and figures, chiefly of everyday people and objects.

Chanakya: or Kautilya, the famous political theorist of the third entury BC, author of the *Arthashastra.* He is also credited with 108 *shlokas* or stanzas on moral themes, once commonly taught to young children during their early training in Sanskrit. Despite their celebrity, they obviously do not compare with the works of Kalidasa.

MIRTH (*Koutukhasya*)

First published in *Sadhana,* Poush 1301 (Dec.1894–Jan.1895)

not even the gods know, etc.: said of the intents of women and the fates of men, in one of the shlokas attributed to Chanakya. (See notes to 'Lucidity'.)

Time is eternal: From Bhavabhuti's play *Malatimadhava* 1.6. The full line (cited in 'Bengali National Literature') refers to 'Endless time and the vast world'.

kirtan: a type of traditional devotional song about the love of Krishna and Radha.

THE MEASURE OF MIRTH (*Koutukhasyer Matra*)

First published in *Sadhana,* Phalgun 1301 (Feb.–Mar. 1895).

mandakranta, upendravajra, shardulavikririta: various elaborate metres of classical Sanskrit poetry.

five spooks: Rabindranath is punning on the common Bengali meaning of *bhut,* a ghost or spook, and its original Sanskritic sense of material elements.

cowrie shell: used as money in old times.

Calcutta Maidan: a large tract of open land in the heart of Calcutta, used as a promenade and sports ground.

rasa of humour: *hasya rasa,* one of the nine rasas stipulated in classical Sanskrit aesthetics.

Siraj-ud-Daulah (ruled 1756–57): the last independent Nawab of Bengal, who lost his kingdom at the Battle of Palashi (Plassey).

Titanias who offer themselves to asses: as in Shakespeare's *A Midsummer-Night's Dream.* Cf. the following reference to Shakespeare's *The Merry Wives of Windsor.*

six systems of philosophy: in classical Indian philosophy, Purva-Mimamsa, Vedanta, Nyaya, Samkhya, Patanjala, and Vaisheshik.

330 million gods: the traditional size of the Hindu pantheon.

A NOVEL *RAMAYANA* (*Apurba Ramayana*)

First published in *Sadhana,* Asharh 1302 (June–Jul. 1895).

Barawaan: Bengali *baroan,* an evening raga.

raginis: Originally, there were 36 *raginis*, 'females' or 'consorts', postulated for six basic *ragas*; but the distinction between them has virtually ceased to matter in present-day classical music.

adi (*rasa*): *Adi* means 'primal, original'. This rasa, also known as *shringar*, is so called as being sexual or amatory in nature.

rasa of death: This is not, of course, one of the nine traditionally-stipulated rasas.

Advaita philosophy: established by Shankaracharya; holds that Brahma the supreme divine being and the universe are one and the same, and that all creatures bear divinity within them in addition to their own identities.

wishing-tree: the *kalpataru*, a mythological tree said to grant all wishes.

Shiva . . . in the cremation ground: Shiva is said to haunt cremation grounds in the company of spirits and ghouls.

Purvi: another evening raga.

a novel Ramayana: What follows is an allegorical interpretation of the life of Rama and Sita after their return from Lanka, as told in the *Ramayana*.

Uttarakanda: 'The Canto of the Aftermath': the final canto of the *Ramayana*, recounting these events.

The Theatre (*Rangamancha*)

First published in the Poush 1309 (Dec.1902–Jan.1903) number of *Bangadarshan*, the famous journal started by Bankimchandra Chattopadhyay in 1872 and revived under Rabindranath's editorship in 1902. Later included in *Bichitra Prabandha* ('Various Essays'), 3 Vaishakh 1314 (16 April 1907).

This essay was directed against the public theatres of Calcutta, where Western-style stagecraft, especially the drop-scene, make-up, and elaborate costumes were almost obsessively cultivated as the surest means to please the public. Rabindranath was opposed to the very concept of 'realism' in the theatre, which, in Bengal, he considered a blind and unimaginative imitation of contemporary British theatre. However, reports indicate that performances of his own plays on the Tagore family stage showed a perceptible presence of 'realism'; nor did Rabindranath show any marked aversion to stage props.

Written when Rabindranath was deeply concerned with new ideals of education and codes of social behaviour, this essay may be considered as the manifesto for a new theatre, an alternative to the commercial enterprises of the time; and still more significantly, as a defence of the kind of drama he would be writing from 1908 onwards, replacing the proscenium stage by an open theatre. In support of this new model for a theatre, he adduces not only the classical dramaturgy of Bharata and the plays of Kalidasa, but also the *jatra* or open-air popular theatre of Bengal.

Even those who appreciated Rabindranath's concern for an open acting space and eschewal of unnecessary detail, could not fully accept his recommendations.

No one, for example, considered the acting of female characters by actual women as a 'crude European barbarism'.

Bharata: the legendary sage credited with composing the *Natyashastra* (Art of Drama), the earliest Sanskrit treatise on dramaturgy: probably dating from the second century AD or later, though sometimes placed before Christ.

tom-tana-nana: meaningless words used to anchor a line of music in Indian classical practice.

an orphan . . . an uxorious husband: The original refers to the art of acting in the feminine gender and the play or play text in the masculine, suggesting a witty parallel with a married couple.

Dushyanta, Shakuntala, Anasuya, Priyamvada: respectively the hero, heroine, and the latter's two companions in Kalidas's play *Abhijnanashakuntalam*. See notes to '*Shakuntala*'.

jatra: the traditional popular theatre of Bengal.

the gardener-woman: a reference to a play (*c.* 1835) based on the traditional story of Bidya–Sundar. The woman gardener Hira, who acts as go-between for the lovers Bidya and Sundar, features in such a scene as described here.

Kanva's ashram: Shakuntala was brought up in the forest retreat or ashram of the sage Kanva.

the cloudy path out of heaven, the sylvan retreat of Maricha: the successive settings of the last act of *Abhijnanashakuntalam*, where the final reconciliation between Dushyanta and Shakuntala takes place.

in another essay: *Atyukti* (Overstatement), published in *Bangadarshan*, Kartik 1309 (Oct.–Nov. 1902), and then in the collection *Bharatbarsha* (3 Phalgun 1312: 15 Feb. 1906).

vishalyakarani, Gandhamadan: In the *Ramayana*, after Lakshmana had been grievously wounded by a special weapon of Ravana's, Hanuman was directed to fetch the herb vishalyakarani, growing on Mount Gandhamadan, to revive him. Unable to identify the herb, Hanuman brought back the entire mountain.

fallen days: The Bengali refers specifically to the Kali Yuga, the last and worst of the four ages of human existence. The events of the *Ramayana* took place in the second age, the Treta Yuga.

Lakshmi's owl, Sarasvati's lotus: The owl is the mount of Lakshmi the goddess of wealth as the swan is of Sarasvati, goddess of learning and the arts. But in fact both deities are represented as seated on a lotus in full bloom.

CHILDREN'S RHYMES
(*Chhelebhulano Chhara*)

First published under the title *Meyeli Chhara* (Women's Rhymes) in *Sadhana*, Ashwin-Kartik 1301 (Sept.–Nov. 1894); later included in the collection *Loksahitya*

(Folk Literature), 10 Shravan 1314 (26 July 1907). The 4th edition of *Loksahitya* (Poush 1345: Dec.1938–Jan.1939) included a second piece under this title, which had originally appeared as the introduction to a collection of children's rhymes published by Rabindranath in the journal of the Bangiya Sahitya Parishad (*Sahitya Parishat Patrika*), 1301 (1884–85). This latter piece has not been translated here.

A *chhara* is most closely rendered in English as a 'rhyme', essentially for children. It is short, composed in a free-flowing lilting metre, structurally loose and often incoherent, and unsophisticated in style. It is commonly marked by striking phrases and lively imagery. Rooted in simple rural life, these verses throb with an intimacy of tone. They were most probably composed by women and transmitted orally down the generations, with continuous change and replenishment.

In earlier times, the *chhara* had not been considered respectable enough for literary scrunity. With a rising awareness of folk culture, a by-product of nineteenth-century cultural nationalism, the English-educated Bengali first felt the urge to collect proverbs, folk tales, folk songs, and rhymes in an attempt to bridge the widening gulf between rural and urban culture.

Rabindranath played a notable part in this cultural agenda. He started collecting *chharas* from the early 1890s during his stay at Shilaidaha (now in Bangladesh) to look after the family estates. His interest in the *chhara* was not anthropological or linguistic but literary. In a letter written while he was planning this essay, he remarked, '*Chhara* has a kingdom of its own, free of rules—a world of clouds.' Although some contemporary critics took Rabindranath to task for his interest in these rhymes, which they found dull, inconsequential, and purposeless, the essay was warmly received, and had a great impact on the Bengali literary community. It started a process whereby the *chhara* acquired a new acceptability in elite culture, so that attempts are being made to revive it with some success.

Puranas: See notes to 'On Changes in the State of Poetry'.

uncultured, non-Sanskritic: The Bengali has the single punning word *asangskrita*, literally 'unrefined, uncultured', but also meaning 'non-Sanskritic'.

formal Bengali: i.e. *sadhu bhasha*: see notes to 'About Language'.

gandharva marriage: a secret and informal marriage ceremony: one of eight forms of marriage recognised in the Hindu scriptures.

shastras: the Hindu scriptures.

Meghadutam: 'The Cloud-Messenger', Kalidasa's famous poem about parted lovers. Commencing with a reference to the first day of Asharh, the first month of the rains, the poem is set against a backdrop of rain and clouds: hence the reference here.

Dada: elder brother.

easy, simple: The Bengali word repeatedly used here is *sahaj*, which combines the senses of 'easy' and 'simple'.

adhibas: certain rites performed on the evening before a wedding.

Bagdi: a low caste Hindu community.

Ulu, ulu: representing the ululation made by women at weddings and other auspicious ceremonies.

People differ in taste: Kalidasa, *Raghuvamsham* 6: 30.

Khoka: a common affectionate appellation for a boy.

koel: a black bird related to the cuckoo.

bangles made of shell, reddle (vermillion) *on your brow*: signs of a married woman. The poem may, then, indicate a husband's effort to win the heart of his new bride, or else an extramarital relationship.

co-wives: The Bengali talks specifically of *bon-satin*, sisters married to the same husband.

the cold within your heart: This would normally indicate lack of love or hardness of heart; but as Rabindranath interprets it two paragraphs later, it signifies 'a heart more soothing than cool water'.

Sita's vow regarding the bow: Sita of the *Ramayana* had vowed to marry the man who could string her father King Janak's great bow (*haradhanu*). Rama not only strung it, but broke it in two in course of his efforts.

Draupadi's . . . feat of marksmanship: Draupadi of the *Mahabharata* had vowed to marry the man who could shoot an arrow through the eye of a suspended fish, taking aim from its reflection in a pool of water. Arjuna performed this feat and won the bride.

sweet things: The rhyme as quoted in this essay has no such reference. However, a test relating to sweet things commonly supplies another stanza to it. Rabindranath no doubt had this in mind, here and in the next paragraph.

Kali Yuga: See notes to 'The Theatre'.

Company bonds: promissory notes issued by the East India Company: a common means of investment in former times and no doubt, as this passage suggests, welcome as dowry.

Senate hall: the central hall of the old Senate House of Calcutta University, where meetings and examinations were held.

Eden Gardens: a public park and garden in Calcutta.

skins: i.e. the outer layer of the rice-grain, removed when rice is polished.

twenty-seven stellar beauties: Traditional Indian astronomy postulates twenty-seven *nakshatras* or groups of stars, each named after its most prominent member, against which the moon is positioned on the successive days of the lunar month. These stellar groups are said to be Daksha's daughters and the moon's wives.

parijat flower: said to grow in the garden of heaven.

great poet of . . . Ujjayini: Kalidasa. The quotation is from his *Meghadutam*, stanza 3. For Ujjayini, see notes to 'Rural Literature'.

mother goddess . . . maiden goddess: *Ambika Puja* and *Kanya Puja*, two forms of the Hindu worship of the female as deity.

Agamani, Bijaya songs: respectively, songs of home-coming and departure, sung at the beginning and end of Durga Puja. At this time, Durga is supposed to come from her mountain abode, where she dwells with her consort Shiva, to visit her parents' home in the plains. The Agamani songs present the mother's longing for her daughter, and the Bijaya songs their farewell lament.

masi: mother's sister.

pisi: father's sister.

Putu: a common affectionate nickname for a girl.

Khoka, Khuku: terms of affection for a boy and girl respectively.

Rig-Veda: Composed *c.*1200 BC, the *Rig Veda* is an anthology of hymns and prayers to various gods such as Indra (the sky-god, later considered the king of the gods) and Varuna (the sea god). The addition of Chandra (the moon-god) is Rabindranath's own contribution.

Michael Madhusudan Datta (or Dutt, 1824–73): a pioneering poet and dramatist, mediator of many European models and influences. He was the first poet to graft elements of Greek mythology onto Bengali poetry.

Devaki's offspring: Krishna.

backdrop: i.e. the *chalchitra*, the background scene or panel against which images of gods and goddesses are set.

broken the pot and stolen the butter: the mischief traditionally wrought by Krishna as a boy, living in a community of dairyfolk.

Vrindavan: the haunt of Krishna in his childhood and youth. Vaishnava literature is full of references to Krishna's playing the flute and sporting under the kadam tree.

RURAL LITERATURE (*Gramya Sahitya*)

First published in *Bharati*, Vaishakh 1306 (April–May 1899) and later included in *Loksahitya* (see headnote to 'Children's Rhymes'). A sequel to 'Children's Rhymes', it analyses the popoular verses on the relation between Shiva (Hara) and his consort Parvati (Gauri), as well as between Radha and Krishna, the dual deities of the Vaishnavas. Only a part of this long essay has been translated here.

Despite his empathy with folk poets, Rabindranath does not totally approve of the values projected in these songs. He complains that they present the conjugal life of Hara and Gauri in terms of such everyday domesticity that they fail to convey the sublimity of the underlying theme. The love of Radha and Krishna too has been not only secularised but vulgarised to the level of crude amusement. He contrasts Krittibas's medieval transcreation of the *Ramayana* in Bengali with the folk songs and poems based on episodes from the epic, finding the latter deficient in edifying themes. This view may be held to smack of puritanism, but it indicates Rabindranath's refusal to romanticise folk culture.

Shravan: The fourth month of the Bengali year, at the height of the monsoon rains.

Pabna, Rajshahi: district towns in north-central Bengal, now part of Bangladesh.

motari: probably a necklace with round beads in the shape of *matar* or peas.

Kalidasa, Bhavabhuti: eminent classical Sanskrit poets.

Manas Sarovar: the famous sacred lake in the Tibetan Himalayas, also celebrated in poetry.

parijat flower: See notes to 'Children's Rhymes'.

Ujjayini: modern Ujjain, a town in central India; the seat of Chandragupta II or Vikramaditya, at whose court Kalidasa is held to have flourished.

shikharini, mandakranta: two elaborate Sanskrit metres.

dhenki: a treadle-like implement for threshing rice.

Meghadutam, Alaka: See notes to 'The *Meghadutam*'.

mendicant Vaishnavi: Such itinerant singers of the sect were, and to some extent still are, a common sight in rural Bengal.

Annadamangal: a long poem narrating the myths of Shiva and Durga, by the eighteenth-century Bengali poet Bharatchandra Ray.

the Kabikankan: Mukunda Chakrabarti. See notes to 'Silent Poet, Untaught Poet'.

royal courts: Bharatchandra was patronised by Maharaja Krishnachandra Ray of Krishnanagar, and Mukunda by Bankura Dev, a ruler of Medinipur (Midnapur).

Kumarasambhavam: See notes to '*Kumarasambhavam* and *Shakuntala*'.

Hara and Gauri: Shiva and Parvati or Durga.

Kabikankan-Chandi: the chief work of Mukunda Chakrabarti (see notes to 'Silent Poet, Untaught Poet'). It recounts the legends and miracles of the goddess Chandi, a manifestation of Durga.

Dharmamangal: a medieval Bengal narrative poem by Ghanaram Chakrabarti (*fl.* 1713), based on earlier works, celebrating the glory of the god Dharma.

Manasar Bhasan: A collective term for the many medieval Bengali works concerning Manasa the snake-goddess.

Satyapir: a rural Bengali god emerging out of the synthesis of Hindu and Islamic tradition, and worshipped by both Hindus and Muslims.

Bholanath: Shiva in his aspect as a wayward all-relinquishing figure, given to narcotics, wandering in cremation grounds with spirits and ghouls.

Umapati: Uma's 'lord' or husband, i.e. Shiva.

Umapati is not to be slighted: as, however, he was by his father-in-law Daksha. Shiva thereupon despoiled the great *yagna* or sacrificial feast convened by Daksha. See notes to 'Presidential Address'.

Menaka: Parvati's mother; the 'aged son-in-law' is therefore Shiva.

the ascetic lord in Kalidasa: Shiva as presented in Kalidasa's *Kumarasambhavam*.

Annapurna: literally, 'one with store of rice', or 'giver of rice': Durga or Parvati in her aspect as universal purveyor.

Lakshmi: the goddess of wealth and prosperity.

the spiritual doctrine they contain: The erotic literature concerning Radha and Krishna has been consistently interpreted in a vein of erotic mysticism.

Vaishnava and non-Vaishnava: the Vaishnava is a special devotee of Krishna.

jatra: See notes to 'The Theatre'.

kathakata: the reading and exposition of the puranas or mythological narratives: a traditional practice, virtually an art form.

The Song of Solomon: the Song of Songs in the Bible, erotic poems interpreted in a mystical light.

Hafiz: the famous fourteenth-century Persian poet, whose *ghazals* or love songs carry a rich vein of mystical Sufi theology.

Bharatavarsha: the ancient name for India.

Pururava: the son of Budha and Ila; lover and consort of Urvashi, the celestial dancer and courtesan. There are many legends concerning his violent passion for Urvashi.

Mahadeva: Shiva.

the third canto (of the *Kumarasambhavam*): This canto recounts Parvati's frustrated attempt to win Shiva by her beauty and sexual charm, and the consequent burning of Madana the love god by Shiva's fury. Parvati subsequently wins Shiva by ascetic meditation.

extramarital love: Apart from his chief consort Rukmini, Krishna had four other chief wives and 16,000 subsidiary wives, but Radha was not among them.

pinda at holy Gaya: Gaya in Bihar is traditionally held to be the most propitious place for offering rites to the dead. The *pinda* is the portion of rice and other ingredients ritually offered to the dead.

Bidya–Sundar: a highly erotic tale of Bidya, princess of Bardhaman (Burdwan), and her paramour and eventual husband Sundar; composed by Bharatchandra Ray (see notes above) as part of his *Annadamangal*; based on earlier works.

dug a tunnel: Sundar used to gain access to Bidya by this means.

society's back . . . the Milky Way: i.e. Bharatchandra has presented in a mundane and physical manner what the Vaishnava poet presents spiritually and intellectually.

being the father of a daughter, etc.: from the play *Avimaraka*, attributed to Bhasa.

the seventh autumnal lunar day: the *saptami* or seventh day of the waxing moon in the autumn month of Ashwin. It marks the start of Durga Puja, celebrating Durga or Parvati's supposed annual descent from the mountains to visit her parents.

Vijaya: the *dashami* or tenth day of the above lunar cycle: the final day of Durga Puja, when Parvati is held to return home to Shiva.

World Literature (*Bishwasahitya*)

This and the next four essays were collected in *Sahitya* (Literature), 24 Ashwin 1314 (11 October 1907). Except for 'Bengali National Literature', they had previously appeared in *Bangadarshan* (see headnote to 'The Theatre')—this piece in Magh 1313 (Jan.–Feb. 1907). It had earlier been read as a lecture on 23 Magh (9 February 1907) at the National Council of Education. The Council had been set up to provide a channel of modern education outside the system and curricula shaped by British interests. As director of Bengali studies at the Council, Rabindranath was asked to deliver a series of extension lectures on Comparative Literature, a discipline yet to take root in the West and almost unheard of at the time in India. The lecture does not indicate an awareness of the few books then available on the subject, nor with the problems of influence and interaction that form the core of comparative literary studies. Interestingly too, though 'world literature' is now distinguished from 'comparative literature', Rabindranath not only equates the terms but actually translates 'comparative literature' as *bishwasahitya* (Sanskrit *vishva*, world, and *sahitya*, literature). He was probably influenced by Goethe's term *Weltliteratur*.

King of Mathura, milkmaid of Vrindavan: Krishna was a cowherd in Vrindavan, where he had sportive and amorous relations with the milkmaids. Subsequently, he ruled as king from Mathura.

Yajnavalkya had told Gargi: In fact the sage Yajnavalkya said this to his wife Maitreyi. The slip is curious, as the episode (related twice in the *Brihadaranyaka Upanishad*, 2.4.5 and 4.5.6) is a famous one. The basic meaning of the passage is simply 'The son is loved not for his own sake but for the sake of one's own self.' Rabindranath glosses it in this way in 'The Philosophy of Literature'. Here, however, he takes *atman* (self) to imply the Supreme Self, into which the love of the self passes.

Rabindranath quotes the passage with *putra* (son) in the singular. The usual reading is in the plural.

atmiya, atman: *Atmiya* (commonly meaning 'a relative') derives from *atman*, self: 'one who is part of or linked to one's self'.

Kuber: the king of the yakshas (see notes to 'The *Meghadutam*'), renowned for his wealth.

a lyric by Balaram Das: beginning *Tumi mor nidhi Rai, tumi mor nidhi*. Rabindranath included the poem in *Padaratnabali*, an anthology of Vaishnava poetry that he co-edited with Shrishchandra Majumdar. Balaram Das was a Vaishnava poet of the sixteenth century.

dervishes . . . in Egypt: A reference to the radical Islamic elements in the complex and widespread opposition to the growth of British power in Egypt from the 1880s.

the brides of the heavens: the *digbadhus*, celestial courtesans or nymphs held to reside in the eight quarters of the skies.

an earlier essay: *Sahityasammilan* (A Literary Convention). It was delivered as a speech at a literary convention on 5 Magh 1313 (22 January 1907)—i.e.

before 'World Literature'—though published only afterwards, in the Phalgun 1313 (Feb.–Mar. 1907) number of *Bangadarshan*.

Bhagirathi: another name for the Ganga or, strictly speaking, one of its upper branches (not to be confused with the Bhagirathi, or Hooghly, that flows past Calcutta). According to legend, King Bhagirath pleased Brahma with his devoted meditation and obtained the boon that the Ganga should come down to earth to wash away the sins of Bhagirath's ancestors.

Airavat: the elephant of Indra, king of the gods. As the Ganga or Bhagirathi was descending to earth, Airavat tried to draw it up in his trunk and was washed away.

the literary stage: As the Bengali clearly indicates, Rabindranath is not talking about dramatic literature. He is referring to all literature as a stage or platform (*mancha*) on which humanity manifests itself.

great time: The Bengali has *Mahakal*, a name of Shiva the destroyer, but also literally meaning 'great time' and hence carrying an implication of abiding or perpetuity.

kirtan: See notes to 'Mirth'.

panchali: See notes to 'Lucidity'.

Panchavati: the forest in central India where Rama, Sita, and Lakshmana lived during their forest exile, and from where Ravana abducted Sita.

Meghadutams: See notes to 'Children's Literature' and 'The *Meghadutam*'.

Vidyapatis: See notes to 'Vidyapati's Radhika'.

Chandra and Surya kings: literally, 'the dynasties of the Moon and the Sun'. The first includes the royal line of Krishna (Yaduvamsa) as well as that of the Kauravas and Pandavas (Puruvamsa) in the *Mahabharata*; the second is the line of the kings of Ayodhya including Rama.

the Mountain King's daughter: i.e. Parvati, daughter of Himalaya. See notes to 'Children's Rhymes' and 'Rural Literature'.

the poor god on Mount Kailas: i.e. Shiva, Parvati's consort, imaged as ascetic and even wayward.

Literary Creation (*Sahityasrishti*)

Delivered as a lecture at the National Council of Education, Bengal on 24 Asharh 1314 (9 July 1907); published in *Bangadarshan*, Asharh 1314 (June–Jul. 1907) and later included in *Sahitya* (see headnote to World Literature).

Dashu Ray's panchali: Dasharathi or Dashu Ray (1806–57) was one of the most famous composers and singers of the panchali, a type of traditional lay or ballad on mythological or other themes.

in Kalidasa's mind: Rabindranath is alluding to the composition of Kalidasa's

Meghadutam. The descriptive details in the previous paragraph are drawn from that poem.

mandakranta: a Sanskrit metre used in the *Meghadutam*.

Vidyapati: See notes to 'Vidyapati's Radhika'.

It is Bhadra, etc.: From a poem beginning '*E sakhi hamari dukher nahi or*', traditionally attributed to Vidyapati (as in the *Padaratnabali* co-edited by Rabin-dranath) but sometimes to Ray Shekhar.

Bhadra: the fifth month of the Bengali year (mid-August to mid-September): a month of monsoon rains, though formally part of *sharat* or early autumn.

Chaitanya: See notes to 'Baul Songs'.

the rasa of love: punning on the literal meaning of *rasa*, moisture or juice.

'*we think we grasp*, etc.: from a Baul song beginning '*Dekhechhi rupsagare maner manush kancha sona*'.

Chandimangal: See notes to 'Silent Poet, Untaught Poet'.

Dharmamangal: See notes to 'Rural Literature'.

Manasa: the snake-goddess, whose legends and praise are the subject of many medieval Bengali poems.

Ketakadas: a seventeenth-century poet.

Annadamangal: See notes to 'Rural Literature'.

The works cited here all belong to the category of *Mangalkabya*, medieval Bengali poems recounting folk legends about the works and glory of gods and goddesses, especially various manifestations of the goddess Durga.

Panchatantra: a Sanskrit collection of fables with morals, ascribed to Vishnu-sharma.

Kathasaritsagara: a collection of Sanskrit didactic tales ascribed to Somadeva Bhatta.

Vidyapati. . . padabali: See notes to 'Vidyapati's Radhika'.

Grierson: Sir George Abraham Grierson (1851–1941), civil servant and philologist.

Raghuvamsham: Kalidas's Sanskrit epic on the lineage of King Raghu, Rama's ancestor.

Bharavi: sixth-century Sanskrit poet, author of *Kiratarjuniya*.

Magha: Sanskrit poet (probably sixth century), author of *Shishupalavadham*.

Henriade: a 1728 poem by Voltaire on King Henri IV of France.

Vikramaditya: a legendary monarch usually identified with Chandragupta II (reigned *c.* AD 380–413). He successfully countered the power of the Shakas or Scythians in India.

Vishvamitra: a renowned sage. Among many other achievements, he guided and trained Rama in the latter's youth, as described in a number of episodes of the *Ramayana*.

Guhaka: King of the Nishadas, a forest tribe; befriended Rama during the latter's forest exile.

Janaka: King of Mithila and father of Sita. He is said to have found the infant Sita among the furrows while ploughing, though in fact this ploughing was in connexion with a ritual and not actual agriculture.

rakshasas: demons; Rama's chief adversaries in the *Ramayana* under their king Ravana. Here, they are being identified with the Dravidians.

Sita: literally, the furrow made by a plough.

breaking the bow: See notes to 'Children's Rhymes'.

Bali and Sugriva: in the *Ramayana*, brothers and successive rulers of Kishkindhya, the kingdom of the vanaras or monkey-tribe. Sugriva agreed to help Rama recover the abducted Sita if Rama would aid him in battle against his brother Bali, who had exiled him. Rama did so and killed Bali; Sugriva thereby became king.

Maya (pronounced 'Moy'): a demon or *danava* renowned as architect and artisan; married his daughter Mandodari to Ravana. His amazing seven-chambered palace is described in the *Ramayana*. Later, in the *Mahabharata*, he is said to owe his life to Arjuna and, in gratitude, to have built a great palace in Indraprastha for the Pandava brothers.

Vibhishana: Ravana's younger brother; allied himself to Rama after falling out with Ravana, and materially helped Rama with secret information about his adversaries.

Kishkindhya: the kingdom of the vanaras or monkey-tribe in the *Ramayana*.

Outram: Major James Outram, prominent soldier and administrator of British India in the mid-nineteenth century. Took part in the action at Lucknow during the 'Mutiny' or Indian Revolt of 1857–58.

shastras: the Hindu scriptures.

the outcaste Guhaka: The Nishadas, of whom Guhaka (see above) was king, were a forest-dwelling tribe outside the pale of the Brahmanical caste system.

lila: See note on p. xii.

at one time: Rabindranath is alluding to the medieval Bhakti movement (fifteenth–sixteenth centuries), and the inflorescence of Bengali literature to which it gave rise.

Kalketu: a hunter in Mukunda Chakrabarti's *Chandimangal* (see notes to 'Silent Poet, Untaught Poet'). He was actually not 'an ordinary mortal', but the son of Indra the king of the gods, born as a human by Shiva's curse.

Dhanapati: a merchant, the chief human character of Mukunda Chakrabarti's *Chandimangal*. See notes to 'Silent Poet, Untaught Poet'.

Chand Sadagar: 'Chand the merchant', a major character in the *Manasamangal* or lay of the snake-goddess Manasa.

the humblest service of the squirrel: When Rama and his followers were building a bridge across the sea to reach Lanka, the devoted squirrel did its bit to help by carrying small pebbles.

Krittibas: the poet of the chief Bengali version of the *Ramayana*.

the Bhagirathi: or Hooghly river, the distributory of the Ganga flowing past Calcutta.

Meghnadbadh Kabya: an epic poem on Rama's victory over Lanka, by Michael Madhusudan Datta (Dutt). Following the Romantic idealisation of Satan in *Paradise Lost*, Michael took Ravana as his hero rather than Rama.

Valmiki: traditionally named as the original poet of the *Ramayana*. See notes to 'The Nature of Krishna'.

payar: a traditional Bengali metre, most often employed in rhyming couplets: the metre of Krittibas's Bengali *Ramayana*. Michael departed from this traditional metre and wrote his epic in blank verse on the English model.

Vayu, Agni, and Indra: god of winds, god of fire, and king of the gods respectively

the pauper Raghava: Raghava (i.e. the descendant of Raghu) is Rama. He was a pauper when he attacked Lanka, having been in forest exile. In a famous line in *Meghnadbadh Kabya*, Pramila, the wife of Ravana's son Meghnad, contemptuously refers to 'the beggar Raghava'.

Chaitra: the last month of the Bengali year (mid-March to mid-April): not usually a time of much rain.

Gangotri: the source of the Ganga in the Garhwal Himalayas.

The Sense of Beauty (*Soundaryabodh*)

The first of Rabindranath's extension lectures at the National Council of Education, Bengal (see headnote to 'World Literature'), delivered on 13 Magh 1313 (27 Jan. 1907); published in *Bangadarshan*, Poush 1314 (Dec.1907–Jan.1908) and later included in *Sahitya* (see above).

brahmacharya: the severe discipline, particularly in the matter of celibacy and other restraint of appetites, enjoined in youth by the traditional Hindu code.

sadhana: See note on pp. xii–xiii.

rasa: The literal meaning of *rasa* is 'juice' or 'moisture'; hence the pun on 'desiccation'.

enemy of the human state . . . the original six: There were said to be six chief vices or 'enemies' (*ripu*) of humankind: lust, wrath, avarice, insensibility, pride, and envy.

the fiery raging goddess: The Bengali names Chandi, an aspect of the goddess Durga, but literally meaning 'the angry one'. The 'gracious goddess of beauty' opposing her is identified as Lakshmi.

King Paushya . . . Utanka: in the *Mahabharata*, Utanka the disciple of the sage Veda was commanded by the latter's wife to bring her the earrings of the wife of King Paushya. On his way to perform this errand, he was enjoined by a figure seated on a bull to consume the animal's droppings. Utanka did so but did not properly purify himself afterwards, for which reason he was unable to see Paushya's queen when he entered her chamber.

practise self-control, etc.: *Manusamhita* 6.49.

depraved impulses: The Bengali specifically mentions the 'six enemies' (see note above).

the tiger and the cow, etc.: a proverbial Bengali expression.

Vishvamitra: In order to satisfy his protégé Trishanku's desire to enter heaven in the flesh, the sage Vishvamitra created an alternative heaven.

dhrupad. . . khayal: In Indian classical music, the dhrupad is a more austere and ordered musical exercise than the khayal.

taan: the extension of a raga in a melody.

the prince who left his kingdom: Gautama, who became the Buddha.

plantain leaf: used as a platter, especially at feasts and community meals.

Forgiveness is the ornament, etc.: a maxim attributed to Kautilya (Chanakya).

Asharh: the third month of the Bengali year, marking the start of the monsoons. Kalidasa's *Meghadutam* is set in early Asharh.

the. . . Yaksha's embassy of love: in Kalidasa's *Meghadutam*, which is echoed through this paragraph. See notes to 'The *Meghadutam*'.

Kumarasambhavam, *Abhijnanashakuntalam*: For the relevant details of these works, see notes to '*Kumarasambhavam* and *Shakuntala*'.

the waters of peace: The Bengali has *shantidhara*, using the metaphor of the holy 'water of peace' or *shantijal* sprinkled on the company at the end of a religious ceremony.

stupa: a Buddhist sacred memorial.

pillars: raised by the emperor Ashoka to accommodate his celebrated edicts.

the bodhi tree in Bodh Gaya: where Buddha achieved liberation.

Lakshmi's [union] with Vishnu: The goddess Lakshmi is the consort of Vishnu the preserving deity, the second aspect of Brahma the supreme being. Beneficence is, however, as much Lakshmi's attribute (besides beauty) as Vishnu's.

Shiva vilifies, etc.: The episode occurs in *Kumarasambhavam* canto 5. The quoted line is from stanza 82.

Truth is beauty, etc.: Rabindranath habitually quotes Keats's line 'Beauty is truth, truth beauty' (Ode on a Grecian Urn', line 49) in this inverted form. Cf. 'The Poet's Defence'.

the being that shines forth, etc.: *Mundaka Upanishad* 2.2.8.

the Elephanta caves: a Shaivite place of pilgrimage near Mumbai (Bombay), with celebrated rock carvings.

temple at Konarka (Konarak): the famous temple of the sun on the Orissa coast.

He indeed is rasa, etc.: *Taittiriya Upanishad* 2.7.2.

BENGALI NATIONAL LITERATURE
(*Bangla Jatiya Sahitya*)

Delivered on 25 Chaitra 1301 (7 April 1895) as a lecture at the annual meeting of the Bengal Academy of Literature, founded in 1893 and later known as the Bangiya Sahitya Parishad. Rabindranath was one of the most active members of this academy. The lecture was published in *Sadhana*, Vaishakh 1302 (Apr.–May 1895) and later included in *Sahitya* (see headnote to 'World Literature').

The eloquent plea for the creation of a 'national' literature reflecting the aspirations of the entire Bengali community, and for the introduction of Bengali at various levels of education, was part of a continuous discourse that had begun with Bankimchandra Chattopadhyay. Bankimchandra's call, as early as 1870, for a 'popular literature' in Bengal had gathered momentum with each succeeding decade. The anxiety about the hegemony of English and the threat to the mother tongue has not lost its relevance in India even today.

shruti: the vedas.

smriti: twenty classic corpuses of theological texts.

puranas: mythological texts.

Bhubaneshwar: the capital of Orissa, site of many famous temples.

Konarka: See notes to 'The Sense of Beauty'.

shastras: the Hindu scriptures.

the old Brahman in the new almanac: In Bengali almanacs, the entry for the last day (*sankranti*) of each month is traditionally accompanied by a crude woodcut of a brahman (*sankranti purush*), emaciated as a sign of his asceticism.

original Ganga: the Adi Ganga: now a narrow stream running through southern Calcutta, once the main channel of the Hooghly or Bhagirathi river.

Kanva and Kanad, Raghava and Kaurava, Nanda and Upananda: These names were probably chosen because of their rhetorical scope for alliteration and quasi-rhyme. Hence they have been retained in translation, instead of being replaced by more familiar terms.

Kanva: an ancient sage, foster father of Shakuntala.

Kaṇad: an ancient sage; founder of the Vaisheshika philosophy, one of the six ancient systems of Indian philosophy.

Raghava: Rama, descendant of King Raghu.

Kaurava: Usually refers to Dhritarashtra's 100 sons, one of the two warring sides in the *Mahabharata*. But the name can be applied to all descendants of King Kuru—i.e. both Dhritarashtra's sons and their adversaries, Pandu's sons or the Pandavas. The present context would suit this extended sense.

Nanda: Krishna's foster father. The name thus indicates the entire segment of Hindu myth, philosophy, and literature centred on the figure of Krishna.

Upananda: Of the many mythological figures of this name, the most likely in this context is Nanda's (see above) younger brother.

Kanauj, Koshal, Kashi, Kanchi: The names seem to have been chosen for the alliteration. They are all places famous in myth and ancient history.

Kanauj: or Kanyakubja, a region of north India and a major centre of ancient Indian civilisation.

Koshal: a region of north India including Rama's kingdom Ayodhya.

Kashi: the holy city of Varanasi.

Kanchi: Kanchipuram, a holy city in south India, renowned as the 'Varanasi of the south': one of the seven sacred cities where a dying soul might obtain *moksha* or liberation.

ashvamedha sacrifice: This involved, *inter alia*, letting a consecrated horse roam for a year, and doing battle to conquer any territory whose inhabitants obstructed its course.

Indraprastha: Yudhisthira's capital, at the site of modern Delhi.

Rajtarangini: the chronicles of Kashmir, composed by Kalhan in the mid-twelfth century.

Nandas: a dynasty of kings reigning in Magadha (present-day southern Bihar) in the fourth century BC.

Vikramaditya: usually identified with Chandragupta II (reigned *c.* AD 380–413). Ujjayini or Ujjain was his capital.

Kalidasa: said to have belonged to Vikramaditya's time and enjoyed his patronage.

Chandvardi: or Chand Vardai, author of the chronicle *Prithviraj-Raso* and court poet of Prithviraj (see following note).

Prithviraj: Rajput hero of the late twelfth century, the last Hindu ruler of Delhi; opposed the advance of Muhammad of Ghur but was defeated and killed by the latter in 1192.

Chanakya: See notes to 'Lucidity'.

Chandragupta: Chandragupta Maurya (*c.* 324–300 BC). Chanakya is said to have played a crucial advisory role in his rise to power.

Shakta: worshippers of Shiva (and his consort Kali).

Vaishnava: worshippers of Vishnu.

Shakta and Vaishnava were the two chief strands of medieval and later Bengali Hinduism, and hence of the religious poetry of the time.

Rammohan Ray (1772–1833), the first major thinker, writer, and reformer of the great religious, social, and cultural movement in nineteenth-century Bengal.

Sarasvati: the goddess of learning.

halls . . . the private and the public: alluding to a Mughal ruler's two halls of audience, the *khas durbar* for private or select audiences and the *am durbar* for the general public.

Vedantasutra: a collection of aphorisms by Badarayana on the doctrine of the Upanishads: the basic text of the Vedanta philosophy.

antecedents: In Bengali, relative adjectives and adverbs nearly always precede the words to which they relate.

Vedantasara: an epitome of Vedanta doctrines.

Brahmasutra: the *Vedantasutra* (see above).

a new Raja: punning on the title of 'Raja' commonly bestowed on Rammohan Ray.

endless time and the vast world: a phrase from Bhavabhuti's play *Malatimadhava* 1.6.

the earliest people to learn English: Rabindranath seems to be thinking specially of the 'Young Bengal' group of the early nineteenth century.

pure mustard oil: the traditional cooking medium among Bengalis.

said in the Bible: Luke 19.26. The translation follows Rabindranath's Bengali rendering.

Sarasvati's lotus: Sarasvati, goddess of learning, is represented as seated on a lotus.

fit for neither the gods, etc.: a proverbial expression.

ask the ground to part: as Sita did towards the end of the *Ramayana* on being suspected and humiliated by her husband Rama.

the king's daughter . . . our second wife: i.e. the language of our rulers and the second language we learn.

our ears suffer molestation: Boxing the bridegroom's ears was a jocular custom of sisters-in-law at a Bengali wedding.

told in fairy tales: Bengali fairy tales often present a king's two wives, the favoured queen or *suorani* and the neglected or discarded *duorani*.

the inner quarters: where the women lived in the traditional household. The implication is that the Bengali race has accepted the language as a wedded wife.

Housewife, aide, friend, etc.: Kalidasa, *Raghuvamsam* 8.67.

The Historical Novel
(*Aitihasik Upanyas*)

First published in *Bharati*, Ashwin 1305 (Sept.–Oct.1898); collected in *Sahitya* (see headnote to 'World Literature').

This essay has its origin in an exchange with Akshaykumar Maitreya, the noted historian and writer, who had criticised Bankimchandra's treatment of history in an article in the journal *Purnima*. Rabindranath made a rejoinder in *Bharati*, Shravan 1305 (July–Aug. 1898). Akshaykumar defended his views in a letter, to which this essay was the reply.

Bankim Babu: Bankimchandra Chattopadhyay, the pioneering Bengali novelist. See notes to 'Baul Songs'.

Nabin Babu: the poet Nabinchandra Sen (1847–1909), author of *Palashir Juddha* (1875), a historical poem on the Battle of Palashi (Plassey).

Freeman: Edward Augustus Freeman (1823–92). He made this observation about Scott in his *History of the Norman Conquest* (Oxford, 1867–79), vol. 5, Appendix.

Sir Francis Palgrave (1788–1861), lawyer and historian. He makes this observation in the Preface to his *History of Normandy and of England* (London, 1851).

Bishabriksha: A novel by Bankimchandra. See notes to 'Baul Songs'.

rudraveena: a stringed musical instrument. As *rudra* literally means 'fierce, angry', and is commonly applied to Shiva, Rabindranath seems to have imaginatively conceived of the instrument as a veena played by Shiva to accompany cosmic destruction. Actually, the instrument has a rather soft sound.

Shiva's horn: another instrument with the same significance.

Mommsen: Theodor Mommsen (1817–1903), the German historian and archaeologist.

an earlier critical essay: the piece in *Bharati*, Shravan 1305, referred to above.

sap and juice: the literal meaning of *rasa*: a pun worked into the metaphor.

Rama *as a villain . . . Ravàna as a righteous man*: as in Michael Madhusudan Datta's *Meghnadbadh Kabya*. See notes to 'Literary Creation'.

Yadu: son of King Yayati, progenitor of the Yadav line to which Krishna belonged.

his complexion was as fair: Krishna is presented as dark skinned, and this indeed is the meaning of his name.

Subhadra: See notes to 'The Nature of Krishna'.

Dwarka: a city on the west coast of India, in present-day Gujarat, said to have been established by Krishna.

Pandavas: the five sons of King Pandu: Yudhisthira, Bhima and Arjuna (by Kunti) and Nakul and Sahadeva (by Madri). One of the two adversary parties in the *Mahabharata*, the other being the Kauravas or 100 sons of King Dhritarashtra, Pandu's brother.

Vedavyasa: or Vyasa, traditionally named as the poet of the *Mahabharata* though perhaps a mythical figure.

dry and wither: again playing on the literal meaning of *rasa*, sap or juice.

A Poet's Biography (*Kabijibani*)

First published in *Bangadarshan*, Asharh 1308 (June–Jul. 1901) and collected in *Sahitya* (see headnote to 'World Literature').

Rabindranath was highly sceptical not only about biographical criticism but about the literary biography itself. He distinguishes between the 'external' and 'internal' facts in the life of a poet and considers the former irrelevant to the 'truth' about him. In a poem on Kalidasa included in *Chaitali* (1896), he celebrates the 'inner life' of the poet, uncontaminated by contemporary events and deducible only from the poet's own work. But the idea is expressed most strongly in the poem *Kabicharit* ('The Poet's Biography'), written in 19[illegible] (*Utsarga*, poem no. 21), and the first essay in *Atmaparichay* ('Self-Introduction', 1943). This last was written for a 1904 anthology of biographical essays, *Bangabhashar Lekhak* ('Writers in the Bengali Language'), edited by Harimohan Mukhopadhyay. To ensure accuracy of fact, living writers had been asked to prepare accounts of their own lives; but Rabindranath wrote instead of his 'inner' life, producing a predictably controversial piece. Again, when Prabhatkumar Mukhopadhyay published the first volume of *Rabindrajibani*, the most comprehensive biography of the poet till then, Rabindranath dismissed it as the life of a grandson of Prince Dwarkanath Tagore.

two massive volumes: Hallam Tennyson's *Alfred, Lord Tennyson*: *A Memoir* (1897). This essay was published as a review of the book.

legend current about Valmiki . . . the heron: The *Ramayana* (*Adikanda*, ch. 2) recounts how one day, beside the river Tamasa, Valmiki saw a heron killed by a hunter while coupling with his mate. Struck by the female's lament, Valmiki came out spontaneously with what are held to be the first verses of Sanskrit poetry, leading up to his composition of the *Ramayana*.

Ravana tears the lovers apart: by abducting Sita.

the war canto in the Ramayana: where Rama and his associates go to rescue Sita.

Ratnakar: Valmiki's original name. He is said to have begun life as a bandit. He reformed on discovering, at the behest of the sage Narada, that his wife and children refused to share the burden of his guilt, although he had turned bandit in order to support them.

the Kabikankan: See notes on 'Silent Poet, Untaught Poet'.

the goddess: Chandi, an aspect of Durga, in whose praise Mukunda Chakrabarti composed his poem.

legend about Kalidasa: Kalidasa is said to have been a foolish yokel married to a clever and learned princess. Her taunts and laments made him educate himself, with the blessings of Sarasvati the goddess of learning, whom he encountered in a forest.

VIDYAPATI'S RADHIKA (*Vidyapatir Radhika*)

First published in *Sadhana*, Chaitra 1298 (Mar.–Apr. 1892); collected in *Adhunik Sahitya* ('Modern Literature'), 23 Ashwin 1314 (10 October 1907).

Vidyapati was a versatile poet of fifteenth-century Mithila (in present-day Bihar), chiefly renowned for his lyrics in praise of Shiva and, more particularly, on the love of Radha and Krishna. His work was extremely popular in Bengal. Many Bengali poets imitated his style so perfectly that a large number of poems not actually by him passed under his name. (Some scholars even suggest that there were two Vidyapatis, one from Mithila and the other from Bengal.) Rabindranath was a great admirer of Vidyapati and the Vaishnava poets of Bengal, whose lyrics are collectively known as *padabali.* He co-edited a collection of Vaishnava lyrics with Shrishchandra Majumdar under the title of *Padaratnabali* (1292/1885; also later editions), and wrote a number of poems in that style and language under the pseudonym 'Bhanusingha'.

Although the Radha–Krishna lyrics are often highly erotic, orthodox Vaishnava scholars read them as expressions of Vaishnava theology. Rabindranath, on the other hand, advocated a secular reading. For him, the Radha–Krishna story is an allegory of the relationship of the mortal to the divine, and its spirit is essentially secular.

Chandidas: a sixteenth-century Bengali poet of disputed identity, author of Vaishnava lyrics and other works on Krishna. There might be more than one poet of this name.

My eyes are birds, etc.: from the song *Jaladbaran dalit anjan* ascribed to Dina Chandidas. In the original, the 'birds' are chakors or partridges, said to drink the moonlight, hence a type of the lover drinking in his beloved's beauty.

Now she'll bind up, etc.: from Vidyapati's verses beginning *Saisab jouban darasan bhela,* on Radha's onset of puberty.

Half the veil slips, etc.: from Vidyapati's verses beginning *Sajani bhala kaye peuna na bhela*, on the first arousal of love in Krishna.

In a new Vrindavan: the entire text of a song on spring by Vidyapati, included by Rabindranath in *Padaratnabali*.

new. In the translation, *new* been used to render both *naba*, new, and *nabin*, fresh or youthful. Vidyapati plays intricately on these two etymologically related words.

Vrindavan: the haunt of Krishna as a child and a lover.

Sweet is the season, etc.: another springtime composition by Vidyapati, also to be found in *Padaratnabali*.

Ever since birth, etc.: These lines, among the most celebrated in Vaishnava poetry and repeatedly quoted by Rabindranath, are from the poem beginning *Sakhi he ki puchhasi anubhaba moya*, ascribed by modern scholars to Kabiballabh but earlier (as here) to Vidyapati. (There is a footnote in *Padaratnabali*: 'This poem is usually ascribed to Vidyapati.') The version in that collection differs somewhat from the text quoted here. The two couplets quoted are not consecutive in all versions of the poem.

THE NATURE OF KRISHNA (*Krishnacharitra*)

First published in the Magh and Phalgun 1301 numbers (Jan.–Mar. 1895) of *Sadhana*; collected in *Adhunik Sahitya* (see headnote to 'Vidyapati's Radhika' above). A review of Bankimchandra Chattopadhyay's highly polemical and recondite treatise *Krishnacharitra,* published in 1886, revised and enlarged in 1892.

Bankim's purpose was to prove the historicity of Krishna, who has been variously presented in Indian epics and legends. He is one of the heroes of the *Mahabharata* and, within that epic, the spiritual preceptor of the *Bhagavadgita*; also a romantic hero of the *Bhagavat Purana* as well as the mythical cowherd of Vrindavana and Radha's paramour. In his anxiety to construct a hero fulfilling the requirements of his version of Hinduism, Bankim rejects the Krishna of the Vaishnava poets and privileges the Krishna of the *Mahabharata* as an ideal man, the only religious teacher without any imperfection. Bankim's ideal Krishna, inspired by Biblical scholarship and a rationalist approach to the life of Christ, was free of erotic as well as miraculous associations.

Despite his sound scholarship and professed objectivity, Bankim's work failed to evoke much favourable response. Orthodox Hindus found his attitude to the romantic Krishna offensive; the Christian missionaries were predictably unconvinced by his reasoning; but the Brahmos, concerned about the repercussions for their movement against puranic Hinduism, were the most vocal critics of all. As an active member of the Brahmo Samaj, Rabindranath shared this anxiety. He recognises Bankim's pioneering role in the historical criticism of Krishna, and admires his rational temper in contrast to the fervour of the Hindu zealots; but he is severe on Bankim's methodology, and finds in him an intolerance and partisanship incompatible with his professed aim.

Rabindranath's respect for Bankim was reciprocated by the latter's affection for the young poet; but they differed significantly in their conception of Hindu thought.

shastras: Hindu scriptures.

Vedavyasa: See notes to 'The Historical Novel'.

Vaishampayana: a disciple of Vedavyasa, said to have recited the *Mahabharata* to King Janmejaya at Vedavyasa's command.

Both the *Vaiyasiki Samhita* or original *Mahabharata* composed by Vedavyasa, and the *Vaishampayan Samhita* or version composed by Vaishampayana, are hypothetical versions that have not come down to us.

Kurukshetra: a place in the Punjab region (now in Haryana state); site of the great battle recounted in the *Mahabharata*.

Kunti: mother of Yudhisthira, Bhima, and Arjuna, the three senior of the five Pandava brothers. Her *daughter-in-law* was Draupadi, married to all the five Pandavas.

Pandavas: See notes to 'The Historical Novel'.

Vidula, Sanjay: Sanjay, prince of the kingdom of Sauvira, remained inert on being deprived of his kingdom by the king of Sind. His widowed mother Vidula thereupon fiercely rebuked him and urged him to war. When Sanjay said that Vidula's sufferings would increase if he were to be killed in battle, Vidula responded that a kshatriya can win peace only by conquering his enemy or sacrificing his life.

kshatriya: the warrior caste.

Arjuna, Bhima: See note on 'Kunti' above.

Bhishma: a hero of immense virtue and stern vows; a character of heroic action and moral authority in the *Mahabharata*.

Karna: the son of Kunti (see above) by the Sun God in her virgin state, and therefore abandoned by her: a virtuous and heroic figure.

Drona: tutor to the Pandavas and Kauravas in weaponry and the art of war.

Bhishma, Karna, and Drona all fought on the side of the Kauravas in the battle of Kurukshetra.

Gandhari: Dhritarashtra's wife, mother of the Kauravas.

Duryodhana: the eldest Kaurava brother, presented in the *Mahabharata* as a vicious and unheroic character.

Gandhari proposes forsaking Duryodhana: *Mahabharata, Sabhaparva* ch. 73.

Draupadi asserts, etc.: *Mahabharata*, *Udyogaparva* ch.81.

Ugrashraba's father: Romaharshana, a leading pupil and disciple of Vedavyasa. He took up the recital of the Puranas at the latter's command.

Ugrashraba: also known as Sauti: a reciter of the Puranas, who heard the *Mahabharata* as recited by Vaishampayana to King Janmejaya (see above) and passed it on to an assembly of sages and ascetics.

five husbands: Arjuna won Draupadi's hand in marriage; but later, following an inadvertent command of their mother Kunti, all five Pandava brothers took her to wife.

Drupad: King of Panchal and father of Draupadi. Drupad arranged a *yagna* or ceremonial sacrifice to obtain a son. In addition to that son, Dhrishtadyumna, the ceremonial altar yielded him this daughter.

swayamvara marriage: one where the bride chooses her own husband. In Draupadi's case, it was by imposing a severe test of marksmanship (see notes to 'Children's Rhymes').

Mr Forster: John Forster (1812–76), historian and biographer. His life of Thomas Wentworth, Earl of Strafford, appeared in 1836 as part of his *Lives of the Statesmen of the Commonwealth.* He was a friend of Robert Browning, as of many other eminent men of his times. Browning's play *Strafford* was first performed on 1 May 1837 and published the same year.

Mr Froude: James Anthony Froude (1818–94). This passage, which Rabindranath quotes in a Bengali version, is from Froude's essay 'Homer'. The English text given here has been cited from *Short Studies on Great Subjects* (3rd edn: Longman, Green and Co., London, 1868), p. 337. In Rabindranath's Bengali version, the gist of the last sentence was placed first.

termites of modern times: A pun in the Bengali. Valmiki is customarily named as the poet of the *Ramayana.* His name derives from Sanskrit *valmik*, termite or white ant, because he was once so absorbed in meditation as not to have stirred even when termites built an anthill over his body.

Shishupala: King of Chedi, destined to be killed by Krishna. The latter agreed to excuse his first 100 misdeeds; but finally killed him after the 101st, which was to abuse Krishna at a great *yagna* or ceremonial sacrifice organised by Yudhisthira and the Pandavas.

yogin: a being of supreme virtue and spiritual discipline, master of the entire range of *yogas* or disciplines of mind and body.

Vishvamitra. . . Vashishtha's cow Nandini: Vishvamitra, king of Kanyakubja (Kanauj), once took shelter while hunting at the forest retreat of the sage Vashishtha. Vashishtha entertained the royal party with the help of his miraculous cow Nandini, who would yield whatever one desired of her. When Vashishtha refused to part with her, even in exchange for Vishvamitra's kingdom, the latter attempted to steal her. Finally, Nandini protected herself by gendering bands of soldiers from each of her limbs. Vishvamitra was overcome at this proof of brahmanic power, and though a kshatriya or warrior by birth, became a quasi-brahman ascetic.

Ravana: king of Lanka; abductor of Sita; villain and chief adversary of Rama in the *Ramayana*.

Kumbhakarna: Ravana's second brother: renowned for sleeping six months in the year, hence awoken to battle against Rama with great difficulty.

Kangsa: the tyrant of Mathura who persecuted Krishna and his parents and was finally killed by Krishna.

Subhadra: Krishna's half-sister and Arjuna's second wife. When Arjuna felt attracted to her, Krishna incited him to abduct her, and defended his conduct before and after the act as worthy of a kshatriya.

Malabari: Behramji Malabari (1853–1912), eminent social reformer who campaigned for widow remarriage among other causes. Rabindranath speaks of him in more favourable vein elsewhere.

The *Meghadutam* (*Meghdut*)

This and the next three essays are from the collection *Prachin Sahitya* ('Ancient Literature'), 28 Asharh 1314 (13 July 1907), though they were published earlier in periodicals. *Prachin Sahitya* is of great importance in the history of Bengali criticism, as of Indian criticism of Sanskrit literature generally, because of its remarkable freshness and freedom from pedantry. With these essays, Rabindranath freed Sanskrit criticism from the age-old prison of philological investigation and the obsolete framework of ancient poetics.

'The *Meghadutam*' appeared in the journal *Sahitya*, Agrahayan 1298 (Nov.–Dec. 1891), before its inclusion in *Prachin Sahitya*. Kalidasa's *Meghadutam* was perhaps Rabindranath's favourite poem, an inseparable part of his mental landscape and, consequently, a crucial text in understanding the nature of his poetic imagination. This chapter, the most substantial among innumerable references and tributes scattered through his works, should be read in conjunction with the poem *Meghdut* from the collection *Manasi* (1890). Both poem and essay were written on dark days of incessant rain, like that evoked by Kalidasa's poem; both present a sequence of evocative scenes tracing the cloud's progress through the sky, bearing the lover's message.

The Sanskrit *Meghadutam* is a poem of 115 stanzas in the stately mandakranta metre. It presents a *yaksha*, a type of demigod, banished for neglect of duties from his homeland in the Himalayas to Ramagiri in central India. On the first day of the month of Asharh, he grows restless at the sight of a rain-cloud and prays to it to convey a message to his wife in the far-off Himalayan town of Alaka. Early commentators like Mallinath divided the poem into two parts. The first, commonly called the *Purva-megham* or 'Early Cloud' (i.e. while it is journeying), describes the various places that the cloud will pass over on its journey to Alaka: it presents fine instances of the celebrated descriptive vignettes of Sanskrit poetry. The second, the *Uttara-megham* or 'Later Cloud' (i.e. after its arrival), is a luxuriant description of the splendours of Alaka.

Ramagiri: commonly identified with the Chitrakut Hills mentioned in the *Ramayana,* in the Bundelkhand region of north-central India; alternatively with Ramtek near Nagpur. The yaksha of *Meghadutam* was exiled here from his Himalayan homeland. The subsequent account, place by place, closely follows the path of the cloud as described by Kalidasa, and often echoes his very phrases.

Dasharna: an ancient kingdom in central India, around modern Bhopal.

Avanti: the ancient name for Malwa in central India.

Udayana and Vasavadatta: Udayana was a famous king of the Vatsa kingdom of central India in the sixth century BC. He carried off King Pradyota's daughter Vasavadatta.

Ujjayini (Ujjain): the capital of Avanti (see above); now a city in Madhya Pradesh.

Vidisha: capital of Dasharna (see above); present-day Bhilsa in Madhya Pradesh.

Vindhya: a range of hills running east and west through central India.

Kailas: a mountain in western Tibet, north-east of Manas Sarovar. The home of the yakshas, from which the hero of *Meghadutam* has been exiled.

Devagiri: the 'hill of the god(s)', the abode of Skanda or Kartikeya as mentioned in *Meghadutam* stanza 44.

Reva: *the* river Narmada, rising in the eastern Vindhyas and flowing west to the Arabian Sea.

Shipra: a river flowing past Ujjayini (see above).

Vetravati: modern Betwa, the river running through Dasharna (see above).

Nirvindhya: the Nevaj, a river running through the Vindhya hills.

hills, rivers: Rabindranath has in mind Kalidasa's compound *naganadi*, 'mountain streams'; but the context of the Bengali suggests the different syntax followed here.

village wives, town wives: echoes *Meghadutam* stanzas 16, 49.

an English poet: Matthew Arnold in 'Isolation' (also known as 'To Marguerite, in Returning a Volume of the Letters of Ortis').

the first clouds of Asharh: a clear echo of a phrase near the start of *Meghadutaṁ*, 'On the first day of Asharh . . .'. Asharh is the third month of the Indian year, and the first month of the rainy season.

Alaka: the capital of the yakshas, where the beloved of Kalidasa's hero lives.

Manas Sarovar: the well-known lake in Tibet, near Kailas (see above) and thus close to the yaksha's homeland. But *Manas* literally means 'the mind' or 'the mind's desires', and Rabindranath plays on the word here.

The breezes from the snowy peaks, etc.: *Meghadutam* stanza 107.

In each other's arms, etc.: from a celebrated poem ascribed to Chandidas, on the love of Radha and Krishna, beginning *Eman piriti kabhu dekhi nai shuni.*

Who took you out, etc., *Lord, your Balaram's,* etc.: the last two lines of a wooing song for Krishna composed by Balaram Das (sixteenth century), beginning *Tumi mor nidhi Rai tumi mor nidhi.* See notes to 'World Literature'.

Kumarasambhavam and *Shakuntala* (*Kumarsambhab o Shakuntala*)

First published in *Bangadarshan,* Poush 1308 (Dec.1901–Jan.1902); collected in *Prachin Sahitya* (see headnote to 'The *Meghadutam*' above).

Kumarasambhavam ('The Birth of Kartikeya') is a poem by Kalidas in seventeen cantos, describing the marriage and union of Shiva and Parvati (Durga) and the birth of their son Kartikeya, the warrior-god who rescues the gods from the invasion of the demons. The last ten cantos have often been held to present a markedly grosser vein, and hence dismissed as not being Kalidasa's work. Rabindranath too found this part offensive to his taste, and justified his view in a poem included in *Chaitali* (1896).

Abhijnanashakuntalam ('Shakuntala's Memento') is a play by Kalidasa drawing its plot from the first book of the *Mahabharata.* It tells how King Dushyanta secretly married Shakuntala, foster daughter of the sage Kanva. He then forgot about her and repudiated her in court, because of a curse of the sage Durvasa. His memory was restored after a ring, the token of remembrance he had given her, was discovered inside a fish. He finally re-encountered her with their son Bharata in the sage Maricha's hermitage.

In *Kumarasambhavam* and *Abhijnanashakuntalam,* Rabindranath found the finest manifetations of ancient Indian ideals of love and duty, sacrifice and piety, and a great vision of life encompassing man, nature, and God.

renouncing, annihilating music: This rendering attempts to capture the implications of Rabindranath's word *bhairabsangit.*

the Great Departure: the *mahaprasthana,* the final journey to heaven undertaken by the five Pandava brothers and Draupadi at the end of the *Mahabharata,* after Yudhisthira's renunciation of the kingdom he had ruled for thirty-six years.

Mount Kailas: a sacred peak in the Himalayas; the setting for a part of *Kumarasambhavam.*

Dushyanta, Shakuntala, [their] union: See notes to 'The Theatre'.

Parvati ('daughter of the Mountain'): daughter of Himalaya, lover and consort of Shiva; identified with the goddess Durga.

Parvati's sorrow and shame: after her initial rejection by Shiva, described in Canto 3 of *Kumarasambhavam.*

the subsequent wedding night: described in Cantos 7–8.

The cool breeze, etc.: The following description draws closely on details in Canto 2, stanzas 25 ff.

kinnaras: a legendary race, half human and half horse: musically gifted, and singers in heaven. Said to roam Mount Kailas.

untimely arrival of spring: Madana arranges for this untoward phenomenon to provide a fit setting to tempt Shiva to love.

bride of the southern horizon: The Sanskrit has the word *dakshina*, which signifies the south as well as a loving wife. The Bengali has *digbadhu* (see notes to 'World Literature').

Kanva's hermitage: See notes to 'The Theatre'.

Gauri ('the fair one'): a name for Parvati.

fish-pennanted god: Madana.

encouraged by the king of the gods: Indra, the king of the gods, sent Madana to tempt Shiva so that Kartikeya might be conceived to save the gods from the demons.

one with neither array, etc.: i.e. Shiva.

a master's curse: alluding to *Meghadutam*, where the yaksha is banished by his lord, Kuber.

a holy man's . . . the law of hospitality: alluding to *Shakuntala*. Absorbed in thoughts of Dushyanta, Shakuntala did not offer due respect and hospitality to the irascible sage Durvasa. He thereupon cursed her that her husband would be unable to recognise her.

turned to ashes by divine wrath: the fate of Madana the love god in *Kuarasambhavam*.

Uma: another name for Parvati: from her mother's cry '*U ma*' ('Ah! Do not!') asking her to desist from the severe ascesis she undergoes to win Shiva.

came like a swaying creeper, etc.: This paragraph is entirely based on elements from *Kumarasambhavam* 3.52–68.

yogin: See notes to 'The Nature of Krishna'. Shiva is the supreme ascetic and yogin.

three eyes: a classic attribute of Shiva.

Kanva's foster daughter: Shakuntala. She is rejected and humiliated by Dushyanta when she goes to claim recognition as his wife and queen.

'*knowing the grace*', etc., '*somehow making her way*', etc.: *Kumarasambhavam* 3: 75.

dispraised beauty, etc.: Ibid., 5:1.

She desired, etc.: Ibid. 5.2.

When dharma, etc.: Ibid., 6.14.

Mahadeva ('the great god'): Shiva.

Shiva himself said as much: in *Kumarasambhavam* 5:65 ff.

My mind is centred, etc.: Ibid. 5.82. Rabindranath renders this line in a different way in 'The Sense of Beauty' to suit the context there.

the Seven Sages: the constellation known in English as the Great Bear. It is held to represent the transformed beings of seven great sages. Shiva encounters them and Arundhati (see below) in *Kumarasambhavam* Canto 6.

'*neither here nor there*' (or 'neither moving nor staying'): a phrase from *Kumarasambhavam* 5.85, describing the state of Parvati (like a river impeded by a hill) when she encounters Shiva at the end of her self-mortification to win him.

Arundhati: the wife of the sage Vashishtha, one of the Seven Sages (see above). Because of her wifely devotion, Arundhati was also transformed into a star, which appears among the Seven Sages.

Seeing her, Shambhu became, etc.: *Kumarasambhavam 6.13.*

Shambhu: another name of Shiva.

cleansed by the auspicious bath, etc.: *Kumarasambhavam 7.11.*

Manu: the legendary law-giver of Hindu civilisation. His dispensation is usually considered oppressive or inimical to women.

They give birth, etc.: *Manusamhita* 9.26.

Kartikeya's birth: This occurs in *Kumarasambhavam* Canto 10.

Madana reduced to ashes: by Shiva, enraged at Madana's efforts to disturb his meditation, in *Kumarasambhavam* Canto 3. Rati, Madana's wife, thereupon breaks out in a long lament, the substance of Canto 4.

Bharata: Shakuntala's son by Dushyanta, who grows up to be overlord of the whole of India (hence the traditional name for the country, *Bharatavarsha*). In the last act of *Abhijnanashakuntalam*, Dushyanta meets and recognises the infant Bharata as a prelude to his reunion with Shakuntala.

holier forest hermitage: that of the sage Maricha, where Shakuntala takes shelter with her son after her repudiation by Dushyanta.

a single boy: i.e. Bharata (see above).

Shakuntala of cleansed mind, etc.: *Abhijnanashakuntalam* Act 7 shloka 21. Rabindranath's Bengali translation (here rendered in English) covers more text than his Sanskrit quotation.

'Mother, who is this', etc.: ibid. Act 7.

SHAKUNTALA

First published in *Bangadarshan*, Ashwin 1309 (Sept.–Oct. 1902); collected in *Prachin Sahitya* (see headnote to 'The *Meghadutam*').

On Kalidasa's play and Rabindranath's response to it, see opening notes to '*Kumarasambhavam* and *Shakuntala*'.

The English translations given here for Rabindranath's Sanskrit quotations from *Abhijnanashakuntalam* owe something to those in the edition by Bidhubhushan Goswami (7th edn., Calcutta, n.d.). All references to the play are by act and, for a shloka or verse passage, its number.

the hermit's foster daughter: Shakuntala was the daughter of the sage Vishvamitra and the heavenly courtesan Menaka. Abandoned by her parents, she was brought up by the sage Kanva.

forest retreat: The word *tapoban* has been translated in this essay as 'forest retreat' or 'forest hermitage'. A literal meaning would be 'a forest of/for ascetic meditation'. As developed by Rabindranath here and elsewhere, such a setting combines the consciousness of nature with the cultivation of the spirit in equal measure, and indeed in interaction. See also note on p. xiii.

Goethe: He read *Abhijnanashakuntalam* in 1791 in Georg Forster's German translation, and wrote an appreciative quatrain that has been translated as follows by Forster:

> Shall I embrace the blossoms of spring, the fruits of the autumn,
> All that enchants and that charms, all that nurtures and fills?
> Shall I embrace in a name all heaven and all of the earth?
> Call I, Shakuntala, thee—all is comprised in one name.

'*Early Cloud*' *and* '*Later Cloud*': See headnote to 'The *Meghadutam*'.

another essay: i.e., '*Kumarasambhavam* and *Shakuntala*'.

five-darted love god. . . Kandarpa: The love god Kandarpa was said to have five floral arrows in his quiver, shot from a floral bow.

ashram: a spiritual or monastic retreat.

gandharva marriage: See notes to 'Childen's Rhymes'.

Rishyashringa: a hermit brought up in exceptional solitude, and thus utterly devoid of knowledge about women and sexual matters.

O King, do not kill, etc.: *Abhijnanashakuntalam* Act 1.

Turn your bow, etc.: Translates Act 1 shloka 10. A more literal rendering would have 'a heap of flowers'; and, for the last two lines, 'Ah! Where is the delicate body of young fawns, and where are your arrows, hard as thunderbolts, falling sharply!' A variant reading has 'heap of cotton' instead of 'heap of flowers'.

They are both forest-dwellers: *Abhijnanashakuntalam* Act 4.

Lips as red, etc.: Act 1 shloka 19, translated fairly closely.

She who never quenched, etc.: Act IV shloka 9; again, quite closely translated, though the Sanskrit is in the present tense, and refers to Shakuntala's delight at the coming of new leaves as her 'highest pleasure'.

Priyamvada: one of Shakuntala's two companions in the forest retreat, the other being Anasuya.

The grass drops, etc.: Act 4 shloka 12: a close rendering.

He whose jaws, etc.: Act 4 shloka 14. More literally, 'My child, the deer to whose mouth, pricked by the sharp points of the kusha grass, you applied the healing oil of ingudi (or inguli)—who was reared on handfuls of syamaka grains, and treated by you like a child—will not move out of your path.'

Uttararamacharitam: See notes to 'On Changes in the State of Poetry'. The refer-ence here is to Sita's state of mind on her return to an unhappy court life after her forest exile and captivity in Lanka.

Durvasa's curse: See notes to '*Kumarasambhavam* and *Shakuntala*'.

O honey-bee, etc.: *Abhijnanashakuntalam* Act 5 shloka 1. Rabindranath's rendering reverses the positions of lotus and mango blossom as given in the Sanskrit.

comic companion: Madhava, a brahman friend of the king, serving as the *vidushaka*, a conventional comic figure in Sanskrit drama.

Sakritkritapranayoyam janah: 'A person only loves once': Act 5.

Queen Vasumati: Dushyanta's crowned queen. In one recension of the play, Dushyanta takes Hamsapadika to be taunting him for neglecting her in favour of Vasumati.

Sharngarava, Sharadvata: inmates of Kanva's forest retreat. With Gautami (see next note), they accompany Shakuntala to Dushyanta's court to claim her rightful place.

Gautami: matron of Kanva's forest retreat.

Maricha: See notes to '*Kumarasambhavam* and *Shakuntala*'.

Do not, do not let the arrow fall, etc.: Quotes, in Sanskrit, Act 1 shloka 10, rendered earlier in a Bengali version.

The elephant terrified, etc.: the latter part of Act I shloka 30.

THE *RAMAYANA*

Written as the introduction to *Ramayani Katha* (1904), a collection of essays by the literary historian Dineshchandra Sen (1866–1939) analysing the characters of the epic; later collected in *Prachin Sahitya* (see headnote to 'The *Meghadutam*' above). Rabindranath's essay is not a mere foreword to Dineshchandra's book but a substantial analysis of the *Ramayana*. The traces of revivalistic and nationalistic fervour do not materially detract from its historical value and critical acumen.

Vyasa and Valmiki: the poets to whom the *Mahabharata* and the *Ramayana*, respectively, are commonly ascribed.

Lakshmana: Rama's devoted brother, his companion in forest exile and in battle.

heroic rasa: the *vira rasa*: see note on p. xi.

Adikanda: the first canto of the *Ramayana*. At its very outset, the great sage Narada recounts the entire history of Rama to Valmiki, thereby inspiring the latter to compose the *Ramayana*.

Lakshmi: the goddess of wealth and prosperity, and thus of all beneficent qualities generally.

domestic stage of life: one of the four *ashramas* (stages or phases) into which Indian tradition divided human life.

Kaikeyi and Manthara: Kaikeyi, the second wife of King Dasharath, intrigued with her attendant woman Manthara to send Rama to exile, thereby ensuring the throne for Kaikeyi's own son Bharata.

rasa of serenity: the *shanta rasa*: see note on p. xi.

LITERATURE (*Sahitya*): 1924

This and the next five essays were included in the collection *Sahityer Pathe* ('On the Road to Literature'), Ashwin 1343 (Sept.–Oct. 1936), enlarged 2nd edition

Chaitra 1352 (Mar.–Apr. 1946). *Sahityer Pathe* is a seminal work. Its component essays, written over a long period of time, record the growth and consolidation of Rabindranath's literary thought. They also proved extremely controversial, initiating animated debate on issues like realism and modernity.

'Literature' is the revised version of a lecture delivered at Calcutta University on 18 Phalgun 1330 (March 1924). Barring a transcript of the lecture by another hand, it was first published in the journal *Bangabani* in Vaishakh 1331 (Apr.–May 1924), and then in *Sahityer Pathe.* The two texts vary in many respects. The Visva-Bharati edition of the Works, chiefly following the latter, merges the two at points (see note below).

mantra: a chant, incantation or spell, usually holy.

Om: the supposed composite sound to which all earthly sounds merge in the hearing of Brahma the supreme being; hence the 'seed-mantra' or mantra most basically expressing the nature of divinity. It bears noting that Rabindranath applies this most sacred of Hindu utterances to the Taj Mahal, a mausoleum raised by a Muslim emperor.

In equating *Om* with 'Yes', Rabindranath has in mind passages like that from the *Chhandogya Upanishad* 1.1.8: 'That which is this (*Om*) is a letter of consent: whatever a person approves, he does so by uttering *Om* only'; and the *Taittiriya Upanishad* 1.8.1: '*Om* is well known as a word of imitation' (i.e. concurrence, approval).

ocean of fatal night: The Bengali carries a pun on *Kalighat*: literally 'black *ghat* (landing-place or jetty)', but suggesting Kalighat, the famous shrine of the goddess Kali in Calcutta, and hence implying pilgrimage.

Jahanara: She looked after her father Shah Jahan, deposed and imprisoned in his old age. She was a poetess of some note. Note again the reference to *Om* in such a context.

I give [the bride] to you: words from the traditional Hindu marriage service.

as is this heart of mine: '. . . so may your heart be': also from the Hindu marriage service. Rabindranath has slightly altered the words of the *Samamantra Brahmana.*

The Meghadutam: Kalidasa's poem celebrating a mutual and romantic love.

Ujjayini, Vikramaditya: Kalidasa's supposed city of residence, and the emperor (otherwise Chandragupta II) whose patronage he is said to have enjoyed. In fact (as Rabindranath points out), there is much uncertainty about Kalidasa's dates and provenance.

Hamsapadikas: used in the plural, generically, of rejected or marginalised paramours: from Hamsapadika, one of Dushyanta's many spent loves in *Abhijnanashakuntalam.* (See 'Shakuntala'.)

panchalis: a type of traditional Bengali lay or ballad, usually on mythological themes. Rabindranath has in mind a specific alliterative style introduced by the famous panchali poet Dasharathi (Dashu) Ray.

pedigreed brahmans: The *kulins* or brahmans of unsullied caste practised many gross abuses of marital conduct in earlier times. *Kulin* men would marry countless wives, with whom they often had little or no contact; while many of the women failed to marry all the same, and had to undergo such sad fates as being ritually married to trees.

the being that shines forth, etc.: See notes to 'The Sense of Beauty'.

Titagarh: a town near Calcutta, the site of jute mills.

Bopadeva (seventh–eighth century AD), author of the widely used Sanskrit primer *Mugdhabodha* and other treatises on Sanskrit grammar.

staff-bearer's rigour: The Bengali (*dandir danda*) carries a double pun: (1) on *dandi*, literally 'one carrying a staff' but specifically a wandering sage or ascetic—hence suggesting ascetic rigour and spiritual discipline; (2) on *danda*, literally a staff or rod but also meaning a punishment or imposition.

the Maidan: the large open space in the heart of Calcutta.

Aurangzeb: The Emperor Aurangzeb is traditionally held to have engaged in bloody persecution of the Hindus, though this view is now questioned.

when I was sailing to Japan: in 1916. The incident is described in *Japanjatri* ('Traveller to Japan'), Rabindranath's journal of this tour.

rudraveena: See notes to 'The Historical Novel'.

The word amrita, etc.: As usual, the translation follows the Visva-Bharati edition of the Bengali Works, which, at this point, alternates between two separate versions of the essay. This paragraph occurs in the version published in the journal *Bangabani*, though the rest of the essay follows the later version in the volume *Sahityer Pathe*. The corresponding paragraph in *Sahityer Pathe* is as follows:

> That image of the storm, of course, is no more. Some day my memory too may disappear. But the picture of frenzy and destruction that was painted that day on the huge canvas of the sky, however transient it might have been, had expressed the immortal in a brief segment of time. The squalid slum next to the jute mill may last longer, but it is already dead.

amrita has two meanings: The literal meaning is 'deathless'; but as the nectar drunk by the gods, endowing them with immortality, it is a *rasa* in the literal sense (fluid, hence drink) and source of joy—the second meaning cited by Rabindranath here.

lives under time's rule and yet does not cooperate with it: a metaphor drawn from the Non-Cooperation Movement of 1920–1.

rupadaksha: The word in this sense was commonly used by Rabindranath's nephew, the artist Abanindranath, in his writings on art.

a university: The lecture on which this essay is based was delivered at Calcutta University (see headnote).

whether art does us any good: In the preamble to the original version of the essay (omitted in *Sahityer Pathe*), Rabindranath mentions a question he was asked by an Indian student (in English): 'Is art too good for human nature's daily food?' He goes on to say that the question mirrors the popular confusion about the social utility of art, and claims that the lecture is an attempted answer. It is to this question that he returns in the last sentence.

Creation (*Srishti*)

The revised version of a lecture delivered at Calcutta University on 20 Phalgun 1330 (March 1924). If we ignore a transcript by another hand, the first version of the present chapter appeared in *Bangabani* in Kartik 1331 (Oct.–Nov. 1924). It was later revised and collected in *Sahityer Pathe* (see headnote to 'Literature' above).

lifted the veil: This phrase is used to remind the reader that Rabindranath might have had Shelley's words in mind: 'Poetry lifts the veil from the hidden beauty of the world, and makes familiar objects be as if they were unfamiliar.' (*A Defence of Poetry*). However, Rabindranath also uses the image in his memoirs (*Jibansmriti*) while describing how he composed the poem *Nirjharer Swapnabhanga* (The Fountain Awakes from Its Dream): 'It was as though suddenly, in an instant, a veil had been drawn away from my eyes.'

A person only loves once: Spoken by King Dushyanta in Kalidasa's *Abhijnana-shakuntalam*, Act 5. See 'Shakuntala'.

Hamsapadikas: See notes to 'Literature'.

Krishna, Vraja, Mathura: Vraja or Vrindavan is the scene of Krishna's life as herdsman and lover; Mathura, the seat of his kingdom in later life. Cf. notes to 'World Literature'.

mace, war-quoit: traditional attributes of Krishna, relating particularly to his role in the Battle of Kurukshetra. The war-quoit is his celebrated weapon, the *sudarshan chakra*.

panchajanya: the conch of Vishnu and hence of his avatar or incarnation in Krishna.

six schools of philosophy: see notes to 'The Measure of Mirth'.

ten avatars of Vishnu: Vishnu is held to have come to earth ten times as avatars or incarnations.

cottah: a measure of land.

yesterday: i.e. in the lecture subsequently made into the essay *Tathya o Satya* (Fact and Truth): the second of three lectures at Calcutta University, 'Literature' and 'Creation' being the first and third.

Jesus said, 'It is easier', etc.: Matthew 19.24. The wording here follows Rabindranath's Bengali rendering.

pleasurable truth: Translates the Bengali *rasasatya*, roughly 'the truth of the rasa', or 'the truth realised through rasa'.

to look upon fleeting appearances, etc.: *Isha Upanishad* 1. The translation follows

Rabindranath's reading. Alternative readings would be '. . . as intended for God to dwell in', and 'Do not covet, for whose is wealth?'

the goddess of joyful abundance: The Bengali has *anandalakshmi*, 'the Lakshmi of joy'. Lakshmi is the goddess of wealth, prosperity, and grace.

lakh: a hundred thousand.

Lord Indra: the king of the gods.

shastras: the Hindu scriptures.

Menaka and Urvashi: celestial courtesans; here taken as emblems of beauty in conjunction with a higher materiality.

parijat: See notes to 'Children's Rhymes'.

Sujata: a woman disciple of the Buddha who brought him food during his period of meditative ascesis.

Martha and Mary: Luke 10: 38–42, John 12.3–8.

THE POET'S DEFENCE (*Kabir Kaiphiyat*)

First published in the avant-garde monthly *Sabuj Patra*, Jyaistha 1322 (May–June 1915) in a formal Bengali (*sadhu bhasha*) verson: this is the version reprinted in the Visva-Bharati edition of the Works and used in this translation. Later collected in *Sahityer Pathe* (see headnote to 'Literature' above) in a colloquial (*chalit*) version.

This essay was written in response to a severe attack on Rabindranath by Radhakamal Mukhopadhyay, an eminent social scientist and professor at Lucknow University. Rabindranath's alleged lack of realism and remoteness from the common people had been condemned by Radhakamal in two articles: *Lokshikshak ba Jananayak* (People's Teacher or People's Leader), *Prabasi*, Jyaisthya 1321 (May–June 1914), and *Sahitye Bastabata* (Realism in Literature), *Sabuj Patra*, Magh 1321 (Jan.–Feb. 1915).

lila: See note on p. xii.

holy narcotic . . . drugged deity: a reference to Shiva in his aspect of a wayward ascetic, given to narcotics, consorting with spirits and ghouls on cremation grounds and waste spaces.

Everything is born of joy, etc.: *Taittiriya Upanishad* 3.6. A variant reading of the last word of the Sanskrit is *prayantyabhisamvishantiti*. 'Joy' has been preferred to the more usual 'bliss' as a translation of *ananda*.

Rabindranath had carried out a revisionary reading of *ananda* (joy) and *bairagya* (renunciation) in the play *Phalguni*, the first version of which had been published in *Sabuj Patra* in Chaitra 1321 (Mar.–Apr. 915), two months before this essay. In the play, the theme of affliction and the poet's role in a world of suffering took on an urgent context: *Phalguni* was staged to raise money for famine victims in Bankura. Much of its argument is repeated in this chapter, especially the account of *lila* and *khela*, both translated as 'play'.

Who would have exerted, etc.: *Taittiriya Upanishad* 2.7.2. *Akasha*, unavoidably translated as 'skies', is supreme space, which is also in the heart.

rasa . . . distillate: a pun on the literal meaning of *rasa*, 'juice, sap'. Rabindranath was clearly following the *Taittiriya Upanishad*, which he continually has in mind in this essay. *Taittiriya* 2.7.2 has: 'He indeed is rasa (*rasa vai sah*); this rasa it is that makes humankind feel joy.'

being, consciousness, and joy: translates *sat*, *chit*, and *ananda*, the three attributes of Brahma, the supreme deity (hence referred to by the compound *sachchidananda*). *Sat* comprises both knowledge and truth, *chit* both consciousness and knowledge.

Vishvakarma: the craftsman or artificer god.

As is our play, etc.: the first line of a song by Rabindranath in *Phalguni*.

Mildness fosters vice, etc.: from the shlokas attributed to Chanakya (see notes to 'Lucidity').

Give with respect: *Taittiriya Upanishad* 1.11.3.

as Shiva drank poison: When the gods and demons churned the sea, a fearsome poison was generated from it. Shiva saved the gods and demons by drinking up the poison and storing it in his throat, which thereupon turned blue (hence his name *Nilkantha*, 'blue-throated').

transcendent capacity of taking trouble: Carlyle, *History of Frederick the Great*, 4.3.

O self-revealed one, etc.: from the *shantivachanam* or benedictory opening of the *Aitareya Upanishad*. The translation given here follows Rabindranath's own Bengali gloss.

Truth is beauty, beauty truth: See notes to 'The Sense of Beauty'.

Modern Poetry (*Adhunik Kabya*)

This essay was written at the instance of the writers associated with the highbrow journal *Parichay*, edited by the poet Sudhindranath Datta, and published there in Vaishakh 1339 (Apr.–May 1932). It was later collected in *Sahityer Pathe* (see headnote to 'Literature' above).

Like other modern writers of the time, the *Parichay* group had an ambivalent relation with Rabindranath, whom they venerated but challenged. According to Amiya Chakrabarti, a distinguished poet and for some time Rabindranath's literary secretary, 'the *Parichay* group of progressive writers of Bengal . . . asked Tagore to publish his ideas on the "modern versus Victorian" controversy which was current in the thirties.' (*A Tagore Reader*, Beacon Press, Boston, 1961, p. 227). This essay was the result

'*the lake bedecked*', etc.: Of many precedents for such images and descriptions in Sanskrit, the closest, perhaps, are the descriptions of lake scenery in Banabhatta's *Kadambari*.

sanctified wisdom: An elaborate play on various senses of the word *sadhu*. It basically means 'virtuous, holy' (hence *sanctified*), and is also used as an expression of praise. But in this context, it moreover refers to *sadhu bhasha*, the formal style of Bengali composition (see headnote to 'About Language').

a favoured pupil, etc.; Kalidasa, *Raghuvamsham* 8.67.

disrobing the world . . . Draupadi: See notes to 'The Significance of a Poem' in this volume.

giant juggernaut: a reference to the chariot of Jagannath, drawn annually at the chariot festival at Puri.

'*I am the greatest laugher*': from Orrick Johns's poem 'Songs of Deliverance' (the section entitled 'No Prey Am I'). Rabindranath cites a few words in English and the rest in Bengali translation.

The food's aroma, etc.: a Sanskrit proverb.

You are beautiful, etc.: Amy Lowell, 'A Lady', from *Sword Blades and Poppy Seed* (1914). Rabindranath cites the poem in his own Bengali translation. His chief departures from the English are given below.

opera tune: 'jatra tune' (*jatra*, the traditional folk theatre of Bengal).
harpsichord: 'sarindi' (also sarangi, a stringed instrument).
eighteenth-century boudoir: 'an old-world drawing-room'.
Smoulder . . . minutes: 'The petals of blown roses wither away'.
sealed spice-jars: 'spices for washing hair, sealed in earthen pots'.
I grow mad: 'My soul is delighted'.

Ayamaham bhoh: literally 'I am here' or 'I have come': Durvasa's words in Kalidasa, *Abhijnanashakuntalam*, Prelude to Act 4.

a poem . . . about red slippers: Amy Lowell, 'Red Slippers', from *Men, Women and Ghosts* (1916); cited by Rabindranath in the original English.

a poem about aesthetics: Ezra Pound, 'The Study in Aesthetics', *Lustra* (1916). Pound actually describes a band of children as struck by the sight of the girl; one of them, named Dante, afterwards has the experience with the fish. Rabindranath cites the poem in a Bengali prose paraphrase.

The winter evening: T.S. Eliot, 'Preludes', *Prufrock and Other Observations* (1917). Rabindranath cites the poem in five instalments, the first two and the last in Bengali translation, the third and fourth in English. In the translated sections, these are the chief departures from the original:

the burnt-out ends of smoky days: 'a smoky day, a burnt-out lamp'.
gusty shower: 'a wet wind'.
newspapers: 'torn newspapers'.
broken blinds: 'broken window-panes'.
dozed: 'drowsed, nodded off'.
the thousand sordid images: 'a thousand tawdry fanciful images'.
your soul: 'your nature'.
fuel: 'cowdung pats' (used as fuel in India).

That is something external: a proverbial phrase derived from the *Chaitanya Charitamrita* or life of Chaitanya by Krishnadas Kaviraj.

more than a thousand years: Li Po's dates are 701–62. Rabindranath probably read these poems in *The Works of Li-Po*, translated by Shigeyoshi Obata (E.P. Dutton, New York, 1928), where the four pieces are titled respectively, 'In the Mountains', 'Nocturne', 'A Summer Day' and 'Two Letters from Chang-Khan—I'. Needless to say, Rabindranath cites them in Bengali translation. His version of the last poem departs substantially at times from Obata's rendering, and may owe something to that by Florence Ayscough and Amy Lowell (*Fir-Flower Tablets*, Constable, London, 1928). The present translations follow Rabindranath's Bengali versions.

a poem by Eliot: 'Aunt Helen', *Prufrock and Other Observations* (1917).

the aghori sect: a sect of worshippers of Shiva (also called Aghor), given to practices generally regarded as repellant or horrific.

Whenever Richard Cody: The poem is 'Richard Cory' by Edwin Arlington Robinson, cited by Rabindranath in Bengali translation. Despite relying on his memory (see his footnote), he makes no major departure except in writing 'Cody' for 'Cory'. There are relatively minor changes as follows:

a gentleman: 'what one calls a gentleman'.

imperially slim: 'slim as a young prince'.

quietly arrayed: 'simple in demeanour, simple in dress'.

richer than a king: 'incredibly (literally, 'impossibly') rich'.

In fine . . . his place: 'Whatever about him we saw, we thought, "If only I were he!" '.

cursed the bread: 'cursed the thick bread' (clearly with unleavened Indian bread in mind).

calm summer night: 'calm spring night'.

The Philosophy of Literature
(*Sahityatattwa*)

Delivered as a lecture at Calcutta University in February 1934. Published in *Prabasi*, Vaishakh 1341 (Apr.–May 1934), and later collected in *Sahityer Pathe* (see headnote to 'Literature').

the One said, etc.: *Taittiriya Upanishad*, 2.6.3.

anubhav: The root meaning is 'to become like'.

a son is dear, etc.: See notes to 'World Literature'.

Poetry is speech imbued with rasa: from *Sahityadarpan* by Vishvanatha Kaviraj, a fifteenth-century rhetorician and literary theorist.

Ever since birth, etc.: See notes to 'Vidyapati's Radhika'.

The body's breeze, etc.: from a poem by Balaram Das beginning *Kishor bayas kata baidagadhi tham*. For Balaram Das, see notes to 'World Literature'.

born of the union, etc.: Kalidasa, *Meghadutam* stanza 5.

'Ten moons fall weeping', etc.: closely echoes a Vaishnav poem by Uddhab Das. There are many parallels in Vaishnav poetry.

Boatman, pick up your oar, etc.: the opening of a Baul song of unknown authorship, from East Bengal.

Listen, Eugenia, etc.: Matthew Arnold, 'Philomela'. The standard text reads 'the bursts come'.

Rama's banishment, Kaikeyi, Manthara, the death of Dasharatha: See notes to 'The *Ramayana*'. Dasharatha died of shock and grief at having had to send Rama into exile.

Alas, for long: from Rabindranath's poem 'Swaying' (*Jhulan*), included in the first volume of his poems in the Oxford Tagore Translations.

Know that knowable being: *Prashna Upanishad* 6.6.

vedana: used here in the root sense of 'feeling'; but the common Bengali meaning of 'pain' cannot be entirely excluded, providing a play with the later 'pain' (*byatha*).

By means of the heart, intellect and mind: These words render, and the whole passage closely follows, *Katha Upanishad* 2.3.9.

Look, here I am: Kalidasa, *Abhijnanashakuntalam*, Prelude to Act 4 (cf. 'Modern Poetry'): Durvasa's call on arriving at Shakuntala's door. She ignored the call and was cursed by him for her lack of respect and hospitality.

Where shall I find, etc.: the opening of a Baul song recorded by Rabindranath from Gagan Mandal, the local *harkara* or postman at the poet's estate at Shilaidaha.

Art is the reformation, etc.: *Aitareya Brahmana 6.27*. The *Aitareya Brahmana* is a sacerdotal text relating to the *Rig Veda*, attributed to the sage Mahidasa Aitareya.

midget incarnation: a humorous reference to the *Vamana Avatar*, Vishnu's incarnation as a dwarf or midget.

Vedavyasa: traditionally held to be the poet of the *Mahabharata*.

Shakuni: In the *Mahabharata*, the Kauravas' maternal uncle, who craftily defeats Yudhisthira at dice to claim his kingdom and his wife.

Bhanru Datta: a comic rustic in Mukunda Chakrabarti's *Chandimangal*.

Kabikankan: See notes to 'Silent Poet, Untaught Poet'.

Hirimba: in the *Mahabharata*, a demoness who consorted with Bhima for a time and bore him a son. She is not presented as a uniformly malevolent character.

Shurpanakha: in the *Ramayana*, a demoness, widowed sister of Ravana. Thwarted in her advances towards Rama, she tries to harm him by various means and finally incites Ravana to abduct Sita.

tease us out of thought: Keats's 'Ode on a Grecian Urn', line 44

It's dark upon the other shore, etc.: a popular children's rhyme. See 'Children's Rhymes', where Rabindranath cites and discusses the full poem, including the 'grammatical error' it contains.

Come and see the cuckoo dance, etc.: another such rhyme, also discussed in 'Children's Rhymes'.

A portly tiger, etc.: a children's poem of which Rabindranath composed several versions. One of them, included in the fantasy *Se* ('That Man'), will be found in the volume of Rabindranath's writings for children in this series.

thumri in the tappa mode: In north Indian classical music, the thumri and tappa were widely held to be relatively light compositions, usually on the subject of love. The thumri has also given its name to a beat, which seems to be the sense here.

chautal composition in the Tori raga: Tori is an austere morning raga. The dhrupad, considered a more serious composition than the thumri or tappa, was usually sung to the chautal beat.

Lalitalabangalata, etc.: Jaideva, *Gitagovinda* 28: '[The tender spring breeze has grown] sweet, having touched the sweet clove-creeper.' Jaideva was a fifteenth-century poet celebrated for his ornate mellifluous style.

Vasantapushpabharanam, etc.: 'Wearing ornaments of spring flowers': Kalidasa, *Kumarasambhavam* 3:53.

Dhritarashtra: who avowedly overlooked the misdeeds of his sons the Kauravas, in particular the eldest, Duryodhana.

the beast of burden: the ass, traditionally used by washermen to carry their bundles of washing.

sajina: a plant with an edible stem.

chalta: a fruit used to make pickles and condiments.

redundant for those who have read my poems: The incident recounted here is the subject of his poem *Karma* ('Work') in the collection *Chaitali*.

rasa of compassion: i.e. the *karuna* or sorrowful rasa.

Uma: i.e. Parvati. Her bridal is described in canto 7 of Kalidasa's *Kumarasambhavam*.

Indumati: daughter of King Bhoja of Vidarbha: queen of King Aja, son of Raghu, and mother of Dasharatha, father of Rama. Her bridal is the subject of canto 6 of Kalidasa's *Raghuvamsham*.

Rammohan Ray: See notes to 'Bengali National Literature'.

Vidyasagar: Ishwar Chandra Vidyasagar (1820–91), one of the most eminent scholars, educationists, and social reformers of nineteenth-century Bengal.

Presidential Address (*Sabhapatir Abhibhashan*)

Rabindranath delivered this lecture in Varanasi on 3 March 1923 at the Bengali Literary Convention of north India. The surviving Bengali text is a partial transcription made by Pradyotkumar Sengupta. It first appeared in the journal *Shantiniketan* in Jyaistha 1330 (May–June 1923), and was one of a number of previously uncollected pieces appended to *Sahityer Pathe* in the Visva-Bharati edition of the Works, vol. 23.

strains of a flute: an implicit allusion to Krishna's flute, to which the poet's soul responds like Radha

the person who asked me: Pramathanath Tarkabhushaṇ, the eminent Sanskrit scholar. He went to Varanasi to take charge of the Indology Department at Benares Hindu University the year this address was delivered. He was chairman of the Convention's reception committee.

Bankimchandra: Bankimchandra Chattopadhyay (Chatterjee), 1838–94, the pioneering novelist, essayist, and thinker of nineteenth-century Bengal.

It is better to die, etc.: *Bhagavadgita*, 3rd discourse, shloka 35.

Vande mataram: 'We praise the mother': the opening of Bankimchandra's famous hymn to the motherland in his novel *Anandamath*. It had already become a hymn and motto of the nationalist movement, and is now India's national song.

external bond . . . chain-gang: The Bengali carries a pun on *shrinkhal*, 'chain', and *shrinkhala*, 'order, rule' (literally, the order or sequence of links in a chain).

the indivisible one: The Bengali has *advaita*, the term used to indicate the oneness of Brahma the godhead with his creation. The word *Shiva* here carries its basic etymological implication, 'the good' or 'the beneficent'.

Daksha's pride in his lineage: Daksha was one of the ten *prajapatis* or great sages, soul children of Brahma himself. This made him disparage Shiva, married to his daughter Sati, and take offence when Shiva did not pay him due homage. Shiva finally despoiled the *yagna* or sacrificial ceremony organised by Daksha. The phrase 'rite of union' above translates Bengali *milan-jagna* (*milan*, union); there is thus an implicit pun in the subsequent reference to Daksha, as *daksha-jagna* is a conventional Bengali phrase meaning total despoiling or ravaging.

disintegration of death . . . concert of the living: The Bengali carries a pun on *panchatwa*, 'resolution into the five elements' (i.e. death: see notes to 'The Five Elements') and *panchayet*, 'a gathering' (literally 'of five people'), applied specially to village councils.

Let us never decry each other: from the *shantivachanam* or benedictory opening of the *Katha*, *Svetasvatara* and *Taittiriya Upanishads*.

It is superficial: *Ehah bahya*: a proverb. See notes to 'Modern Poetry'.

Rama's foot . . . Ahalya: Ahalya was condemned by her husband, the hermit Gautama, to a thousand years' invisible, unfed, and (in some recensions) stone-like state because of her adultery. She was freed by the coming of Rama to Gautama's hermitage during Rama's forest sojourn.

The Poet Yeats (*Kabi Yeats*)

First published in *Prabasi*, Kartik 1319 (Oct.–Nov. 1912) and later included in the collection of essays *Pather Sanchay* (Treasures of the Road), Bhadra 1346

(Aug.–Sept. 1939). The collection consists of essays written before and during the poet's tour of England and America in 1912.

This essay was written in England, soon after Rabindranath's first meeting with Yeats. It must be borne in mind that at this time, Yeats was yet to produce his greatest volumes of verse. On his side, his initial enthusiasm about Rabindranath's work—he wrote a perceptive introduction to the English *Gitanjali*—soon subsided, and the relationship between the two soured shortly after Rabindranath's receipt of the Nobel Prize in 1913.

Yet we must remember that in 1931, Yeats wrote to Rabindranath: 'What an excitement it was, the first reading of your poems, which seemed to come out of the fields and the rivers and have their changelessness!' And Rabindranath, in his message after Yeats's demise in 1939, wrote: 'Today my mind goes back to the time when I first met Yeats, full of exuberant life and youthfulness. The same picture of the glowing genius of a magnificent personality will, I am sure, remain unfaded in memory of all time. I shall cherish to the end the fact that my life was linked with the memory of one of the rarest poets of modern Europe.' (*The English Writings of Rabindranath Tagore*, ed. Sisir Kumar Das, Delhi: Sahitya Akademi, 1996, vol. 3, p. 845).

the Vaishnava poets: See notes to 'Vidyapati's Radhika'.

Bankimchandra: See notes to 'Baul Songs'.

Bangadarshan: See notes to 'The Theatre'.

Comte: Auguste Comte (1798–1857), the French positivist philosopher. Positivism was a major influence on the work and thought of many nineteenth-century Bengali writers, including Bankimchandra.

Mill: John Stuart Mill (1806–73), the English philosopher.

George Moore (1852–1933), Anglo-Irish novelist: His *Hail and Farewell* (1911–14) is an autobiographical work in three parts.

A certain critic . . . writes: Of the two excerpts, Rabindranath quotes the first in Bengali translation and the second in the original English.

The True Nature of Literature
(*Sahityer Swarup*)

First published in the Vaishakh 1345 (Apr.–May 1938) number of *Kabita*, a journal exclusively devoted to poetry and the discussion of poetry, edited by the poet and critic Buddhadev Basu (Bose), 1908–74. It was later made the title-essay of a collection of Rabindranath's late writings on literature, published posthumously on 1 Vaishakh 1350 (April 1943).

Rabindranath had been persistently criticised for his alleged failure to address the problems of contemporary life and face hard reality. The attack became strongest and most strident towards the end of his life, with the emergence of

Marxist criticism in Bengal. This essay is his final apologia for his conception of poetry.

makes a prospective bride stand, walk, etc.: part of the orthodox procedure for inspecting and selecting the bride in an arranged marriage.

'*Truth is beauty*': Rabindranath habitually quotes Keats's line in this form. See notes to 'The Sense of Beauty'.

Gosainpara: a typical rustic place-name.

if its ornaments jingle: The Bengali carries a pun on *alankar,* literally 'ornament' or 'jewellery' but used by extension of rhetorical figures.

at Indra's court: i.e. among the celestial gods, Indra being their king.

sex, pathos, and *revulsion*: In the Bengali, Rabindranath ironically uses the names of three formal rasas of Sanskrit poetics, *adi, karuna,* and *vibhatsa.*

husking-pedal: or dhenki, an implement worked by the foot to husk rice by pressure.

the ashok tree flower: as suggested in Kalidasa's *Meghadutam* stanza 77 and his *Kumarasambhavam* 3: 26.

wrist-watch, . . . spectacles, . . . hair brushed back: All these, even the spectacles, were regarded as signs of foppery.

the natey plant is lopped off: part of an old rhyme used to wind up children's tales: 'My tale is finished, the natey plant is lopped off', etc.

The Prose Poem (*Gadyakabya*)

This essay was based on the notes of a lecture delivered at Shantiniketan on 29 August 1939. It appeared in *Prabasi,* Magh 1346 (Jan–Feb. 1940), and was collected in *Sahityer Swarup* (see headnote to 'The True Nature of Literature'). It should not be confused with the essay *Kabya o Chhanda* (Poetry and Metre), which also appeared originally under the title *Gadyakabya* in the journal *Kabita* in Poush 1343 (Dec.1936–Jan.1937).

Rabindranath formally introduced the prose poem in the poetical collection *Punascha* (1932); but his experiments with the form had begun much earlier, when he was preparing the English *Gitanjali.* He found models for such a rhythmic structure in the Upanishads, the Psalms of David in the English Bible, and in Whitman's *Leaves of Grass.* His first conscious and serious experiments in the mode occur in *Lipika* (1922), though the pieces there are, as a rule, not arranged as verse but printed in short prose-like paragraphs. Gradually, he overcame his diffidence in this respect.

Rabindranath wrote quite a few essays and letters explaining the features of this new form. All of them are to be found in *Chhanda,* the collection of his writings on Bengali metre, edited by Prabodhchandra Sen.

either through the intellect, etc.: *Mundaka Upanishad 3.2.3, Katha Upanishad* 1.2.23. Rabindranath probably had the former passage in mind, as his preceding sentences closely echo its context.

People differ in taste: Kalidasa, *Raghuvamsham* 6:30.

Vararuchi's lament: See notes to 'Prose and Verse'.

a poem about . . . Satyakam: *Brahman*, composed on 7 Phalgun 1301 (February 1895): collected first in *Chitra* (1896) and subsequently in *Katha* (1900). This poem is in verse. Rabindranath also composed a prose poem on the subject, which remained in manuscript in a draft of the essay *Gadyachhanda* (Prose Rhythm).

anushtubha (or anushtupa), trishtubha, mandakranta: Sanskrit metres.

a group of unnamed writers, etc.: referring to the Authorised or King James Version of the Bible (1611). The translators were established clerics and scholars, but their names were not attached to the translation.

Yajur Veda: the third of the four Vedas.

mantra: a chant or incantation, especially as a prayer to a deity.

Satyendra: Satyendranath Datta (1882–1922), poet and follower of Rabindranath. He is well known for his facility with rhyme and metre.

Lipika: a collection published in Bhadra 1329 (Aug.–Sept. 1922), though the pieces had appeared earlier in various journals. They are intensely poetical in nature but printed as continuous prose, divided into paragraphs.

Mohammadi: a weekly (later monthly) journal, founded in 1903 and edited by Maulana Muhammad Akram Khan. Primarily an organ of Bengali Muslim society, the *Mohammadi* attracted contributors from other communities, Rabindranath among them.

Shesher Kabita (The Last Poem): a romantic novel by Rabindranath (published Bhadra 1336, Aug.–Sept. 1929) with many poems embedded in the narrative.

Introduction to the Bengali Language
(*Banglabhasha-Parichay*)

This translation comprises sections 3 to 5 of the work of this title, published by Calcutta University in 1938. It does not follow any specific model of linguistic analysis, but presents the basic grammatical structures of the Bengali language with a wealth of detail and acute insight. It is the only analytic account of the Bengali language by a creative writer. Its style and approach are comparable only to *Bishwa-Parichay* ('Introduction to the Universe'), the work of popular science composed by Rabindranath in late life.

the word white is very white: Bengali *sada*, white, also means 'plain, simple, straightforward'.

seer: a measure of weight.

Her body's breeze, etc.: See notes to 'The Philosophy of Literature'.

The liquid grace, etc.: the opening of a poem by Gobinda Acharya or Gobinda Das on Radha's love for Krishna: included in the *Padaratnabali* co-edited by Rabindranath. Gobinda was a Bengali poet of the twelfth century.

labanya: the Sanskrit word of which *labani* is a poetic derivative.

the War: i.e. the First World War.

Mangalkabya, Mukundaram: See notes to 'Silent Poet, Untaught Poet' and 'Literary Creation'. The reference is to a specific *Mangalkabya*, Mukunda(ram)'s *Chandimangal*.

the goddess: i.e. Chandi, an aspect of Durga.

the power of good: The Bengali carries a pun on *Shibashakti*, 'the power of Shiva' as well as 'the power of good'.

Manasamangal: poems about Manasa the snake goddess. There are a number of such medieval Bengali poems.

Prahlad: a legendary devotee of Vishnu. He battles great odds to reach his adored god.

Shelley . . . man held captive: The reference is to Shelley's *Prometheus Unbound*.

Manthara: See notes to 'The *Ramayana*'.

Bhanru Datta: See notes to 'The Philosophy of Literature'.

In Java: Rabindranath visited Java in 1927.

Hanuman and Indrajit: an episode from the *Ramayana*. The heroic Hanuman, Rama's faithful follower from the monkey-tribe, fought Indrajit or Meghnad, Ravana's son.

About Language (*Bhashar Katha*)

This piece was first published in *Sabuj Patra* in Chaitra 1323 (Mar.–Apr. 1917). It served (with modifications) as an introduction to the collection *Bangla Shabdatattwa* ('Bengali Linguistics'), Agrahayan 1342 (Nov.–Dec.1935). This was the expanded second edition of the volume originally published as *Shabdatattwa* ('Linguistics') in 1315 (February 1909).

The essay appeared in *Sabuj Patra* at a time when its editor Pramatha Choudhuri had launched a frontal attack against the established formal style of Bengali (*sadhu bhasha*) in an effort to establish the colloquial style (*chalit bhasha*) in its place. Rabindranath gave him full support. He had himself used *chalit* from an early date in his travelogues and in private correspondence, but he fully abandoned *sadhu bhasha* only in 1916.

sadhu language: See headnote. In Bengali, *sadhu* also means 'honest, virtuous, laudable'; hence the subsequent pun on 'refinement and honest speech'.

colloquial Bengali: The Bengali term used here is *prakrit*, which means 'natural' and hence 'unrefined, colloquial'. 'Prakrit' is employed as a generic term for the group of Middle Indic dialects that arose in counteraction to Sanskrit (literally 'refined, cultured'). In classical Sanskrit drama, non-brahmans and women speak various kinds of Prakrit.

Sabuj Patra (literally both 'green leaf' and 'green page'): an avant-garde journal of its time, where this essay was first published: founded in 1917 by Pramatha Choudhuri, who married Rabindranath's niece Indira Debi.

Kshanika (Momentary Pieces): a collection of Rabindranath's poems published in 1900.

Mathur: where Krishna reigned as king.

Vrindavan: where Krishna spent his childhood and youth as cowherd and lover.

Europe Jatrir Patra (Letters of a Traveller in Europe): There is no work by Rabindranath with this title. He seems to be referring to his 1881 volume, actually entitled *Europe Prabasir Patra* (Letters of a Sojourner in Europe). Later, he published *Europe Jatrir Diary* (Diary of a Traveller in Europe) in two parts, in 1891 and 1893. The second part was reprinted in 1936 in a single volume with *Europe Prabasir Patra* under the title *Paschatya-Bhraman* (Travels in the West).

Shantiniketan: a collection of Rabindranath's speeches, sermons, etc. delivered at Shantiniketan; published in seventeen vols. in 1909–16, and later collected into two vols. in 1935.

a man and his younger brother's wife: In a traditional Bengali household, it was forbidden for a woman to show her face to her husband's elder brother or to address him directly.

they banished Sita. . . golden image: In the *Uttarakanda* ('Canto of the Aftermath') of the *Ramayana,* it is recounted that Rama, after banishing Sita to the forest, held an *asvamedha-yagna* or horse-sacrifice at which a golden image of Sita was built and displayed.

Bhagirath: See notes to 'World Literature'.

taddhita pratyaya: In Sanskrit grammar, a *pratyaya* is a derivational suffix (as opposed to a *vibhakti* or inflectional suffix); *taddhita* is the term used to denote derivation from nouns, pronouns, and adjectives (as opposed to the *krit-pratyaya* derived from a verb stem).

chayita, chaoniya: hypothetical forms created by inappropriately adding Sanskrit endings to the non-Sanskritic stem *cha* (*i*), 'to want, to wish'.

Michael: Michael Madhusudan Datta. See notes to 'Children's Rhymes'.

Bopadeva: See notes to 'Literature' (1924).

Count Okuma: Shigenobu Okuma (1838–1922); Prime Minister of Japan, 1898 and 1914–16. Rabindranath met him in Japan in 1916. He also enlisted Okuma's aid in 1918 for the Indians falsely accused of conspiracy in the famous San Francisco trial.

Alaler Gharer Dulal (published in book form in 1858): generally considered the first novel in Bengali, written by Pyarichand Mitra under the pseudonym Tekchand Thakur. Noted for its marked use of colloquial Bengali forms in a narrative basically written in the *sadhu* or formal style.

Rammohan Ray: See notes to 'Bengali National Literature'.

Sara Bridge: the railway bridge over the Padma referred to at the start of the piece.

Chant of the Flowers: A reference to *phuler kirtan*, a particular type of the *kirtan* or Vaishnava songs or chants about Krishna and Radha.

habe, hacche: colloquial or *chalit* forms of the verb 'to be, become, happen', whereas *haibe, haitechhe* are formal or *sadhu* forms

hayen, haiba, kariba, haibek, karibek, karaha, chalaha, kariha: archaic forms which had disappeared by Rabindranath's time, though the alternatives he cites alongside them also belong to formal language or *sadhu bhasha*.

jela, jeyechhi, jeyechhilum: unacceptable forms adding colloquial (*chalit*) endings to a modified version of the Sanskrit stem *ya-*.

Ami-o jabo tumi-o jabe: Literally 'I-too shall-go you-too shall-go.'

bedding, pillows, etc.: The first sentence featuring these items (but not books) does not have any conjunction.

good things should be accomplished without delay: a Sanskrit proverb.

Birbhum: Probably Rabindranath mentions this district in particular, here and later, as the one where Shantiniketan is located.

Genu, karnu: in place of the standard *gelam/gelum, karlam/karlum*.

bheyer be, cheler dam: The standard *chalit* forms would be *bhaiyer biye, chaler dam*.

Impending threat of the Partition of Bengal: the cause of the great nationalist upheaval of 1905, in which Rabindranath played a leading part.

The Bengali of Maktabs and Madrasas
(*Maktab-Madrasar Bangla Bhasha*)

This essay appeared in *Prabasi*, Bhadra 1339 (Aug.–Sept. 1932). It has a specific social context: it was reacting to an earlier *Prabasi* article (Vaishakh 1339, Apr.–May 1932) by Rameshchandra Bandyopadhyay, also entitled *Maktab-Madrasar Bangla Bhasha*, decrying a Bengali style dominated by Perso-Arabic words for the benefit of Bengali Muslims. This was presented as part of a larger agenda of defining the Muslim identity in linguistic terms. A programme for the Islamisation of Bengali was first clearly spelt out by Nawab Abdul Latif, who told the Hunter Commission in 1882 that while the 'upper-class' Muslim should be instructed in Urdu, the primary education of the 'lower-class' Muslim should be conducted in a Bengali free of 'the super-structure of Sanskritism of learned Hindoos and supplemented by numerous words of Arabic and Persian origin' (cited in Badruddin Umar, *Purba Banglar Sangskritir Sangkat*, Calcutta, 1971, pp. 189–90). The tendency was encouraged by the separatist politics that flourished in the 1920s and 1930s under the banner of the two-nation theory. It should be emphasised, however, that the majority of Bengalis, irrespective of religion, opposed attempts at such communalisation of their language.

maktab: an Islamic primary school.

madrasa: an Islamic high school or traditional Islamic college.

Prabasi: a well known journal of the time, published first from Allahabad and later from Calcutta, edited by Ramananda Chattopadhyay (Chatterjee). Ramananda was Rabindranath's admirer and associate, and the latter wrote frequently for *Prabasi*.

the original books: Rameshchandra cites four in his abovementioned article: Muhammad Mubarak Ali's *Maktab Madrasa Sahitya*, parts 1 and 4, and Muhammad Shahidullah's *Maktab-Madrasa Shiksha*, parts 2 and 3.

Mag (pronounced 'Mawg'): a term used generically of the Myanmarese, and particularly of a community of Arakanese once notorious for banditry along the Bengal coast. Hence the expression used here, *mager mulluk* (the land of the Mags), a Bengali phrase for a lawless, anarchic land.

hajar, sahasra: words for 'thousand', from Persian (*hazaar*) and Sanskrit respectively.

In the instances that follow, the context makes it clear which words are of Persian or Perso-Arabic and which of Sanskrit origin.

Hyperion: The original lines, opening the poem, are:

Deep in the shady sadness of a vale
Far sunken from the healthy breath of morn,
Far from the fiery noon, and eve's one star,
Sat grey-haired Saturn, quiet as a stone.

The Persian and Arabic words substituted here are as follows:

saya-i-ghamagin, Persian, 'shadow of sorrows'; *nafas-i-hayat*, 'breath of life' (Arabic *nafas*, breath + Persian *hayat*, life); *afza-in*, Perso-Arabic, 'increasing' or 'refreshing of'; *atshin*, Persian, 'fiery'; *bamoo-i-safid*, Persian, 'with hair of white' or 'turning grey of hair'; *khamush*, Persian, 'silent'; *sang*, 'rock, stone'.

Maulvi Sahab: A Maulvi is a traditional Arabic scholar and teacher; *Sahab* is a respectful Arabic term of address.

tambu: a word of obscure but supposedly Islamic origin.